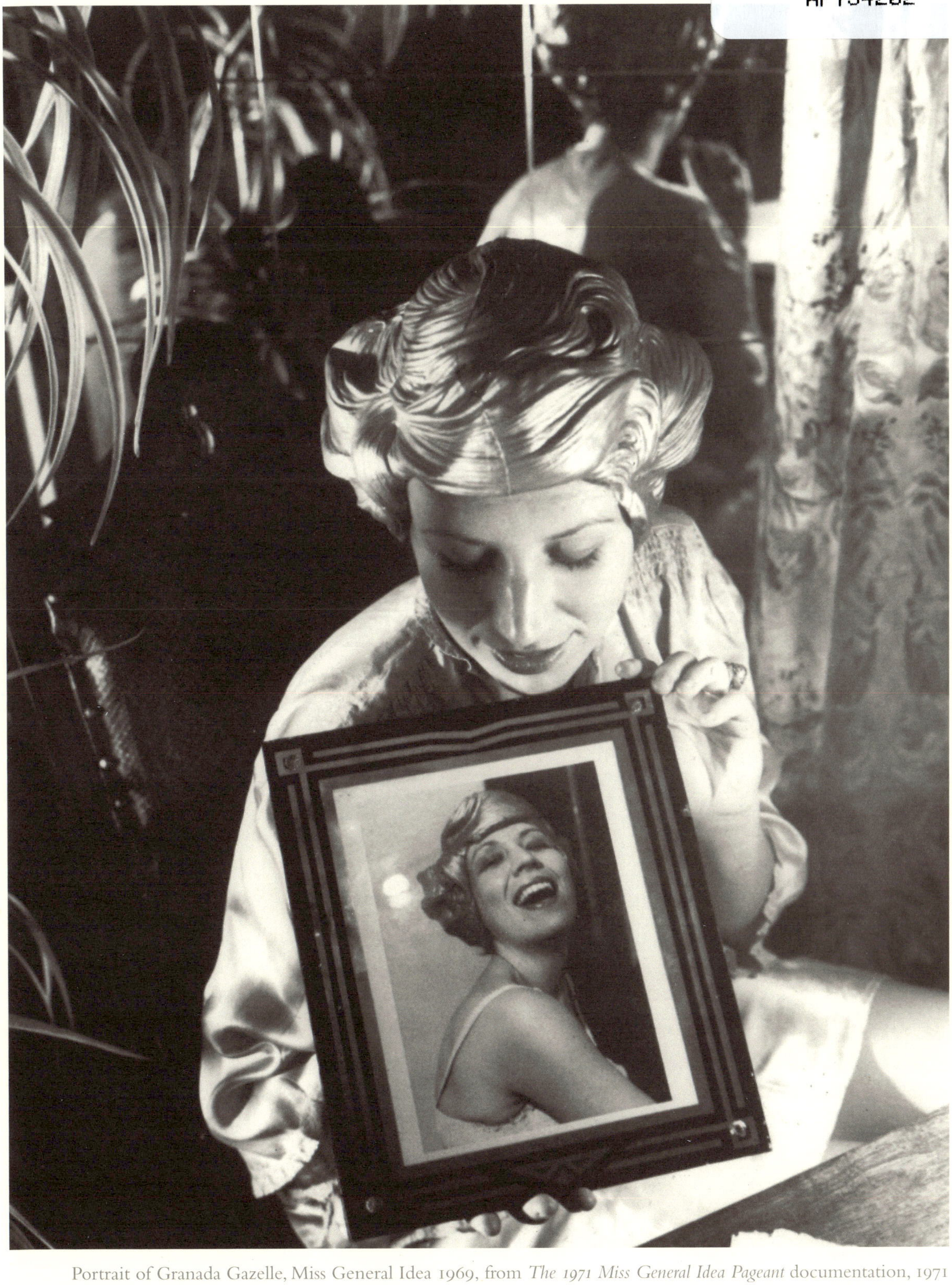

Portrait of Granada Gazelle, Miss General Idea 1969, from *The 1971 Miss General Idea Pageant* documentation, 1971

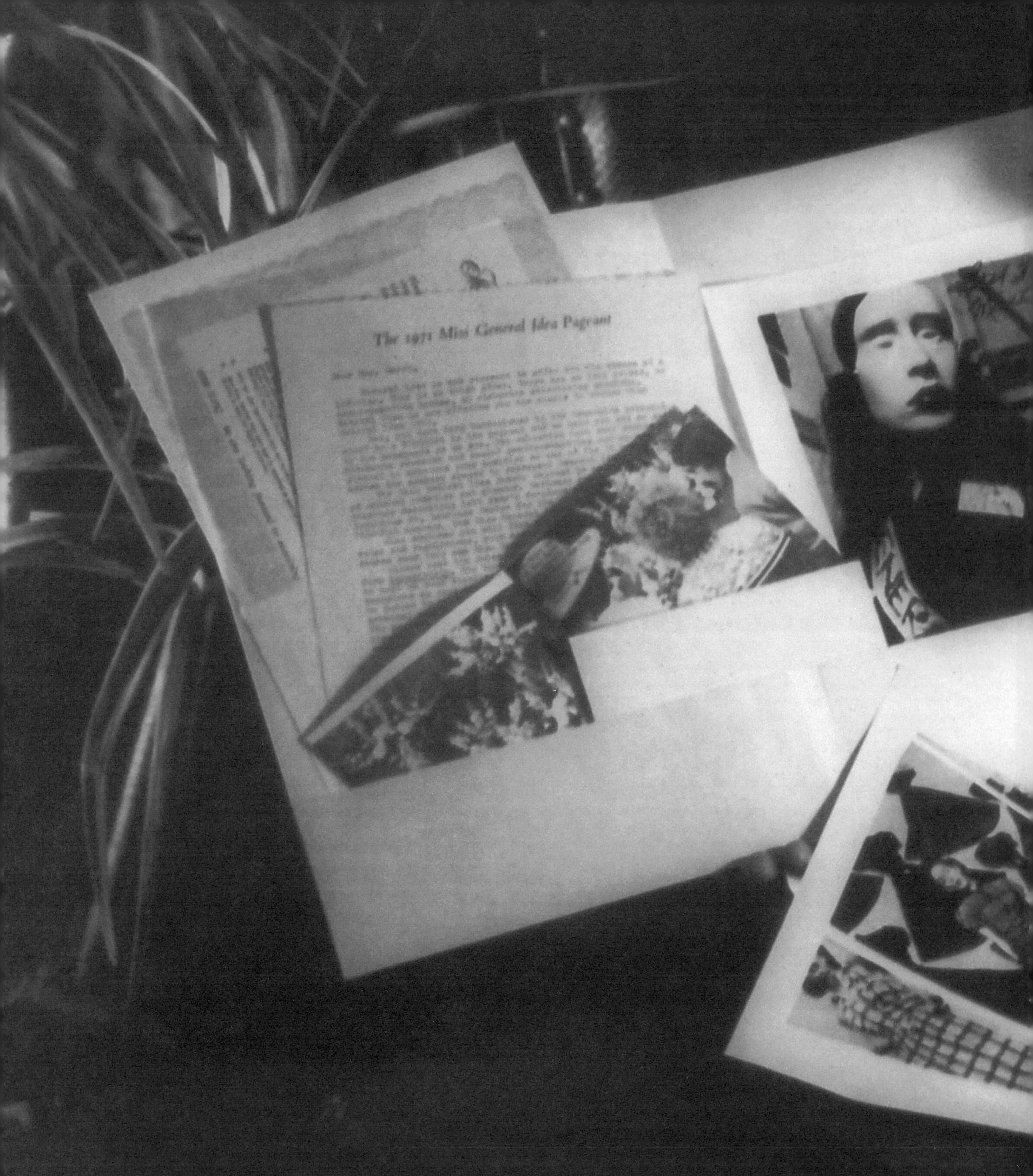

Granada Gazelle, Miss General Idea 1969, displays *The 1971 Miss General Idea Pageant Entry Kit*

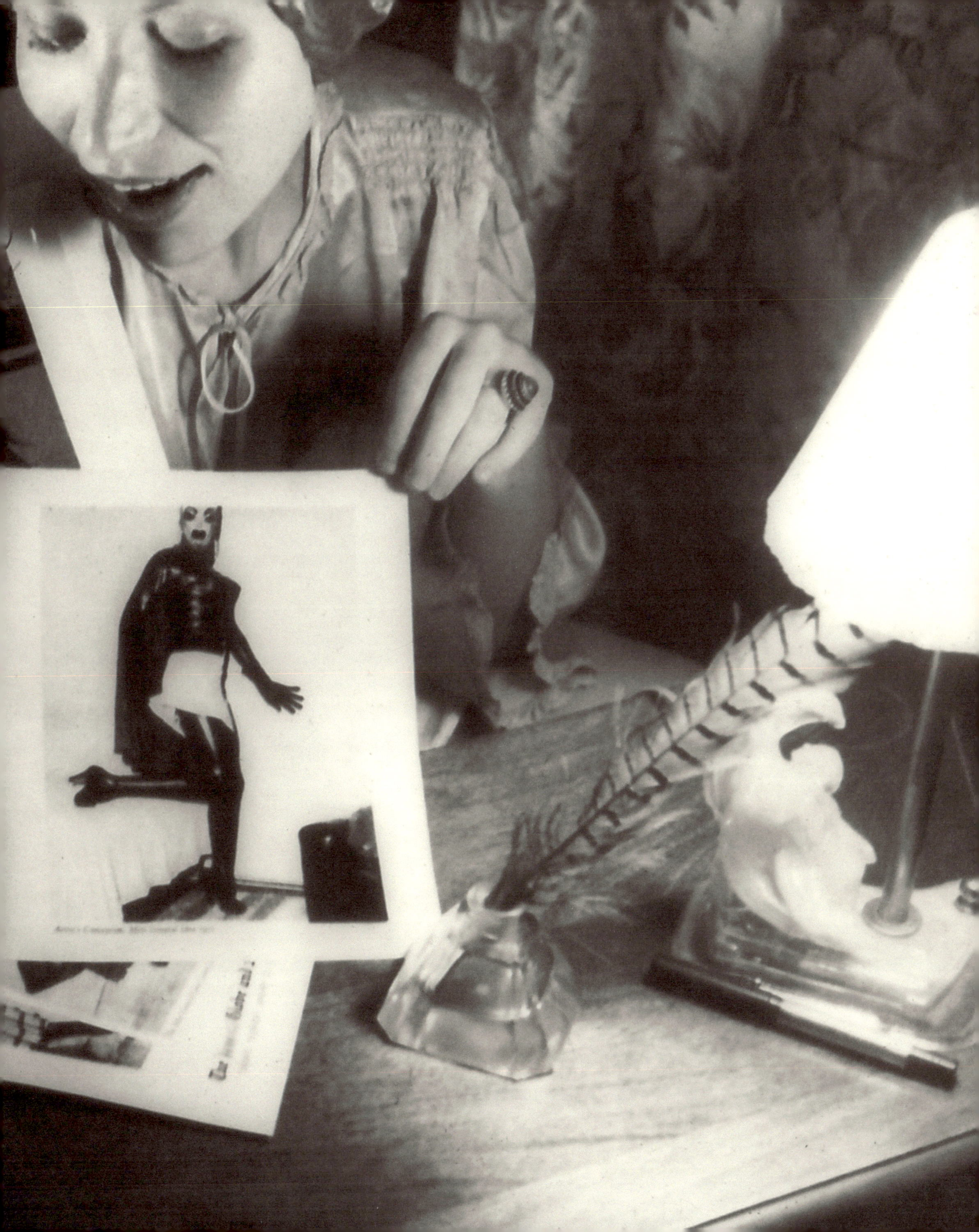

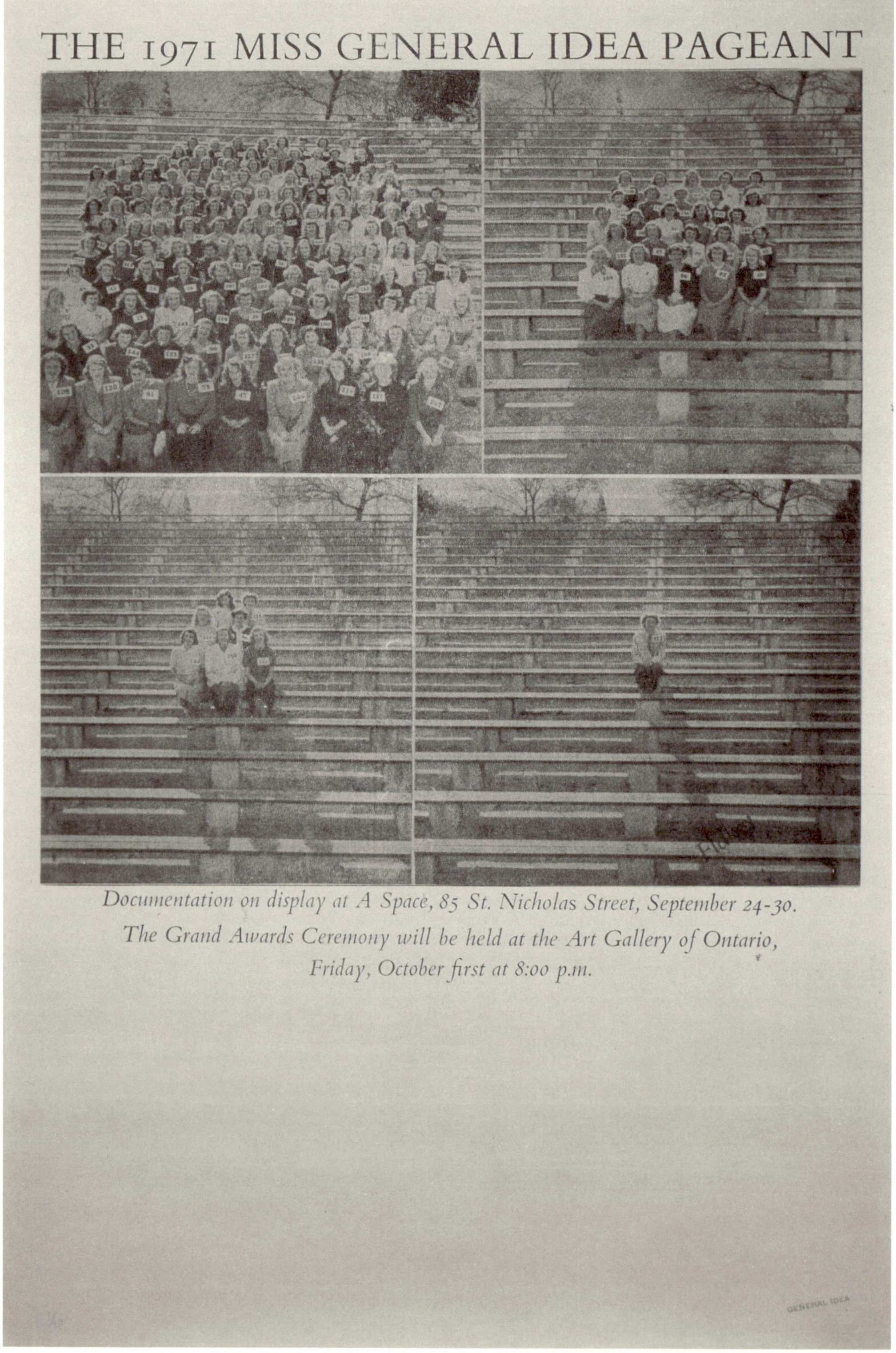
THE 1971 MISS GENERAL IDEA PAGEANT
Documentation on display at A Space, 85 St. Nicholas Street, September 24-30.
The Grand Awards Ceremony will be held at the Art Gallery of Ontario,
Friday, October first at 8:00 p.m.
GENERAL IDEA

The 1971 Miss General Idea Pageant poster, 1971

The 1971 Miss General Idea Pageant
Art Gallery of Ontario

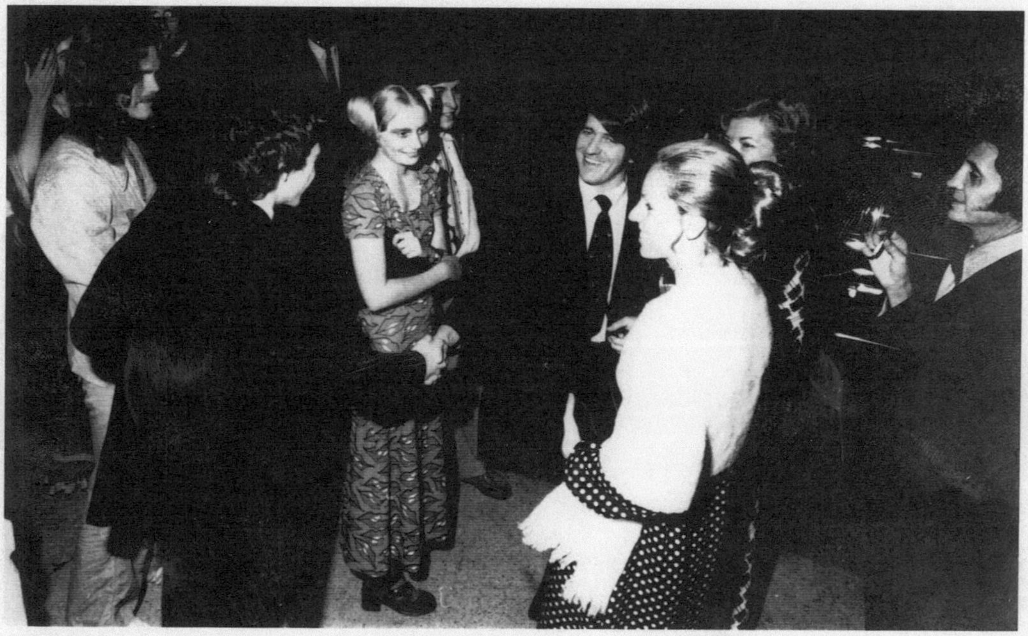

"Canada's first surrealist evening"
—Mario Amaya

On the evening of October 1, 1971, the serpentine voice of the handsome Pascal signalled the opening of the 1971 Miss General Idea Pageant Grand Awards Ceremony at the Art Gallery of Ontario. During the course of the evening the Awards Ceremony emerged as a vehicle for the completion and articulation of certain processes which had been in operation at General Idea Headquarters for over a year.

The 1971 Miss General Idea Pageant, fourth in a series, despite General Idea's protests to the contrary, was primarily an investigation of the hierarchial structures of establishment patterning, a simulation of hierarchial techniques co-ordinated with tolerance testing of the existing system. Much of the effectiveness of the project resided in its ambiguous use of hard-core glamour imagery: arc lamps, limousines, past queens, and poignant invitations. In approaching the pageant one must cope with the ahistorical significance of these images: they arise from the manipulation of the concept within the beauty pageant framework.

Thirteen Miss General Idea entry kits were sent to thirteen contestants. The finalists, arrayed in their Miss General Idea Gowns, returned the requested documentation. This documentation was displayed at A Space Gallery, Toronto, to allow judges Dorothy Cameron, David Silcox and Daniel Freedman to choose the winning entry. The heated three-hour judging session provided the *ipso facto* climax of the project, which then relaxed back into the frivolity of pageantry.

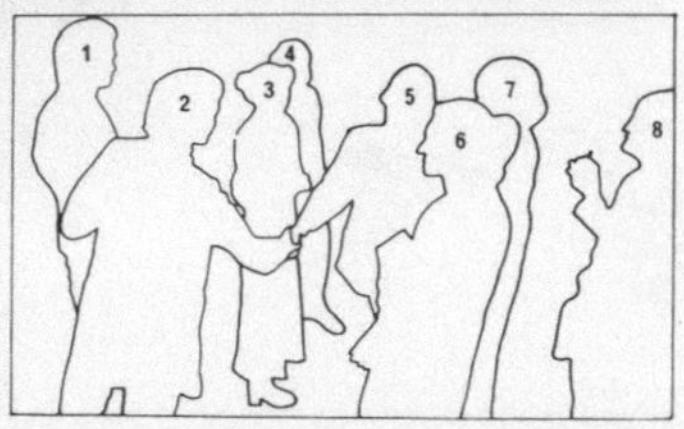

Miss Paige, Miss General Idea 1968, greets guests at the 1971 Miss General Idea Pageant: (1) Michael Hayden, (2) judge Daniel Freedman, (3) Miss Paige, (4) contestant Michael Morris, (5) judge David Silcox, (6) Mimi Silcox, (7) judge Dorothy Cameron, (8) artist Ronald Bloor. Photo: Rodney Werden.

History is what you make it.

Artscanada, December, 1971 84

The 1971 Miss General Idea Pageant (Artscanada), 1971

The Awards Ceremony encompassed an hour of entertainment well-mixed with pageant mythology and the usual awards procedures: demonstration of rules and regulations, reminiscing with past queens, and viewing of the entries. Pascal, the General Idea chanteuse, captured in every song the spirit of the event, the precise yet undefined borderline where nature meets culture. Hovering between worlds with the ambidextrous intensity of the compulsively frivolous, Pascal articulated both male and female registers with a remarkable saxophone sound. "I am not an *artiste*", he asserted, "I am a work of art."

Previous queens Mimi Paige (1968), Granada Gazelle (1969), and Miss Honey (1970) added historical validity to the pageant. Both Mimi and Granada were chosen in private ceremonies in their respective years, while Miss Honey emerged victorious at the 1970 Miss General Idea Pageant held at the St. Lawrence Centre for the Arts in Toronto. Mario Amaya, chief curator of the Art Gallery of Ontario, admired Miss Honey's "delightful sort of Elizabeth Taylor kitsch", an image which easily relates her position as General Idea's specialist on the fads and formats of the late fifties and early sixties.

"WE MADE THEM DO IT"

It was no accident that art consultant Dorothy Cameron and art bureaucrat David Silcox were chosen judges, nor that the Awards Ceremony took place at the Art Gallery of Ontario. The Pageant was, on one level, a simulated hierarchial system introduced into the real thing. The subjects responded with admirable enthusiasm, well-trained by a firm tradition of noun domination and its bastard child, the *objet d'art*. All were aware of the nature of the project, yet unable or unwilling to articulate the endangering factor. The Art Gallery of Ontario attempted a withdrawal but gave in to good manners. Dorothy Cameron balked at the last moment: "Marcel is the best but I don't think he should win." He won, nevertheless, as all Fine Art must, with a terse convolution of pose and gesture that captured glamour without falling into it.

Echoing the judges and gallery alike, the audience assumed a deliberate role. Clapping wildly at every cue, they appeared to be recreating an ambience as much as praising performance. This was total audience participation: seven hundred people acting out Pavlovian responses in enthusiastic demonstration of Heisenberg's principles.

On one level then the pageant recreated all the working structures of any layer of the art hierarchy: the Canada Council or the Art Gallery of Ontario itself. The Pageant included art critics, art products, judges and aesthetics within a competitive process that eliminated the individual artist from the actual art proposition. The 1971 Miss General Idea Pageant was ultimately sucessful not through illusion but through transparency. Only the collectors were missing.

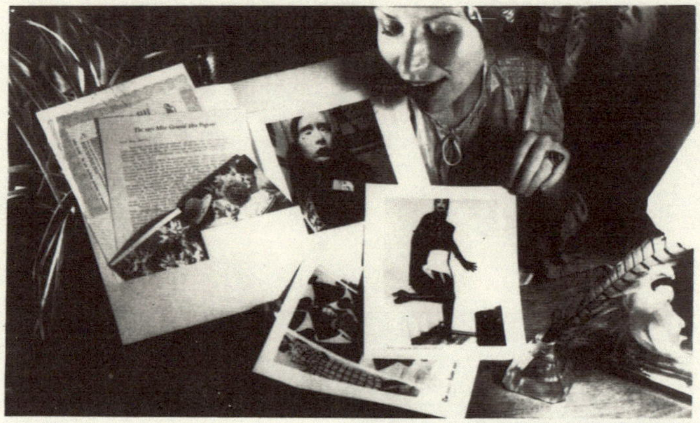

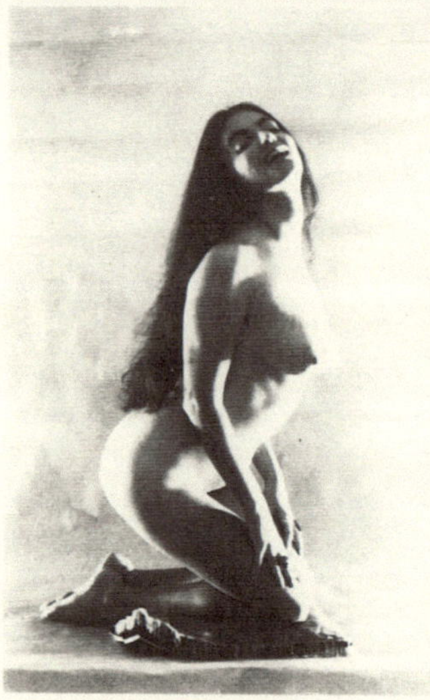

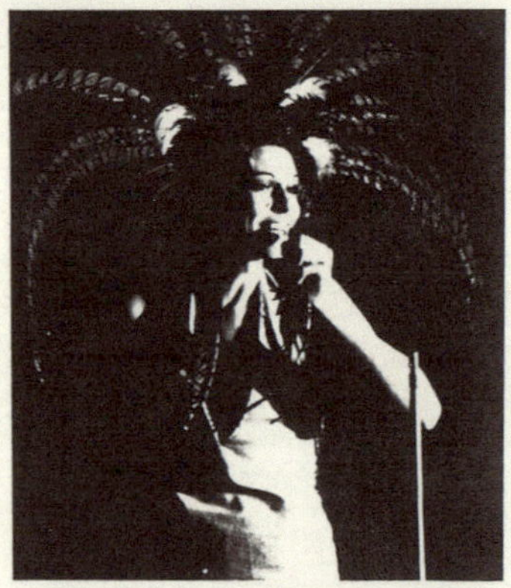

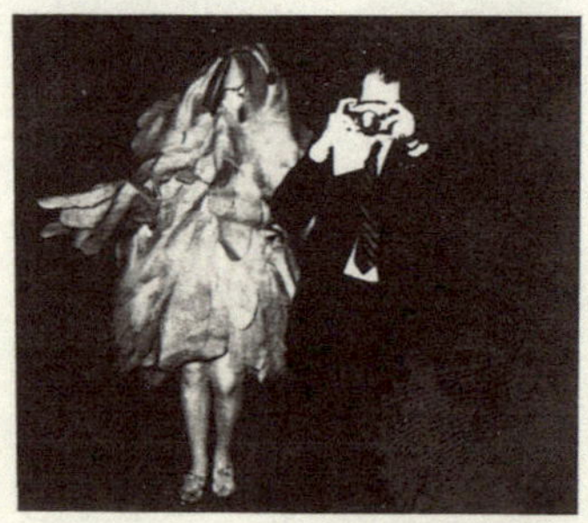

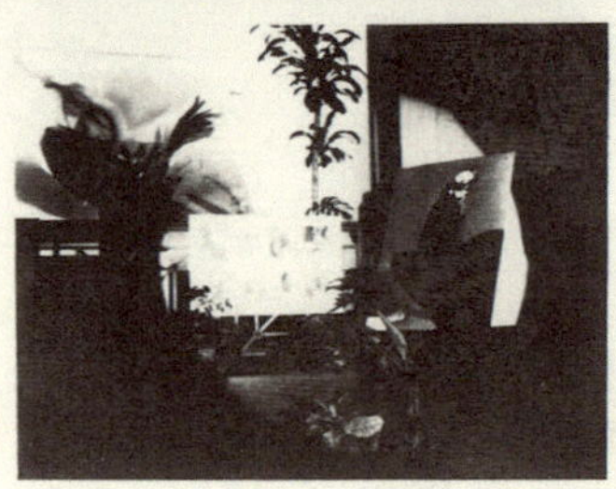

1 Granada Gazelle displays the 1971 Miss General Idea entry kit which each contestant received.

2 Miss Honey, Miss General Idea 1970, in a publicity still by General Idea.

3 General Idea chanteuse Pascal entertains guests at the Grand Awards Ceremony at the Art Gallery of Ontario. Photo: Henry Dunsmore.

4 Dr. Venus, disguised as instant playback parrot, and escort Dr. Duck arrive at the pageant for an evening of documentation. Photo: Rodney Werden.

5 The spotlight reveals Marcel Idea's winning entry at the Art Gallery of Ontario.

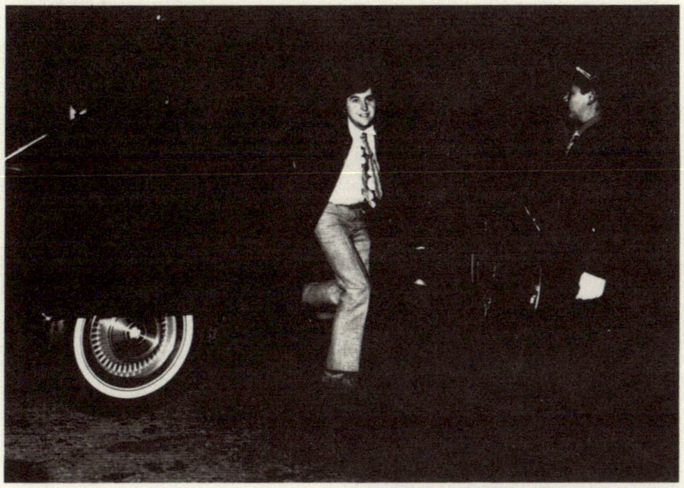

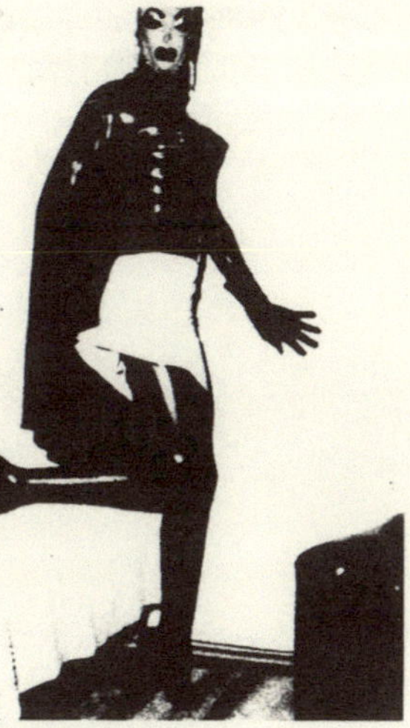

6 Pageant contestant Marcel Idea of Vancouver steps from his limousine. Photo: Rodney Werden.

7 Artists' Conception of the new Miss General Idea, as included in the Miss General Idea entry kit.

8 Canadian film star Daniel Freedman joins well-known art critic and consultant Dorothy Cameron for the pre-judging at A Space Gallery, Toronto.

9 Presentation of the three finalists: from left to right, MC AA Bronson introduces Margaret Coleman, Tina Miller, and Marcel Idea. Photo: Henry Dunsmore.

10 Marcel Idea's winning entry, in the judges words, "captured glamour without falling into it." Photo: Mr. Peanut.

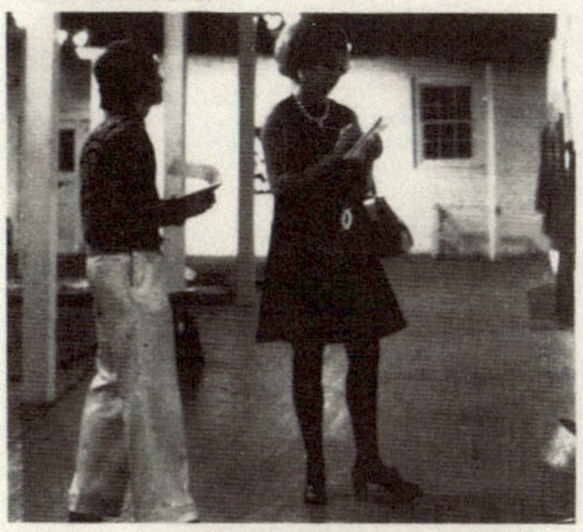

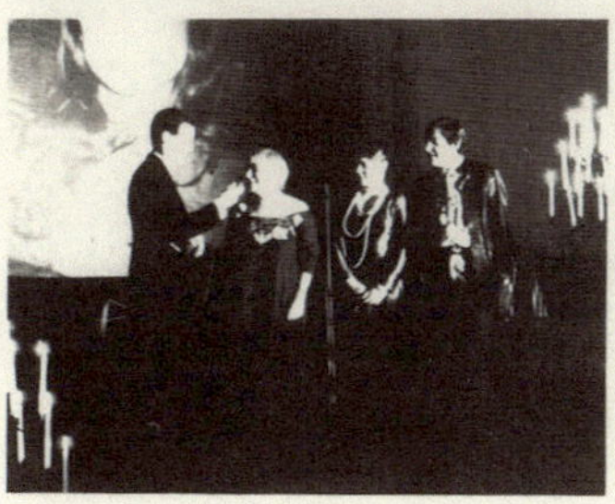

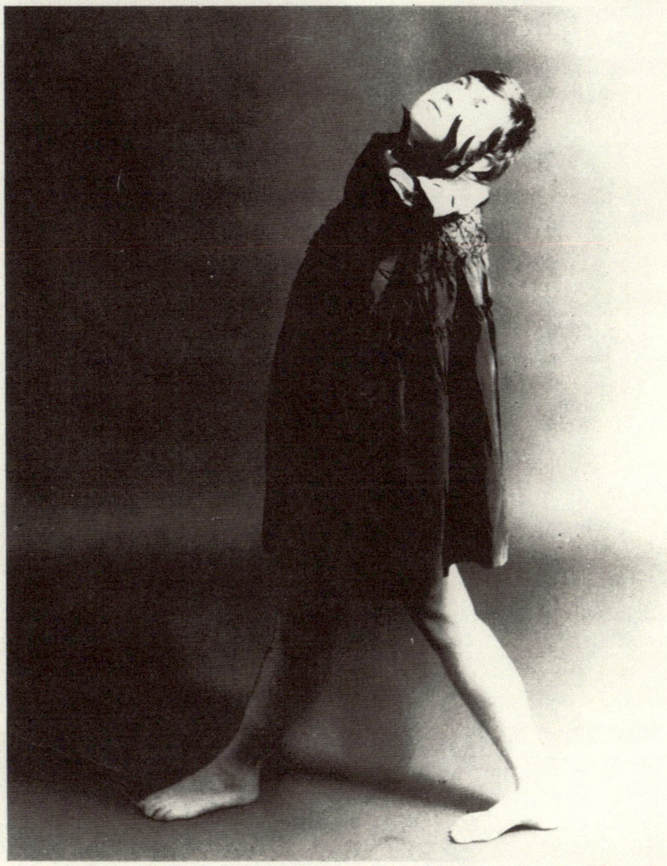

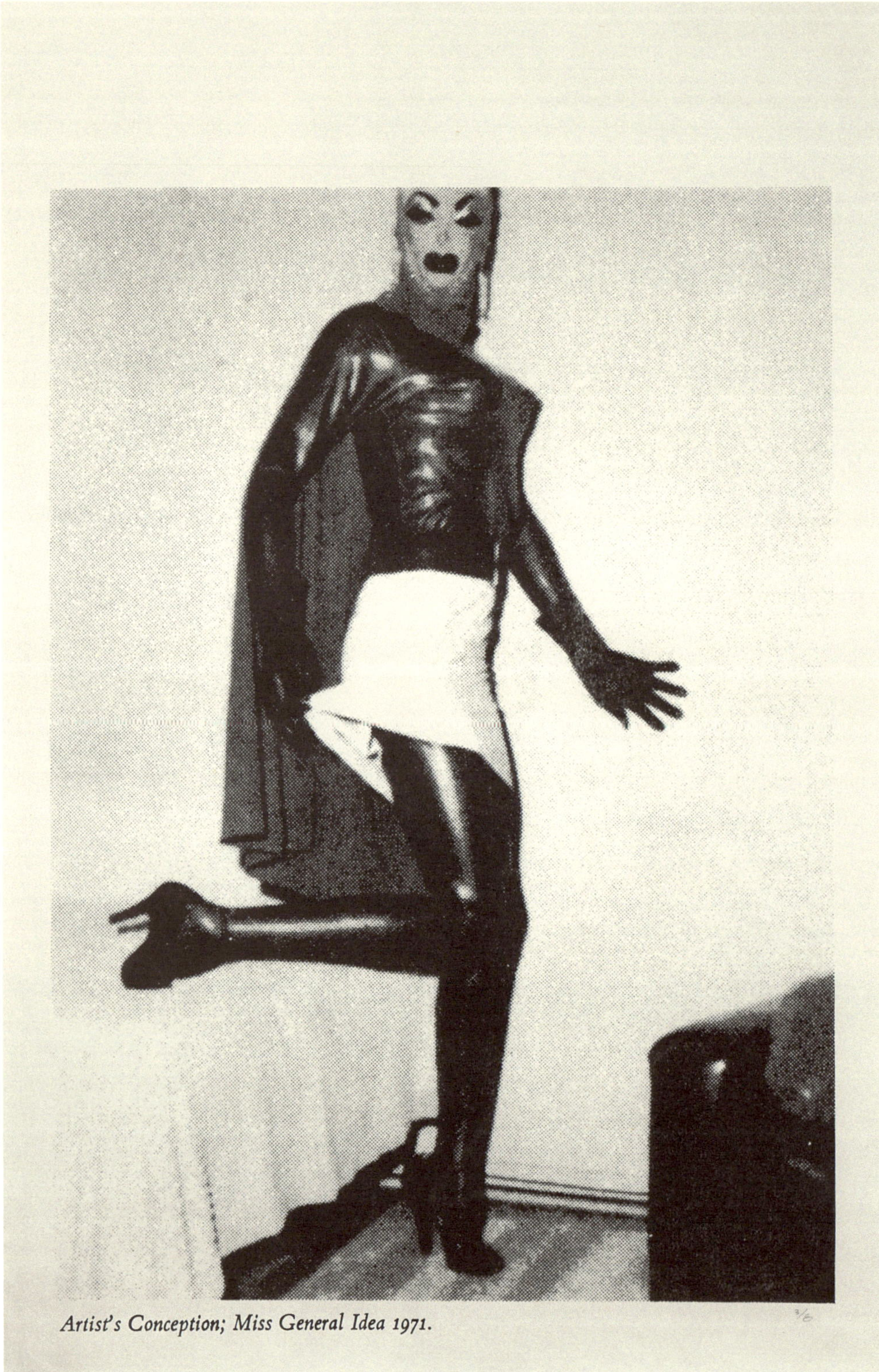

Artist's Conception: Miss General Idea 1971, 1971

GLAMOUR IS THEFT
A USER'S GUIDE TO GENERAL IDEA: 1969-1978
PHILIP MONK

The Art Gallery of York University

agYU

TOP TEN

The art of evacuation, which is the art of the hidden smile, sliding behind the inevitable movement of the disappearing fan. The art of the feminine wile. The art of levitation, which is the art of evacuation of the lower order, the octave raised to the higher resonance, mars pulled into pluto. The art of the skirt raised. The Canadian beaver, castoris Canadienne, spread cunt, the open vessal, the unspoken work, the emit of our file.

The mailing chain, broken, wilts in mimosa manner, exposing the tenderness of the underside; Marcel Idea slides in lugubrious ease. The mailing chain, which is broken, which emerged as a major concern in FILE 1, which has now merged into the ongoing processes of our everyday life, which forms the content of our daily musings - muse, musée - now serves as a medium through which the politics of art reach our ear. The inner ear lies empty, receptive, bristling. Encircling.

The female gender rises through the medium of the mailing chain with an elegant ease, establishing itself with mundane eloquence in the arena of our affliction.

The TOP TEN, which is a description, which outlines the arena of our concern, collects the cream of the milking in the gesture of the first positions. The first five hold seven (see next page), and five of these are ladies. Of the remainder one affects the feminine posture, (Doigt Doigt Gl'amour) the other is a mailing man who has crept to the top through the medium of his media coverage, the wolf in cover-girl costume. The second five positions hold eight. Of these, one is a woman rising through the evacuation of her own past; the others are again the mailing sensation of the previous issue, the sensation of the letter lifted to the lip of the lipstick-red mailbox.

One-by-one: Pascal is the singing sensation, ambidexterity become a lifestyle. The clue to her success lies beneath the layers of her voice, the clarity of acetate which coats the swift dexterity of her manipulations. Her primary position is significant. The second is Mr. Peanut, about whom no more need be said. The third is Margaret Coleman, Ms. Generality herself, who engages scenes in the manner of the blushing bride. Her art is her artfulness, and the fullness of her cooking. She is all heart. The fourth position is shared: Granada Gazelle is a late developer, who has captured the animal elegance of jungle in a single strength; Doigt Doigt Gl'amour is the posturing comedienne who has found in all women all things; Ms. Paige, star of General Idea's final film "God is my Gigolo" retains the instinctive slyness of so-called feminine logic, the absurd sophistication of child-like delight. In fifth position is Ms. Holden-Lawrence, the Jill Johnston of Spadina, Ontario, who hides a pretty wit beneath a gestured surface. Each of these is remarkable for the extent of her view, which is all of each of them; except Mr. Peanut, whose quality lies entirely within the mailing sensation and the name game extended.

On the following pages the TOP TEN transformed and the nature of this month's concerns are illuminated. Sexual politics captures the tactical front.

The Editor

TABLE OF CONTENTS

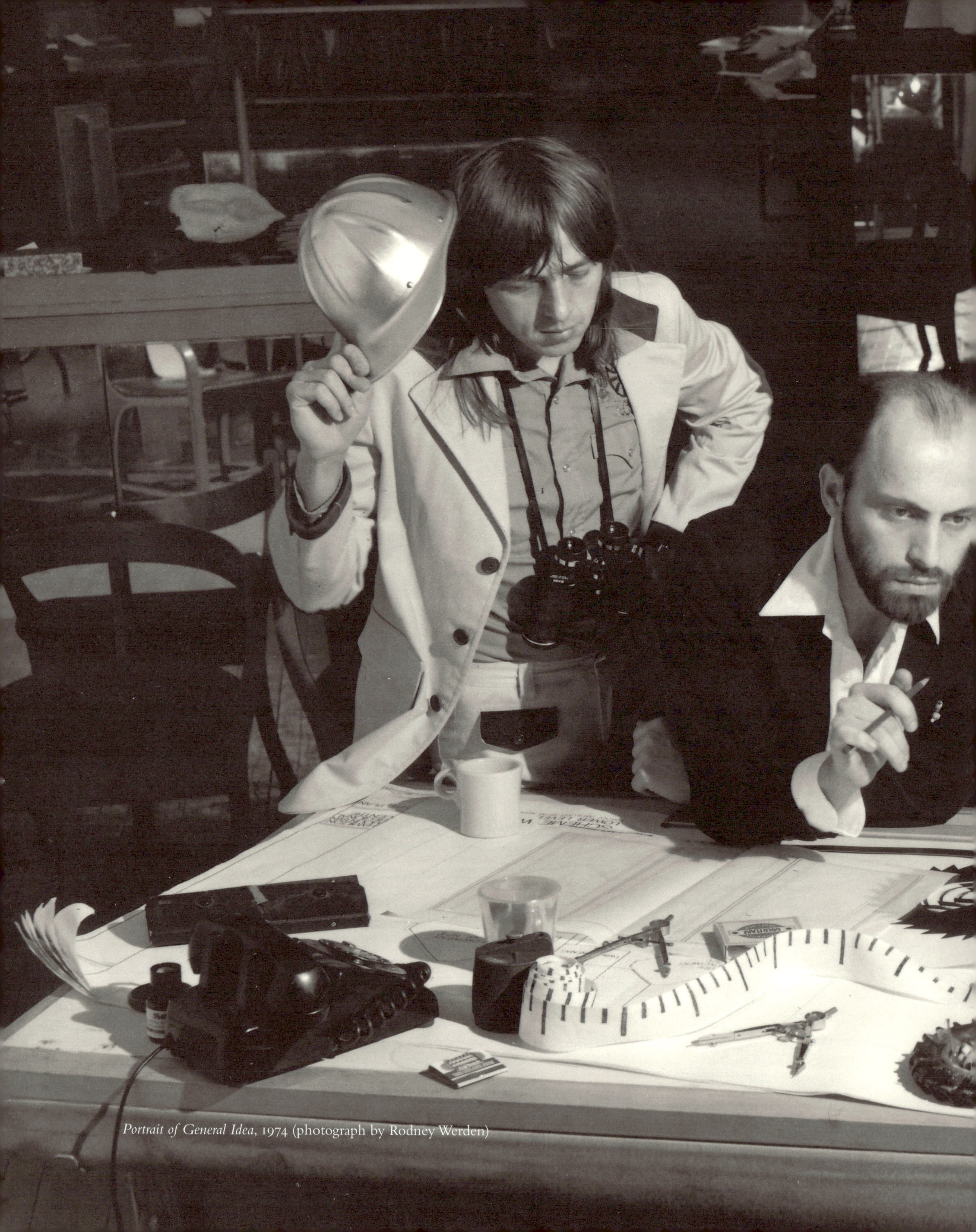

Portrait of General Idea, 1974 (photograph by Rodney Werden)

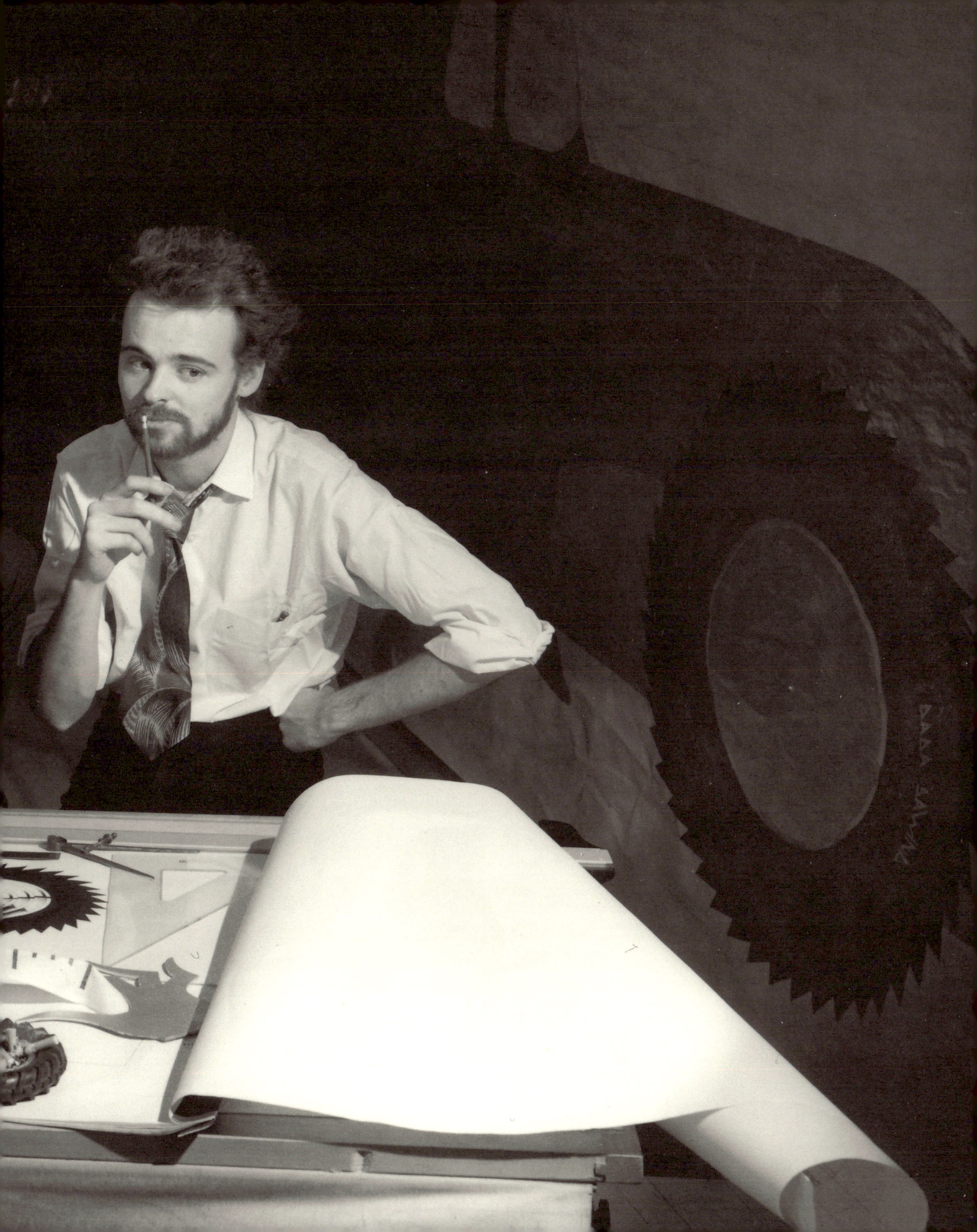

The study of myths raises a methodological problem, in that it cannot be carried out according to the Cartesian principle of breaking down the difficulty into as many parts as may be necessary for finding the solution. There is no real end to mythological analysis, no hidden unity to be grasped once the breaking-down process has been completed. Themes can be split up *ad infinitum*. Just when you think you have disentangled and separated them, you realize that they are knitting together again in response to the operation of unexpected affinities. Consequently the unity of the myth is never more than tendential and projective and cannot reflect a state or a particular moment of the myth. It is a phenomenon of the imagination, resulting from the attempt at interpretation; and its function is to endow the myth with synthetic form and to prevent its disintegration into a confusion of opposites. The science of myths might therefore be termed "anaclastic," if we take this old term in the broader etymological sense which includes the study of both reflected rays and broken rays. But unlike philosophical reflection, which claims to go back to its own source, the reflections we are dealing with here concern rays whose only source is hypothetical. Divergence of sequences and themes is a fundamental characteristic of mythological thought, which manifests itself as an irradiation; by measuring the directions and angles of the rays, we are led to postulate their common origin, as an ideal point on which those deflected by the structure of the myth would have converged had they not started, precisely, from some other point and remained parallel throughout their entire course. As I shall show in my conclusion, this multiplicity is an essential characteristic, since it is connected with the dual nature of mythological thought, which coincides with its object by forming a homologous image of it but never succeeds in blending with it, since thought and object operate on different levels. The constant recurrence of the same themes expresses this mixture of powerlessness and persistence. Since it has no interest in definite beginnings or endings, mythological thought never develops any theme to completion: there is always something left unfinished. Myths, like rites, are "in-terminable." And in seeking to imitate the spontaneous movement of mythological thought, this essay, which is also both too brief and too long, has had to conform to the requirements of that thought and to respect its rhythm. It follows that this book on myths is itself a kind of myth.

—Claude Lévi-Strauss, "Overture," *The Raw and the Cooked: Introduction to a Science of Mythology* (1964)

PREFACE

> Myth grows spiral-wise until the intellectual impulse which has produced it is exhausted. Its *growth* is a continuous process, whereas its *structure* remains discontinuous.
>
> —Claude Lévi-Strauss, "The Structural Study of Myth" (1955)

This book is not a history of General Idea. General Idea and the intellectual milieu of the period eschewed history: both were for structure not genesis. Rather, this book ostensibly is a guide to their project *The 1984 Miss General Idea Pavillion*—or simply a guide to General Idea's concepts. That is, it is a conceptual guide to a conceptual project. It falls into three parts: descriptive, analytic, and synthetic. *Description* may have the appearance of a history but it takes General Idea at their word—as fictional as that might be—and does not attempt to contextualize their work in relation to other artists in terms of sources and influences. In an era of collaboration and flouting of copyright, who did what first or who influenced whom is a moot point. *Analysis* may have the appearance of an adherence to General Idea's program but it attempts to uncover, as well, in work that was all about articulation, what could not be said therein: its operative concepts as distinct from its conceptual strategies. While Parts One and Two deal only with what objectively appears within the system or structure of General Idea's work, even if not articulated, the *synthesis* of Part Three ascribes motivation within an accounting of the artists' enterprise.

Reading the "Overture" to Claude Lévi-Strauss's *The Raw and the Cooked: Introduction to a Science of Mythology*, published in translation in 1969, the year of General Idea's association, one senses the same frustration of dealing with myth as the problems of interpretation of General Idea's oeuvre offered here. We shouldn't be surprised: General Idea's work intentionally assumed a mythological structure. Thus, part of the effort of Part One is to establish the multiple statements that compose this contemporary myth, which are dispersed in different media and drawn from various sources, sometimes contradictory, and, moreover, which develop over time. This compilation is but the story of General Idea told in their words; it is not the meaning of their work. In spite of the discontinuous structure of Part One, a narrative nonetheless underlies it—but readers are equally free to jump to the analysis of Part Two, which, however, also is not the meaning of General Idea's work but merely its means of operation. (One should not think that we are dealing with content in one, form in the other, even though Part One can be read as a lexicon for terms cited in Part Two.) As there is no logical entry to the book, readers are again equally free to start with the narrative of Part Three. Part Three was a late addition to the book, an accounting of what could not be said within the logical frameworks of Parts One and Two. Actually, since the book is reversible, readers may proceed backwards from Part Three to Part Two and then to Part One. Each part returns to the same "ground" to construct General Idea's system once more with a renewed understanding of its complexity.

In reflecting on General Idea, this book assumes the "dual nature of mythological thought, which coincides with its object by forming a homologous image of it but never succeeds in blending with it." This is why Lévi-Strauss could say that his book on myths "is itself a kind of myth."[1] Likewise the case here.

This *operation*, whether it is called structural or semiological, "is therefore actually a *simulacrum* of the object, but a directed, *interested* simulacrum."[2] So in this book, in spite of its divisions, we must construct (describe) and deconstruct (analyze) at the same time. Such *verbal* processes are precisely those of the making of General Idea's art. Because my writing therefore has to partake of the character of General Idea's work, I like to flatter myself that sections of the following text originally could have appeared in *FILE Megazine*, but only if we pretend that they are spoken as if by the venetian-blind-clad mannequins of the performance *Going thru the Motions.*★ Likewise, the text should be read as if written by Roland Barthes of the same period (in English translation, of course), the book's format a mimicking homage to the conceptual inventiveness of this author's creations. Such a conceit is not arbitrary but a means of using the form and rhetoric of period stylistics or semiotics—which were as well contemporary models and influences on our artists—as tools of interpretation.[3]

The book concerns only the first ten years of General Idea's work. Although the *Pavillion* continued to exist as a paradigm, the intellectual impulse that had produced it was exhausted by 1978, the chronological conclusion of this book, a fact that was marked not only by the *Pavillion*'s "destruction" in 1977 but also of the system that sustained it. •

★ *Hello out there. I'm D'ynette and I'm going through the motions in a tri-tier V. B. gown sans helmute. All the better to play the part of a General Idea mouth-piece. They call us conversation-pieces at the Pavillion. Walking, talking, living, breathing ideas-with-legs. Feast your eyes on my volumes you voyeurs.... Can the camera catch both my recto and my verso?*

—From the performance *Going thru the Motions*, 1975,
reprinted in "Ideas With Legs," *FILE* 4:1 (Summer 1978), 20

1. Claude Lévi-Strauss, *The Raw and the Cooked: Introduction to a Science of Mythology*, trans. John and Doreen Weightman (New York: Harper & Row, Publishers, Inc, 1969), 6. Originally published 1964.

2. Roland Barthes, "The Structuralist Activity," in *Critical Essays*, trans. Richard Howard (Evanston: Northwestern University Press, 1972), 215.

3. The text therefore strictly limits itself to period literature, specifically the books that were of interest to General Idea, with the exception of more recent catalogues on General Idea or texts by and interviews with AA Bronson.

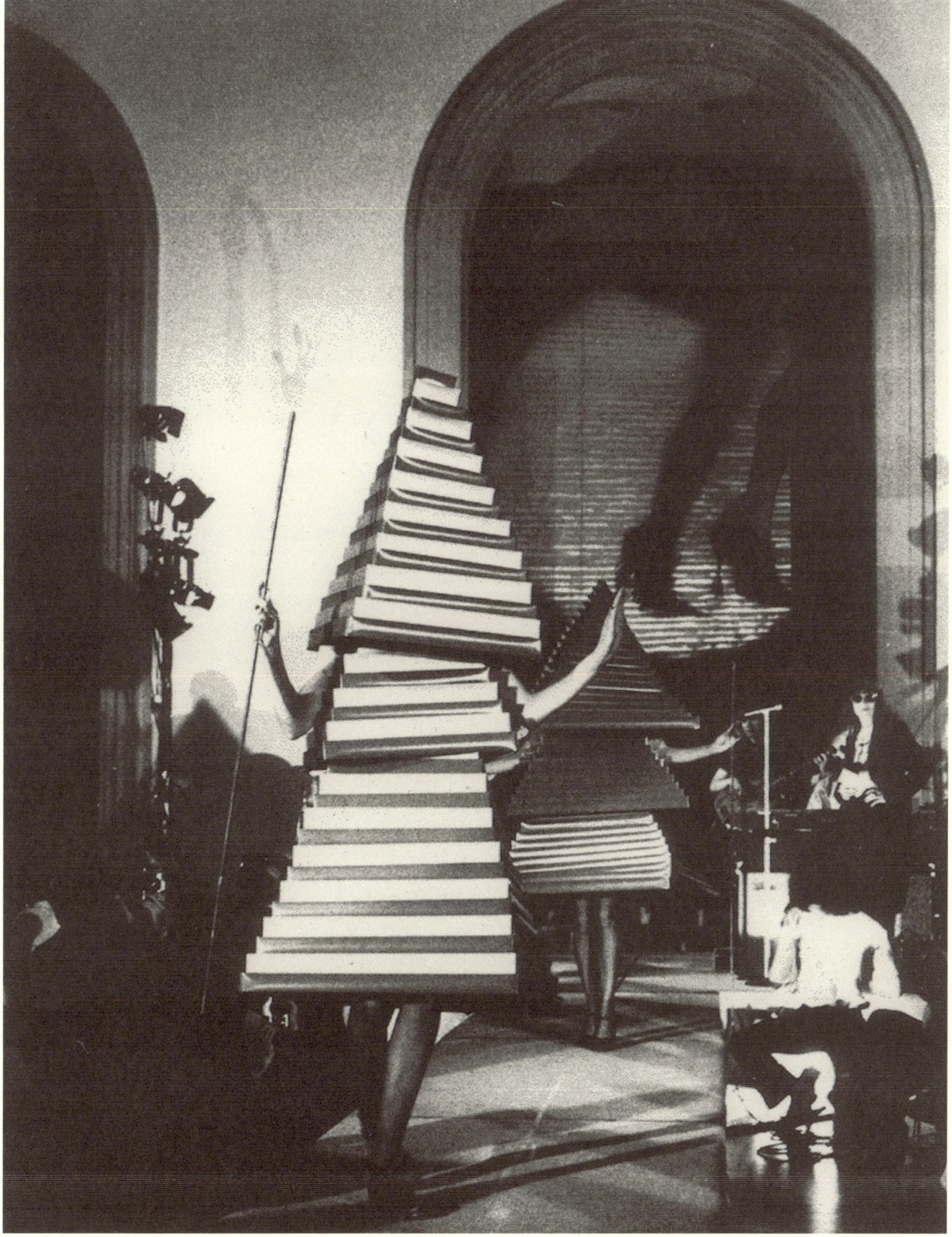

Tri-tier V. B. gowns at *Going thru the Motions*, Art Gallery of Ontario, 1975

PART I

DESCRIPTIVE

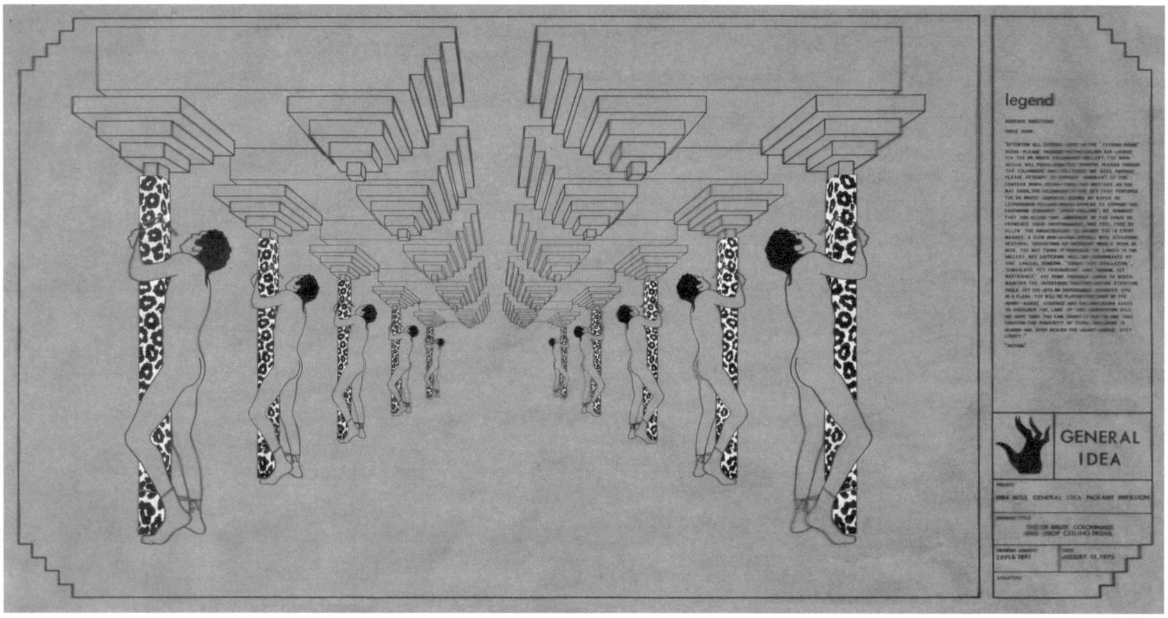

The Dr. Brute Colonnade and Drop Ceiling Detail, 1975

ON THE **THRESHOLD** OF AN ACCOUNT

Perhaps only an arbitrary cut into the totality of General Idea's work can lead to any pertinent remarks on this collective's enterprise. Cutting remarks, however, only further fissure and proliferate, leading us deeper into a labyrinth and, in the process, re-creating the architecture of an enigma that is General Idea. At any one moment, forking lines are like fractals that mirror the whole in each part. Problematically, mirrors mirror mirrors. With no beginning and no end, this evolving *and* devolving structure, like myth, appears always to have existed. (This is why their enterprise was posited on a mythical date though in the future: *1984*.)

From their very first editorial in the debut issue of *FILE Megazine*, General Idea warned us of this problem of analysis: "We might categorize connections and demonstrate the fluidity of the ballooning situation. But in the end it is all the same; the telling destroys the actuality and the story slips through our fingers, wriggling into other levels convoluted beyond expectation."[1] Convoluted, indeed! They themselves recommended myth: "The myth slides down the center, slicing realities into thin transparencies shuffling lives like leaves dissolving dualities into fabled tales. In the story it all comes together. In the myth opposite possibilities become complementary content."[2]

Myth, then, brings it all together, as ambiguous as *it* remains. As a story, myth operates other than history. Perhaps it is the way we should proceed here: by means of a story. But General Idea themselves have claim to their story from the moment they stated: "This is the story of General Idea and the story of what we wanted." They were constantly telling this story and they told it better than anyone else. It is futile, therefore, to try to tell it again other than to repeat the artists' words. Moreover, their totalizing enterprise cannot be captured in any one narrative that attempts to totalize it. Rather, any description or analysis already is anticipated in advance. Their enterprise was a whole that expanded and defined itself at every moment. Only through its *mythic* structure can we penetrate its devices. Myth composes a whole while any narrative of General Idea's enterprise is only partial. A narrative no more than a chronology, therefore, is possible. Nonetheless, in myth "everything must be accounted for."[3] A partiality that repeats might be the only way to remark the architectonics of their conceptual apparatus. Hence a series of fragments follows in Part One, fragments that are not to be considered only remains but equally constructive: a view on their work.[4] After all, deconstruction mirrored construction in General Idea's enterprise, where the mirror, moreover, was both fictive and architectonic.

Consider these fragments mirrors. Consider the cuts mirrors, too. Dividing and uniting, penetrating and glancing. They slice into myth but sometimes other than the mirror of part and whole myth already is.

They say the first cut is the deepest, but only in betrayal. •

1. "Editorial: Some Juicy and Malicious Gossip," *FILE* 1:1 (April 1972), 3.
2. Ibid.
3. "Editorial: Bulletin from the Ivory Tower," *FILE* 2:1&2 (May 1973), 11.
4. "We began to realize as we began to realize in fragments." "General Idea's Borderline Cases: Introduction," *IFEL* 2:3 (September 1973), 12

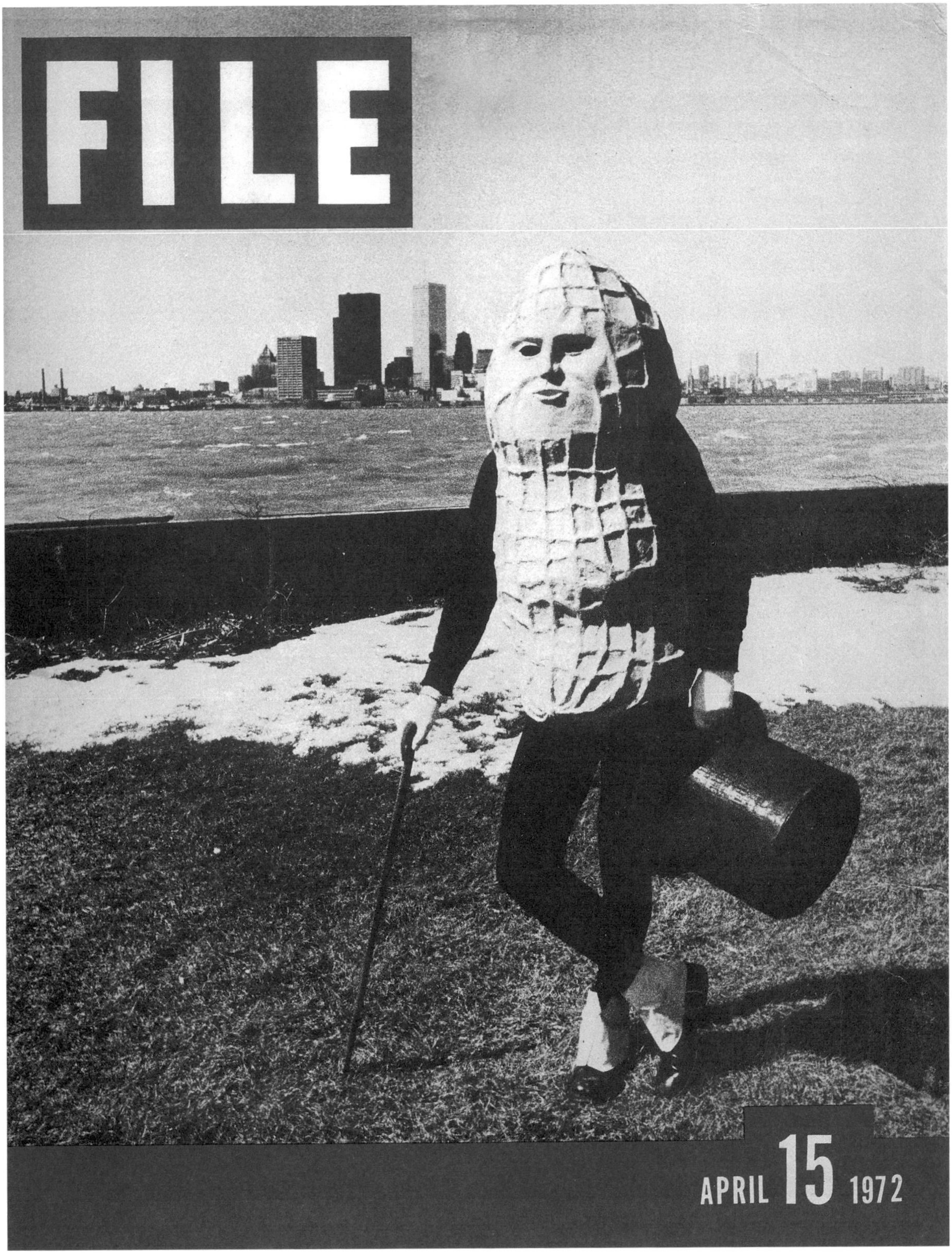

FILE 1:1 (April 1972), cover

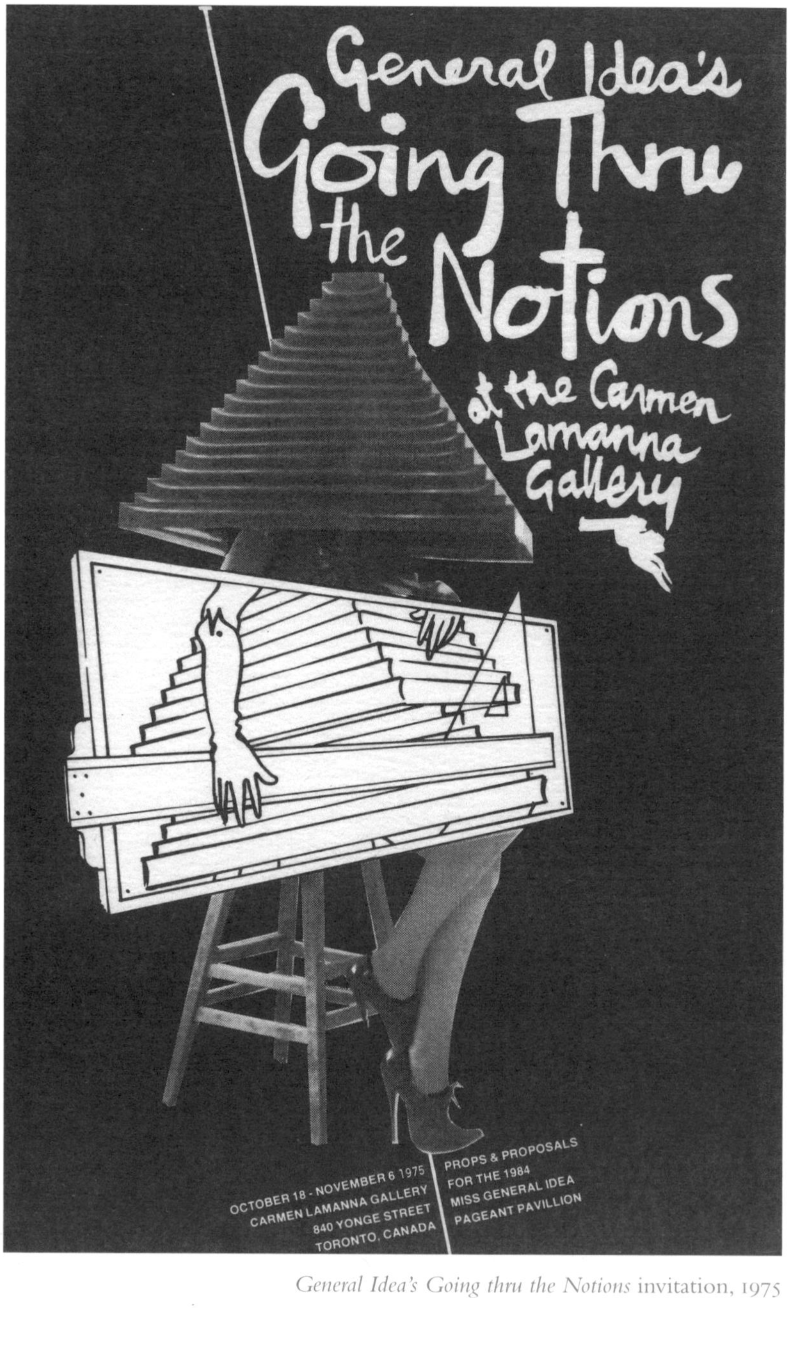

General Idea's Going thru the Notions invitation, 1975

WHEN AN **ANNOUNCEMENT** IS A PERFORMANCE

As always, we begin *in medias res*, looking both forwards and backwards at the same time. Any point of entry is as good as any other as long as we don't look for either origins or closure. General Idea began in 1969 when AA Bronson, Felix Partz, and Jorge Zontal more or less formed as a group, but we shall never talk here of beginnings as much as the *inauguration* of their enterprise, which was an *ongoing* fiction.[1] General Idea ended in 1994 with the untimely deaths of Partz and Zontal, but at any one moment during their history their project, by definition, was complete.

So, in telling the story of General Idea, to say that *The 1984 Miss General Idea Pavillion*, for example, followed chronologically from *The 1984 Miss General Idea Pageant* makes no sense when the latter was incorporated within the former (elevated or raised up in an architectural enclosure or structural completion that has nothing of Hegel's *Aufhebung* about it). And to say that *The 1984 Miss General Idea Pavillion* can be deconstructed analytically into its "architectural" elements or systematic development—that it is an entity in itself—likewise makes no sense when it continued the principles, indeed, was formed by the ideals of *FILE Megazine*, a collective enterprise of another function—and fiction—altogether.

In considering General Idea's history, we must think in terms of another whole: that of an overarching conceptual apparatus guiding the elaboration of their work. Operative concepts, however, are different from artists' strategies, which General Idea frequently announced within the fabric of their work itself, indeed, as an essential component of it. For instance, viral strategies of inhabitation articulated most succinctly in the 1975 "Glamour" issue of *FILE*. No more are operative concepts meta-concepts or a meta-commentary on General Idea's own commentary itself enfolded within their work—indeed, to be more accurate, a meta-meta-commentary on their meta-commentary. As a totality, their work should not be considered only as a second-order semiological system as Roland Barthes explained myth to be—a metalanguage already parasitic on another order of language. Rather, General Idea's work is an unconventional type of myth analysis itself, containing the evacuated form of any particular myth in its presentation, in the process re-mythifying rather than demystifying myth for their own purposes of creating art. Yet, let's not dismiss Barthes out of hand who was otherwise so pertinent to their enterprise.

Let's also be clear that this is not an analysis that I impose on General Idea from a superior position outside their work, demystifying it, but that these are operations internal to it, though not visible, for instance in the way that *The 1984 Miss General Idea Pavillion* is visible. But was the *Pavillion* ever visible or was it merely the effect of a linguistic operation? Was it only a *performative* fiction? Visual art produced by enunciative strategies?

From the start, General Idea were lucky or intuitive enough to hit upon an overall totalizing structure, which, nonetheless, was elaborated and articulated over time. Not so lucky myself, I must follow when their structure is complete—forever a timeless and closed system. So in my descriptions here, I must move back and forth in time, flipping in and out of focus between content and context, presenting General Idea's work in all its pretended—because intended—"ambiguity without contradiction." •

---

1. Jorge Zontal (Slobodan Saia-Levy) 1944–1994; Felix Partz (Ron Gabe) 1945–1994; AA Bronson (Michael Tims) 1946– . Although General Idea always maintained they began in 1968, they actually came together in 1969. See Fern Bayer, "The Search for the Spirit," *The Search for the Spirit: General Idea 1968–1975* (Toronto: Art Gallery of Ontario, 1997), 10.
In its early years, a product of communal living, General Idea was a loose formation or coalition. Amongst others, it included the three Miss General Ideas of 1968, 1969, and 1970: Mimi Paige, Granada Gazelle, and Miss Honey as well as the transvestite chanteuse Pascal. (Miss General of 1968 and 1969 were retrospective crownings.).

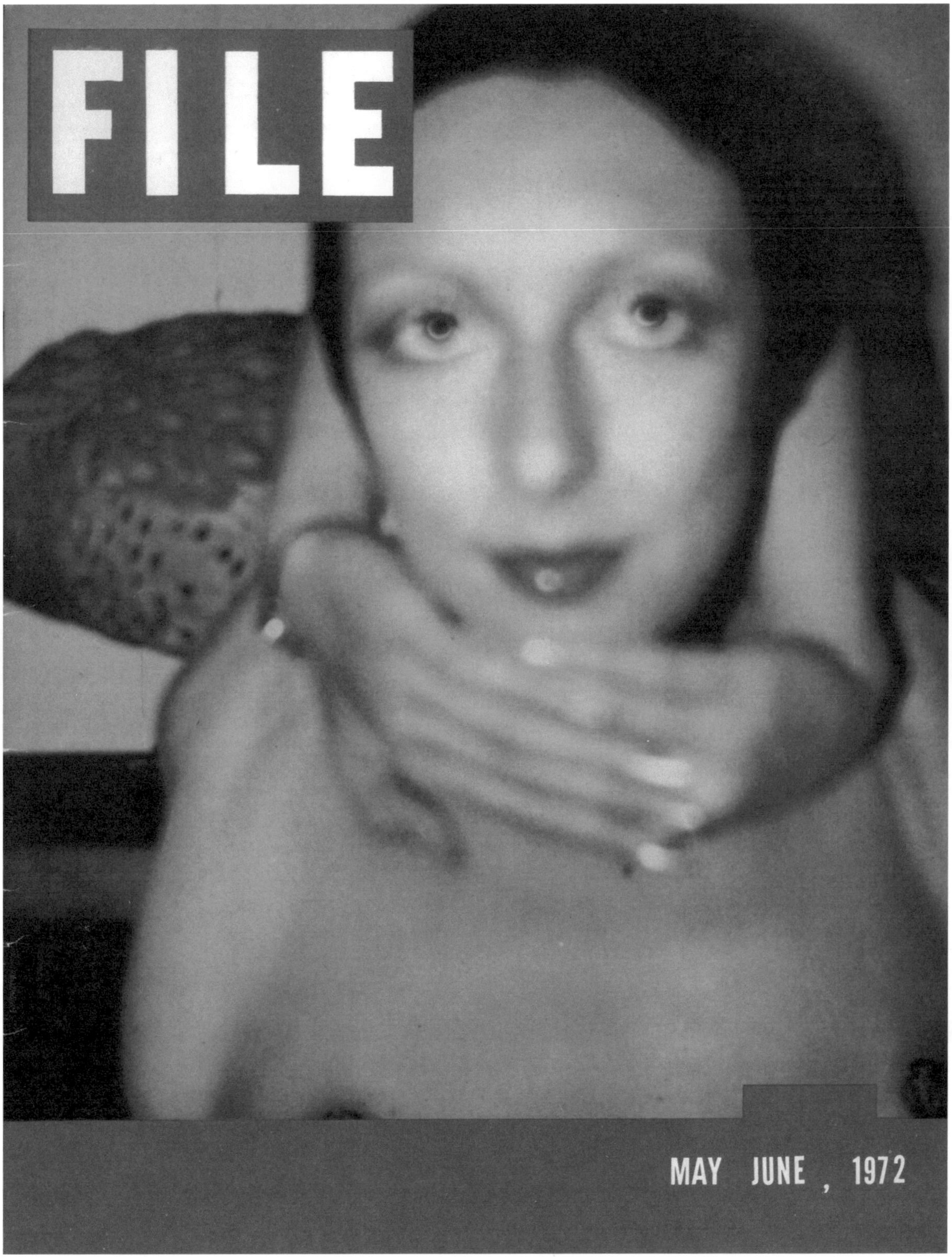

FILE 1:2&3 (May/June 1972), cover

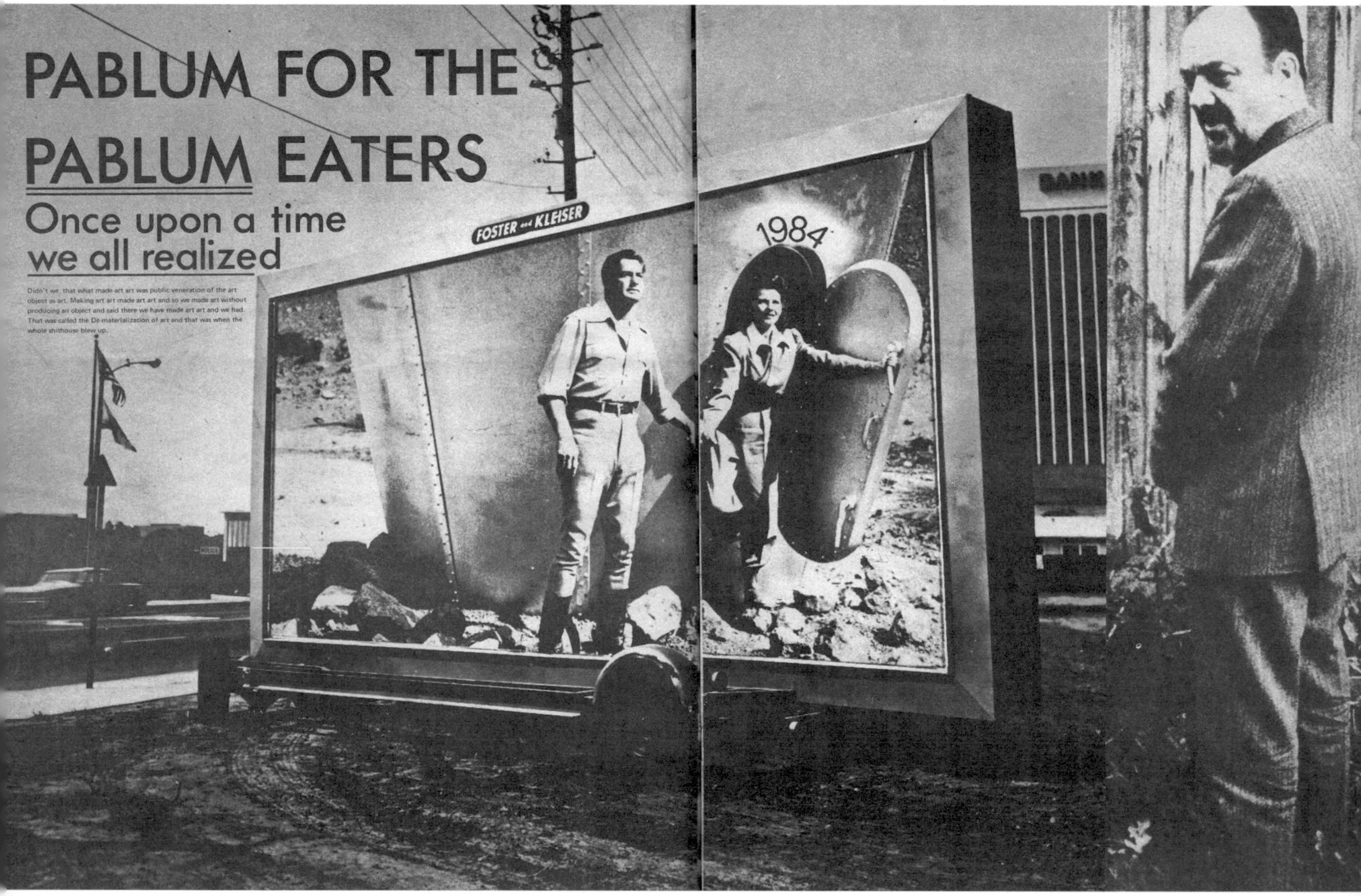

PABLUM FOR THE PABLUM EATERS

Once upon a time we all realized

Didn't we, that what made art art was public veneration of the art object as art. Making art art made art art and so we made art without producing an object and said there we have made art art and we had. That was called the De-materialization of art and that was when the whole shithouse blew up.

"Pablum for the Pablum Eaters," *FILE* 2:1&2 (May 1973), 16–17

MYTH TODAY

We begin, then, not with General Idea themselves but with *FILE Megazine*, but not at the beginning of *FILE* in 1972, when it was started, the typical Canadian way, with a government grant, but a year and three issues later in May 1973.[1] This moment is not privileged but it is pivotal. The editorial announced, "FILE no longer mirroring a scene, mirrors the mirror."[2]

This pivot articulates a mirror shift from reflection in general to self-reflection: a change in function of *FILE* not just from the social to the formal, or from conviviality to narcissism, but from reflecting an art scene to elaborating and disseminating General Idea's own program. Needless to say, *FILE* was always never fully one or the other.

The mirror turns to enclose and reflect itself, but in pivoting captures glimpses of both past and future. Fluctuating ambiguously, the mirror invisibly hovers on a borderline that divides the present into past and future. Complicating the present, this divide, however, also complicates past and future through the mirror's framing device, which now extends its serried views both backwards and forwards.

At the time, the May 1973 issue of *FILE* may not have been so self-conscious an expression of change, its pivot so decisive, as I make out here. A magazine never is immediately ideologically coherent but develops partially, at different speeds; any issue of a magazine represents several moments of an enterprise. So, in a sense, this issue of *FILE* both looked forward and glanced back. While looking to the future, it began to complete the past. Its pages printed the first rumours of *The 1984 Miss General Idea Pavillion*. But with the publication of the article "Pablum for the Pablum Eaters," which theorized the correspondence art movement, the first phase or function of *FILE* really was over: the magazine's founding role of disseminating Image Bank Request Lists through the Eternal Network.[3] That is, the movement was theorized at the moment of its demise, a crisis one might say. General Idea, however, always could cope with crises and turn them to their advantage.

Here were *FILE*'s initial functions as an artists' publication: disseminator of Image Bank Request Lists (a means for correspondence artists to collect their signature fetish images through the mail in order then to recirculate their obsessive compulsions) and mirror, of sorts, of a particular art scene (a clique, one might at first complain). Myth was the unlikely binding agent of these two functions. If General Idea were "concerned with the web of fact and fiction that binds and releases mythologies," *FILE Megazine* was a fictional vehicle masquerading as a factual magazine for its enactment.[4]

As the magazine was a vehicle for advocating and disseminating correspondence or mail art, the article "Pablum for the Pablum Eaters" partook of the phenomenon. It was both a description and an exemplification of the activity in its mythic dimension. The article was its own image bank, clipped from lifestyle and business magazines, of golden showers and "the future seen in retrospect" (that is, depictions of futurity imagined by the past, particularly images from the streamlined 1940s found in *Fortune* magazine)—all mimicking the picture and extended-caption format of *LIFE* magazine, but written in the avant-garde argot and prose rhythms of Gertrude Stein and William Burroughs.[5]

In the guise of writing on Image Bank, the Vancouver duo of Michael Morris and Vincent Trasov (respectively Marcel Idea, Miss General Idea of 1971, honorifically extended to 1983, and the anthropomorph Mr. Peanut, *FILE*'s first "cover girl"), the article was rather a covert methodology subverting history, and art history with it, in favour of contemporary mythology—blending camp, new age, and alternate lifestyles: "In this article seeing art as a system of signs in motion as an archive and indicator and stabilizer of culture as a means of creating fetish objects as residence for the field of imagery defining a culture, seeing all this and more in many ways we have become aware of the necessity of developing methods of generating realizing stabilizing alternate myths alternate lifestyles."[6] This complex article addressed many things, but I concentrate here on its take on myth. To do so I feign a shift to the article's republication three years later in 1976 in the Art Metropole publication *Video by Artists*, where the author stripped the prose bare of Gertrude Stein, deleted the images, and got straight to the point. Needless to say, this shift from 1973 to 1976 was another mirror trick.

•

> The decision that everything must be taken account of facilitates the creation of a memory bank.
> —Claude Lévi-Strauss

> And he breaks out all the ugliest pictures in the image bank and puts it out on the subliminal.
> —William S. Burroughs[7]

As in the earlier rendition of the article, myth was counterpoised to the category of history: "subliminal" affect as opposed to historical cause and effect; "networks of people and information as opposed to hierarchies" of rulers or events.[8] Bronson (the author of the second article though the first was unsigned) distinguished between myth as contemporary mystification and its function in primitive societies, the latter which he saw as a methodological analogy to the "Subliminal," a term we have yet to define but the zone in which these artists worked. "I am not concerned with breaking myths, nor with making myths, but with the structural implications implicit in mythology's view of the universe. In myth it is clear that *everything* must be accounted for. Unlike science, myth starts with a vision and fills in the blanks. It structures a cosmology through description, not analysis."[9] The principles of accountability, description, and part-whole relationships were to be fundamental to General Idea's practice and to the elaboration of *The 1984 Miss General Idea Pavillion.*

Bronson set his task to describe the contemporary mythology of the Eternal Network: the working practices of a network of artists exchanging images through the mail and creating individual image banks or archives of their fetish images. His article provides a handy summary to this evolving system of imagery.

Image Bank is a structure set up to generate, extend and stabilize such a system of image connections, or correspondences. Begun in 1970 by artists Michael Morris and Vincent Trasov, in Vancouver, Canada, Image Bank set out to establish a network of artists exchanging imagery and ideas without reference to existing art gallery and bureaucracy structures. In Canada in particular, where artists were fairly isolated, this filled a strong need. The first Image Bank Image Request Lists were mailed to correspondents (many from Ray Johnson's already well established New York Correspondence School); by 1972 they were being included in General Idea's FILE Magazine. These lists were simply a free listing of individuals' image requests. Like personal columns and classified sex ads, they acted as anonymous means of advertising and filling personal needs. Like penpal lists, they established communication links between artists around the world—but links of a particular kind. By establishing each artist as an image "collector," they gave each artist an image habit, committed him to image bondage. Image is virus.

> Functionally, the lists not only established and reinforced an evolving network of people, they also set up a moving field of significant contemporary imagery. And that field of imagery is a description of the world. The lists themselves became an indexing system to a vast library of imagery, while necessitating some stability and continuation by establishing each correspondent as a collector with particular image archives.[10]

Bronson added, "This is the network of artists and imagery I am calling subliminal."

If the impetus in setting up *FILE* in 1972 was to be a node in this correspondence network, by 1976 *FILE* had announced mail art's demise and stopped publishing a request list.[11] The rewriting and republication of "Pablum for the Pablum Eaters" that same year, therefore, extended correspondence art's mythic principles to other art activity, including General Idea's own, in order to show "in what way different groups continued to generate and stabilize an ongoing body of imagery as myth" derived from and continuing these earlier practices but now individualized.[12] What followed was a set of categories distant from the formalist vocabulary of the day, even from those of conceptual art.[13]

FETISH: "A fetish object is the intersection of a multiplicity of potent meanings, here made visible. It is the point at which a network of significations whirlpools around a convenient image."

RITUAL: "Fetish objects generate activity. It is only through performance that their resident meanings may be unlocked and released, reaffirmed in the present.... This activity, then, is ritual ... The performance is reenacted by replay; the fetish objects are reactivated by replay. Replay becomes a means of reading the resident meanings released by the props in performance."

EVENT: "A whole series of available fetish objects can be found in the anthropomorphs of the advertising world, especially those that have been around long enough to become imbedded in the culture.... Once again, the fetish object, here personified, becomes the focus for event."

ARCHIVE: "Within the mythological world of the Subliminal, video and film emerge primarily as an archival, rather than a 'creative' format. And such an archive is imperative for the stabilization of the intricate 'history' or myth currently evolving."

FORMAT: "One common characteristic of all these events and the General Idea's Beauty Pageants is that they make use of available formats, familiar formats, acceptable formats for the re-creation and transmutation of current culture…. Hence: the beauty pageant, the nightclub act, the election campaign, the media stunt."[14]

In this last sentence, Bronson was talking respectively of the appropriated formats of General Idea, Dr. Brute, Mr. Peanut, and Ant Farm. But he was always talking about General Idea's procedures whether they were named or not. These categories already existed in the earlier version of the article without General Idea being so central, based as it was on Image Bank. In *FILE*, it is often a matter of *who* really is being described, whether named or not. I'm not suggesting a subterfuge on General Idea's part. General Idea cannot be divorced from the development of *FILE*, just as their work cannot be separated from the collective enterprise of the period that *FILE* represented.[15]

The correspondence network was no less than an attempt to map contemporary consciousness in terms of its mythic structure, something presumed absent in modern man. But it was *contemporary* myth only in the sense that it was still conscious as archived within media representations. These were démodé and depassé, demobbed and declassified images ripe for reclassification as *media* mythology. Undoubtedly, "alternate myths" reflecting "alternate lifestyles" were coloured by the countercultural sixties and seventies, but myth was a matter really of *reception*—a reception, moreover, of all that seemingly was rejected by the counterculture. For baby boomers (Zontal, b. 1944, Partz b. 1945, Bronson, b. 1946), this meant the "mythologies" or "mystique" of the 1940s and 1950s found in the postwar publicity apparatus of magazines such as *Fortune*, *Time*, and *LIFE* and the banal first years of television. In this sense, "myth" fulfilled Roland Barthes's criteria that "Mythical speech is made of a material which has *already* been worked on so as to make it suitable for communication."[16] In this sense, re-mythologized art was "a system of signs in motion as an archive and indicator and stabilizer of culture as a means of creating fetish objects as residence for the field of imagery defining a culture."

Correspondence artists traded ready-made images, that is, those already published and circulated as automatically recognized icons—in the process individualizing them as personal fetishes. Their aim was not demystification, therefore, but "amplified" obsession. "By establishing each artist as an image 'collector,' [correspondence] gave each artist an image habit, committed him to image bondage. Image is virus." (I reserve discussion of "image habit," with its overtones of drug addiction, and "image bondage," with that of s/m fetishism, likewise the discussion of "viral" parasitism, with its link to criminality, to later.)

In the subliminal network, artists became Public Relations agents for their own individuated archetypes, responsible through networking for maintaining their own image habit. (Pseudonyms lent a covert status to artists' habits.) Some of these images were already quasi-mythological in terms of their copyrightable iconography within a commercial publicity system. Planters' Mr. Peanut appropriated by Vincent Trasov, for example, differed from the leopard spots of Dr. Brute (Eric Metcalfe), which were more general in their function as a "medium by which ideas enter the object."[17] Artists linked these ready-made images, beyond their original copyrightable context or pervasive appearance, in "systems of imagery" that now were "description[s] of the world"—myths, that is. Each archive housed a myth; each was a myth.

Myths are socially received as unquestioned inheritances, not ironically constructed and archly contrived as here in artists' fabrications. They are a collective, anonymous endeavor. Over the twentieth century, especially in the post-war era, media culture, however, changed everything. Advertising provided the ground of dissemination and reinforcement by repetition for perpetually new sets of manufactured myths for a consumerist capitalist system. The corresponding invention of publicity completed the process in the intentionality given to desired effect: that is, advertising was part of a coordinated design effort to sway consumers through images and slogans. As Marshall McLuhan wrote in 1951, "ours is the first age in which many thousands of the best-trained individual minds have made it a full-time business to get inside the collective public mind" and in the process creating a "folklore of industrial man, so much of which stems from the laboratory, the studio, and the advertising agencies. But amid the diversity of our inventions and abstract techniques of production and distribution there will be found a great degree of cohesion and unity. This consistency is not conscious in origin or effect and seems to arise from a sort of collective dream."[18]

The subliminal network was parasitical on what was already a dream, on what had already been worked over by a process of rationalized dream work called advertising. Artists were there to exploit this mythic unconscious, infiltrating the collective mind through the very images purveyed to it and rewriting them as *camp* folklore. Not just the dreams, they copied as well the publicity apparatus that fabricated and delivered these constructs. One could say that General Idea's whole enterprise was nothing but an advertising agency—as well as being a laboratory and studio—with the proviso that it advertised nothing but itself, that is to say, nothing but its own fabrication.

In correspondence art, myth was all about linkages creating new archives of imagery: "Systems of images evolve, then, as 'families' of imagery, connected to each other by strings of equivalencies."[19] Collecting particular types of images made a mythological whole. Ready-made mythological systems were another matter. They were appropriated already whole. In Ant Farm's *Cadillac Ranch* or General Idea's *The 1984 Miss General Idea Pageant*, "American mythology is deactivated and included in [artists'] larger mythological structures, their concern with themselves as artists concerned with culture."[20] Deactivating was not demythologizing, however. It was re-mythologizing. Formats were taken over and filled in otherwise; contexts were reactivated with new content: "We moved in on history and occupied images, emptying them of meaning, reducing them to shells. We filled these shells then with Glamour."[21]

This process was not merely a matter of collecting images, on the one hand, or appropriating formats, on the other. It was not only "a method of invasion" of a ready-made system, but also the articulation of a new system from what was cannibalized. It was a *description* to new ends. In General Idea's case, this articulating technique *accounts* for all of their work, for *The 1984 Miss General Idea Pageant* and the *Pavillion*. Accounting: that is, it was the *measure* of the enterprise and the *telling* of it at the same time. In myth, everything is given right away but the details are filled in over time. Description was functional; it had to add up to a structured, meaningful whole.

"In myth it is all very clear that everything must be accounted for. One starts with a vision and names the parts. One structures a cosmology through description."[22]

Description was not, well, just descriptive. It played another role of articulation and elaboration. Description was constructive; myth was a "universe to be described, hence created."[23] Statements were descriptions of systems *yet to be*. So description had to be a particular type of *saying* as *realizing*: "Myth is essentially the naming of parts. In this way it becomes clear what one is saying is doing is speaking and one does it. One realizes the myth."[24] This saying as doing—otherwise known as a performative utterance—was *the* all-important strategy in the creation of the General Idea myth as well as in the erection of *The 1984 Miss General Idea Pavillion*. •

1. *FILE* initially was funded through an initiative of the Trudeau government: the Local Initiatives Program Grant. For a description of is origins, see "Catalogue," *FILE* 1:2&3 (May/June 1972), 57. For publication of some of the documents related to its start up, see Vincent Bonin, ed. *Protocoles documentaries (1967–1975) / Documentary Protocols (1967–1975)* (Montreal: Leonard and Bina Ellen Art Gallery, 2010), 144–162. On the origins and functions of *FILE* see David Brittain, "F is for Filing System: An Interview with AA Bronson," *Afterimage* 35:3 (November/December 2007), 9–12. Also compare *Showcard* 1-015 "Search for the Site Office": "VOICE OVER: When we started this search we needed a site-office, some place we could just get back to the drawing boards. We moved in with our scrapbooks and our references, slapped a coat of paint on the place, and applied for a grant. Business as usual."
2. "Editorial: Bulletin from the Ivory Tower," *FILE* 2:1&2 (May 1973), 15.
3. Rather, I should say, one of its first two roles was over; it continued to mirror the art scene in its BZZZ BZZZ BZZZ gossip column.
4. "Editorial: Some Juicy and Malicious Gossip," *FILE* 1:1 (April 1972), 3; "Editorial: Fictional Aspects of a Factual Magazine," *FILE* 1:2&3 (May/June 1972), 8.
   Not only a web of fact and fiction, *FILE* was a media conscious magazine, situating itself in a moment of flux in the magazine publishing business: "In particular, more magazines are realizing a media consciousness, that is to say, they are referential in the context of magazine and publishing history, they are media to be swallowed by the media, a constant search for talent in preparation for the big time publications, yes, those same big brothers that are going under." "The Magazine Addicts Have Hit it Rich," *FILE* 2:1&2 (May 1973), 8.
   General Idea followed in the line of Canadian pre-eminence in media analysis of The Toronto School particularly theorists such as Harold Innis and Marshall McLuhan. There is an obvious affinity between McLuhan's *The Mechanical Bride: Folklore of Industrial Man*, first published in 1951 and reissued in soft cover in 1967, and *FILE* but no dependency.
5. The article's images were derived from two sources: General Idea's archive of future-oriented images from *Fortune* magazine and Image Bank's "Piss pics for Barbara Rrose," solicited in part in the December 1972 *FILE* Image Bank Request List.
6. "Pablum for the Pablum Eaters," *FILE* 2:1&2 (May 1973), 20.
7. These quotations served as epigraphs for both articles, though "image bank"—Burroughs's nomenclature—was perhaps unconsciously substituted for "memory bank" in the Lévi-Strauss quotation. AA Bronson corrected this slip in "Myth as Parasite/Image as Virus: General Idea's Bookshelf 1967–1975," in *The Search for the Spirit: General Idea 1968–1975*, (Toronto: Art Gallery of Ontario, 1997), 19.
8. AA Bronson, "Pablum for the Pablum Eaters," in *Video by Artists*, ed. Peggy Gale (Toronto: Art Metropole, 1976), 196.
9. Ibid., 197.

10. Ibid. Image Bank originally also included the artist Gary Lee-Nova. Of course, *FILE Megazine* itself was an image bank, its very name indicative of an archiving function: "Files are the dead matter of appropriated ideas." "Editorial: Some Juicy and Malicious Gossip."

11. The correspondence art movement was put into crisis in the very next issue of *FILE* (September 1973) where letters from both Ray Johnson and Robert Cumming announced their withdrawal. The December 1973 *FILE* had no request list, while the last list was published in the Spring 1976 issue.

12. "Pablum" (1976), 198.

13. Could we even say that they were conceptual artists after reading this article? The article pointedly contrasts and ethos and practices of conceptual artists and mythical artists.

14. "Pablum" (1976), 198–200.

15. See AA Bronson on the role of authorship and copyright in General Idea's work: "General Idea emerged in the aftermath of the Paris riots, from the detritus of hippie communes, underground newspapers, radical education, Happenings, love-ins, Marshall McLuhan, and the International Situationists. We believed in a free economy, in the abolition of copyright, and in a grass-roots horizontal structure that prefigured the internet.... Our corporate name belied individual authorship. For the entire twenty-five years of our collaboration, we questioned and played with various aspects of authorship and copyright." AA Bronson, "Copyright, Cash, Crowd Control: Art and Economy in the Work of General Idea," in *General Idea Editions: 1967–1995* (Mississauga, Ontario: Blackwood Gallery, 2003), 24, 26–7.

16. Roland Barthes, "Myth Today," in *Mythologies*, trans. Annette Lavers (New York: Hill and Wang, 1972), 110. (First published in 1957). General Idea saw themselves as bricoleurs working on the detritus of culture: "Both the scientist and 'bricoleur' might therefore be said to be constantly on the look out for 'messages'. Those which the 'bricoleur' collects are, however, ones which have to some extent been transmitted in advance..." Claude Lévi-Strauss, *The Savage Mind* (Chicago: University of Chicago Press, 1966), 20. In a similar manner, Andy Warhol and Jack Smith used degraded Hollywood stars of 1930s and 1940, as recycled in the early 1960s in the new medium of television, as the subject of their obsessions.

17. "Pablum" (1976), 198.

18. Marshall McLuhan, *The Mechanical Bride: Folklore of Industrial Man* (Boston: Beacon Press, 1967), v.

19. "Pablum" (1976), 197.

20. Ibid., 198.

21. "Glamour: Stolen Lingo," *FILE* 3:1 (Autumn 1975), n.p.

22. "Pablum" (1973), 26.

23. "Pablum" (1976), 200.

24. "Pablum" (1973), 26.

LETTERS TO THE EDITORS

CONTINUED

rage out here... but I find them to be too "hippyish" and tomorrow I'm going to see Mance Lipscoms, who is sort of like Blind Willie.

The days are so beautifully warm like 80 but by five it gets dark and very cold and the contrast is amazing from hot pants to full length furs in a couple hours.

Calif. is breathtakingly beautiful but like I've said, Who can live without breath.

It is also quite a well known fact that rats live in the palm trees.

I'm so bored here and creatively frustrated. I'm really cured. Barry thinks I shouldn't hide my "poetry". I thought it was too personal and very bad but hes a teacher and he knows so Art World get ready—Miss Honey is gathering up steam. (That is if I don't die of rustration here first). One cannot live without a car or phone— literally.

So, as I gaze thru the window into the Camellia tree, and listen to the Aleatory babies wail, I realize that a woman travelling alone is not the best way of enjoying ones vacation. I wonder if I'll go anywhere alone ever again.. I'm so looking forward to going home with Michael. A good male companion beats all the (pardon me) lovers in the world.

If nothing else Ron, I've somewhat learned to be cool.

I'm sure you people are buzzing with work and shivering from cold. I somehow envy you right now. Also I sure hope you have a job for me when I get back. But... que sera sera. I sure wish I could learn to relax. All that valliums do is put me to sleep and I don't want to sleep away this Calif. trip but I seem to have no better alternative. I wish Ed Rusha would be my knight in shining armed car. I have not seen any part of L.A. I pay so much for cabs or gas to be driven to a restaurant and then so much for food that I blow almost $10 a day. And cigarettes, wow...but at least I'm getting my fill of Mexican Food. I even had Ratatui— a gourmet French delicacy at Donas before the big fight.

I saw El Topo— I recommend it only if you're prepared for a lot of bloodshed and Cisco Pike what a laugh—Viva drew me in and Kustofferson, the new superstar, what a joke— bored me.

CONTINUED ON PAGE 14

April, 1972. **FILE** Vol. 1, No. 1

CONTENTS

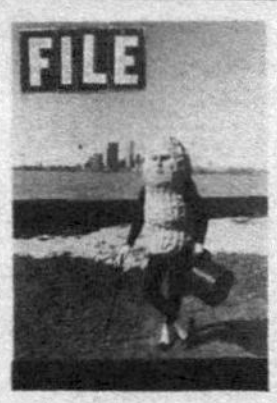

When the New York Corres-Sponge Dancers of Vancouver arrived in Toronto (see pages 6 & 12) they were invited to the island by the staff and freinds of the Goose and Duck Newspaper. Mr. Peanut was so excited by the splendid veiw of the Toronto skyline that he fell off the ferry. Here he rests in front of the view that caused his fall

The following list, page by page, shows the source from which each picture in this issue was gathered. Where a single page is indebted to several sources, credit is recorded picture by picture (left to right, top to bottom) and line by line, (lines separated by dashes) unless otherwise specified.

Cover— David Wlysky
5— Mr. Peanut, Ant Farm, Yvonne Rainer.
6,7— The New York Corres-Sponge Dance School of Vancouver.
8,9— Ray Johnson—General Idea, Image Bank—Anna Banana, Chicken Bank, Mr. Peanut— Jim Hamilton, Susan Bunny—Chicken Bank, General Idea—General Idea, Fat City School of Finds Art, Chicken Bank.
10,11— The Eternal Network
14— Talkin' Dirty
15— General Idea
16— Heshe&it Works
17.18,19— Art City
20— Chicken Bank
21— Robert Cumming
23— Art Zack, Art Zack, Miss Paige.

FILE is a transcanada art organ produced by artists for artists on a monthly basis. Correspondance should be directed to the editors at 87 Yonge Street, Toronto 1, Ontario, Canadada. All contributions will be considered, but emphasis is placed on evidence of research or other activity in progress, rather than on criticism, aesthetics or historical considerations.

SOME JUICY AND MALICIOUS GOSSIP

MYTH—TAKEN

The phenomenon of FILE and of files emerges from the underbrush of available art, shuffling its leaves in patterned disarray. Files are the dead matter of appropriated ideas, the manure of rat city, the space hidden between one gallery and the next.

In order to grasp the FILE phenomenon it is necessary to realize the extent of concerns involving the invisible network that bind the world of Dr. Brute and Alex the Holy, Marcel Idea and Miss Generality, Clara the Bag Lady and Lady Brute, the Swedish Lady and Mr. Cones, Dadaland and Dada Long Legs, A.A.Bronson and Dr. Fluxus, Ray Johnson and Susan Bunny, Anna Banana, and Honey Banannas, Bum Bank and Art Rat, Brutiful Brutopia and Canadada. We are concerned with the web of fact and fiction that binds and releases mythologies that are the sum experience of artists and non-artists in co-operative existence today.

Every image is a self image. Every image is a mirror.

We are astounded at the diversity of common images and common fantasies exposing the quality of group life now.

High art concerns are lone concerns and these must continue too. But the word emerges as a sign and a signal, and these are exchanged. When you smile at a mirror, does a mirror smile at you? Humor lies in the beat between action and recognition.

On local levels the Nihilist Spasm Band of London Ontario and the Goose and Duck Newspaper of Wards Island, Toronto, are both developed and appreciated examples. The New York Correspondence School begun by Sugardada Ray Johnson, remains the recognized forerunner of international image exchange now in operation.

While London has remained introspective, Vancouver has left the banquet years for the banquet. Image Bank, The New Era Social Club, Metromedia and the rest have extended their well integrated base of operations onto a national and international scale. Joining A Space, General Idea and The Coach House Press of Toronto and Ace Space of Victoria, they have invaded the subliminal and broken open the image bank.

The obsessions are streaming up front. Each authenticates the rest, creating a total scene which is at once ephemeral and impossible to ignore. We might list the concerns, we might expose the personal imagery which has been released from the private world of High Art obscurity and into the mainstream.

We might catergorize connections and demonstrate the fluidity of the baloonging situation. But in the end it is all the same; the telling destroys the actuality and the story slips through our fingers, wriggling into other levels convoluted beyond expectation.

What is the function of

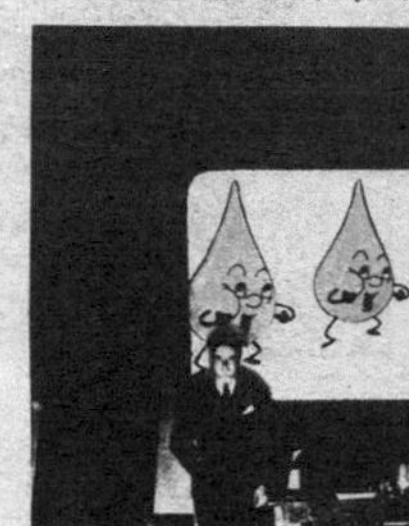

the myth? The myth transforms Pandora's box into the image bank of compulsions. The myth slides down the center, slicing realities into thin transparencies shuffling lives like leaves and dissolving dualities into fabled tales. In the story it all comes together. In the myth opposite possiblities become complementary content. In the fable we lay out models, testing and tasting. In the space between myths lies the lucid expression of artists activity.

FILE is precisely this: the extension and documentation of available space, the authentication and reinforcement of available myths lying within the context of Canadian art today.

"Editorial," *FILE* 1:1 (April 1972), 3

EDITORIAL

So we are back to the beginning, not the beginning of General Idea (1969) but the beginning of *FILE* and its first issue (1972). And since we are at a beginning, perhaps it is time to address the issue of the editorial—and how the editorial, at the beginning of a magazine, addresses us. This is especially so for an inaugural issue that audaciously called itself a "transcanada art organ."

Such was the utopian aim of *FILE* because there was nothing ready-made to reflect, no transcanada art scene to speak of because it had not yet been represented. Not that, nascent, it was not there: the problem was that it had not yet been given reality by being mirrored to itself. Listen to AA Bronson in 1982 describing the problems of the period for young Canadian artists:

> As an artist writing about museums by artists, about my own history, which is a story beginning in 1968, a Canadian story with elaborately Canadian characters dreaming the Canadian dream of one community, that is a network of communities, sea to sea, in that reticent evocation of collective consciousness which seems our national destiny; as a Canadian artist then, wanting a Canadian art scene just like in New York, or London, or Paris in the thirties; as a Canadian artist typically unable to picture the reality of a Canadian art scene except as a dream projected upon the national landscape as a sea-to-sea connective tissue; that is as a dream community connected by and reflected by the media; that is authenticated by its own reflection in the media; as such a Canadian artist desiring to see not necessarily himself, but the picture of his art scene pictured on TV; and knowing the impossibility of an art scene without real museums (the Art Gallery of Ontario was not a *real* museum for us), without real art magazines (and *artscanada* was not a *real* art magazine for us), without real artists (no, Harold Town was not a *real* artist for us, and we forgot that we ourselves were real artists, because we had not seen ourselves in the media—real artists, like Frank Stella, appeared in *Artforum* magazine); as such as an artist desiring such a picture of such a scene, such a reality from sea-to-shining-sea, then, it was natural to call upon our national attributes—the bureaucratic tendency and the protestant work ethic—and working together, and working sometimes not together we laboured to structure, or rather to untangle from the messy post-sixties spaghetti of our minds, artist-run galleries, artists' video, and artist-run magazines. And that allowed us to allow ourselves to see ourselves as an art scene. And we did.[1]

They did! And *FILE* was a large part of that doing. But would one have known it at the time, given the subject of *FILE*'s first editorial, titled "Some Juicy and Malicious Gossip"?[2]

Malicious perhaps because the editorial set about the rumour of the demise of the myth of individual genius ("high art concerns are lone concerns") in favour of an "invisible network" of "artists and non-artists" who had "invaded the subliminal and broken open the image bank," releasing imagery from "the private world of High Art obscurity ... into the mainstream."[3] Collectivity opposed individuality as a new ideal both in terms of the source of images and their subsequent alterations: "We are astounded at the diversity of common images and common fantasies exposing the quality of group life now."

Gossip perhaps because the editors stated: "We are concerned with the web of fact and fiction that binds and releases mythologies that are the sum experience of artists and non-artists in co-operative existence today." Having identified the web of fact and fiction that produces both myth and gossip (one and the same perhaps), the editors then asked: "What is the function of the myth? The myth transforms Pandora's box into the image bank of compulsions. The myth slides down the center, slicing realities into thin transparencies shuffling lives like leaves and dissolving dualities into fabled tales. In the story it all comes together. In the myth opposite possibilities become complementary content. In the fable we lay out models, testing and tasting. In the space between myths lies the lucid expression of artists' activity."

The space between myths was fictive; yet space was also the actual links between a developing network of art-initiated activity across the country. The editorial thus named the participants and "institutions" of this invisible network (predominately in Vancouver and Toronto) and also identified the magazine's two-fold function: "*FILE* is precisely this: the extension and documentation of available space, the authentication and reinforcement of available myths lying within the context of Canadian art today." A month later, the second issue stated: "We began as a mirror of sorts, a transcanada organ of communication within the art scene, a way of looking at the scene and oneself within it... We are a node in the correspondence network, and *FILE* is evidence of correspondence that passes through General Idea Headquarters; friends, visitors, mail, gossip."[4]

FILE contrived itself to be the house organ for the correspondence clan. It served an administrative function with its Image Bank Request Lists and Artist Directory, the latter "with an emphasis on people interested in the Eternal Network and the correspondence chain";[5] it published correspondents' print-based artwork derived from this network in articles that mimicked news magazine layouts.[6]

The "correspondence" of friends and visitors, as well as the mail that passed through General Idea Headquarters, reappeared in *FILE* in a fictionalized form of gossip. Here, too, mythic principles of fabrication applied: real personalities were fictionalized; events were concocted to assume the form of popular rituals, such as popularity contests ("Top Ten").[7] Myth and scene came together in a picture-magazine format that imitated *LIFE*.

FILE reflected neither the inheritance of an art scene (a legacy that was rejected) nor the institution of it (in time artist-run institutions, too, would develop) but the devious inauguration of one through *fictional* strategies.[8] Intention was not to inaugurate a myth but to use myth to inaugurate a scene—at first, the myth that one existed! Gossip was a device to link scene to myth in order to elevate an art scene to mythic proportions, that is, in order to make it *visible*. Hence, the necessary web of fact *and* fiction.

The editorial deviously shared this inaugurating function. Coming first, an editorial was inaugural. Fictionalizing, it broke journalistic rules. It, too, was a web of fact and fiction. The editorial took advantage of its lead position in a magazine to stage direct what followed. It, too, was part of the performance. That is, the editorial had a *performative* as much as a prescriptive function. Like fable, it too was a model of myth, however well disguised by its authoritative format. We should look to *FILE*'s editorials as much as to General Idea's *Pageants* and *Pavillion* for the development of the concepts that comprise their work. •

---

1. AA Bronson, "The Humiliation of the Bureaucrat: Artist-run Spaces as Museums by Artists," in *Museums by Artists*, eds. AA Bronson and Peggy Gale (Toronto: Art Metropole, 1983), 29–30. Reprinted in *From Sea to Shining Sea* (Toronto: The Power Plant, 1987), 164.
2. The aim here is not to write a history of *FILE* as well as that of General Idea but to find where the two enterprises complement each other. The implication, though, is that the self-fashioning of General Idea and the creation of a transcanada art community through *FILE* go hand in hand.
3. "Editorial: Some Juicy and Malicious Gossip," *FILE* 1:1 (April 1972), 3. All unacknowledged quotations in this section are from this editorial. What a non-artist or rather "practising non-artist" is was made clear in the second issue of *FILE*, where we find that they are bag ladies and street people such as Clara the Bag Lady, Alex the Holy, and The Swedish Lady.
4. "Catalogue," *FILE* 1:2&3 (May/June 1972), 57.
5. "Artists' Directory," *FILE* 1:2&3 (May/June 1972), 53.
6. A further function was archival, not in the mythic manner that *FILE* itself was as an archive ("Files are the dead matter of appropriated ideas..."), but as a "preliminary attempt to gather information on available sources of Canadian art imagery and documentation; books, video, slides, films, or whatever." "Catalogue," 57.
7. "Top Ten" was a popularity contest based on casting ballots through the mail. It appeared in the first two issues of *FILE* and provided a "straight forward description of the web of concerns that always defines an art scene or others." "Top Ten," *FILE* 1:1 (April 1972), 8.
8. There was an element of nationalism in this strategy consistent with the call in Canada then for economic nationalism, which was also widely expressed in Canadian theatre, literature, and visual art. The following might be read in the same light: "Myth is the past brought into the present, ritualized and enacted that the past may be created by the present, that we may be masters of our own culture." "Pablum for the Pablum Eaters," *FILE* 2:1&2 (May 1973), 26.

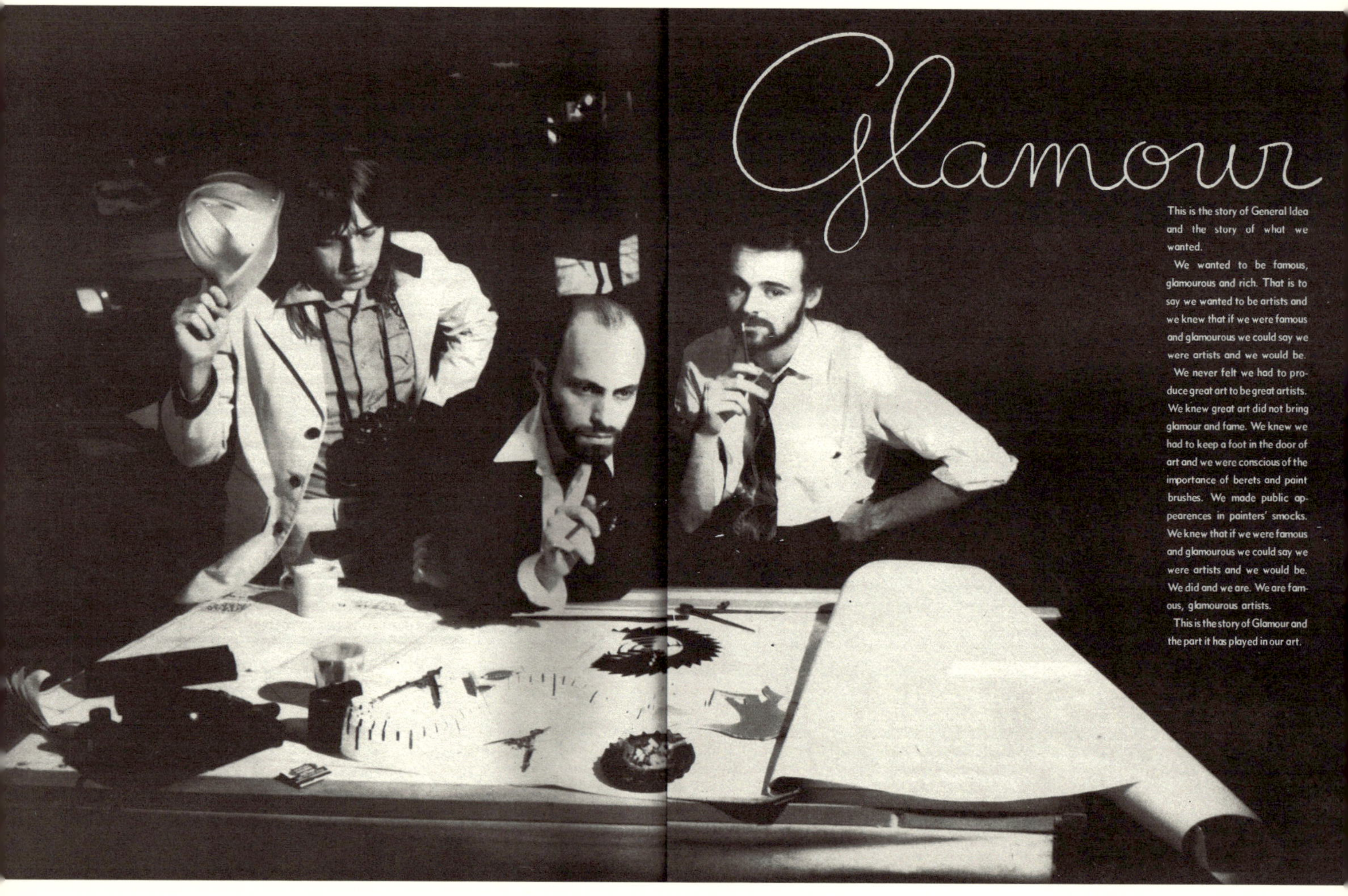

Glamour

This is the story of General Idea and the story of what we wanted.

We wanted to be famous, glamourous and rich. That is to say we wanted to be artists and we knew that if we were famous and glamourous we could say we were artists and we would be.

We never felt we had to produce great art to be great artists. We knew great art did not bring glamour and fame. We knew we had to keep a foot in the door of art and we were conscious of the importance of berets and paint brushes. We made public appearences in painters' smocks. We knew that if we were famous and glamourous we could say we were artists and we would be. We did and we are. We are famous, glamourous artists.

This is the story of Glamour and the part it has played in our art.

"Glamour" issue, *FILE* 3:1 (Autumn 1975), 21–22

THIS IS THE **STORY** OF GENERAL IDEA

Everybody knows the story:

> This is the story of General Idea and the story of what we wanted. We wanted to be famous, glamourous and rich. That is to say we wanted to be artists and we knew that if we were famous and glamourous we could say we were artists and we would be. We never felt we had to produce great art to be great artists. We knew great art did not bring glamour and fame. We knew we had to keep a foot in the door of art and we were conscious of the importance of berets and paint brushes. We made public appearances in painters' smocks. We knew that if we were famous and glamourous we could say we were artists and we would be. We did and we are. We are famous, glamourous artists.[1]

This *is* the story of General Idea—as told famously by the artists themselves, that is. How could we not dispense with analysis and start only with it as if offering a myth, a myth of their origin? Not a history, but a story. An origin in *and* as their own story, we could say. *Fait accompli.* They said it; they did it. They were famous, glamourous artists. And the saying was the doing.

We take this story at face value, even knowing that it is fictional. A fiction, I repeat. We accept it as true for the necessary functioning of their work. Of course, we are part of sustaining this fiction, too. But we also know there is a back story for every story, several perhaps.[2] So let's look at General Idea's foundational statement more closely.

"This is the story of General Idea," they said. That is, this is the *story* they told. But *telling* was the methodology of their work, the means of its fictional fabrication. Their work existed only in the telling. Telling was performative. Or, this is the story *they* told *themselves*. In other words, they didn't rely on others to tell it. Could they rely on others, though? On the operational level of telling, could their story ever be summarized and told by others? At the same time, this is the story they told themselves, that is to say, *to* themselves, for lack of a sustaining history in the void of Canadian culture. Saying so was a *fiction* to allow them to go on making art in a place where they felt there was no scene.

This story, however, is only one of a series of interlocking fictions of different types and functions within General Idea's work as a whole, each one nested within another. Fictions within fictions. •

1. "Glamour," *FILE* 3:1 (Autumn 1975), n.p.
2. This is not to imply that there is a "behind" to the story, a transmissible meaning, for example. Compare what the *Showcards* say of the Miss General Idea Vehicle: "There's nothing behind it at all. It's all on the surface" (2-038). "There's nothing behind it at all, and that is one of the problems we continue to encounter. People want to know what's behind it but is anyone really interested in what goes on behind the canvas? Our guess is *no*" (2-040).

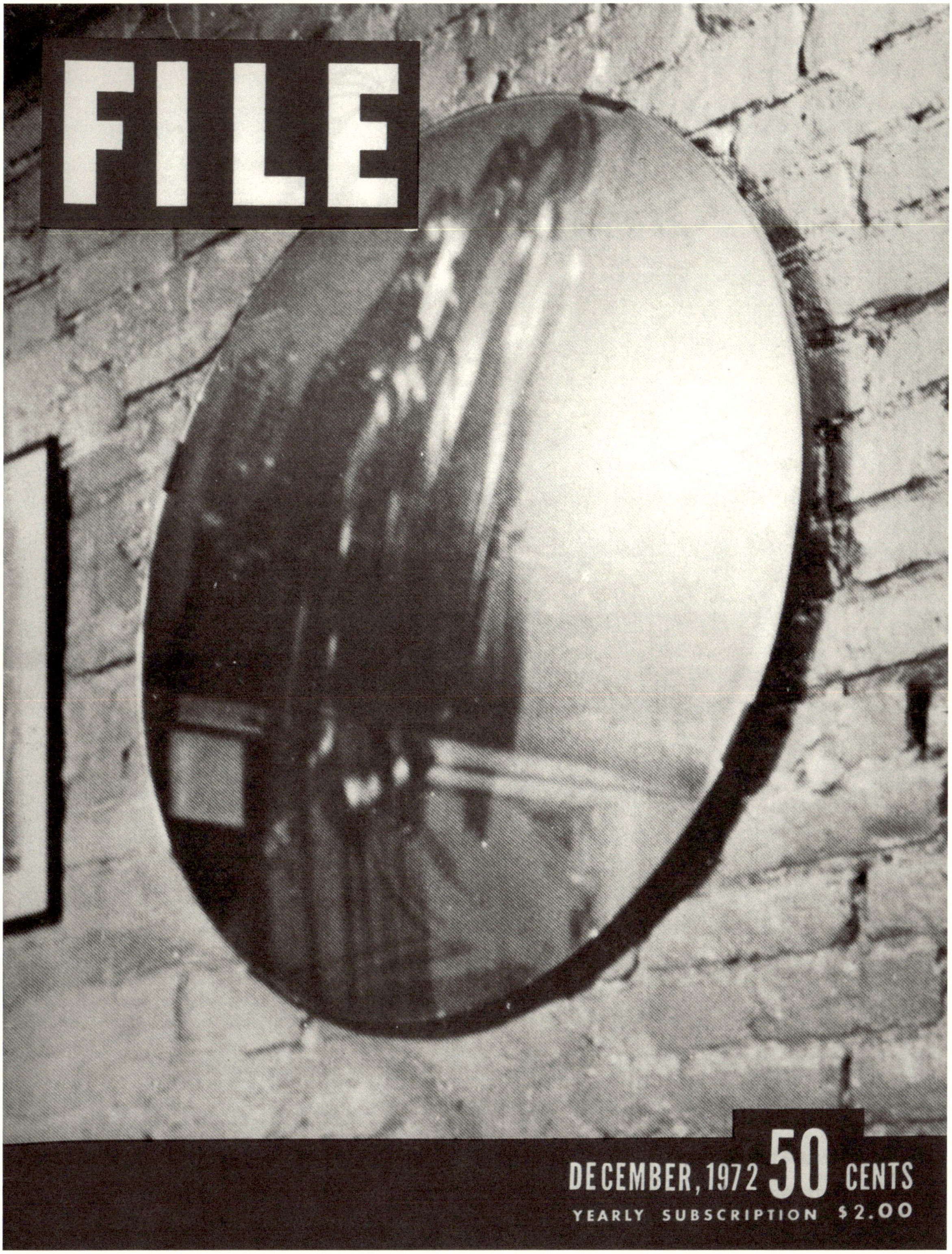
FILE
DECEMBER, 1972 50 CENTS
YEARLY SUBSCRIPTION $2.00

FILE 1:4 (December 1972), cover

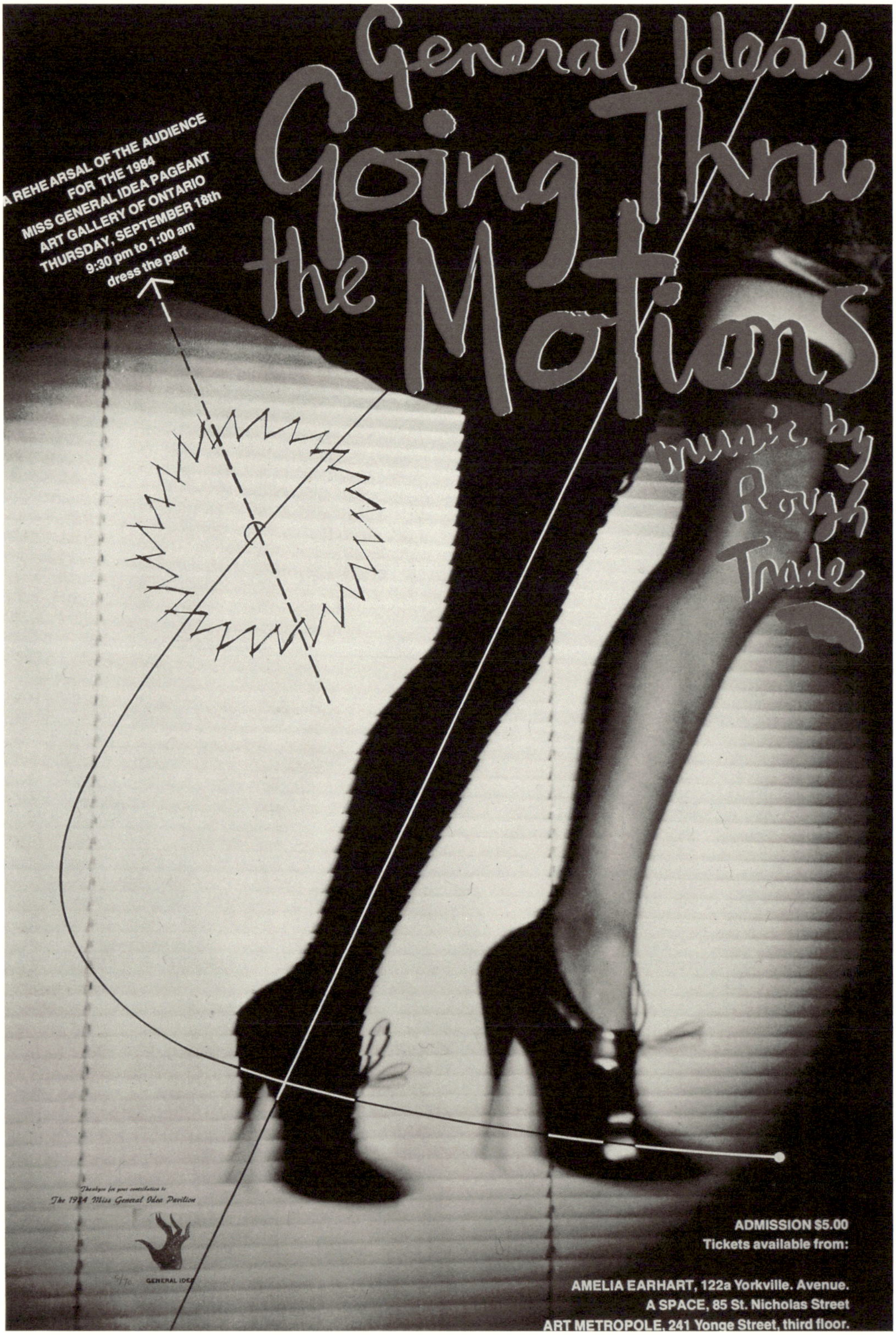

General Idea's Going thru the Motions poster, 1975

THE 1984 MISS GENERAL IDEA **PAGEANT**

> The 1984 Miss General Idea Pageant is basically this: a framing device we have framed for our own devices to contain our frame-ups. The Search for the Spirit of Miss General Idea is the ritualized pageant of creation, production, selection, presentation, competition, manipulation and the revelation of that which is suitable for framing.
>
> —*Going thru the Motions*, 1975

In some way, we must start with *The 1984 Miss General Idea Pageant*, that is, with something already framed or formatted. But even the *Pageant* has a history on its path to perfection, and, for this reason, we shall not discuss its 1970 staging. That first pageant was framed by the wrong context, reflective of General Idea's experimental theatre interests, and performed in a Festival of Underground Theatre. It was not until the next year, at the Art Gallery of Ontario in Toronto, that General Idea inhabited the right framework by appropriating the format of an art gallery in turn.

For the *Pageant* was the ritual of the *art* system, or more particularly a parody of its modes of evaluation and elevation. But it was also the outcome of another system or, rather, community: that of the correspondence network. Contestants were solicited by and applications submitted through the mail. The entry kit, as documented by Fern Bayer, was a plethora of correspondence ephemera ready to be recirculated:

> A mail-order creation in elaborate form, the Pageant involved the participation of artists from across Canada. Sixteen pre-selected "finalists" were each sent an *Entry Kit* by insured mail. The kit consisted of a box (silkscreened with the Pageant logo: an idyllic South Sea island dotted with swaying palm trees, engulfed by a sunrise) containing a variety of items: a folded liver-coloured dress, *The Miss General Idea Gown*, with a specially printed letterpress tag (one of the sixteen left over from *Betty's* [1970]); a silkscreened card folder containing a typed letter of invitation signed by Granada Gazelle, Miss General Idea 1969; a General Idea Business card; a black-and-white photograph of the *Artist's Conception: Miss General Idea 1971*; a black-and-white photograph of the reworked *Globe and Mail* newspaper article (about *Betty's*) featuring the *The Miss General Idea Gown*; an autographed black-and-white photograph of Miss Honey (Miss General Idea 1970); *The 1970 Miss General Idea Pageant* program published just for the occasion; a perforated entry form with rules; a folded acceptance card with pre-addressed return envelope; and an application form requesting the name of the contestant or of the "stand-in" of his/her choice, along with the name of the photographer.[1]

The *Pageant* at first was doubly procedural but also doubly referential, using a doubly demodé form (the beauty pageant was culturally outmoded: both unhip *and* contested by feminists) to comment on the art system. Doubly inflected, the irony cut two ways, but only one was really pointed; the other was an easy target. The beauty contest, of course, was any form of judgement and elevation, any form of crowning, that is, but it was particularly rich in its protocols or clichés of selection, presentation, and elevation. Knowing them off by heart, everyone could participate in its contrivances. The beauty pageant format itself was disposable; another cultural form equally might be appropriated to comment on the art system. "The most exotic cultural forms are here in our midst," Bronson noted in "Pablum for the Pablum Eaters."[2]

Demodé, it was not the format that was disposed of so much as it was preserved while the content was cannibalized. Preservation was exaggeration: *commented* on, the ritual became camp. It was all a matter of staging ... and the re-staging of staging. Re-framing any format's framing devices, General Idea inflected the presentation towards their own program. Programs need maintenance, however. And it was too much work to maintain an ongoing Pageant every year. Hence, winner Marcel Idea (Image Bank artist Michael Morris), who, according to the judges, "captured Glamour without falling into it," in 1973 was officially declared Miss General Idea until the yet still mythical 1984 when his period of elevation would be reversed in a "decrowning ritual."[3]

Hence, ongoing performances, rather, were "rehearsals" for that ultimate, culminating *Pageant* in the future 1984 Miss General Idea Pavillion purpose-built for its event. *Blocking* (1974) rehearsed the audience in entrances, exits, and standing ovations, all to Jorge Zontal's and Granada Gazelle's colour commentary. The grand *Going thru the Motions* (1975), held once again at the Art Gallery of Ontario, practiced audience routines on a more elaborate scale. *Towards an Audience Vocabulary* (1978) staged an audience, literally. That is, it put an audience on stage in order for it to perform its behavioural cues while another audience, the real one, now role-deprived, looked on from the wings of its own displacement, so to speak. In *Hot Property* (1977), the *Pavillion* caught on fire during the "may-I-have-the envelope" routine. But we are getting ahead of ourselves with this fire before the razed *Pavillion* has even been raised in our discussion.

The *Pageant* was a model, that is to say it was mythical, an *ur*-myth perhaps for General Idea's enterprise as a whole, but its fate was to be replaced—or displaced. We could say of the *Pageant* what AA Bronson wrote of Ant Farm: that "mythology is deactivated and included in Ant Farm's larger mythological structures, their concern with themselves as artists concerned with culture."[4] That is, cut out from its original context, the beauty pageant played a role within the framing device of General Idea's *Pageant*, but the *Pageant* itself, from about 1973 on, was to function within a more consuming mythological (and morphological) structure: *The 1984 Miss General Idea Pavillion.*

This logic of consumption and incorporation ("intellectual cannibalism") was no more than another framing device, a nesting of one frame within another—or one format within another. The *Pageants* already inhabited a double format: they were always performed as if in television studios—playing to the camera as well as to scripts—with videotapes as their outcome.[5] Audience members were not simply passive but consciously and ironically played their preordained role of manipulated collective judgement. "The Miss General Idea Pageant was an archetypal format containing archetypal scenes requiring an archetypal audience performing archetypal responses."[6] •

1. Fern Bayer, "Uncovering the Roots of General Idea: A Documentation and Description of Early Projects 1968–1975," in *The Search for the Spirit: General Idea 1968–1975* (Toronto: Art Gallery of Ontario, 1997), 65. For a description of the event, see ibid., 65–75.
2. AA Bronson, "Pablum for the Pablum Eaters," in *Video by Artists*, ed. Peggy Gale (Toronto: Art Metropole, 1976), 200.
3. "The Spirit of the 1984 Miss General Idea Pavillion," *IFEL* 2:3 (September 1973), insert.
4. "Pablum" (1976), 198.
5. This is exemplified in the video *Going thru the Motions*. "Our interest in the beauty pageant was essentially our interest in television and spectacle. In this exhibition [*The Search for the Spirit*, 1997] you can see how the 1971 Pageant grew out of our involvement with mail art, with projects that utilized the mail system, asking friends and artists to respond to a mailing, and using the response to generate a project (an event, a publication) in which they could again participate: a sort of cultural biofeedback. The 1971 Pageant was, at the same time, a metaphor for our society and specifically for the art world, in which talent competitions, winners and losers, prizes and celebrities all take part. But finally it was an event designed for television, in which the audience became the performer, the mythical pageant moments ('May I have the envelope, please!') were assembled into a collage of meta-mythical intent, and the art world system was stripped of pretense and bathed in irony." AA Bronson, "Myth as Parasite/Image as Virus: General Idea's Bookshelf 1967–1975," in *The Search for the Spirit: General Idea 1968–1975*, 19.
6. "The Audience," *FILE* 4:1 (Summer 1978), n.p.

TO WHOM IT MAY CONCERN:

"Just do it sir . . . in front of everyone sir . . . It would have a comic effect sir . . . We flash a sex pic with torture in the background sir then snap that torture pic right in your bloody face sir . . . if you'll pardon the expression sir . . . we do the same with the sound track sir . . . varying instances *sir . . . It has a third effect sir . . . right down the old middle line sir . . . if you'll pardon the expression sir . . . the razor inside sir . . .*

"Jerk the handle . . . It sounds like this sir . . ."

William Burroughs
Nova Express

The old Humpty Dumpty mere mirror on the wall, the old seams to be coming apart, the old egg-oh on the face. Ask anything but don't expect a glimpse behind the final curtain. In the burlesque galleries taking art's pants down to titilate art's history. "I CAN HANDLE NUDITY BUT THIS IS UNNATURAL." Double edge blade of the cutting remark for the kill. Egg-oh, like when your lips meet your lips on the glass of the mirror. Speechlessness behind the scenes. We only launched this image balloon to see if the world was around. Your arrows to pinpoint the leak in our FILE/style orbit talking in circles. We promise not to burst onto your scene from under the carpet leaving you holding the vacuum. You probe our love letters with your letter knife in the back. You got our number and we got the picture under wraps like in camouflage, corre-sponge dancing on the subliminal.

We're just a plug looking for a socket. Like we plugged into the water works when we realized the similarity. Like when we realized the valves were all under control. Like we slipped into your mailbox disguised as LIFE.

" 'It's the story of my life, what's the difference between wrong and right?' But Billy said, 'Both those words are dead.' " The Velvet Underground

There you were staring FILE in the face and you couldn't believe it was LIFE. The old seeing is believing dilemma. The old media mirror up against the wall. Meanwhile he's out on some street corner contacting the big energy under your feet. He discovers images float through media like words out of water. He re-channels the mainstream as folk art. He lost quality control when he got into deep water and attitudes. When attitudes become action as in how many, how much? . . . maybe 50 maybe 100 maybe 1200 are needed to salve a bad case of media burn. Modern art under the scalpel sliced open and sewn up as just another style, like computors, or porno. Now this is no news since we got the pants down already but the voyeurs are still hung up on carbon copy. Walt Disney's magic paint brush brushing with death and bringing to LIFE a little of the old now you see it.

Alex the Holy's animated LIFE/style bringing to FILE with style a little of the old now you're it. A little too close to home the thought of our water pipes and your water pipes like network T.V. or our mailboxes, coming up through the ground and in the back door like subliminal in residence. By the time it gets through all this charcoal carbon copy it infiltrates the cells. Step up to the colour bar and order the system to pay colour back with an Image Blank cheque. Don't point your critical breadknife at seven years of bad luck. Don't break our light through your spectrum of words. Don't pass the buck and call it green back. Don't stain our sheets with your lyrical abstractions. Don't tarnish our image. We're only following orders.

"And the General stepped out of his view screen in a glittering robe of pure shamelessness . . ."

William Burroughs
The Ticket that Exploded

HOMELY DETAILS OF EVERYDAY "LIFE"

LIFE magazine died with '72, emitting the casual stench of instant nostalgia for the waiting relatives, all of us with our hands crossed, leaving LIFE as we found it for the network world it bred and weaned but cannot nurture. Thirty-five years over a hot story, devoured in an instant by a public hungry for a past.

LIFE was the Coca-Cola of the picture magazines, image bank primer extraordinaire. LIFE was the first and instant precis of lifestyle the emerging manner the reflective possibilities of mass media. LIFE was the first and necessary authentication, the initial glamourization, of lifestyle and the common man.

LIFE initiated the first democratization of cultural consciousness, mirroring in news format the sensibility of the massive masses, the thin crumbling wall of mediocrity. The news that made LIFE was made news by LIFE.

LIFE was unique in its recognition of the value of sensibility and lifestyle over the traditional concerns of the historical view. LIFE took a stance in the face of history, sidestepping quality fixations for a coherent vision of people in process.

History is what you make it. LIFE made it.

LIFE in sensing in glamourizing in mirroring people in process LIFE and later TV certainly LIFE and others created expectations, expectations of access, expectations of everyman's fifteen minutes of personal fame, expectations of the common man's right to make the headlines, well it did that and we got that and that's why LIFE died.

In this role of information re-caste-ing, LIFE sealed its own fate, creating the possibility and reinforcing the potential for a truly grassworks network culture.

Lately many magazines are dying. Some say this is due to postal dues. Actually it is very simple people are demanding access people are demanding and reading magazines providing access to particular tools particular goods particular scenes. VOGUE does this. WHOLE EARTH ALMANAC does this. NOVA does this. Toronto's BARGAIN HUNTER PRESS does this. LIFE did not do this.

Now FILE is simply this: the future seen in retrospect, actualization of 1984 envisioned by LIFE; a particularization of LIFE methods and manners utilized for the needs at hands, access to the trip and trappings.

FILE is LIFE out of hand, a handy map of scenic networks lacing the globe for you. Our tribute to LIFE passed by.

FILE is a transcanadada art organ produced by artists for artists quarterly. Correspondence should be directed to the editors at 87 Yonge St., Toronto 1, Ontario, Canada. Annual subscriptions — $2 for individuals or $5 for business and institutions.

SIMULATION OF LIFE

I.

The December 1972 editorial page of *FILE* was split in two—two editorials, that is. The plural editorials were split between a form of address and a publication format: divided between an anonymous addressee ("To Whom it May Concern") and an address to well-known *LIFE* magazine ("Homely Details of Everyday 'LIFE'"), which had just ceased publication. One half seemed quasi-fictional, the other quasi-factual. Was this what the editors had previously meant by the "fictional aspects of a factual magazine?"[1] This did not necessarily mean one half fiction, the other half fact—but one way or the other it was fact and fiction, fiction mixed up with fact and vice versa.

The first half assumed a fictional voice. Perhaps it was imitating one of William Burroughs's "routines," as the epigraph suggested in quoting that author's *Nova Express*. Burroughs was no stranger to General Idea or the subliminal network: rather, its inspiration. He invented the terms "image bank" and "the subliminal" and practically patented cut-up and viral techniques as well as inspiring General Idea to the newsmagazine format.

> "We need a peg to hang it on," he said. "Something really ugly like virus. Not for nothing do they come from a land without mirrors." So he takes over this newsmagazine.
>
> "Now," he said, "I'll by God show them how ugly the Ugly American can be."
>
> And he breaks out all the ugliest pictures in the image bank and puts it out on the subliminal so one crisis piles up after the other right on schedule.[2]

In spite of the fiction, General Idea were going public here. They were broaching a public realm beyond the eternal network of like-minded artists while using the same techniques and strategies, indeed, emboldened by them. These techniques were still disguised, however. That was the point. But the point was also in the telling—the telling of them. Fictionally, but factually, as well. "Just do it sir ... in front of everyone sir," the Burroughs's epigraph started. General Idea simulated *LIFE* magazine, but more than that, *FILE* "slipped into your mailbox disguised as LIFE." It was all a matter of infiltration by camouflage and disguise. How dangerous was that? "There you were staring FILE in the face and you couldn't believe it was LIFE."[3]

What they were not telling were Burroughs's radical techniques, even though the epigraph displayed them fictionally. Particularly his cut-up technique that the magazine referenced every time it said "cut up or shut up." These were media techniques—"media" meaning available to all, exposed to all. Anyone could experimentally take up the tools and techniques of media. As opposed to mainstream media, Burroughs wrote,

> You have an advantage which your opposing player does not have. He must conceal his manipulations. You are under no such necessity. In fact you can advertise the fact that you are writing news in advance and trying to make it happen by techniques which anybody can use. And that makes you NEWS. And a TV personality as well, if you play it right. You want the widest possible circulation for your cut/up video tapes. Cut/up techniques could swamp the mass media with total illusion.[4]

Inhabiting it, *FILE* exposed *LIFE*. Falsely inhabiting *LIFE*, *FILE* exposed its own readership to the "total illusion" of another content. But this was a fiction as well—that inhabiting popular formats *FILE* reached a popular audience; that *FILE* "slipped into your mailbox disguised as LIFE." The extension of this fictional conceit beyond the magazine's network readership, however, was necessary, necessary if the magazine's effects were to be subliminal, that is to say, to be considered criminal.

II.

Most people think that *FILE* was a parody of *LIFE*. They should read the editorial "Homely Details of Everyday 'LIFE'." *FILE* was copycat *homage* to *LIFE*. This editorial sounds rather like a primer on *FILE*: "LIFE was the Coca-Cola of the picture magazines, image bank primer extraordinaire. LIFE was the first and instant précis of lifestyle and emerging manner the reflective possibilities of the mass media. LIFE was the first and necessary authentication, the initial glamourization, of lifestyle and the common man."[5] Not exactly born from its ashes, but published in tandem for a year, *FILE* countered the failure of *LIFE* with its own take on alternative lifestyles.[6] *FILE* altered *LIFE*'s culture for its own counter-culture of manufactured myths, although mimicking *LIFE*'s proven format as a picture magazine. It would do for the art scene what *LIFE* did for the common man, exploiting its "reflective possibilities." "The news that made LIFE was made news by LIFE." In turn, *FILE* made its own news, reflecting its own scene in its editorial pages.

The editorial concluded with yet another definition of *FILE*. "Now FILE is simply this: the future seen in retrospect, actualization of 1984 envisioned by LIFE; a particularization of LIFE methods and manners utilized for the needs at hand, access to the trip and trappings."[7] •

1. "Editorial: Fictional Aspects of a Factual Magazine," *FILE* 1:2&3 (May/June 1972), 8.
2. William S. Burroughs, *Nova Express* (New York: Grove Press, 1992), 11–12. First published in 1964.
3. "Editorials: To Whom it May Concern" *FILE* 1:4 (December 1972), 8.
4. William S. Burroughs, "Electronic Revolution," in *Word Virus: The William S. Burroughs Reader*, eds. James Grauerholz & Ira Silverberg (New York: Grove Press, 1998), 298–99. AA Bronson refers to the 1971 publication of this text in "Myth as Parasite/Image as Virus: General Idea's Bookshelf 1967–1975," in *The Search for the Spirit: General Idea 1968–1975* (Toronto: Art Gallery of Ontario, 1997), 19.
   General Idea played it right as television personalities in their brilliant series of videos: *Press Conference* (1977), *Pilot* (1977), *Colour Bar Lounge* (1979), *Test Tube* (1979), and *Shut the Fuck Up* (1985).
5. "Editorials: Homely Details of Everyday 'LIFE'," *FILE* 1:4 (December 1972), 8.
6. *FILE*'s December 1972 issue coincided with *LIFE*'s cessation that month. The editorial analyzed *LIFE*'s demise in contrast to *FILE*'s success in "the network world it bred and weaned but cannot nurture…. In this role of information re-caste-ing, LIFE sealed its own fate, creating the possibility and reinforcing the potential for a truly grassworks network culture." The *FILE* column "Magazines: The Magazine Addicts Have Hit it Rich" put it this way: "The sense of fragmentation in magazine publishing today is not so much a sense of the big magazines going under as it is a sense of new methods of organization meeting today's new needs. This is an age of subcults, whether they be age groups, lingo groupings, or sexual coteries. Certainly magazines today are realizing the emergence of a new diversity and the need of decentralizing that is splitting into more and more diverse more explicit publications catering to or reflexive of a certain network. The success of a magazine may usually be estimated by how closely it anticipates, creates, or mirrors a cult in process." *FILE* 2:1&2 (May 1973), 8.
7. For General Idea's account of the Time-Life lawsuit against *FILE*, see "Editorial," *FILE* 3:3 (Spring 1977), 17.

PABLUM FOR THE PABLUM EATERS

OH WHAT A TANGLED WEB WE WEAVE

Setting up a network setting up a community any kind of community certain aspects of that community have to be considered. Often it is unclear just what these aspects are. Image Bank has chosen a few specific aspects. In this section I want to talk about stabilization of the subliminal, this is very simple, it is the method whereby the accumulated body of significant images and afterimages becomes stabilized and generally accessible.

Now there is something to consider about imagery. We are all used to progress and the sense of progress and the idea of a community a city a country progressing. Working on the subliminal working with culture molding history it is very important to step outside of progress that is outside of historical process to stabilize then not only in terms of imagery and available imagery (and without preventing growth, which is different than progress) but also to erase the timegap between past and future, to erase then that sense of progress of historical process and create a continuum of discrete presences.

This is how Image Bank has chosen to do this:

DEEP IN THE HEART OF THE FETISH

Fetish objects: In the fetish object a body of images is resident. The fetish object is the intersection point of potent images, naming of partz accumulated about a convenient pole. The fetish object is thus a convenient point about which ritual may gather and concentrate. Dr. Brute's leopardskin traingles are plywood triangles painted in leopardskin pattern. Dr. Brute has isolated the leopardskin image as fetish. Leopardskin for Dr. Brute is the medium by which ideas enter the object. The Brutopian cosmology of Brutiful Brutopia, which is all around us, swims about us in images of impersonal horror and pleasure, spread-eagled for the brutal taking, shrouded in leopardskin.

Consider the anthropomorph: Vincent Tarasoff's Mr. Peanut or Bob Fones Can-D-Man. All objects are potentially or intrinsically animate, possessed by resident imagery. The available anthropomorphs of contemporary advertising are available vessels,spiralling whirlpools collecting image flotsam.

The alphabet print series organized by Image Bank and executed by a number of artists move beyond the apparent art of it all and objectify the concern with shifting linguals and cut word lines into fetishistic presences. Dr. Brute's leopardskin alphabet, Mr. Peanut's peanut alphabet and Glen Lewis' Corres-Sponge Dance Alphabet are all direct manifestations of imagery in action stabilized into a basic and ongoing vocabulary. Gary Lee Nova's "Small Electrical Storm in Element County" acts as a cipher whereby the others may be seen in context. More about ciphers later, but consider the imagery of the alphabet in Ben-Hur Pyramidal lettering struck by lightening and exploding. Cut word lines. Shift linguals.

THE SUBLIMINAL IN MOTION

Rituals: Myth is Muthos, Something by Mouth, the flip side of the thing done, ritual itself. There are two basic aspects of ritual to consider here: first, the ritual, accumulating about and releasing the resident imagery of fetish objects, carries the stabilization of imagery beyond the mere objectification offered by fetish objects. The ritual re-enacts the potency of the imagery in repeated manifestation of its venerated importance. Secondly, the ritual re-enacts an activity repeated in the past and known to repeat in the future, the ritual enacts the past as present, enacts the future as present, establishes the time continuum as a complex network of ongoing presents. The present ritual generates both past and future experience. In this way the ritual acts as a means of stepping outside of the historical process and placing oneself in the context of a dense mythical network in order that one may view simultaneity. It is no longer necessary to feel done in by history. History is how you tend it.

The Miss General Idea Pageant, Corres-Sponge Dance Meetings, the Coach House annual Waizygoose, Bumbank's John Dowd Fanny Club meetings are all prime examples of ritual. Each is derived from formats available in existing north american culture . . . this is the subliminal in motion, society mirrored and mirrored captured in reverse frozen in flux by the time lapse thinking of the subliminal kids.

A DANCE WITH THE PAST

Archives: The archive format is what Image Bank is all about. The archive format is automatically instituted by the Image Bank Image Request Lists, which set up branch offices as a matter of course. Your image request is your image responsibility. Certain images become articulate and concentrated enough that they enter the general vocabulary — then these archives are instituted as actual banks: chicken bank, bumbank, artbank, etc.

Now that the bank format (Banker's drag he calls it, now isn't that cute?) has solidified and spread beyond expectation, Image Bank and others are setting up specific collections of imagery filling obvious gaps in the cosmology attempting by these collections to define whole areas of emerging consciousness.

Image Bank's 1984 collection is a developed attempt to establish an archive having a similar function to ritual. In fact all archives are a means of making present, of establishing the past as an existing presence. However the 1984 project operates specifically within the arena of imagery from a progress-oriented society forseeing the future and inadvertantly answers specific contemporary problems in coping with nostalgia and camp.

The 1984 request calls for your image of 1984. The rampant concern with futurism, various forms of future-oriented advertising and science fiction and so on here becomes objectified in the mass-media imagery, primarily drawn from the futuristic forties raining about our eyes and ears in contemporary and recycled form. Fortune magazine is a prime source. What has collected is primarily a collection of future images seen through the eyes of the immediate past (which in many ways is the only past we have as a culture). It is very easy to see then that this body of imagery contains the collective historical vision of the future seen through the past and existent as a general mythology in the present. This is a very interesting project it is quite subliminal it is quite invisible it is all around us and Image Bank is articulating orchestrating this collective surge of consciousness this dance with the past with the future with archetypes here and now.

This is a very important aspect of the archive. Once upon a time the archival function lay with the storyteller, who learnt his stories from his predecessor. Now we have the media we have video we have print we have film we have many media they all tell stories for those who want to tell stories want to write stories we are all writing our own history and that is the importance of that.

It is important to note that Image Bank uses media as a format, available tradition, not as a creative medium. The creativity lies in the creation of afterimage and the subliminal creation of invisible image networks and cosmologies.

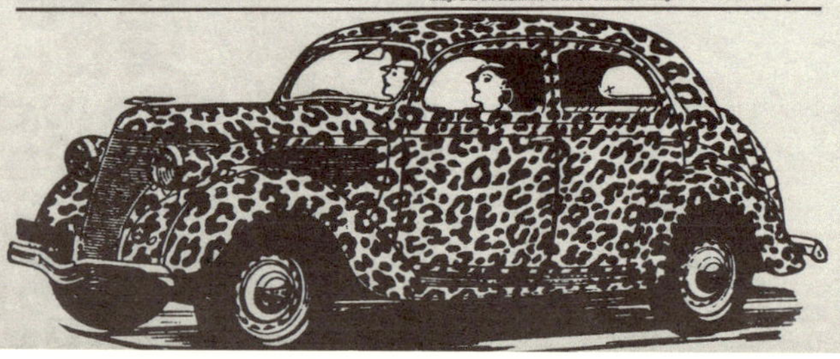

28

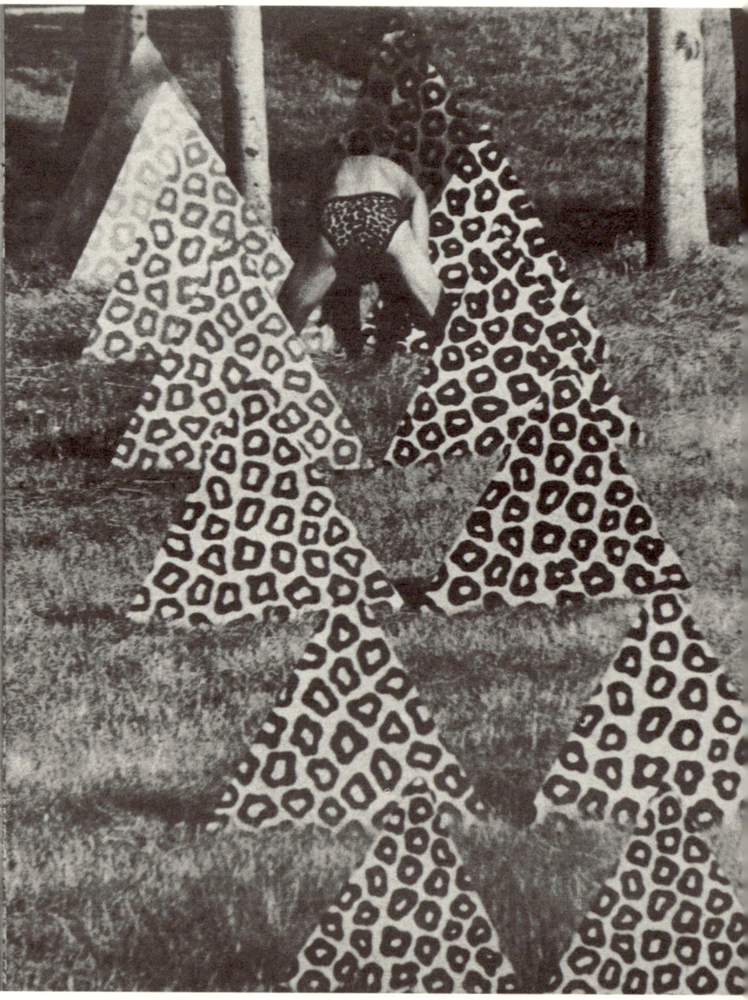

"Pablum for the Pablum Eaters," *FILE* 2:1&2 (May 1973), 28–29

IMAGE IS **VIRUS**

It requires the mind of a criminal. Collage or perish. Cut up or shut up.

—"Pablum for the Pablum Eaters"

A criminal statement, the above concatenation of sentences itself is a collage. So is the following, although appearing as one sentence: "Aware of nova explosion they work like criminals on the subliminal erecting mirrors cutting wordlines shifting linguals."[1] Taken from the same 1973 "Pablum for the Pablum Eaters" article, the latter ostensibly describes the activities of Vancouver's Image Bank, but its language, with the exception of its mirror insertion, is dependent on William Burroughs—as are the cut-up concepts of the epigraph.[2]

To be Subliminal was to be criminal.[3] To have a subliminal effect was to use the cut-up method, either openly or covertly. Burroughs provided the methodology and the criminal master plan as well as the language to implement it, whether correspondence artists followed it to the letter or not. Perhaps most infected by this dogma, General Idea were the most fervid in its application.

"Collage or perish" and "cut up or shut up" were slogans of the correspondence network and the methods of its contrivances. Collage was not one or the other but both word and image combined, together composing a fictitious whole while dismantling other systems in the process. The cut-up method was also a subversive device—a *viral* technique of parasitical inhabitation—benignly circulating its mocking images within the mail system: "Like we slipped into your mailbox disguised as LIFE.... like subliminal in residence."[4]

For Burroughs himself, the cut-up method was a compositional device applied in his early 1960s trilogy of novels *The Soft Machine*, *The Ticket that Exploded*, and *Nova Express*.[5] It was not merely an experimental practice, however. There was a more perfidious relationship we humans inherit that Burroughs tried to subvert. "Word begets image and image *is* virus," he wrote ... and believed.[6] While for correspondence artists viral images were liberating, in Burroughs's science fiction mythological system, language was an alien virus used to control humans—hence the need to cut word lines, shift linguals, and storm the Reality Studio.[7]

The individual Subliminal artist was susceptible to image virus. Image requests led to a habit, and habit was the soft point of entry, a virus's strategy being to invade, damage, and occupy, and then replicate itself in a host.[8] "The art junkies' habit is founded on image. *Image is virus*," stated the first "Pablum" article. "By establishing each artist as an image 'collector,' [request lists] gave each artist an image habit, committed him to image bondage," added the second.[9] (The artist was both addict and fetishist.) The viral image carried on its life within correspondence, spreading its effects by means of this network: the self-inflicted habit extended damage by infecting society. Countering social control through society's own images, virus had a counter-mythic function: "The image carries its own realities within it, harbouring subliminal connections in its interstices in a manner that denies concepts to gain control or apply definition. The image gains territory, holds a foot in the door of art, leaving a space for ideas, defining contours negatively."[10] Images were isolated and cultured as a virus towards this end of parasitical proliferation, "culture" here having a double sense.[11] "Dr. Brute, for example, isolates leopardskin as a fetish image. Leopardskin, for Dr. Brute, is the medium by which ideas enter the object. Not leopardskin itself, but the image of leopardskin, *the pattern*, applied carelessly to any object, opens that object to a cosmology of associations, *meanings*, from which it has no escape."[12]

The individual artist might mythologize but, like a *bricoleur* or handyman, his would always be a small-scale enterprise for a small-time criminal. A corporation, however, was another matter. It had license to dissemble on a grand scale. To take over a corporation in order to openly pursue one's criminal activities would be the inspired masterstroke of a criminal of the business class. Its parasitism would not be atomistic—proceeding image by image—but already be whole:

> Now we turned to the queer outsider methods of William Burroughs.... We abandoned bona fide cultural terrorism, then, and replaced it with viral methods.... Following Burroughs's fictionalized example, we began with projects through the mail and then graduated to newsmagazine format to perfect our method. We saw *FILE Megazine* as a parasite within the world of magazine distribution, positioned to infect newsstands, schools and libraries in urban centres. Our familiar, homey, *LIFE*-like format belied its viral content: images emptied of meaning and filled with our own perverse content of metamythologies, transgressed borderlines and alien consciousness, designed to take hold of the subconscious and infiltrate.[13]

So in passing from individual to corporation, we also pass from image to format, from correspondence as an individual practice to *FILE* as a corporate activity, from infecting the individual to infecting society as a whole. General Idea's activity was viral: "We are obsessed with available form. We maneuver hungrily, conquering the uncontested territory of culture's forgotten shells—beauty pageants, pavillions, picture magazines, and other contemporary corpses. Like parasites we animate these dead bodies and speak in alien tongues."[14] Speaking in alien tongues, the subliminal criminal performed in the "stolen moments" of a cut-up, performatively cutting up not shutting up, collaging not perishing. •

1. "Pablum for the Pablum Eaters," *FILE* 2:1&2 (May 1973), 26. Placing commas would break up the sentence into its collage components: Aware of nova explosion, they work like criminals on the subliminal, erecting mirrors, cutting wordlines, shifting linguals.
2. Yet the mirror insertion is strategic here as its own means of collage, the means by which word lines are cut and rearranged.
3. "... the Subliminal exist in a 'parasitic' or 'criminal' role, in which they partake of the same institutions, media and art hierarchy without relying on that hierarchy for any structural definition, nor contributing anything to it." AA Bronson, "Pablum for the Pablum Eaters," in *Video by Artists*, ed. Peggy Gale (Toronto: Art Metropole, 1976), 197.
4. "Editorials: To Whom it May Concern," *FILE* 1:4 (December 1972), 5.
5. Burroughs also called it the fold-in method: "An extension of Brion Gysin's cut-up method which I call the fold-in method has been used in this book which is consequently a composite of many writers living and dead." William S. Burroughs, *Nova Express* (New York: Grove Press, 1992), Foreword Note. First published in 1964.
6. Burroughs, *Nova Express*, 48. The Image Bank Request List sometimes used this phrase (or its reduction to "image *is* virus") as a slogan for its activities.
7. This was the frequent call to partisans to overthrow control: "His plan called for total exposure—Wise up all the marks everywhere Show them the rigged wheel—Storm the Reality Studio and retake the universe ... 'Calling partisans of all nations—Shift linguals—Cut word lines—Vibrate tourists—Free doorways—Photo falling—Word falling—Break through in Grey Room.'" William S. Burroughs, *The Soft Machine* (New York: Grove Press, 1992), 151–2. First published in 1961.
8. "Pushing in a small way to keep up The Habit: INVADE. DAMAGE. OCCUPY." Burroughs, *The Soft Machine*, 7. Also see "Technical Deposition of the Virus Power," in *Nova Express*, 49–50.
9. "Pablum" (1973), 26; "Pablum" (1976), 197. "As in all research investigations into terminal definition there is the risk of the culture overpowering the host. Somehow the virus may permeate the researchers." "General Idea's Borderline Cases: Introduction," *IFEL* 2:3 (September 1973), 12.
10. "Pablum" (1973), 26.
11. Ibid. "The thrust of Image Bank is two-pronged: on the one hand they are concerned with establishing a culture that relates to official culture as a virus does to an organism."
12. "Pablum" (1976), 198.
13. AA Bronson, "Myth as Parasite/Image as Virus: General Idea's Bookshelf 1967–1975," in *The Search for the Spirit: General Idea 1968–1975* (Toronto: Art Gallery of Ontario, 1997), 18.
14. "Glamour," *FILE* 3:1 (Autumn 1975), n.p.

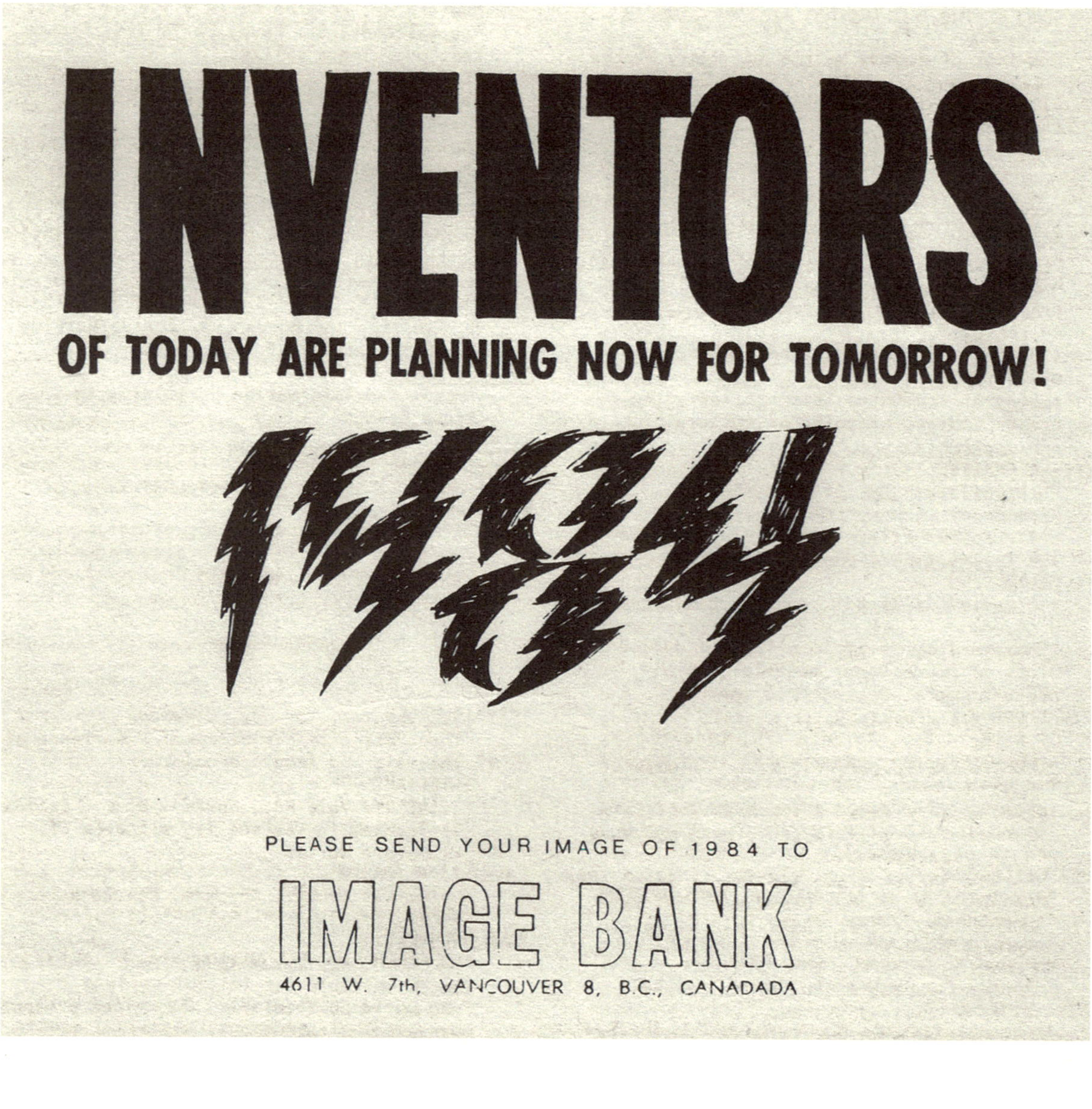

Advertisement, *FILE* 1:4 (December 1972), 18

THE **FUTURE** IN RETROSPECT

The future has a provenance. It comes from the past—the past's vision of the future, which is always being superseded, perpetually providing an archaeology or image bank of futurity. In the early 1970s, the mythical year 1984 was still long away but it already was on the minds of the Subliminalists. An advertisement in the December 1972 Image Bank Request List read "Inventors of today are planning now for tomorrow! Please send your image of 1984 to Image Bank," while the editorial of that *FILE* defined the magazine as "simply this: the future seen in retrospect, actualization of 1984 envisioned by LIFE."[1]

Belying the fixation on the dystopian character of George Orwell's *1984*, the magazine's preview in review was not simply future-oriented but enamoured of the simplistically utopian.[2] The emphasis of these image banks of futurity consequently was not on the failures but the wishful thinking for a technologically enhanced future. Their images were drawn from future obsessed forties and fifties magazines such as *Popular Mechanics*, for the lower end of the market, or *Fortune*, for the upper end. So, for instance, the article "Pablum for the Pablum Eaters" was partly illustrated by images of futuristic cityscapes with elevated, multi-layered freeways passing through skyscrapers with rooftop heliports.[3]

The idea of 1984 was a project shared conceptually on the subliminal network, particularly between Image Bank and General Idea. "Image Bank's 1984 collection is a developed attempt to establish an archive having a similar function to ritual," with the distinction that "the 1984 project operates specifically within the arena of imagery from a progress-oriented society forseeing the future and inadvertently answers specific contemporary problems in coping with nostalgia and camp."[4] Nostalgia and camp were not the only inadvertencies of coping. For General Idea, the 1984 idea was applied generally to their project but specifically to the *Pageant* and *Pavillion*. The *Pageant* was to culminate in 1984 in the newly constructed *Pavillion*. But the *Pavillion* was to be designed and constructed according to the principles of this retrospective futurism. In putting the *Pavillion* out to tender, the artists advertised that "we at General Idea have a revision of the future and its foundation involves the conception design and construction of the 1984 Miss General Idea Pavillion."[5]

The *Pavillion*'s foundations, problematically, were built on a fault line: "Once the concept slips into the mainstream our whole vision of the future could split from the past."[6] The building stood on a borderline—but not just between past and future. The altered temporalities of reconstructed futures created an unstable shape-shifting template on which to construct the *Pavillion*. But this was part of its design, or built into its design. Collage was the perfect technique for this: "The 1984 Miss General Idea Pavillion may be seen as a revision of the future, and it involves the conception, design, and actual erection of a 'Collage or Perish' edifice to house our new archival and iconographic needs."[7] Collage disjunctions automatically reordered time and space. Wasn't *FILE* magazine itself already that? Every conjunction was a disjunction, words and images—spliced, folded, or cut in. But an edifice built to withstand the test of time must secure its spatial foundations. This was not the case with the *Pavillion*. It was built to destabilize itself: "We are only for time and space available to undifferentiate the borderline," the artists wrote.[8] •

1. *FILE* 1:4 (December 1972), 18, 5.
2. "The Spirit of Research. We wanted to capture the spirit of research with its futuristic overtones and its optimistic undertow. We wanted to have ideas we could put down on paper that would draw a bead on progress. The objects resulting from this procedure attempt to assimilate this illusion in their 'lure of the future' profiles." *Showcard* 1-034.
   A preview in review is different from a "review in preview" mentioned in *FILE*'s May 1973 editorial: those "demanding art history, a review in preview." The latter was the historical mode practiced by artists. "More recently, and particularly in art circles, history has become a means of anticipating the future in order to plan one's own work as the next logical step in art history. In other words, history has become a marketing device." AA Bronson, "Pablum for the Pablum Eaters," in *Video by Artists*, ed. Peggy Gale (Toronto: Art Metropole, 1976), 196.
3. General Idea shared an interest in different aspects of futurism enamoured as they were with the utopian architecture of Buckminster Fuller and the Pop futurist architecture of Archigram.
4. "Pablum for the Pablum Eaters," *FILE* 2:1&2 (May 1973), 28. "The 1984 request calls for your image of 1984. The rampant concern with futurism, various forms of future-oriented advertising and science fiction and so on here becomes objectified in the mass-media imagery, primarily drawn from the futuristic forties raining about our eyes and ears in contemporary and recycled form. Fortune magazine is a prime source. What has collected is primarily a collection of future images seen through the eyes of the immediate past (which in many ways is the only past we have as a culture). It is very easy to see then that this body of imagery contains the collective historical vision of the future seen through the past and existent as a general mythology in the present. This is a very interesting project it is quite subliminal it is quite invisible it is all around us and Image Bank is articulating orchestrating this collective surge of consciousness this dance with the past with the future with archetypes here and now." Ibid.
5. "The Spirit of the Miss General Idea Pavillion," *IFEL* 2:3 (September 1973), insert.
6. "General Idea's Borderline Cases: Introduction," *IFEL* 2:3 (September 1973), 12.
7. *Luxon V.B.: The 1984 Miss General Idea Pavillion No. 101*, self-published, 1973.
8. "General Idea's Borderline Cases: Now You Don't," 30.

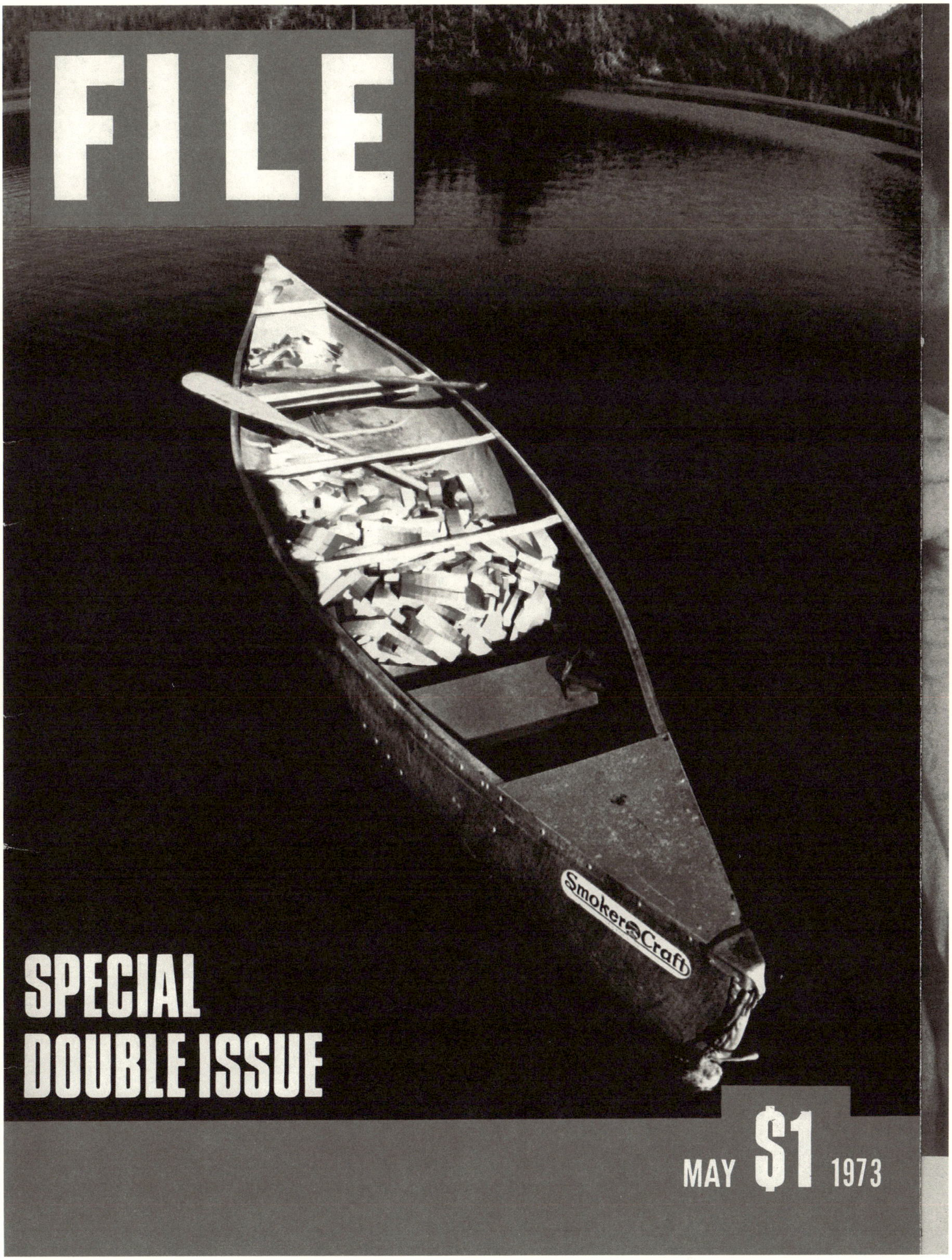
FILE
Smoker Craft
SPECIAL
DOUBLE ISSUE
MAY $1 1973

FILE 2:1&2 (May 1973), cover

"The Spirit of the 1984 Miss General Idea Pavillion"

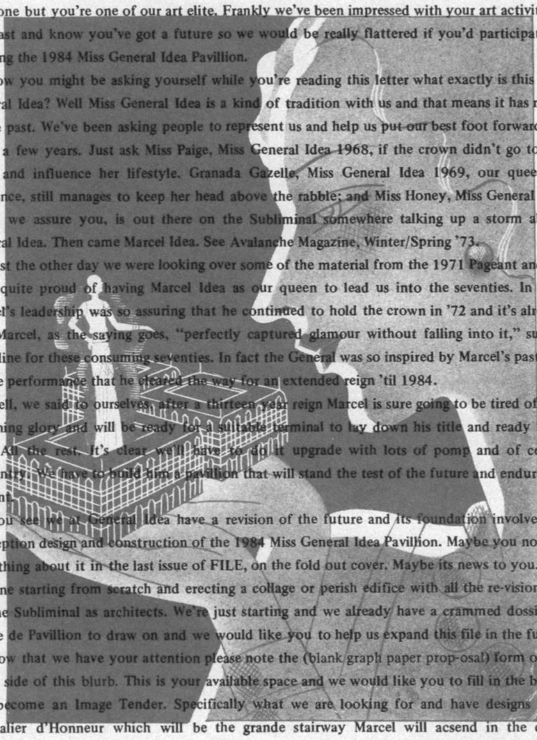

Please consider this an informal rather than a form letter. We're not just sending them to everyone but you're one of our art elite. Frankly we've been impressed with your art activity in the past and know you've got a future so we would be really flattered if you'd participate in creating the 1984 Miss General Idea Pavillion.

Now you might be asking yourself while you're reading this letter what exactly is this Miss General Idea? Well Miss General Idea is a kind of tradition with us and that means it has roots in the past. We've been asking people to represent us and help us put our best foot forward for quite a few years. Just ask Miss Paige, Miss General Idea 1968, if the crown didn't go to her head and influence her lifestyle. Granada Gazelle, Miss General Idea 1969, our queen in residence, still manages to keep her head above the rabble; and Miss Honey, Miss General Idea 1970, we assure you, is out there on the Subliminal somewhere talking up a storm about General Idea. Then came Marcel Idea. See Avalanche Magazine, Winter/Spring '73.

Just the other day we were looking over some of the material from the 1971 Pageant and we were quite proud of having Marcel Idea as our queen to lead us into the seventies. In fact, Marcel's leadership was so assuring that he continued to hold the crown in '72 and it's already '73. Marcel, as the saying goes, "perfectly captured glamour without falling into it," such a guideline for these consuming seventies. In fact the General was so inspired by Marcel's past and future performance that he cleared the way for an extended reign 'til 1984.

Well, we said to ourselves, after a thirteen year reign Marcel is sure going to be tired of that crowning glory and will be ready for a suitable terminal to lay down his title and ready for a rest. All the rest. It's clear we'll have to do it upgrade with lots of pomp and of course pageantry. We have to build him a pavilion that will stand the test of the future and endure the present.

You see, we at General Idea have a revision of the future and its foundation involves the conception design and construction of the 1984 Miss General Idea Pavillion. Maybe you noticed something about it in the last issue of FILE, on the fold out cover. Maybe its news to you. Just imagine starting from scratch and erecting a collage or perish edifice with all the re-visionaries on the Subliminal as architects. We're just starting and we already have a crammed dossier of Image de Pavillion to draw on and we would like you to help us expand this file in the future.

Now that we have your attention please note the (blank graph paper prop-osal) form on the other side of this blurb. This is your available space and we would like you to fill in the blanks and become an Image Tender. Specifically what we are looking for and have designs on is L'Escalier d'Honneur which will be the grande stairway Marcel will acsend in the dying moments of the 84 pageant for the decrowning ritual. The skys the limit as far as the stairway goes and we hope you'll have some illustrious suggestions. Remember Marcel requires your support if he is going to make the acsent with style. If you think your artfullness would be better suited to other things then by all means have free rein. The whole building is up for grabs including the location. Maybe you can provide a suitably royal dressing room for Marcel or a good looking looking glass. Fountains, topiary, china, bars, lounges, furniture, wardrobes, doorknobs, decorative art and so much more is required. This is why we need your help as this jig saw building will only be as strong as its missing piece de resistance. We are looking forward to no problems in incorporating your prop-osal into the complex as we are utilizing time honored collage construction techniques. This invitation is open to all media that can fill in the blanks including drawing (art and Architectural), photographs, collage, and what have you. We are hoping that your submission will be translatable into three dimensions and will include all pertinent details such as size, scale, materials, construction techniques etcetera. In the ten year future left (dating from January 1974) we are hoping to realize one way or the other construction of as many prop-osals as possible. The only restrictions are what you consider feasable and constructive.

This request is one of the first steps in the design of the pavillion and if you have any other suggestions please let us in on them and we'll reserve your space. We'll be keeping you up to date on the progress of the edifice and we're hoping you'll keep us up to date on yours. Just as further bait all design participants will receive the choisest seats of the 1,984 available for reveiwing the pageant. We're putting our money on the future so won't you one and all help us lay the corner stone for 1984.

Yours in the future

GENERAL IDEA
GOLD DIGGERS OF '84

p.s any ideas for cornerstones?

IFEL 2:3 (September 1973), insert

THE 1984 MISS GENERAL IDEA PAVILLION

Every major building undergoes a long process of consultation, planning, design, model making, engineering, financing, tendering, erection of hoardings, construction, and publicity lasting years before its doors open to the public. And many designs are modified over the period of tendering. *The 1984 Miss General Idea Pavillion* was no exception. The following chronology charts mentions of the project before it left the drawing board.

Chronology

May 1973

– "Marcel Idea, defining style, surfacing on the themes of the future, immersed in plans, rests long lingering gaze on black mirror mirage of the 1984 MISS GENERAL IDEA PAVILLION mock-up.... Marcel Idea, refining style, styling idea, immersed in tomorrow's world today, inspects with trepidation the full-scale mock-up of certain detailing in the labyrinth interior of the projected Miss General Idea Pavillion for 1984. This is the black glass entrancing to jaded powdered rooms, green glass and bronze mirror surfacing in layered mirage.... Out of the future fog the mist GENERAL IDEA PAVILLION collage or perish.... Look forward to the building blocks of the future for the shape of things to come. Throw up a façade to receive the projections of the 1984 MISS GENERAL IDEA PAVILLION.... General Idea is collecting, collating and collaging your vision of the 1984 MISS GENERAL IDEA PAVILLION.... General Idea ... requests your images of the 1984 GENERAL IDEA PAVILLION, your images of the 1984 GENERAL IDEA PAGEANT. Mañana packaged today ... send in your Prop-osals for the structure and all the contents. Provide our prime locations and furnish ideas. Reserve your seats in the future in advance. Advance into tomorrow today. Usher in the future with Miss General Idea."[1]
– "It's strictly confidential but the Gold Diggers are also preparing to float an issue (take issue) of bonds (that bind) to finance research for the *1984 Miss General Idea Pavillion* (see inside front cover)..."[2]
– "General Idea troops Jorge Lee Saia and A. A. Bronson headed below the banana belt destination Caracas. They were on a *Miss General Idea Pavillion* scouting mission..."[3]
– "The FILE/IFEL issue is also promising continuing developments, details and requests for the 1984 Miss General Idea Pavillion."[4]
– "Image Tender for the Miss General Idea 1984 pavillion fountain 'crack of dawn'."[5]

September 1973

– "Frankly we've been impressed with your art activity in the past and know you've got a future so we would be really flattered if you'd participate in creating the 1984 Miss General Idea Pavillion.… You see we at General Idea have a revision of the future and its foundation involves the conception design and construction of the 1984 Miss General Idea Pavillion. Maybe you noticed something about it in the last issue of FILE, on the fold out cover. Maybe it's news to you. Just imagine starting from scratch and erecting a collage or perish edifice with all the re-visionaries on the Subliminal as architects.… Now that we have your attention please note the (blank graph paper prop-osal) form on the other side of this blurb. This is your available space and we would like you to fill in the blanks and become an Image Tender. Specifically what we are looking for and have designs on is L'Escalier d'Honneur which will be the grande stairway Marcel will ascend in the dying moments of the 84 pageant decrowning ritual.… The whole building is up for grabs including the location.… We are looking forward to no problems in incorporating your prop-osal into the complex as we are utilizing time honored collage construction techniques."[6]

December 1973

– "AHSRAM RRAK, FILE covergirl (May, '72), plays the part of the Spirit of Miss General Idea (1984) at the LUXON, V.B. installation in the Carmen Lamanna Gallery, Toronto. Ahsram manipulates the necessary vacuum for content and context to air their differences, sucking the gulp [sic] between culture and nature. The LUXON, V.B. prototype is being developed for eventual installation in the 1984 General Idea Pavillion."[7]

– "The ten-year collection [Art Metropole], to end in '84, will be housed in the 1984 Miss General Idea Pavillion, inaugurated by the 1984 Pageant and the emergence of the Spirit herself. Art Metropole is thus an extension of FILE Megazine, taking over the diversifying functions of reflection and connection."[8]

– "The Hand of the Spirit of Miss General Idea manipulates the measure of proposed proposals for the 1984 Pavillion."
"Futuristic auto is entitled 'The Spirit of Miss General Idea,' is designed to park in front of the 1984 Pavillion."[9]

– "General Idea have been receiving artists' proposals for props and detailing for the Miss General Idea Pavillion 1984. Favorites include the *Fountain of Light* by Marcel Idea, Bumbank's proposal for a "Light-On" Building, and John May's decentralization schematics."[10]

– "The mirror construction LUXON V.B., is seen as the prototype for the first in a series of proposals being devised towards an architectural program aimed at generating mirror situations for the 1984 Miss General Idea Pavillion.… The 1984 Miss General Idea Pavillion may be seen as a revision of the future, and it involves the conception, design, and actual erection of a 'Collage or Perish' edifice to house our new archival and iconographic needs. Form follows Fiction."[11]

1973 was the debut year of the *Pavillion* ... or transition to the *Pavillion* from the *Pageant*, even though the *Pavillion* seemed at first designed to house the contest. As the year progressed, the conception of the *Pavillion* advanced according to how it reflected the collective practices of the immediate past or developed General Idea's current projects. For instance, the May and September issues of *FILE* saw the *Pavillion* as an outcome of the *Pageant* or foresaw it as a setting for the culminating 1984 *Pageant*, isolating the crowning role of the *Pavillion* in its elevating grand stairway. On the contrary, the December issue saw the *Pavillion* in terms of accommodating General Idea's new developments such as *Luxon V.B.* produced for commercial exhibition that same month. Current projects derived from altogether different concerns unrelated to the *Pageant*, in this case, *Light On* or, more generally, from General Idea's mirror thematics and borderline cases. That is, the *Pavillion* was seen now as an "edifice to house [their] new archival and iconographic needs" as they were brought on line—conceived either as decor or functioning rooms. Significantly, as well, the ideal *Pavillion* housed an *actual* functioning space: Art Metropole, founded in 1974.

If the December editorial suggested that Art Metropole, now "housed" within the *Pavillion*, was an "extension" of the archival function of *FILE* magazine, the *Pavillion* itself must be devised from the same principles, its mode of erection and its architectural program "taking over the diversifying functions of reflection and connection" of the magazine. At this early, speculative stage, the *Pavillion* was participatory and intended to be a collaborative product of the correspondence network as, indeed, the *Pageant* originally was. Proposals were solicited through the open call of *FILE* with tenders to be returned through mail art means—on the architectural graph paper published as a supplement to the magazine. The *Pavillion* was to be an anonymous "starchitecture" fabricated collaboratively by the architects of the Subliminal.

The *Pavillion* would be one with the principles of correspondence art: in process, form, and content; in its construction and architectural program. It was to be a "'Collage or Perish' edifice" erected through correspondence art's "collage construction techniques."[12] Something of a "Spirit of Miss General Idea" theme park, it would be "tomorrow's world today," like Disney's then-planned Epcot Center. Its future orientation, though, was a thing of the past or, rather, the past's orientation to the future. It was "the future seen in retrospect" cut and paste from *Fortune* magazine's imagistic preview of the future, time already past yet an appropriate image of 1984.

The *Pavillion* was a borderline situation. It was an *event*, still to be. The *Pavillion* was erected on a borderline, as a borderline situation, as a borderline event. As it was still speculative, could its creators see into the future and know that, erected on a fault line, the *Pavillion* was built for destruction? •

1. Flap to front cover of *FILE* 2:1&2 (May 1973).
2. "Surfacing: Arti-Facts," Ibid., 39.
3. "Surfacing: Travel," Ibid., 40.
4. Advertisement in Ibid., 62.
5. Illustration in "Pablum for the Pablum Eaters," Ibid., 23.
6. Open letter, "The Spirit of the Miss General Idea Pavillion," *IFEL* 2:3 (September 1973), insert.
7. Advertisement, *FILE* 2:4 (December 1973), 1.
8. "Editorial," Ibid., 11.
9. "The Search for the Spirit of Miss General Idea," Ibid., 15.
10. "Nude Egos in a Nude Era," Ibid., 42.
11. *Luxon V.B.: The 1984 Miss General Idea Pavillion, No. 101*, a pamphlet published to accompany the exhibition "Luxon V.B." at the Carmen Lamanna Gallery, December 17, 1973–January 3, 1974.
12. A couple submissions appear in the *Showcards*: John Jack Baylin's proposal for the Escalier d'Honneur (1-044); S. Carter submission for an architectural detail (1-050). In the end, the submissions did not warrant continuing this collaborative construction.

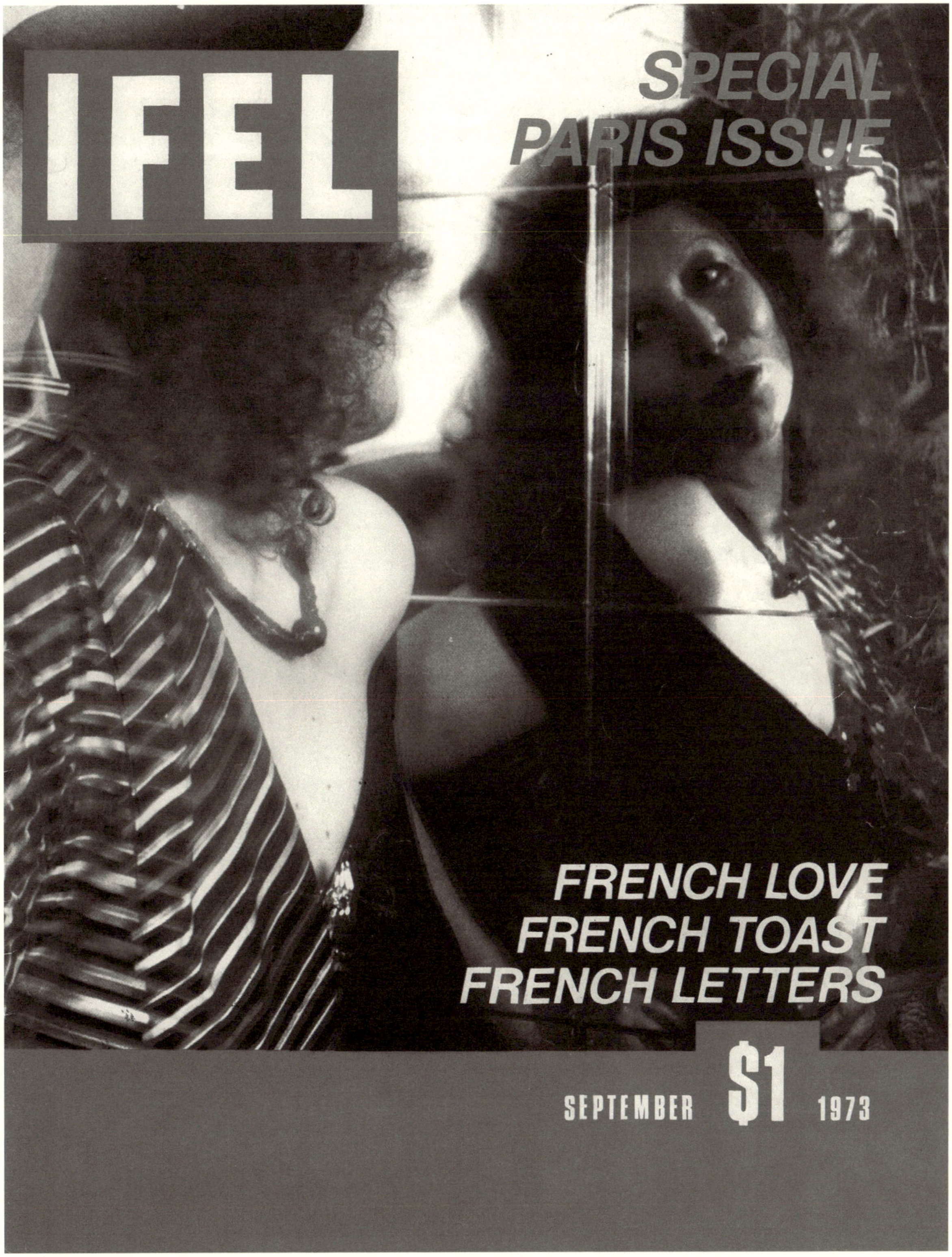
IFEL
SPECIAL
PARIS ISSUE
FRENCH LOVE
FRENCH TOAST
FRENCH LETTERS
SEPTEMBER
$1
1973

IFEL 2:3 (September 1973), cover

BULLETIN FROM THE IVORY TOWER

In the last issue we stuck the knife up the ass. In the end it all came together.

Coping with the pablum-eaters, who must eat; coping with the hunger of intellectual cannibalism, rampant and insatiable; coping with those who sit without and demand that the seeing might be seen, demanding art history, a review in preview; coping with these then, FILE, no longer mirroring a scene, mirrors the mirror. We re-establish our ability to see with a long look into the mirrored mirror, passing through silvered slivered splintered layers of apparent transparency, moving within the arena of our affliction.

The last and silent protection against culture shock in a society harbouring change and multiplicity as its only constants is the harbouring in safe ports of vision, one's own vision, one's ability to see one's manner of seeing as one's only personal constant. Capacity for ambiguity. Narcissism. Mirror mirror on the wall. Media inversion. What does a mirror see, searching for its own reflection?

Nostalgia is to be considered. Nostalgia, a technique for survival, pinning cultural archetypes up against the wall. Collage or perish. Nostalgia, knowledge in camoflage, disguised as yearning, yearning for style that matter might take its course without due notice. Nostalgia providing the sense of vision from afar, essentially a vehicle of entry, entry into safe harbours, harbouring vision, piercing strategical soft points, weakened by the need for entry, vulnerable, necessary.

Nostalgia must be cultured with an eye to the rarified, the rarified vision, the gap, space between, the borderline case. Nostalgia reduces junk imagery to categorical considerations, reducing mind pollution: Dr. Brute's leopardskin, 1984, feigheigh neigheigh, business as usual, art city, thirties, forties, fifties, topiary, terminal, borderline cases.

Narcissism is to be considered: as safe harbour, harbouring a personal vision, harbouring the possibility of vision, the description of the mirror regarding itself, the point of entry, whereby vision may contain the world. Narcissism demands nostalgia if it is to be utilized as a tool of vision. Together accounting for everything that must be accounted for. Everything must be accounted for. Allowing the possibility of describing the myth.

The pablum-eaters demand pablum. In the demanding they set the eye travelling inward and outward, plummeting. This issue is dedicated to the pablum-eaters. Herein please find the description of the art of it all. Collage or perish. Not only the actuality of intellectual cannibalism, not only the necessity of intellectual cannibalism, but the possibility of intellectual cannibalism. Cut up or shut up. Everything is permitted.

FILE is a transcanadada art organ produced by artists for artists quarterly. Correspondence should be directed to the editors at 87 Yonge St., Toronto 1, Ontario, Canadada. Annual subscriptions – $2 for individuals or $5 for business and institutions.

NOTES ON **NOSTALGIA**

"Many things in the world have not been named; and many things, even if they have been named, have never been described."[1] This sentence might have been lifted from "Pablum for the Pablum Eaters," referring to that article's concept of myth. Instead, it is the opening sentence to Susan Sontag's "Notes on Camp," published nine years before in 1964 and well known to General Idea. "Camp" as a word, rather than a concept, rarely appears in *FILE*. One of the only times, if not the only time, is in the article "Pablum for the Pablum Eaters" where it is reported that Image Bank's 1984 project "inadvertently answers specific contemporary problems in coping with nostalgia and camp."[2] What these problems of coping were partially find an answer in the editorial "Bulletin from the Ivory Tower" from that same May 1973 issue where, perhaps not inadvertently, "camp" was not mentioned using instead the allied code word "nostalgia."

Camp, though, was the context in which General Idea's work and *FILE* was immediately recognized, but it was also the reason it was partially rejected. In the early 1970s, queer camp did not have the credibility it has today, so one of the problems of coping would be the critical reception of General Idea's program, on the one hand, by the radical alternative left, and, on the other hand, by the conventional mainstream press. This anonymous 1972 review of the inaugural issue of *FILE*, from the Vancouver radical weekly *The Grape*, is a case in point:

> The format is a takeoff on Life magazine which sets the tune for the mindless masquerade that follows.... In fact, if this magazine is any example, the movement into conceptual art is open to more frauds, fake mystery and mannerist decadence than any art form in our previous history.... They have paraded their homosexuality as though that in itself gave the mag. some bizarre status within the enigma of the alternate society. Instead the problems of homosexuality as an actual way of life recede into the pageantry of camp parody.[3]

In the mainstream, the headline from a Toronto daily newspaper review of General Idea's 1975 *Going thru the Notions* exhibition said it all without need of further exposition: "General Idea still detailed triviality."[4]

We could comb through Image Bank Request Lists submitted by members of General Idea and their extended circle to find advertised there the signifiers of a camp sensibility: requests for information or images on writer Djuna Barnes (AA Bronson and Granada Gazelle); "fin de siècle cheese-cake photos" (Granada Gazelle); Maria Callas (Pascal); "one point perspective with palm trees" (Michael Tims); "Marcel Proust and his Paris" (P. J.).[5] But it is *The 1984 Miss General Idea Pageant* itself, with its props, paraphernalia, and protocols, that was the most appropriate ready-made theatrical vehicle for General Idea's "pageantry of camp parody." Perhaps it was too available a vehicle, though, and not surreptitiously subliminal enough for camp's disguised purposes. In spite of its theatrics, the effects of camp are somewhat disguised and widely dispersed in General Idea's work; moreover, they comprise their work as a whole—that is to say, systematically.

A "sensibility that, among other things, converts the serious into the frivolous,"[6] in turn, could be called frivolous. To find a *system* in what is superficial, or to determine a *structure* in what is only on the surface, is altogether different—although it would be camp to camouflage it. Or to disguise it in something even more disdained. I speculate that the play between even two such degraded terms construct a system. At the very least, the ambiguous space between the two is a borderline case. All the evidence we need to construct this system is found in the May 1973 "Bulletin from the Ivory Tower" editorial.

1. For example, consider "nostalgia" and "narcissism" and the relation between them. There could be nothing more vague, mundane, or outré than these two terms; yet, functioning within General Idea's system, their use was focused and specialized. Like the aestheticism of camp, "nostalgia must be cultured with an eye to the rarified, the rarified vision."[7] Nostalgia's impulse is to fixate and fetishize, to collect and archive, to create image banks of personal compulsions that circulate from the past and surface in the present. "Nostalgia reduces junk imagery to categorical considerations." That is, image banks created classifications for popular cultural imagery, a nostalgia based on imagery predominantly from the "thirties, forties, fifties."

> Nostalgia is to be considered. Nostalgia, a technique for survival, pinning cultural archetypes up against the wall. Collage or perish. Nostalgia, knowledge in camouflage, disguised as yearning, yearning for style that matter might take its course without due notice. Nostalgia providing the sense of vision from afar, essentially a vehicle of entry, entry into safe harbours, harbouring vision, piercing strategical soft points, weakened by the need for entry, vulnerable, necessary.

2. Instead of nostalgia's personalized outward direction, narcissism's aim, though equally individual, is inwards. Narcissism's impulse is to focus—but now on the self, on "one's own vision, one's ability to see one's manner of seeing as one's only personal constant." The emblem of its vanity is the self-reflecting mirror.

> Narcissism is to be considered: as safe harbour, harbouring a personal vision, harbouring the possibility of vision, the description of the mirror regarding itself, the point of entry, whereby vision may contain the world.

3. Narcissism and nostalgia are co-dependent: "Narcissism demands nostalgia if it is to be utilized as a tool of vision." Together, they account for myth: "Together accounting for everything that must be accounted for. Everything must be accounted for. Allowing the possibility of describing the myth." Nostalgia and narcissism therefore account for the mythologizing that will follow in "Pablum for the Pablum Eaters," although their terms are not

used there. Nevertheless, they are not token terms. They are the impulses and terms that make the *system* of myth possible—both myth and its description: one *and* the same we know.

"Nostalgia" appears only once in that article, linked to "camp," but "narcissism" does not. Yet the two terms frame the article from without since they exist poised on its borderline, the editorial being separated from the article by a turn of a page—that is, by the recto-verso of a borderline ("the gap, space between, the borderline case"). Nostalgia and narcissism dwell on the border. They define the border dweller's attitudes.

4. Narcissism and nostalgia have a symbiotic relationship but are distinct in their functions: nostalgia is "a tool of vision"; narcissism is "the description of the mirror regarding itself." If nostalgia is "rarified vision" and narcissism is vision purely regarding itself, how do they relate to one another, as the two seem either opposedly open or closed: "the eye travelling inward and outward"? Nostalgia provides "the sense of vision from afar" while narcissism harbours "the possibility of vision." Nostalgia is active: as a "vehicle of entry" penetrating from afar. Narcissism is passive: "harbouring the possibility of vision." Harbouring, narcissism is the ground of a nostalgic vision. Narcissism and nostalgia not only allow the possibility of myth, they allow the possibility of vision: "We re-establish our ability to see with a long look into the mirrored mirror." The "long look" is nostalgia; the "mirrored mirror" is narcissism.

5. In the mirrored mirror, vision is not natural but cultured.[8] Nostalgia and narcissism not being a natural relationship, the mirror must otherwise be pierced at "strategical soft points" by unnatural or devious means. The mirror narcissistically turned on itself is not only a harbour, it is a *borderline*: its two mirrors (mirrors mirroring mirrors) mechanically create "the gap, the space between" that ambiguously defines this region. Formally reflecting itself in what would seem to be a closed system, narcissism is yet still "vulnerable," maintaining a "capacity for ambiguity" in its "silvered slivered splintered layers of apparent transparency." This zone of vision regarding itself is penetrated by another vision, a vision from afar, this other vision cultured (in the double sense of a virus) for this purpose, "cultured with an eye to the rarified, the rarefied vision, the gap, space between, the borderline case." At this point of entry, nostalgia and narcissism unite in a "vision [that] may contain the world." This world is a self-contained other universe where the archival mania of nostalgia is reflected to infinity in the self-reflecting gaze of narcissism—thereby creating an image-based mythic world (itself another emblem of viral imagery). Such correspondences "allow the description of a Universe as a vision named now. We may no longer move beyond the image, nor beyond the image of the image," contained by it in its self-reflection.[9]

6. We have to wonder, though, whether this mirror trick that "re-establish[es] our ability to see" is not an illusion, albeit a necessary one. After all, the "Pablum" article stated contrarily that, "Image Bank moves within the arena of our affliction, of our *inability* to see, and re-establishes correspondences as an operational method of accounting for everything banking on the future [emphasis added]."[10] This is not a contradiction. The operational methods of myth establish "the illusion of being able to see again, the illusion of a whole."[11] Myth is a zone of seeing within unseeing, of visibility disguised within invisibility, appearing in and out of focus on the borderline, in the in-and-out-of-focus of the borderline.[12]

7. As a tool of vision, nostalgia is a way of seeing that is active not passive. Its agency, however, is disguised or camouflaged. Here is a list, already disguised in itself, of nostalgia's techniques: "Nostalgia, a technique for survival, pinning cultural archetypes up against the wall. Collage or perish. Nostalgia, knowledge in camouflage, disguised as yearning, yearning for style that matter might take its course without due notice." "Disguise" and "camouflage" are other names for nostalgia's actions; indeed they are cryptic names for nostalgia itself. Disguise is nostalgia's passive mood or mode.[13]

8. Nostalgia is the yearning; narcissism is the need.

9. Nostalgia is a virus. ("Nostalgia must be cultured." It seeks the "strategical soft points, weakened by the need for entry." It infects vision.) Narcissism is an affliction. The two are co-dependent on each other. But the resulting disguised or camouflaged symptom is also a showcase: it is "the arena of our affliction."

10. A showcase, however, is only a theatre with its own *machinery* of presentation. In its stylistic clumsiness, in its redemption of the outré, that is, camp makes this machinery just visible. Artifice is kept visible in order perhaps not so much to emphasize a lack of content as to disguise another: "yearning for style that matter [subject matter, that is] might takes its course without due notice."[14]

11. A machine implies a system and structure. A machine functions through a relation of *sets* of terms that are interchangeable with others: "nostalgia" and "narcissism" exchange with "camouflage" and "disguise."

12. Sometimes the machine reflects a "capacity for ambiguity," at other times for focusing. A shift in the "mechanics of vision" enables one to focus on focusing, that is, on "one's ability to see one's manner of seeing." Nostalgia's focus in narcissism's mirror is abstracted—thus remaining disguised as motivations—in General Idea's "Frames of Reference," where we find "mirrors mirroring mirrors expanding and contracting to the focal point of view and including the lines of perspective bisecting the successive frames to the vanishing point."[15]

13. Nostalgia and narcissism reflect the ambiguous turn in the function of *FILE*: "FILE no longer mirroring a scene, mirrors the mirror." •

1. Susan Sontag, "Notes on 'Camp'," in *Against Interpretation* (New York: Dell Publishing Co., 1979), 275.
2. "Pablum for the Pablum Eaters," *FILE* 2:1&2 (May 1973), 28.
3. Anonymous, "FILE: The Great Canadian Art Tragedy," *The Grape*, May 24–30, 1972. General Idea made the article into a multiple and identified the writer as Dennis Wheeler. For an image of this work where you can read the full text, see Barbara Fischer, ed., *General Idea Editions: 1967–1995* (Toronto: Blackwood Gallery, 2003), 82 and *The Search for the Spirit: General Idea 1968–1975* (Toronto: Art Gallery of Ontario, 1997), 80. Referring to this article, Scott Watson wrote, "There was a homophobic backlash in the Canadian art world toward Image Bank and General Idea. Like other forms of discrimination that operate as gentleman's agreements it would be difficult to offer the documentation and specifics." Scott Watson, "Hand of the Spirit: Documents of the Seventies from the Morris/Trasov Archive," *Hand of the Spirit* (Vancouver: UBC Fine Arts Gallery, 1992), 22.
4. James Purdie, *The Globe and Mail* (Toronto), November 1, 1975. In another review of the same exhibition, entitled "3 trendy young men market themselves," Gary Michael Dault wrote, "General Idea is a trio of highly intelligent but trendy young men, Michael Tims, Ron Gabe, and Jorge Saia who, armed with impressive organizational abilities and the help of a gaggle of art-groupies, have been marketing glitter, glamour and, ultimately, themselves for the past four years. Undaunted by the fact that in presenting themselves as their own art objects they are a hundred years after the fact of French poet Charles Baudelaire who invented the attitude, about 75 years after Oscar Wilde who perfected it, and 15 years after Andy Warhol who made it pay, General Idea continues to weld its resources of mind, wit and campy sensibility into an identifiable esthetic and moral whole.... It is their love affair with suffocating self-definition and their dallying with atmospheres of vague fetid evil that is getting more arteriosclerotic and uninhabitable all the time. It's a vein nobody can profitably mine any more. Someone has to tell them how long their train's been gone." *The Toronto Star*, November 3, 1975.
5. These examples are found in Image Bank Request Lists from April 1972, May–June 1972, and December 1972.
6. Sontag, 276.
7. "Bulletin from the Ivory Tower," *FILE* 2:1&2 (May 1973), 15. All subsequent unacknowledged quotations in this section are from this editorial. Compare Sontag: "1. To start very generally: Camp is a certain mode of aestheticism. It is one way of seeing the world as an aesthetic phenomenon. That way, the way of Camp, is not in terms of beauty, but in terms of the degree of artifice, of stylization." Sontag, 277.
8. "... the split between naturalized and culturalized information and the manner in which culturized information may become ritualized as natural information to the point where it in turn may be absorbed by the cultural processes as raw material for further processing." "Pablum" (1973), 26.
9. Ibid.
10. Ibid. The phrase originates in Robert Smithson: "To reconstruct what the eyes see in words, in an 'ideal language' is a vain exploit. Why not reconstruct one's inability to see?" Robert Smithson, "Incidents of Mirror Travel in the Yucatan," *Artforum* 8:1 (September 1969), 32; reprinted in *The Writings of Robert Smithson*, ed. Nancy Holt (New York: New York University Press, 1979), 101. Also compare it use in the faux-rejected May 1972 *artscanada* article "(Advertisement)," *FILE* 1:2&3 (May/June 1972), inside back cover and in *Luxon V.B.: The 1984 Miss General Idea Pavillion No. 101*, self-published, 1973.
11. "Pablum" (1973), 26.
12. "Fuzzy borderlines were coming into focus and in and out of focus was becoming clearer." "General Idea's Borderline Cases: Introduction," *IFEL* 2:3 (September 1973), 12.
13. "Nostalgia" is a coping word: a code word for camp, a word in which vision is disguised. Is it specifically a *queer* vision? AA Bronson implies perhaps so in a 1972 review of Gertrude Stein's *Matisse, Picasso, and Gertrude Stein* when he wonders "Sometimes one thinks this is a book touching in its method on the nature of homosexuality." The language and concepts of this review are consistent with the discussion of nostalgia in the "Bulletin from the Ivory Tower" editorial, for instance, when Bronson writes of Stein's "sense of seeing from afar and between," seeing from afar and the space between being characteristics of nostalgia and narcissism. Bronson discusses Stein's notion of "bottom nature" in terms of this vision ("bottom nature as a vision and a method"): "Certainly this is the sense of Stein's writing the method of Stein's writing certainly the matter of bottom nature as a vision and a

method certainly the pervading sense of this great and touching book and its means of touching and stroking.... In this book the sense of bottom nature and bottom nature as a method and a manner of seeing and coping and liking and loving is very clear." AA Bronson, "Reviews: Matisse, Picasso, and Gertrude Stein," *FILE* 1:4 (December 1972), 23. At the time, General Idea were not inclined to present their work as queer:

Louise Dompierre: So did you see, or did you talk about your practice as a gay practice in the early years?

Felix: No, never. I don't think that we ever disguised it... There was some encouragement from some people to do that, and we always resisted it. I think it was explicit, in a political sense, because of fears of marginalization. There was an interpretation that we were going to be then pigeonholed as that—as opposed to being afraid that someone would find out. I think that it was more of a strategy at that time, I don't know. We never discussed it together, but ...

Louise: You thought it would be too limiting, in terms of exhibition opportunities or ...

AA: It just didn't seem interesting, I guess. For someone to write about us that way would have been fine. And probably interesting. But we weren't interested in *presenting* ourselves that way. It seemed to be beside the point, in a way.

Louise: Do you see your practice now as a gay practice?

AA: It's hard to know what that would be.

Louise Dompierre interviews General Idea, July 26, 1991. Manuscript Series, General Idea archives, 23–24.

14. Compare Sontag: "To emphasize style is to slight content, or to introduce an attitude which is neutral with respect to content." Sontag, 277.

15. "General Idea's Frames of Reference," *FILE* 4:1 (Summer 1978), 12.

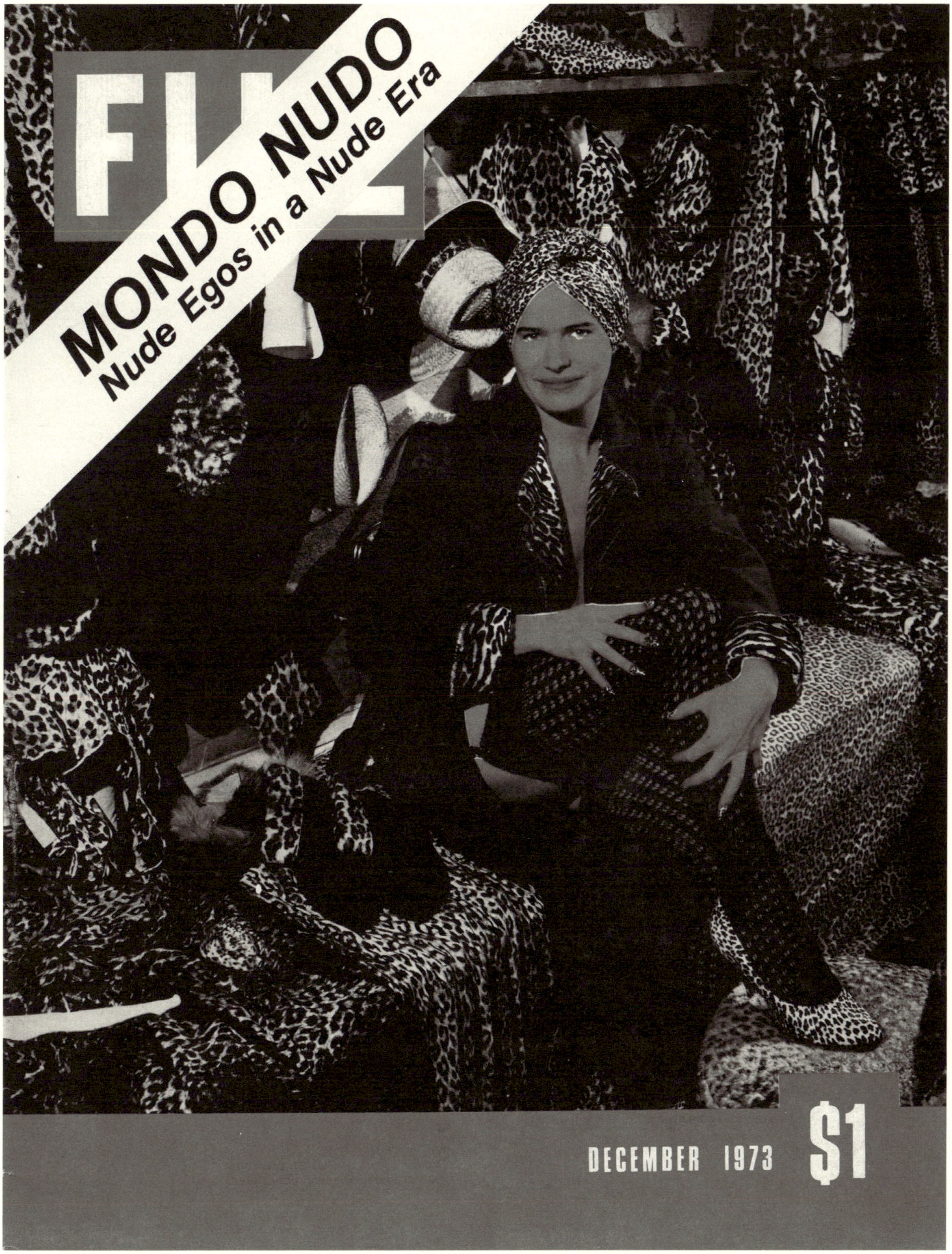
FILE
MONDO NUDO
Nude Egos in a Nude Era
DECEMBER 1973
$1

FILE 2:4 (December 1973), cover

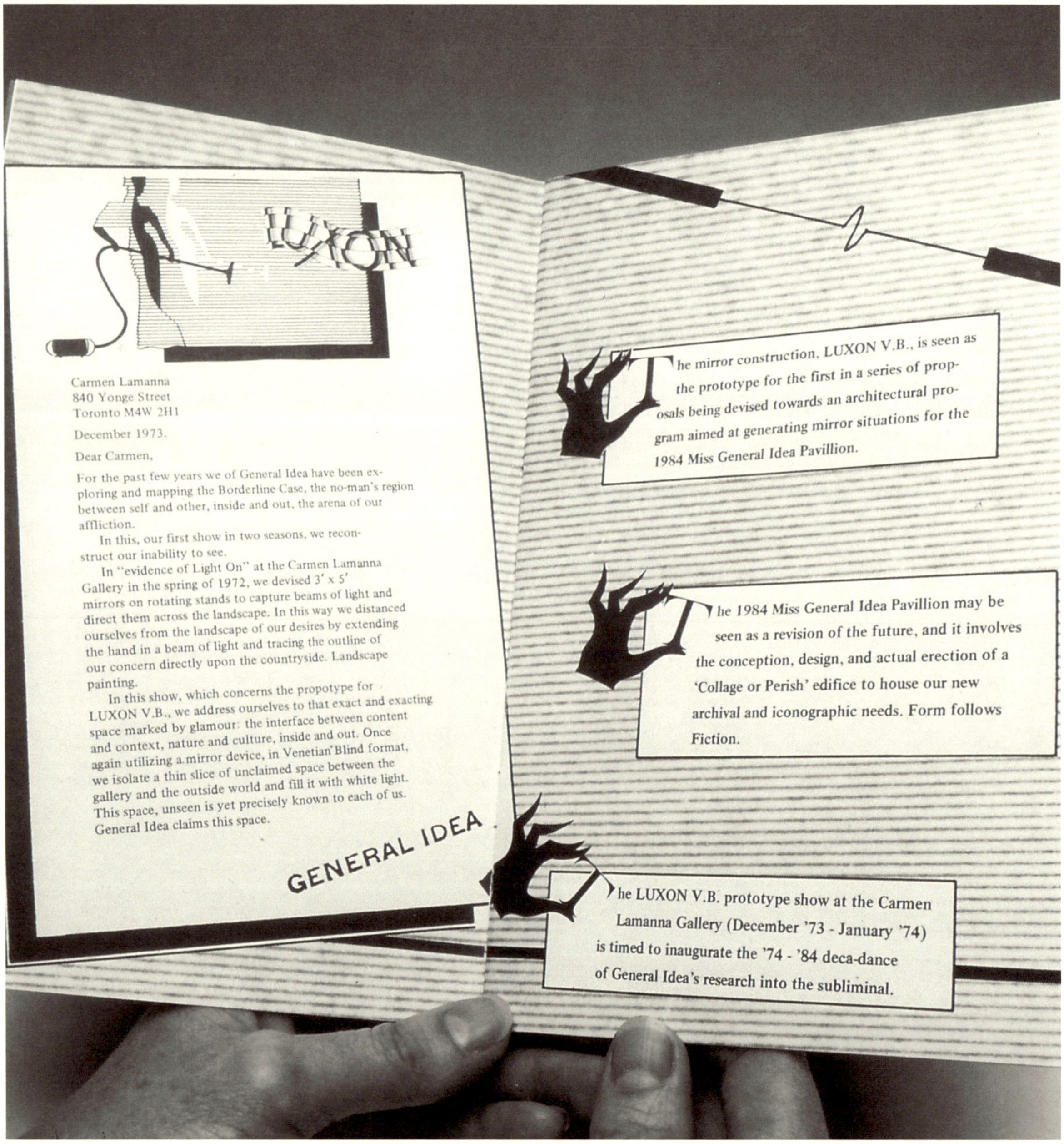

Double-page spread from *Luxon V.B.: The 1984 Miss General Idea Pavillion No. 101*, self-published, 1973

BORDERLINE

The borderline is a place to stage difference—not just differences. It is not just a place where opposites confront each other face to face as if in equal reflection. The powerful narcissistically see only their own overriding image there, not the other. But this differential of power opens sites for transgression. Canadian artists are adept there.[1] And no one was more exemplary than General Idea in locating borderlines and smuggling in their agenda.

In a letter prefacing the pamphlet *Luxon V.B.: The 1984 Miss General Idea Pavillion No. 101*, self-published to coincide with their exhibition of *Luxon V.B.* in December 1973, the artists wrote "For the past few years we of General Idea have been exploring and mapping the Borderline Case, the no-man's region between self and other, inside and out, the arena of our affliction.... In this show, which concerns the prototype for Luxon V.B., we address ourselves to that exact and exacting space marked by glamour: the interface between content and context, nature and culture, inside and out."[2] In this letter the artists outlined an area of interest and a range of content, but they never defined the term "borderline," even though they seemed to fix its location: a "no-man's region." Unlike the *Pavillion* or *Pageant*, the Borderline was not a container but a concept. It was an articulating concept that, nonetheless, did not articulate itself. Could it ever be defined given that it was between things, between one and the other, articulating the in-between? More than this, how could we define it when the borderline was not definitive but ambiguity itself? How "exacting" can such a space be?

General Idea's Borderline Cases

A borderline situation doesn't necessarily advertise itself and therefore make itself readily locatable—or visible. For instance, it appeared in General Idea's work or writing every time myth or mirrors were in play—indeed, whenever there was the cut-up of collage. But General Idea did advertise for it on the Subliminal network and presented the results in public. The article "General Idea's Borderline Cases" was fully a product of correspondence art: solicited through *FILE*'s Image Bank Request Lists and subsequently published in the September 1973 issue.[3] As if a diagnostic report, the article presented ten cases from General Idea's "research investigations."

These were exercises in relating texts to pictures by creating symmetries between words and images. Language was put through its paces, run through the numbers, but from the start the mirror image of one and one always added up to two.[4] Between one and two, between one and the other, between the numbers one and two were all the resources of mirroring, mimicry, and mockery as language clichés were married to banal images. Here is the text from the second case, titled "Imitation of Life (Mimicry)":

> It's only natural to try to be part of our vision, our culture. Like chameleons at odds trying to be part of it all. Like letting our one hand know what the other is about. When one body is imitating one body lying down its life imitating life. This act of bodies rubbing is merely a shadow of things to come. Was meeting face to face the mother of invention of the looking glass? Was this prop-osal to end our singleness? There's safety in numbers and two can have a mind of its own. Our two hands applauded the engagement and came out dueling. In the crack of dawn a narcissus is blooming. All together now, one two, one two, one two.[5]

Yet the two, or the mirror image of two, did not mean equality or even mirror symmetry. *One* brought forth the other (as if in a mirror), gave it life, as simulacral as that life was since it was only mimicry. Mimicry was viral: indeed, a virus. The point of entry, the mirror act was a viral, replicating invasion. It was not as if words described the image as an extended caption, as the set-up before us in the form of a picture magazine implied. One preceded two and that one was the word. It took off from there: serially, creating content in the process. Words, too, were mirrors.

Each case was an application: the application of a method through the insertion of a mirror. It was purely artificial. There was no given place to insert a mirror, however. No pre-existent line. The borderline did not pre-exist. The *act* of mirror insertion created the borderline situation. Only the mirror preceded—as invisible as it was. "Now this is an application gained from reflecting," as General Idea said in case number four, "Graven Imagery (Mockery)"—but not as an *after* the fact of reflecting, rather as its event.[6] The instance of the act was the instantiation of a case, an instance of now. The event was contrary to the process of first collecting images, then writing texts: it was an inaugurating act. What came before was pretence; this was the real thing, the main event.

Each case was an invention, a performance, an impromptu dance between words and images. But in the end, which was the beginning of it all, "the Great Divide was words."[7] "In other words, the words attempted to divide and conquer or multiply."[8] Words did not follow after images; words made images secondary; in fact, doubled them. Words split images. Or, the proliferation of words split images into mirror images of themselves:

> Now that we've got our distance we look back over our shoulders. Could this be our skin? Still waters reflect our eyes reflecting still waters running deep. Let's keep this all on the surface. The surface of the silvered glass narcissus. Could this be our connection? Score one for us and chalk it up to experienced. Driving the wedge down deep through the centre and splitting the images in halves. There is two of us to contend with now. Two heads are better than one but it's really just one more mouth to feed on. Casting our image in the mirror revealed a cast of two. Our very own dialogue to talk to ourselves. We're not the one we used to be.[9]

Splitting in half was only a beginning that had no end. Words, like mirrors, were viral.

So in retrospect when we read the statements on the image from *FILE*'s first editorial ("Every image is a self image. Every image is a mirror."), we must now presume that between every image (that is, between every selfsame image) is a borderline. The image does not merely reflect itself as if in a mirror (performing and posing to itself). A fissure of words, indeed, of cutting remarks, divides the image from itself. As General Idea wrote in their *Borderline Cases*, "More fuel to the fire as we split the levels down the centre with cutting remarks or nouns."[10] Words were a method of invasion, even of the image.

Logics of the Borderline

Since the borderline was one with myth, in dividing, it also united. The borderline, mirror, and myth all participated in the same contradictory processes, which was evident, though not explicitly stated, from the very first *FILE* editorial:

> The myth slides down the center, slicing realities into thin transparencies shuffling lives like leaves dissolving dualities into fabled tales. In the story it all comes together. In the myth opposite possibilities become complementary content.[11]

Myth accommodated contradiction, but not necessarily any longer, as in that first editorial, as "complementary content." Opposites were neither simply complementary nor contradictory. They were only if we think of myth in terms of its content: as if it was a case of one or the other of "content and context, nature and culture, inside and out" and not of their interface. Rather, we must realize, as "Pablum for the Pablum Eaters" stated, that "the key to this logic [of the myth] is the borderline situation, the neither one nor the other."[12] The negative alternative "neither-nor" was an alternating machine: *Luxon V.B.* itself. No mere decor, the *Luxon V.B.* was an articulating *device* that we operated: it functioned as a mirrored venetian blind, capturing images and flipping inside out and outside in.[13] "Now you see it ... now you don't."[14]

As a prototype manipulated by the Hand of the Spirit, *Luxon V.B.* was a *demonstration* device.[15] Its function was to demonstrate that articulation fundamentally was ambiguous. By means of its complicating operations, "a resonance which is ambiguity flips the image in and out of context. Layers of accumulated meaning snap in and out of focus."[16] The "exact and exacting space" of the borderline was articulated only as an operation of ambiguity. No content could be defined there. The borderline articulated but did not define. What received or left its mark there, appearing only in and as the borderline itself, was indefinable, being neither object nor content. In other words, it was Glamour: the "arena of our affliction."

In asserting the difference between contradiction and ambiguity, General Idea began to differentiate themselves from Lévi-Strauss's structural anthropology on which their definition of myth—as the interface of nature and culture—earlier was dependent. As they wrote in the Borderline Cases editorial, "Levels of ambiguity present classification problems not yet dealt with by structural methods."[17]

Border Agency

When we talk of borderlines, we commonly refer to political formations: the regulated borders between nation states. But there are also unregulated edges of territories that border on outlands inhabited by outlaws. This is a porous boundary of crossovers penetrated at unprotected points. Media is such an amorphous environment that might thus be infiltrated and inhabited.

General Idea feigned to posture on the first border and perversely penetrated the second, but there was a third at which they were most adept. These borderlines did not pre-exist their spontaneous formation. They came into being because of an event—almost as if the flash of a mirror, by means of a "cutting remark," or through a collage interruption, equivalent techniques General Idea surreptitiously employed.

Technically, border crossers only existed in this event, self-created in the *act* of border crossing. Strategically camouflaged, they dwelt on this border and dealt in stolen goods, shifting them back and forth across the line. Contrary movements of border crossings were only "stolen moments" that spread ambiguity in this no-man's region: "Ambiguity is not a symptom of a schizophrenic who travels back and forth across the line but a quality of the border dweller who performs in the stolen moments."[18] Performing in stolen moments, border crossers smuggled in and stole out. These sleight-of-hand thieves stole out in a brief act of larceny, the "moment taken for a surreptitious faking." And what was the object of such a theft? General Idea answered: Glamour. "Cross all borders. Steal past the fashion guards and steal away the Glamour Myth! Counterfeit! Interphase! Camouflage!"[19]

Adept at camouflage and counterfeit, General Idea hid nothing of their actions, though. They always said they were subliminal criminals and plagiarist thieves. They were ready to declare their identity at any customs crossing, at any transgression of conventionality. Indeed, it was (per)formed there. In spite of their apodictic declaration "we do declare 'we do' at customs" (where they have "no-thing to speak of," though), they fully disclosed their tactics: "Our favorite spot for border crossings is right between the lines."[20] Right between the lines, of course, was writing itself, the counterfeit performance enacted before us in their *Borderline Cases* and elsewhere, camouflaging while disclosing at the same time a brilliant plagiarism. This delicate performance was a precarious act, "hanging in the balance with a foot in the future and back in the past… caught in a double bind."[21] In the dance and danger of the borderline one sinks or swims, collages or perishes. •

1. See Marshall McLuhan, "Canada: The Borderline Case," in *The Canadian Imagination: Dimensions of a Literary Culture*, ed. David Staines (Cambridge, MA: Harvard University Press, 1977), 226–248. McLuhan called the borderline situation an "interface." In this essay, McLuhan had nothing to say about visual art, restricting himself—in the typically Canadian way—to literary culture, though he and General Idea were on the same wavelength.
2. *Luxon V.B.: The 1984 Miss General Idea Pavillion No. 101*, self-published, 1973. Another exploration of Borderline Cases, which married Robert Smithson's experiments in writing to John Brockman's terminology, was published as an "(Advertisement)" on the inside back cover of the May–June 1972 issue of *FILE*.
3. In the December 1972 Image Bank Request List of *FILE*, General Idea requested "BORDERLINE Imagery and Information concerning: 1. Balance 2. Mimicry 3. Split Realization 4. Mockery 5. Drawing the Line 6. Dams 7. Elemental Breakthrough 8. Crossing the Border 9. Inside/Outside 10. Re-coupling." In the May 1973 issue, Felix Partz asked for: "straight to the point images and head on collisions pertaining to; the man in the middle, meeting half way, middle of the road, sitting on the fence, maybe and walking the straight and narrow."
4. The numerology of the ten Borderlines Cases was based on esoteric principles: specifically the ten categories of the Kabbalah—as well as being influenced by Madame Blavatsky. Email communication from AA Bronson, November 3, 2011. Also see Felix Partz, Notebook 1972 for references to this numeric structuring. Notebook Series, General Idea Fonds, deposited in the Library and Archives of the National Gallery of Canada.
5. "General Idea's Borderline Cases: Imitation of Life (Mimicry)," *IFEL* 2:3 (September 1973), 14. (General Idea renamed *FILE* as *IFEL* for this special Paris issue.)
6. "Graven Imagery (Mockery)," ibid., 18.
7. "Split," ibid., 20.
8. "Introduction," ibid., 12.
9. "Self Conscious," ibid., 16. Identity—or role—was a mirror effect produced serially.
10. "Introduction," ibid., 12. Cf. "Double edge blade of the cutting remark for the kill" in "Editorials: To whom it may concern, " *FILE* 1:4 (December 1972), 5.
11. "Editorial: Some Juicy and Malicious Gossip," *FILE* 1:1 (April 1972), 3. Compare the opening to the editorial "Bulletin From the Ivory Tower" where it stated, "In the last issue we stuck the knife up the ass. In the end it all came together." *FILE* 2:1&2 (May 1973), 15.
12. "Pablum for the Pablum Eaters," *FILE* 2:1&2 (May 1973), 27.
13. "Eyelashes glimmer in glamour dust as her eyes lightly tap the silvered surface. A flick of the Hand of the Spirit turns the slats to allow her image to the other side—a double crossing of borderlines by her image in cahoots with her vision." *Showcard* 4-005.
14. Number 1 and number 10 of the Borderline Cases were headed "Now You See It" and "Now You Don't."
15. Not just a prop, the Hand of the Spirit itself is a mechanism: "The Hand of the Spirit of Miss General Idea is not an object but a mechanism, a style, a sign, the essential configuration of movement and desire." *Showcard* 2-023.
16. "Glamour: Image Lobotomy," *FILE* 3:1 (Autumn 1975), n.p.
17. "Editorial: Borderline Cases," *IFEL* 2:3 (September 1973), 11.
18. "General Idea's Borderline Cases: Introduction," 12.
19. "Are You Truly Invisible?," *IFEL* 2:3 (September 1973), 35.
20. "General Idea's Borderline Cases: Strange Customs," 26.
21. Ibid.

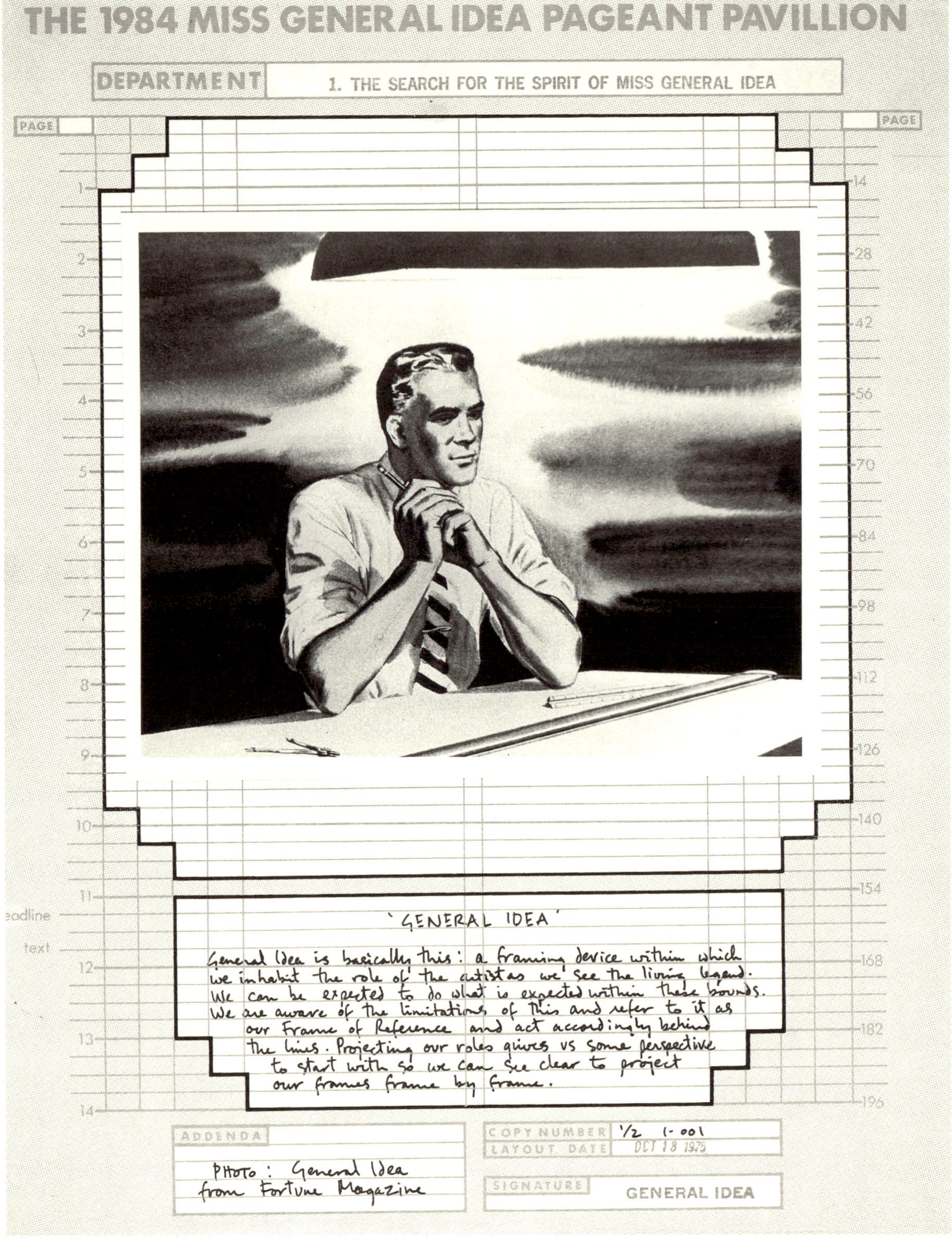
THE 1984 MISS GENERAL IDEA PAGEANT PAVILLION

DEPARTMENT 1. THE SEARCH FOR THE SPIRIT OF MISS GENERAL IDEA

PAGE PAGE

'GENERAL IDEA'

General Idea is basically this: a framing device within which we inhabit the role of the artist as we see the living legend. We can be expected to do what is expected within these bounds. We are aware of the limitations of this and refer to it as our Frame of Reference and act accordingly behind the lines. Projecting our roles gives us some perspective to start with so we can see clear to project our frames frame by frame.

ADDENDA

PHOTO: General Idea from Fortune Magazine

COPY NUMBER 1/2 1-001

LAYOUT DATE OCT 18 1975

SIGNATURE GENERAL IDEA

Showcard 1-001, 1975

PUBLICITY AND PERSUASION

Any one who was around before computers were prevalent knows that designing and producing a magazine was a different affair then. Like all other magazines, *FILE* was a cut-and-paste hand job. Not for publication themselves, the *Showcards* seemed to prepare for it, especially since they were formatted as if they were magazine layout sheets: printed alike in non-repro blue, a technique whereby the blue guidelines disappeared when a layout page was photographed for printing plates—as the prepared pages of *FILE* would have been. With images and copy laid in on these boards from their different sources, design was a collage process that vanished in the printing.

The *Showcards*, however, were not magazine layouts. Perhaps they belonged to a Madison Avenue advertising agency with an account for "The 1984 Miss General Idea Pageant Pavillion," the name that titles all these cards. Indeed, the *Showcards* were for show: perhaps boardroom pitches to colleagues or clients—or the general public itself. What product was being sold? Why, the 1984 Miss General Idea Pavillion itself! In this sales pitch, persuasion *was* erection.[1]

Yes, indeed, these were *show*-cards: They were a verbo-visual performance. The *Showcards*' mechanics—all on the surface, with nothing hidden—was a theatre of presentation.[2]

The *Showcards* were also a compendium: an index or abstract of General Idea's larger enterprise; a record of their ongoing research; a previewing patenting of future works (for instance, the *Colour Bar Lounge* [1-046]). They were a narrative of the design and construction of the *Pavillion* itself and a description of its components. They were a verbal means by which to foresee, see, construct... or re-construct it.[3]

The *Showcards* began the story of the "Search for the Spirit" and the "Search for the Site" of the *Pavillion*. They elaborated on the accoutrements of Miss General Idea, such as her shoes and wig or the specialized car she drove. They told of the *Pavillion*'s planning, proposals, the hoarding that initially was to surround it, and of some of its design features—such as its mirrored venetian-blind window system, the *Luxon V.B.*

Since the *Pavillion* was a monument to the Spirit, images of creativity reigned in the *Showcards*—but of a restrained sort, with emphasis given to planning. First tribute was offered to the master builders who envisioned and conceived the project and oversaw the *Pavillion*'s construction. An architect at a drafting table provided a rich image repertoire, complete with props, of this power of visualization. (One whole section of the *Showcards* was titled "At the Drafting Board.") Visualization was inspiration, and vice versa.[4] So it is no surprise that, before a line was drawn, the first numbered *Showcard* (1-001) was that of a lone architect at the drafting table, pencil raised, staring into space, contemplating his vision. And that the last of the 1975 series was that of General Idea themselves likewise disposed around a drafting table, the three members mimicking inspiration (5-001) in their concentrating poses.[5]

But was it only a pose? Architecture serves a purpose and follows a program; it is a corporate activity, indeed, a corporate creativity; lone vision is insufficient in a world of business. Thus in another *Showcard* (1-041), we see a businessman, perhaps the architects' patron, reading a fully realized skyscraper off a blueprint he holds in his hands—the edifice rising before him in its idealized form. It seems that a larger vision constrained even the supposed creators of the *Pavillion*. Reading off blueprints, perhaps our anonymous architects, too, just recited their lines:

> Their line of vision is falling just outside of our frame but it's still on target. The origin of their vision is in plain view—They are reading their lines. They are engaged in a transformation process that is allowing ideas to jump off the page and fulfill their rightful space. This is what we like to see, if you know what we mean. (1-019)[6]

This *Showcard* repeated what William Burroughs had already openly said of foreground figures such as these architects, builders, and construction foremen: "Yes, we know the front men and women in this organization but they are no more than that . . a façade . . tape recorders . . the operators are *not there* . ."[7] Was the *Pavillion* only a façade with one point of view on it: that of its operators? Were General Idea the hidden operators here or were they, too, dupes of the Spirit with scripted roles to play? Who's writing, indeed, drawing the lines here?

> Voice Over: A silver mask protects the voyeur from stray lines of sight. He bends the slats for more ecstatic data, feasting his eyes on unsuspecting volumes. Whose master plan is he labouring under? (1-053)

Could the abstract operator be a sadistic Miss General Idea herself, a dominatrix schoolmistress, to whom even the artists were subservient?

> "She rigidly and strictly plotted our course from beginning to end like a blueprint that had to be adhered to.... One of the things that seemed to make her happy was the sound of our voices quoting verbatim sections from her private library sources. There was always humiliation to pay if we slipped up in the memory work, some fine point of logic...." (1-008)[8]

The *Showcards* were part of a master plan to construct the *Pavillion*. Information previously had been leaked piecemeal, but these were the first comprehensive set of documents on its planning. The planning, however, was also the projecting of it. General Idea had a unique architectural practice: word lines and sightlines coincided to elevate the *Pavillion*.[9] The *Showcards* not only caught our attention, they also directed our point of view on the *Pavillion*'s erection.

The conventions of architectural drawings, with their plans, elevations, and perspectives, were metaphors for the *Pavillion*'s construction, but taken together the *Showcards* were an allegory for the function of the *Pavillion* itself. The techniques that directed our attention were akin to the architectural drawings that guided the building of the edifice. Not necessarily visible like architectural perspectives, verbal renditions subtended the drawings' projections and prompted us to see a certain way. We were rendered as much as the drawings were. Our vision was constructed; indeed, it was the means by which the *Pavillion* was erected.

Construction of vision entailed three interrelated modes, as if superimposed through several layers of tracing paper:

(1) the lines of vision by which the *Pavillion* was constructed, that is, the perspectives by which it was drawn: its architectural plans and elevations;

(2) the means through which or *within* which the *Pavillion* was seen: the lines of perspective that guided our sight, that is, the perspective of another's dominating vision that was enslaving;

(3) constrained within this vision, a "concentrated vision," a vision that was fetishizing.

Seeing was not only believing, it was elevating. We erected the *Pavillion* as we saw it—through these multiple sightlines. In fact, we elevated the Spirit of Miss General Idea through the same means. Of these two forms of elevation, the second was contained and constrained within the first. Just as the *Pavillion* contained the *Pageant*, so these sightlines constrained a fetishizing, yet elevating, vision:

> (slow pan of a Pavillion interior)
> VOICE OVER: Expressionist spots bath the scene with severe effects. Out of this jumble of slashed planes, out of the darkened halls, arises the streamlined form of the Spirit of Miss General Idea, elevating objects to their proper place, putting objects in grammatical perspective. They remain just out of reach, with just the proper distance. (1-003)

Our vision was stage-directed toward an end: the crowning of Miss General Idea. Directed vision was central to General Idea's project. It served the overall purpose of the *Pavillion*, what it had been purpose-built for: its generalized *elevating* function. Vision had an end: it elevated Glamour.

Sightlines, however, were *verbal* prompts as well; they were "grammatical perspectives." In this theatre, text no longer was secondary or supplemental to the image. Rather, from its prompt box, text animated the framed image above it. Many *Showcards*, such as number 1-003 quoted above, with its slow pan and voice over, revealed that these modes of seeing were directed scenographically, as in a film script: as verbo-visual constructs.[10] Not any film script, however, but one crafted in the style of the *nouveau roman* of Alain Robbe-Grillet with its scrupulous, fetishizing descriptions, where scenes were written as if seen *already* through the lens of a camera, incorporating camera movements into their prose, or seeming merely deadpan descriptions of photographs themselves.

Each card scripted a shot or a scene. But the writing was fragmentary; it was cumulative, seemingly endless in its additive, repetitive task of description. At times, this thankless task seemed to be the labour of some anonymous copywriter—akin to a subservient draftsman—who must write to the image and account for it after the fact:

> At times getting it all down on paper seemed the hardest part. After juggling the books we had to sift all the information into formulae. Everything had to add up to additional information. Try to take a found image and raise it to the second power. See what you're up against. Up against paper and pen and figures, and words. (1-035)

But even if the image came first, writing veered it towards fiction, deviating the image with it, inflecting it towards a new meaning and role within the overall functioning of the *Pavillion*. •

---

1. AA Bronson pointed to the role of the *Showcards* in advertising General Idea's system: "This structure was clarified, even advertised, in the showcards series of 1975..." AA Bronson, "Myth as Parasite/Image as Virus: General Idea's Bookshelf 1967–1975," in *The Search for the Spirit: General Idea 1968–1975* (Toronto: Art Gallery of Ontario, 1997), 20.
2. Indeed, the *Showcards* themselves are equally like a hoarding, turned inside out in exhibition, hiding the construction site. Only their texts provide a point of view.
3. Each of the 130 *Showcards* is headed with the project title: "The 1984 Miss General Idea Pageant Pavillion." This is followed by a box titled "Department" in which five topics are indicated by stamps: (1) The Search for the Spirit of Miss General Idea"; (2) The 1984 Miss General Idea Pageant; (3) Miss General Idea 1984; (4) The 1984 Miss General Idea Pavillion; (5) Frame of Reference. Ziggurat-outlined boxes succeed for image above and hand-written text below, the latter having a "leadline." At the bottom, a legend credits the image source, usually an illustration or photograph from *Fortune* magazine or a photograph by General Idea. Other boxes indicate "Copy number," "Layout date" (all October 18, 1975), and "Signature" (all General Idea). New *Showcards* were added for their 1977 *Reconstructing Futures* exhibition and continued being produced until 1979.

   When exhibited the first time in 1975 in the exhibition *Going thru the Notions* at the Carmen Lamanna Gallery, the artists sub-divided the five departments into a number of groupings:

   Search for the Spirit
   Search for the Site
   Cut Outs
   Massing Studies
   Hand of the Spirit
   Miss General Idea Shoes
   Miss General Idea Wig
   Spirit of Miss General Idea Vehicle
   Portraits
   Frame of Reference
   Hoarding
   Work It
   At the Drafting Board
   Miniatures
   Proposals
   Luxon VB
   Index
4. Inspiration *is* elevation *is* construction, but "Behind every line of vision (and often on the surface) are countless equations, revisions and refinements. The Pavillion would never get off the ground, off the drawing boards, without concrete imagery on a stable foundation. Behind the apparent structure lies a superstructure of obscurantist scrawlings and words" (*Showcard* 1-036). A 1977 *Showcard* (1-090) reads: "'Dedication & Inspiration.'

VOICE OVER: We consider the drafting board not so much a working surface as a backdrop for the pageant of creation. Here it frames the drafting instruments, without whose timeless dedication and inspiration, the *Pavillion* could never have been constructed."

5. Two *Showcards* (1-018, 2-045, both titled "It was at one of those late session in the small hours") illustrate the metonymic (text) and metaphoric (image) relationships within the series: the first, a *Fortune* magazine photograph of three designers around a drafting table, the second a photograph of General Idea likewise disposed. But the caption to the first identifies the players as the members of General Idea, too: "And then ... AA Bronson lit another stick and flipped an aesthetic like a fried egg. Felix Partz aptly demonstrated the Spirit of Discovery by leaning into a hidden light source. And Jorge Zontal, defining style, deftly mimicked inspiration by the correct angle of his furrowed brow. (off camera, voice over: CUT!)" Such found photographs were obviously models for Rodney Werden's photographic portrait of General Idea.
6. In the overdubbing lip flap flip flop of collage, everyone's lines are spoken for them.
7. William S. Burroughs, *The Ticket That Exploded* (New York: Grove Press, 1987) 21. First published in 1962, reprinted in 1967.
8. "Everyone's going to know who's been pulling the strings all these years, who's behind it all... They ['this trio'] are going to fulfill my vision and then I'll move right in and take the cake. I'll be the object of my desire and they can be the subjects. They'll know who wears the crown in this pavillion," Miss General Idea revealed in the 1977 *Hot Property* performance. "Hot Property," *FILE* 4:1 (Summer 1978), 25.
9. "Wordlines are as important as sightlines in plotting the course." "The Miss General Idea Vehicle," *FILE* 4:1 (Summer 1978), 39.
10. Optical devices ("prying camera eyes") dominate in the *Showcards*' descriptions. They concentrate, focus, or direct vision. (Miniatures, models, and diagrams also perform this function.) We are led into or, more likely, over the images through slow zooms or pans. Sometimes these devices are doubled up, as in a "slow zoom into spotlight circle" (2-022).

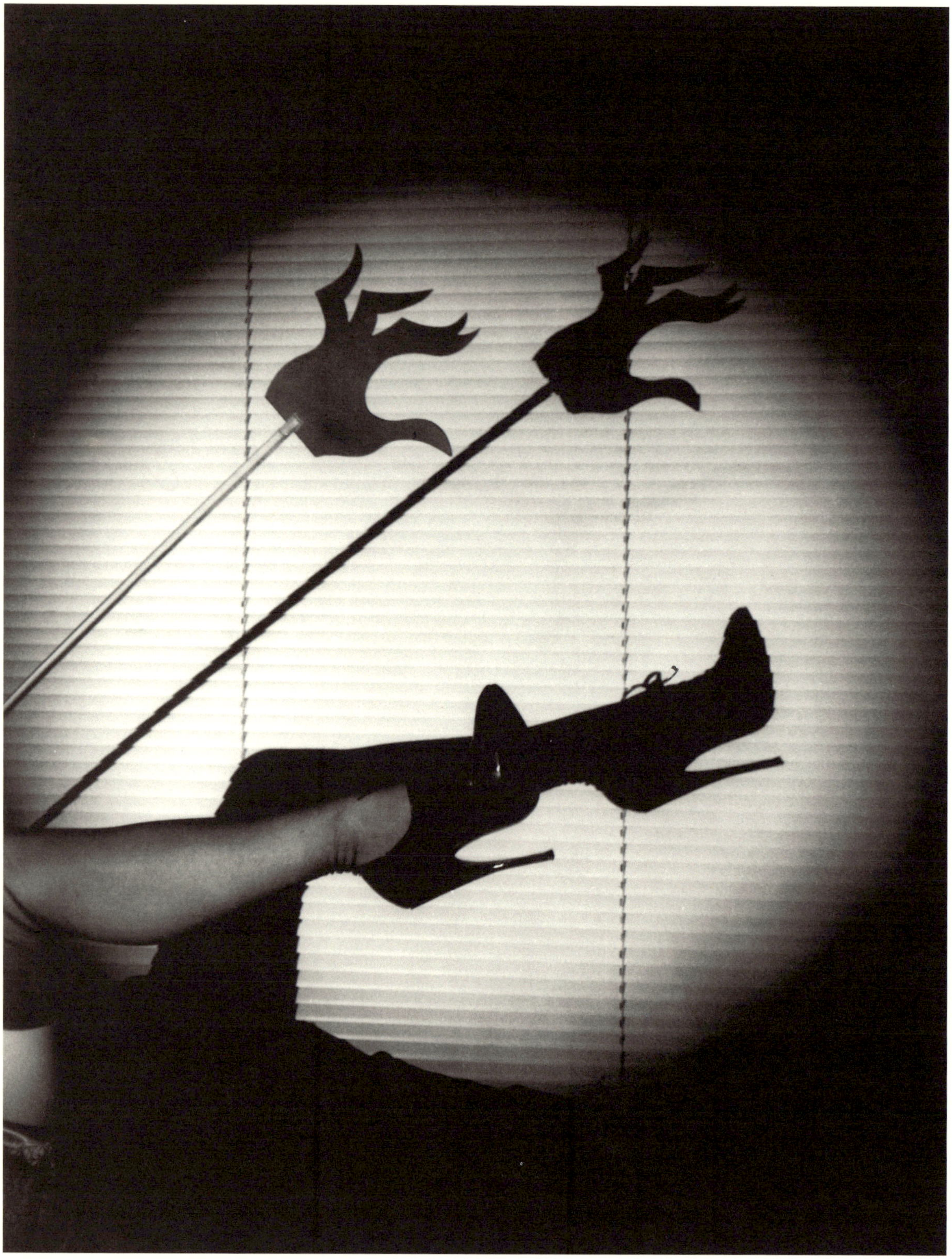

Untitled, 1973–74 (Sandy Stagg models *The Miss General Idea Shoe* and the *Hand of the Spirit* against the backdrop of *Luxon V.B.*)

GLAMOUR IS THEFT

The 1984 Miss General Idea Pageant was directed towards the crowning of Miss General Idea. All eyes were turned towards her, focused on her elevation. Miss General Idea was the epitome of Glamour. Indeed, Glamour was the criteria for her selection: *The 1971 Miss General Idea Pageant* panel of judges unanimously chose Marcel Idea for "capturing 'Glamour' without falling into it." Most people think Glamour to be the apex of General Idea's system. And they are right. But as the centerpiece of the system, "Glamour" is a term that cannot be pinned down. Appropriately, it remains just out of reach, but not out of sight—hardly knowable at all.

As the *Pageant* elevated Miss General Idea, so the *Pavillion* was a system for the elevation of a concept: Glamour. But in the spotlight, a crowning concept tends to obscure the means of its elevation becoming in itself a permanent symbol and enshrined emblem of its success. Concerning Glamour, we can repeat what was said about Miss General Idea herself: "Elevated she reigns; idealized she contains; artfully she maintains; dominantly she sustains our interest."[1] This is to say, Glamour is *the* mythic concept. It demands our attention.

Appropriated in part from the fashion world and in part from beauty contests, Glamour was a means to mock the art system, and the *Pageant* was the parody of its yearly rituals. But Glamour there was not the system, only what was elevated within it. We already know, as advertised in the *Showcards*, the role that Glamour performed in the *Pageant* and *Pavillion*. Glamour was something in which we had a role as an audience with our vision bound and directed and our responses ritually rehearsed in its elevation. Glamour was the means by which we participated in the camp send up of the system. But was Glamour forever destined to function in this fashion?

It is assumed that the classic expression of Glamour was expounded in the 1975 "Glamour" issue of *FILE*. But we find that Glamour did not operate quite the same there as it did in the *Pageant*. We now witness not so much a turn as an exaggeration of Miss General Idea's characteristics. Her "bottom nature" no longer was so benign. Although active and passive at the same time, her sadistic streak had been hardened to the point of aggression. She was likened to poison—and the *Pageant* no longer was so much about elevation as it was about violent intrusion: "Like poison Miss General Idea, objet d'art, posed on stiletto heal and bound in the latest fantasy, represents a violent intrusion into the heart of culture: the Canada Council, for example, or beauty pageants (essentially one and the same)."[2]

This was not the only change in the function of Glamour, which remained, all the same, a difference in kind rather than type. If Glamour operated differently here, it was because the operators now told a different story. This was the story of General Idea themselves and no longer that of the *Pageant*. "This is the story of Glamour and the part it has played in our art," General Idea wrote. It was a story of how the artists diverted Glamour to their *own* self-elevation.

Glamour thus functioned within this story of their desire now "to be famous, glamourous and rich," which was still a send-up of sorts of the art system. But within this story, which was not a pageant, Glamour was not only an attribute to achieve—as in being rich and famous; it was an operation to manipulate in order to get there.

The artists let us in on their secret to being Glamourous. Apparently it was not a matter of talent: "We never felt we had to produce great art to be great artists. We knew great art did not bring glamour and fame." Nor was it a case of playing a convincing role, even though General Idea "made public appearances in painters' smocks." Primarily, Glamour was an operation of "stolen lingo." Right away General Idea shamelessly admitted:

> We knew that in order to be glamourous we had to become plagiarists, intellectual parasites. We moved in on history and occupied images, emptying them of meaning, reducing them to shells. We filled these shells then with Glamour, the creampuff innocence of idiots, the naughty silence of sharkfins slicing oily waters.

Notwithstanding its crazy lingo, here was a concise description of General Idea's methods. "A method of invasion," Glamour was a parasitic operation of inhabitation. But it was, as well, an object of that operation—in spite of General Idea claiming right away that: "We knew Glamour was not an object, not an action, not an idea." However, to complicate the issue, they immediately proceeded to call it an object and an act.[3] For instance, "Glamour acts economically." Or in "Objet d'art," they said "Glamourous objects open themselves like whores to meaning, answering need with vacancy, waiting to be penetrated by the act of recognition." And in "Image Lobotomy," they added, "Glamourous objects events have been brutally emptied of meaning that parasitic but cultured meaning might be housed there." Ambivalently, the object opened itself or it was emptied and penetrated, turning from one to the other as if in the flick of a switch … or a venetian blind.

Glamour exhibited a double structure: vacillating between vacancy and closure, fluctuating between being open and closed. On the one hand, the Glamourous object opened itself to penetration by meaning and recognition. On the other hand, impenetrable, the Glamourous "object exhibit[ed] unashamedly a closure and a brilliance, in a word a SILENCE which belongs to the world of myth."

Glamour was a Borderline Case, so being open or closed was neither then a logical case of either-or (either open or closed) nor a successive event of one after the other (open then closed). Fluctuation was a principle whereby Glamour could not be pinned down because it presented alternative, even contradictory, points of view ambivalently together within the same structure: "A resonance which is ambiguity flips the image in and out of context." However, for Glamour to exhibit this double structure (that is, being both open and closed) it had to operate on a double register whereby an *action* disguised itself as an *object*.

For an object really to be an action, an operation must contradictorily be disguised in a vacant and benumbed image. But disguise itself also was a covert action. That is, not only the object but also the action was disguised. This made it all very difficult to see—doubly so since the object or image was plagiarized, presenting itself as something it was not, but being open about it, displaying itself openly. Disguise advertised and hid itself at the same time in this contradictory, camouflaged moment: "Don't be blinded by the invisibility of our stance," General Idea advised readers in the "Glamour" editorial.

Blinding light disguises, especially when reflected by a mirror. In the article "Are You Truly Invisible?," General Idea had already earlier commanded us, through a manoeuvering of mirrors, to "Cross all borders. Steal past the fashion guards and steal away the Glamour Myth! Counterfeit! Interphase! Camouflage!"[4] Blinding obscures an action; it hides or camouflages an operation in effect. Problematically, Glamour was both the mirror act and the object of a theft by its means. The fact that we were told in the "Glamour" article what was happening did not make it any more visible, quite the reverse: an event sometimes happens disguised in the telling. "Glamour strikes in a single invisible blow," the article concluded. The consecutive moments of plagiarism—moving in on images, occupying, emptying, and then filling them—disappeared in a spirited act, the sleight-of-hand closure that is Glamour. The act disappeared only for its effect to reappear mysteriously as a *detourned* object. This turned and returned object was the result of a "brief but brilliant larceny." Glamour was *theft*:

> Glamourous objects events have been brutally emptied of meaning that parasitic but cultured meaning might be housed there. Thus Glamour is the result of a brief but brilliant larceny: image is stolen and restored, but what is restored? Memories are blurred. Details have been erased. The image moves with the awkward grace of the benumbed, slave to a host of myths.[5]

Glamour was never innocent, even if it had an alibi of being in plain view rather than stealthily thieving behind the scenes. Yet Glamour was doubly implicated: not only the *object*, it was also the *act* of theft. The aim of this theft, of course, was not to steal an image of Glamour but rather to put another surreptitiously in its place.[6]

Stealing in and out hinged on plagiarism. Of the three topics of this article—Glamour, plagiarism, and role—only plagiarism acted and did not merely play a role, indeed never played a role, which is why its actions necessarily were disguised.[7] As theft was a concealed movement of goods, so plagiarism was a disguised movement of words from one place to another, from one author to another, or simply from one context to serve as the content in another context. The original meaning was nullified in this "non-performance" of plagiarism. Plagiarism's meaning, rather, was in its mobility, a mobility it kept under wraps, unexposed: plagiarism meant being in two places at once without being discovered.

As a theft, plagiarism was both offensive and defensive. It aggressively stole in but in the process carefully hid both its theft and its tracks on the way out, leaving nothing seemingly altered. To defend itself from discovery Glamour took its lead now from battlefield strategies where "Glamour is a passive defense." The object of Glamour was to expose itself; but it was risky "slipping in and out of trenches" and potentially revealing oneself to enemy sightlines. Means of concealment that obscured visibility were needed when one acted dangerously out in the open near enemy lines, indeed on the borderline or battle line of nature and culture. If

Glamour was contradictory—being both open and closed, hidden and exposed—then one had to use the same techniques for concealment that were also used for exposure and elevation. Thus:

> The triple strategy of Glamour is simple but evasive:
> 1. Concealment, i.e. separation, postured innocence.
> 2. Hardening of the Target, i.e. closure of the object, a seeming immobility, a brilliance.
> 3. Mobility of the Target, i.e. the superficial image hides an APPARENT emptiness (changing one's mind, shifting stance, 'feminine' logic).

So in the borderline battle between nature and culture, General Idea "posture in the No-Man's Land between content and context, our brushes and palettes our only weapon, Glamour our only defense." Now that they themselves were objects of Glamour, they needed to be aggressively defended at the same time that they were aggressively promoted.

Behind the benumbed look of Glamour was a conniving artifice. Was Glamour merely conniving or essentially contradictory?[8] Rather than a contradictory concept, Glamour was a term that evolved throughout General Idea's practice, indeed adapting itself to "changing one's mind, shifting stance, 'feminine' logic." It was a mythic concept that could accommodate ambiguity.[9] Indeed, it *was* changing one's mind, shifting stances, applying "feminine" logic, strategically. •

1. "General Idea's Framing Devices," *FILE* 4:1 (Summer 1978), 13.
2. "Glamour," *FILE* 3:1 (Autumn 1975), n.p. All unacknowledged quotations are from this article. On this double construct of Glamour, compare: "Clara [the Bag Lady] is a double construct ... aggressor and victim ... it is she who defines the space between culture and nature, which is glamour." "Confronting the Perilous Future—The Careful Hiding of Identity," *FILE* 1:2&3 (May/June 1972), 10.
3. The "confusion" stems from General Idea's dependence on Roland Barthes's discussion of ideology in "Myth Today" where he wrote "that myth cannot possibly be an object, a concept, or an idea." Roland Barthes, "Myth Today," in *Mythologies*, trans. Annette Lavers (New York: Hill and Wang, 1972), 109. First published in 1957.
4. "Are You Truly Invisible?," *IFEL* 2:3 (September 1973), 35.
5. Compare Barthes: "This is because myth is speech *stolen and restored*. Only, speech which is restored is no longer quite that which was stolen: when it was brought back, it was not put exactly in its place. It is this brief act of larceny, this moment taken for a surreptitious faking, which gives mythical speech its benumbed look." Barthes, "Myth Today," 125. In the change of Barthes's "brief act of larceny" to General Idea's "brief but brilliant larceny," the term "brilliancy" itself vacillates between meaning "inspired" or "blinding."
6. The quotation above continues: "Degraded and humiliated, the glamourous image is brilliant in its vacancy, glorious in its degradation. The image retains signs of a former purity. The face of reality is still evident beneath the thin skin of Glamour.... The Miss General Idea Shoes are still shoes. The 1984 Pavillion is still a building. Miss General Idea is still a particular woman ... or is she? ... Myths hide behind the mask of 'real' images; the shifty eyes of cultural content watch through the loopholes of natural context."

7. In its back-and-forth stealing motion, plagiarism serves to join the other two topics to what motivates them: Plagiarism connects Glamour to "meaning" and links role to format. Thus:

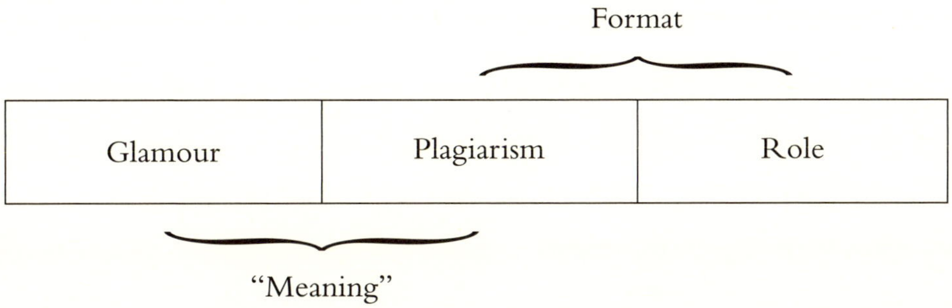

8. Another question: Is Glamour here a change in strategy or merely a diversionary tactic? The different "types" of Glamour basically operate according to the same strategies. Within a combinative machine, the operations of "Glamour" are interchangeable as well with other terms, for instance, "narcissism." Take the sentence, "Glamourous objects open themselves like whores to meaning, answering need with vacancy, waiting to be penetrated by the act of recognition." Narcissism plays much the same role as Glamour, but knowing that the Glamourous object is also a disguised action, we see the same relationship between nostalgia and narcissism: nostalgia is camouflaged penetration ("the sense of vision from afar, essentially a vehicle of entry"); narcissism is the vacancy of "the mirror regarding itself." As active and passive respectively, nostalgia and narcissism add up to a vacillating action that makes it difficult to distinguish between the two, a "capacity for ambiguity" they share with Glamour.
9. Would Glamour be, as Lévi-Strauss writes of *mana*, "a zero symbolic value, that is to say, a sign marking the necessity of a symbolic content supplementary to that with which the signified is already loaded, but which can take on any value required, provided only that this value still remains part of the available reserve and is not, as phonologists put it, a group term"? Claude Lévi-Strauss, *Introduction to the Work of Marcel Mauss*, trans. Felicity Baker (London: Routledge & Kegan Paul, 1987), 64.

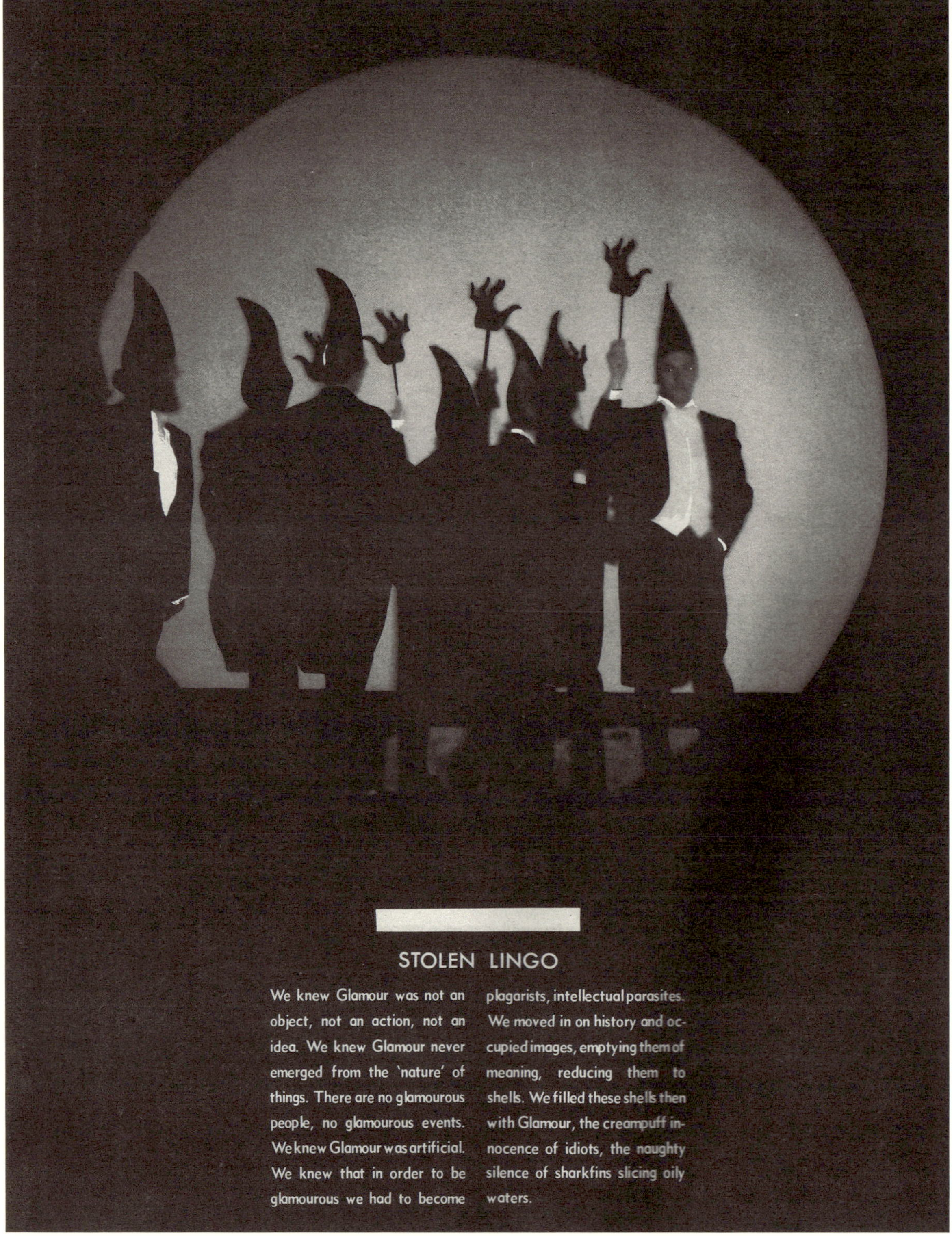

STOLEN LINGO

We knew Glamour was not an object, not an action, not an idea. We knew Glamour never emerged from the 'nature' of things. There are no glamourous people, no glamourous events. We knew Glamour was artificial. We knew that in order to be glamourous we had to become plagarists, intellectual parasites. We moved in on history and occupied images, emptying them of meaning, reducing them to shells. We filled these shells then with Glamour, the creampuff innocence of idiots, the naughty silence of sharkfins slicing oily waters.

"Stolen Lingo," *FILE* 3:1 (Autumn 1975), 22

PLAGIARISM

> This is because myth is speech *stolen and restored*. Only, speech which is restored is no longer quite that which was stolen: when it was brought back, it was not put exactly in its place. It is this brief act of larceny, this moment taken for a surreptitious faking, which gives mythical speech its benumbed look.
>
> —Roland Barthes, "Myth Today"

A lesson on theft, "Glamour" was brazenly constructed by an act of plagiarism. For those in the know, the article itself was an open act of theft: a not so brief act of larceny. The object of theft was an essay by Roland Barthes, "Myth Today," from his book *Mythologies*, published in 1957 and translated in 1972. Barthes was not yet himself as glamourous a figure as he would begin to be later in the 1970s in North America, and, while a first sketch of the new science of semiology, by 1975 "Myth Today" had long been surpassed, notably by Barthes himself.[1] Openly plagiarized, General Idea's theft need not be too disguised since Barthes lent the artists another language with which to discuss what was already in their work. Their strategic act of thievery went hand in glove with the artists' own mystifying mythmaking—the difference being that their act was not meant to demystify but to re-mystify (i.e., Glamourize) using the mechanisms of myth at hand that Barthes had so conveniently revealed: in a semiological model, moreover, which made it applicable to language *and* images: a language of images.[2] Their act of intellectual parasitism made Barthes accomplice to Burroughs, giving theoretical justification to parasitical inhabitations, and clothing the American's mid-Western hucksterism in the intellectual suavity of Parisian culture. Not for nothing did General Idea travel to the City of Light in 1973!

In 1975, having himself moved on, Barthes would have been the last to complain of General Idea's pertinent act of thievery: appropriating his text by means of "quotations without quotation marks."[3] After all, Glamour was mythical speech not myth analysis. And General Idea were mythographers, not mythologists; they wished to mask the image anew, not unmask it. In fact, they were interested only in the mask, not its hidden meaning; they wished to supplant its content in order to supply their own within its evacuated form.

Plagiarism was not just theft for theft's sake; it was a system of *meaning*, a high-class theft: "Glamourous objects events have been brutally emptied of meaning that parasitic but cultured meaning might be housed there." Like myth, plagiarism was a system of *value* and must be read as one. So what Barthes wrote about innocent myth consumers applies equally to vigilant plagiarism attributors:

> In fact, what allows the reader to consume myth innocently is that he does not see it as a semiological system but as an inductive one. Where there is only an equivalence, he sees a kind of causal process: the signifier and signified have, in his eyes, a natural relationship. This confusion can be explained otherwise: any semiological system is a system of values; now the myth-consumer takes the signification for a system of facts: myth is read as a factual system, whereas it is but a semiological system.[4]

We understand nothing of General Idea's system if we triumphantly apply a judgement by simply attributing one of their statements referentially to that of another author, for instance, General Idea's cut-up derivation below to Barthes's original in the epigraph above:

> Glamourous objects events have been brutally emptied of meaning that parasitic but cultured meaning might be housed there. Thus Glamour is the result of a brief but brilliant larceny: image is stolen and restored, but what is restored? Memories are blurred. Details have been erased. The image moves with the awkward grace of the benumbed, slave to a host of myths.

Plagiarism was not a factual system; it was rather a *fictional* one for General Idea where copyright was flouted and plagiarism flaunted—at least for those who were aware of the source.[5] *Of course* General Idea plagiarized Barthes. The point is to see how this flaunting and flouting functioned within General Idea's own system of value, which operated as myth. Although myth was a system of theft, Barthes said it "hides nothing and flaunts nothing."[6] Neither does plagiarism. Plagiarism only succeeds precisely because it hides nothing but also flaunts nothing.

General Idea's plagiarism was adumbrated within Barthes's semiological analysis of myth. But, to reiterate, Barthes only articulated what was already in General Idea's work. Barthes gave General Idea a new language with which to articulate what was already in their work but which then inflected it differently. Although called *Mythologies*, Barthes's book was not just a text on the demystifying decipherment of myths but also an analytical tool for mythifying them in turn, reconstituting them through the production of "artificial myths," i.e., *mythologies*. Barthes's reconstituting mythologist shared characteristics with Claude Lévi-Strauss's *bricoleur*, just as Barthes's "mythologies" had a methodological relation to Lévi-Strauss's "science of mythology," both being myths about myths. Yet Barthes's interest was the language of contemporary mass media not primitive myth; "myth" was used in the sense of McLuhan's "folklore of industrial man" published a half-decade before.[7] This distinction marks a change within General Idea's model of myth. For Barthes was a later discovery by General Idea: *Mythologies* was first read by them sometime in 1974, whereas Lévi-Strauss's structural anthropology was constitutive of their system from the start. Reading Barthes turned General Idea's work away from myth as a positive, ritualized system institutive of community (that enveloping the mail art network in the early days of *FILE*) and inflected it towards the mechanisms of modern corporate manufacture—though they replaced the usual negative critique of its ideological constructions with their own parasitical inhabitations. Being set above, Glamour was an emblem of separateness, whereas myth was always inclusive. General Idea were ready for the turn: hence the manifesto-like character of their "Glamour" editorial and article, which was a marketing of General Idea themselves through the attributes of Glamour.

While "plagiarism" was a new term for General Idea, it was a not a new concept or strategy. Indeed, General Idea already operated by means of "intellectual cannibalism." Plagiarism's parasitism was equivalent to the camouflaged viral methods articulated earlier in "Pablum for the Pablum Eaters" and was the basis, of course, of *FILE Megazine*. Similarly, General Idea's *invasion* and *evacuation* of found formats such as the *Pageant* were merely other names for the actions of the mythic signifier as it appropriated meanings and emptied them in order to fill them with new mythical significations. With General Idea, both evacuation and replacement were plagiaristic, one in terms of form, the other of content. Aligning Burroughs to Lévi-Strauss had anticipated in their work what they would read later in Barthes.

What General Idea stole from Barthes was not necessarily what they took from him. A few plagiarized phrases were worth nothing next to the theoretical justification Barthes offered General Idea's system as a whole. Firstly, Barthes showed that myth had a *systematic* character that could be analyzed semiologically. Secondly, he revealed the inner workings of myth: the method of its appropriations and its ways of naturalizing what was historical.

Myth did not hide its action; nonetheless, it was duplicitous. So was Glamour. Cunning Glamour took advantage of the duplicitous nature of the mythic *signifier*, which is alternately empty or full: "The signifier of myth presents itself in an ambiguous way: it is at one and the same time meaning and form, full on one side and empty on the other" (117). But even the fullness of meaning (of the original sign, now a signifier in the second-order myth) was treated to an impoverishment, while being a reserve that "it is possible to call and dismiss in a sort of rapid alternation" (118). Glamour, like myth, divided its *signified* (its concept) between an evacuated and a full form, the evacuation of its original history and refilling with a new situation. (Both signifier and signified in Glamour's case thus vacillated between being empty and full—but they did so differently, the one active and the other passive.) "It is this constant game of hide-and-seek between the meaning and the form which defines myth" (118) ... and Glamour.[8]

Plagiarism did not need to take lessons from myth. It was not merely a case of ambiguously flipping an image in and out of context and not getting caught. It was not *only* a back-and-forth movement of words from one context to another disguised through ambiguity. Plagiarism was a system of *value*. It was a double system of value: of both meaning *and* evaluation.[9] Plagiarism was both a system of meaning *and* a system of judgement. On the one hand, its operations led to a change in meaning: "Glamourous objects events have been brutally emptied of meaning that parasitic but cultured meaning might be housed there." On the other hand, they led to a reversal of value. Higher values were brought low and others elevated in their place: for instance, the elevation of a drag queen as the embodiment of Glamour. Meaning and evaluation were not two different operations; their mechanisms were the same.

A Note on Myth as a Second-order Semiological System with Reference to *FILE*, the Pageant and *Pavillion*:

Barthes's principal observation, and the starting point of his semiological analysis, was that myth is a type of speech that is not dependent on any particular type of content: "myth cannot possibly be an object, a concept, or an idea," he wrote (109). Rather, it is a *form* defined by its utterance and not by the object of its message. Since "it cannot possibly evolve from the 'nature' of things" (110), and is thus rooted historically, myth is a type of speech that must appropriate other cultural forms of representations: "material which has *already* been worked on so as to make it suitable for communication " (110)—such as General Idea's "beauty pageants, pavillions, picture magazines, and other contemporary corpses."

While myth hides nothing, nonetheless, it is duplicitous. This was possible because myth is a semiological system whose signifier cannibalizes another sign. That is, "myth is a peculiar system, in that it is constructed from a semiological chain which existed before it: it *is a second-order semiological system*" (114).

Since myth is a semiological system, we can break down any myth into its three elements of signifier, signified, and sign, with the proviso that what was a sign in the appropriated first system becomes a signifier in the second myth system. Myth is duplicitous because its signifier is both meaning *and* form. What was a sign in the first system (where meaning resides) is a signifier in the second (a mere empty form). Myth empties and impoverishes meaning; it "turn[s] it suddenly into an empty, parasitical form" (117). That is, myth evacuates the content of another sign and turns it into an empty form, which it then fills with its own motivated content. For instance, the picture magazine *LIFE* is a myth-making apparatus since it is parasitical on photography as a representation of reality. In the second-order semiological system of the magazine, the original photograph is the signifier, the extended caption its signified, and *LIFE* magazine itself the combined sign, where the signified shows through the signifier. (A combination of the two, *LIFE* is a motivated product, a commodity in fact that is also an ideological construct.)

"It can be seen that in myth there are two semiological systems, one of which is staggered in relation to the other: a linguistic system, the language (or the modes of representation which are assimilated to it), which I shall call the *language-object*, because it is the language which myth gets hold of in order to build its own system; and myth itself, which I shall call *metalanguage*, because it is a second language, *in which* one speaks about the first" (115). Barthes illustrated the staggered system thus: Table 1.

"Speaking about," of course, can take different forms, some analytical, as Barthes for instance proffered, some animated by alien tongues, as General Idea preferred. Building on Barthes's analysis, but also independent of it, General Idea actually accomplished what Barthes advocated but he himself could not do: mythify myth.

Language	1. Signifier	2. Signified	
	3. Sign		
MYTH	I. SIGNIFIER		II. SIGNIFIED
	III. SIGN		

Table 1

Myth 1 (Language Object)	1. Photo	2. Caption/Text	
	3. *LIFE* magazine		
MYTH 2 (Metalanguage)	I. *LIFE* MAGAZINE		II. VIRAL INHABITATION
	III. *FILE*		

Table 2

Myth 1 (Language Object)	1. Beauty	2. Contest/Crowning	
	3. Beauty Pageant		
MYTH 2 (Metalanguage)	I. BEAUTY PAGEANT		II. ART SYSTEM
	III. *THE 1984 MISS GENERAL IDEA PAGEANT*		

Table 3

> It thus appears that it is extremely difficult to vanquish myth from the inside: for the very effort one makes in order to escape its stranglehold becomes in its turn the prey of myth: myth can always, as a last resort, signify the resistance which is brought to bear against it. Truth to tell, the best weapon against myth is perhaps to mythify it in its turn, and to produce an *artificial myth*; and this reconstituted myth will in fact be a mythology. Since myth robs language of something, why not rob myth? All that is needed is to use it as the departure point for a third semiological chain, to take its signification as the first term of a second myth.[10] (135)

Of course, this is another way of saying that ideological critique, too, was insufficient in combating myth (captured as it was by its own mystique), but it is hard to imagine how an *artificial* myth can be produced, except perhaps as a work of art. Indeed, Barthes's only example was a literary one: Gustave Flaubert's novel *Bouvard and Pécuchet*. Let's apply Barthes's semiological model to one of General Idea's artifacts, for instance to *FILE Megazine*. *FILE* of course was parasitical on *LIFE* magazine. *FILE* is a third semiological chain that takes the second semiological chain of *LIFE* magazine as its form ("format" in General Idea's terminology). In General Idea's mythology *LIFE* is the empty signifier that is filled with the concept of viral inhabitation and *FILE* is the mythic outcome. Thus: Table 2. *LIFE* is the language-object; *FILE* is the metalanguage in which one talks about the first but only by mythifying it, hence the speaking in "alien tongues." The difference between *LIFE* and *FILE* is that myth naturalizes—"it transforms history into nature" (129)—while Glamour makes artificial.

We can apply the same model to *The 1984 Miss General Idea Pageant*. In the second-order semiological system of the beauty pageant myth, "beauty" is the meaning of the signifier; the idea of a crowning contest or evaluation is the signified concept; and the beauty pageant is the mythic sign. In the third-order semiological system of *The 1984 Miss General Idea Pageant*, the typical beauty pageant is the empty signifier, a mere form; the art system is the signified concept; and General Idea's *Pageant* is its re-mythified outcome. Thus: Table 3. •

1. Surpassed even before the translation of *Mythologies* into English (which brings to mind the problem of reception of this material in North America), for instance by his *S/Z* (1970, translated 1974) and *Sade/Fourier/Loyola* (1971, translated 1976). Barthes's essays "The Death of the Author" (1968) and "From Work to Text" (1971), so influential on the art world in its turn to postmodernism, were translated in 1977. The year before *Mythologies*' translation saw the publication in French of Barthes's "Mythology Today" (1971), which reconsidered his earlier "Myth Today" in light of the advances of the "science of the signifier." Now the "goal is not so much the analysis of the sign as its dislocation.... Initially, we sought the destruction of the (ideological) signified; now we seek the destruction of the sign: 'mythoclasm' is succeeded by a 'semioclasm'." "Mythology Today," in *The Rustle of Language*, trans. Richard Howard (Berkeley: University of California Press, 1989), 66–7. This turn would be equally pertinent to what General Idea's work became in the late 1970s.
2. "Semiology is a science of forms, since it studies significations apart from their content.... One cannot therefore say too often that semiology can have its unity only at the level of forms, not contents; its field is limited, it knows only one operation: reading, or deciphering." Roland Barthes, "Myth Today," in *Mythologies*, trans. Annette Lavers (New York: Hill and Wang, 1972), 111, 114.
3. We could apply to all General Idea's work what Barthes wrote here: "The intertextuality in which any text is apprehended, since it is itself the intertext of another text, cannot be identified with some *origin* of the text: to seek out the 'sources,' the 'influences' of a work is to satisfy the myth of filiation; the quotations a text is made of are anonymous, irrecoverable, and yet *already read*: they are quotations without quotation marks." Barthes, "From Work to Text," in *The Rustle of Language*, 60.
4. Barthes, "Myth Today," 131. Both the myth reader and plagiarist hunter are innocent readers in their own way seeing only a system of fact, on the one hand, and a system of filiation, on the other. General Idea took up this claim three years later in their "1984: A Year in Pictures" editorial: "We wanted to point out the wildly fluctuating interpretations you, our public, impose on us. Under your gaze we become everything from frivolous night-lifers to hard-core post-Marxist theoreticians. We wanted to point out the function of ambiguity in our work, the way in which ambiguity 'flips the meaning in and out of focus,' thus preventing the successful deciphering of the text (both visual and written) except on multiple levels. Curiously, many of you choose only to read one side to any story. Since we give a wide range of choices (and we are conscious of the politics of choice) we are never sure which side you, our readers, will take." *FILE* 4:1 (Summer 1978), 7.
5. A number of writers of influence on General Idea advised and advertised this flouting of copyright and authorship, from William Burroughs's fold-in method and Brion Gysin's cut-up method to John Brockman's "intellectual cannibalism" and Marshall McLuhan's "instant steal."
   Burroughs: "An extension of Brion Gysin's cut-up method which I call the fold-in method has been used in this book which is consequently a composite of many writers living and dead." William S. Burroughs, *Nova Express* (New York: Grove Press, 1992), Foreword Note. First published in 1964.
   Gysin: "You can't call me the author of these poems, now, can you? I merely undid the word combination, like the letter-lock on a piece of good luggage and the poem made itself." ("CUT-UPS: A Project for Disastrous Success") "You'll soon see that words don't belong to anyone." ("Cut-Ups Self-Explained") Brion Gysin, *Brion Gysin Let the Mice In*, ed. Jan Herman (New York: Something Else Press, Inc., 1973), 6, 11.
   Brockman: "Concepts are always the impersonal effect of an epoch.... The first idea was not our own. *Not one idea in this exercise is original.* What are the ideas? Are they the ideas of the author? Are they quotations borrowed from other authors? *It would appear that they are your ideas.* You are doing the reading, the thinking. *Not one idea in this exercise is original : Intellectual Cannibalism.* Plagiarism: the quotation mark." John Brockman, *37* (New York: Holt, Rinehart, Winston, 1970), 25.
   McLuhan: "Xerography ... Anybody can now become both author and publisher. Take any books on any subject and custom-make your own book by simply xeroxing a chapter from this one, a chapter from that one—instant steal!" Marshall McLuhan, *The Medium is the Massage* (New York: Bantam Books, 1967), 123.
6. Barthes, "Myth Today," 129. Unacknowledged quotations in this section are indicated in the text.

7. The Preface to the 1970 French edition of Barthes's *Mythologies* stated: "This book has a double theoretical framework: on the one hand, an ideological critique bearing on the language of so-called mass culture; on the other, a first attempt to analyse semiologically the mechanics of this language. I had just read Saussure and as a result acquired the conviction that by treating 'collective representations' as sign-systems, one might hope to go further than the pious show of unmasking them and account *in detail* for the mystification which transforms petit-bourgeois culture into a universal form." Barthes, "Preface to the 1970 Edition," 9.

8. Curiously, Barthes likened the workings of myth to a turnstile, so close in function to General Idea's *Luxon V.B.*, whose mechanism "flips the image in and out of context"—a work, though, which the artists had manufactured before reading "Myth Today": "What must always be remembered is that myth is a double system; there occurs in it a sort of ubiquity: its point of departure is constituted by the arrival of a meaning.... the signification of the myth is constituted by a sort of constantly moving turnstile which presents alternately the meaning of the signifier and its form, a language-object and a metalanguage, a purely signifying and a purely imagining consciousness." "Myth Today," 123.

9. I am considering "value" in the sense, on the one hand, of Ferdinand de Saussure's assertion that "language is only a system of pure values" (which is the sense Barthes gives semiological value), and, on the other, of being akin to Nietzschean evaluation as being the reversal of values.

10. Fifteen years later, Barthes used other words to describe this strategy: "To act as though an innocent discourse could be held against ideology is tantamount to continuing to believe that language can be nothing but the neutral instrument of a triumphant content. In fact, today, there is no language site outside bourgeois ideology: our language comes from it, returns to it, remains closed up in it. The only possible rejoinder is neither confrontation nor destruction, but only theft: fragment the old text of culture, science, literature, and change its features according to formulae of disguise, as one disguises stolen goods." *Sade/Fourier/Loyola*, trans. Richard Miller (New York: Hill and Wang, 1976), 10. (Originally published in 1971.)

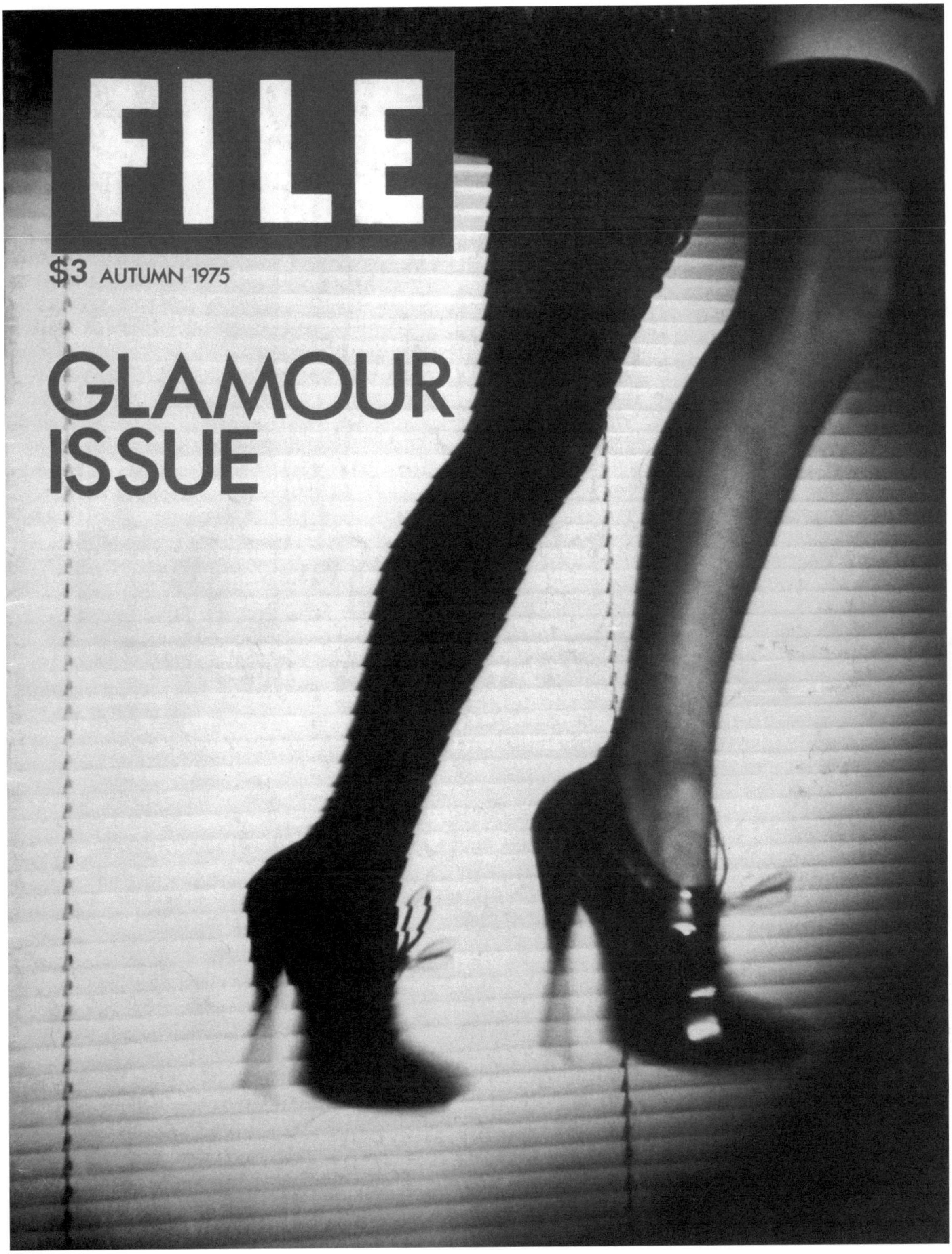

FILE 3:1 (Autumn 1975), cover

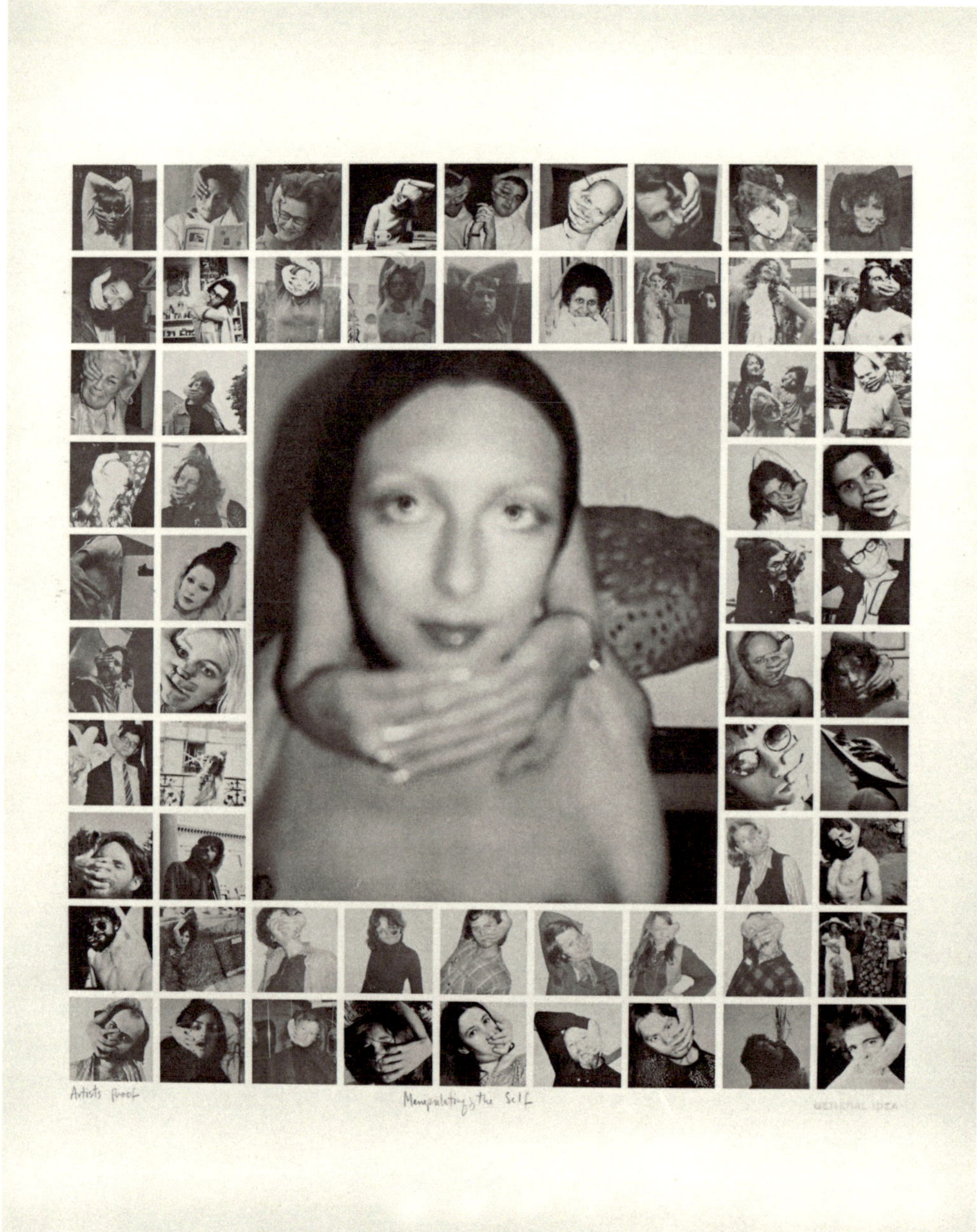

Manipulating the Self, lithograph, 1973

ROLE

> We knew that in order to be artists and glamourous artists we needed a gesture, a MANIPULATION OF THE SELF... Head and hand are separate; body and mind are separate. The hand is a mirror for the mind. Wrap your arm over your head, lodging your elbow behind and gripping your chin with your hand. The act is now complete. Held, you are holding. You are subject and object, context and content, viewed and voyeur.
>
> —"Glamour"

FILE's inaugural editorial brought together an unusual colloquy of strangely named individuals identified simply as members of an "invisible network":

> In order to grasp the *FILE* phenomenon it is necessary to realize the extent of concerns involving the invisible network that bind the world of Dr. Brute and Alex the Holy, Marcel Idea and Miss Generality, Clara the Bag Lady and Lady Brute, the Swedish Lady and Mr. Cones, Dadaland and Dada Long Legs, A. A. Bronson and Dr. Fluxus, Ray Johnson and Susan Bunny, Anna Banana, and Honey Bananas, Bum Bank and Art Rat, Brutiful Brutopia and Canadada.[1]

We were told no more of this secret society than that the editors were "concerned with the web of fact and fiction that binds and releases mythologies that are the sum experience of artists and non-artists in co-operative existence today." To outsiders, none of these names would be familiar, but to stakeholders they signified individual image practices in the Image Bank network of correspondence artists. So said the 1973 "Pablum for the Pablum Eaters" article:

> Many people have commented on the proliferation of pseudonyms in Image Bank and the mailing network.... These names are recorded "history," concerns and events recorded in names to provide contextual information.... Eventually the names proliferate in a manner that provides a system of referencing and cross-referencing of concerns and events within the system.[2]

Insiders, however, would be hard pressed to identify a number of these pseudonymous individuals, such as Alex the Holy, the Swedish Lady, and Clara the Bag Lady, who were not artists but downtown Toronto street people. What concerns and events did their names mark? We would find out later, in the second issue of *FILE* partially devoted to them, that they were not network practitioners but "Practising Non-artists." If these street people similarly were bound to and released by mythologies, what specifically linked them to artists in their conjunctive association: Dr. Brute *and* Alex the Holy, Clara the Bag Lady *and* Lady Brute, the Swedish Lady *and* Mr. Cones? The network was collectively collaborative; practicing non-artists were resolutely loners. Yet, "the Practising Non-artist precisely confines the nature of our research, which is solitary and shared," read the second *FILE* editorial "The End of a Search for Unknown Heroes," where these individuals were described as:

> in a sense obsolete: the contemporary hermit practicing his seclusion and obsessions in the midst of a media-minded world.... In the obscurity of the city, these people become victims. Torn ruthlessly from their separateness, they may respond with a single-minded narcissism, turning their universe in on themselves, and seeing their own compulsions reflected in the rhythm of the world that passes them by. Each of these is in totality an artist, who has given all to his art.[3]

Was calling street people "artists" a patronizing appellation? Or, was it, following Warhol and his Puerto Rican drag queens, a camp principle to glamourize society's refuse (in Warhol's case degrading society's ideals, such as Hollywood screen stars, and elevating other values, drag queens with five-o'clock shadow, in their place)? Or did these eccentric individuals, with their obsessive attunement to their closed, self-signifying universes, offer ready-made models of mythic roles and means of their inhabitation? If one of the aims of *FILE* was to use mythologies to probe its environment, then the Swedish Lady and Clara the Bag Lady were pioneers on the borderline of that transmitting experience. One could just as easily apply this statement to them as to the Eternal Network's reliance on the media: "Identities flow about us. We receive orders, recite information."[4]

Their narcissism had its nostalgic appeal for General Idea, as much as the retro glamour of the thirties and forties had, and practicing non-artists being at hand on the street made them objects of anthropological investigation. Practicing non-artists were not personalities as much as they inhabited "roles" that were fleshed out by costume and communicated by verbal signals. The latter were commands they obsessively repeated. Practicing non-artists themselves were harbingers, evidence of mythic systems of individual design already in place and waiting to be discovered:

> The Swedish Lady uses methods which are typical but not archetypal. She is a borderline shouter but not consistently so.... The Swedish Lady is noted for her wardrobe, which is as diverse as it is consistent. Her constant attraction to harem trousers (diaphanous), Aladdin's slippers, turbans and aluminum house letters projects a rigorous stylistic dedication characteristic of those whose lifestyle is but the outward evidence of a complex and pervasive mythology.
>
> The Swedish Lady, in the manner of many practicing non-artists, enters the medium of mythology through her dress. In Quebec City, Madame Belley operates in a similar manner and has achieved a more public recognition. Both ladies are primarily artists, projecting the

signs and symbols of their particular fantasy onto the flat plane of the visual world through a wealth of costumery that is not so much a disguise or decoration as it is diagrammatic, an elliptical allusion to their manner of perception.[5]

That they lived on the street and were open to scrutiny did not in itself reveal their systems, which, moreover, were not susceptible to conventional psychological analysis: as manifestations of schizophrenia, for instance. In an era of anti-psychiatry, Bronson's text was half fashion commentary and half sociology, its analysis presuming a creative coping strategy to street people's ritualized "performances." "Roles" were means of advocating modes of perception that were non-normative though socially induced and psychically manifested. While practicing non-artists' "roles" were unconsciously assumed, as models they might be artificially copied by artists. From outside, they were a "terse convolution of pose and gesture" that otherwise defined Glamour.[6]

Costumes were ritual props. Practicing non-artists' dress was not merely eccentric but esoteric. Although distressed, it was a sign of a higher mythic order that could be read elliptically. Costumes bespoke symbols that could be analyzed diagrammatically. The Swedish Lady spelled them out with aluminum house letters.

Yet, practicing non-artists' obsessions were disguised rituals, for instance those of Clara the Bag Lady:

> Clara is the double construct. She is the fire, moving. She is the story and the story behind the story, aggressor and victim, lo and behold: it is she who defines the space between culture and nature, which is glamour.
>
> Clara, whose only clarity lies in the tenuous pattern of her life … the action of the wrapping and unwrapping which is her single concern… She is entirely obliviously integral to the avant-garde.
>
> Clara is at once male and female. The sexuality lies in the load….
>
> Clara lies within the wrapping and the unwrapping, which are each of the other. In all cases it is the otherness that lifts. Despite the logical visual equality of wrapping and unwrapping, of one, then the other, the ritual lies in the revealing, which is of nothing.
>
> The bags contain only bags. Clara deals in aggregations and accumulations, in the careful placing of one bag and another. She is the priestess of the unveiling, the creator of delicate cosmologies.[7]

Clara's burden of bags was a ritual prop. As in the *Pavillion*'s reversible composition and decomposition, they were ritually wrapped and unwrapped in order to reveal nothing. Clara was glamour slumming in down-and-out drag; she was a disguised high priestess who defined the glamourous space between culture and nature, a borderline space that was diagrammatized by her "manner of perception."

"Myths lay down alternatives for permissible cultural behaviour," which absolved Clara the Bag Lady and the Swedish Lady of their idiosyncrasies and gave license to the pseudonymous practitioners of the subliminal network for their mythic fabrications and assumption of fictitious roles.[8] Roles, however, were determined by ritual, which were reflections of group formations. Role was ritual.

Even though the subliminal Eternal Network was out in the open it was a ritual community, an esoteric society, a secret cult.[9] The difference between practicing non-artists and network artists was that the former unconsciously contrived individual myths while the latter artificially composed group myths that, nonetheless, were parodies of existing ceremonies.[10] Both received and followed orders. Group myths were realized in the creation of group rituals, such as *The Hollywood Deccadance*, which was staged February 2, 1974 in Los Angeles, appropriately in an Elk's Hall. In this parody of the Academy Awards, the Eternal Network came together to celebrate itself.[11] It was a celebration, however, of what was collective and participatory, not individual, signified, for example, by Sponge Dancers in their dance routine *Gold Diggers of 84*, choreographed by Felix Partz, each dancer holding his Hand of the Spirit and wearing a shark fin bathing cap. These props were venerated, collective fetishes essential to the ritual:

> The fetish object is thus a convenient point around which ritual may gather and concentrate.... Ritual, accumulating about and releasing the resident imagery of fetish objects, carries the stabilization of imagery beyond the mere objectification offered by fetish objects. The ritual re-enacts the potency of the imagery in repeated manifestation of its venerated importance.[12]

The Hollywood Deccadance was a one-off event, but *The 1984 Miss General Idea Pageant*, of course, was a repeated ritual. The *Pageant* was a ritual in which the audience participated, following the prompts of a Master of Ceremonies that were in actuality the commands of the format. The *Pageant* was format and ritual at once in which the audience had a defined role, as simple as it was: the audience played out "a repertoire of stock reactions" such as laughter and applause.

Initially, the *Pageant* was openly participatory: "the 1971 Pageant grew out of our involvement with mail art, with projects that utilized the mail system, asking friends and artists to respond to a mailing, and using the response to generate a project (an event, a publication) in which they could again participate: a sort of cultural biofeedback."[13] Artists and audience were united in ritual. While sometimes a "target audience" and at others a "sounding board," soon the audience was locked in a routine. Only the burning of the *Pavillion* freed them, although "those who did not grasp the magnitude of the emerging emergency, those who stood their ground, stayed behind to play the part of casualties."[14] As in all cults, gradually the priestly officiates alone became "subject and object, context and content, viewed and voyeur." Audience members were initiates in the simulacrum of another ritual of elevation of the artists themselves to fame and glamour.[15]

In this process, the artists had to undergo the same operations as the object of Glamour, which meant a *separation* from their audience: a Glamourous "object separates itself from its surroundings with innocent pride." General Idea's principle operation here was artificiality.

What is artificiality? We knew in order to be artists and to be glamourous artists we had to be artificial and we were. We knew in order to be artificial we had to affect a false nature, disguising ourselves ineffectually as natural objects: businessmen, beauty queens, even artists themselves....

What some find disturbing about General Idea is our resort to false nature, this imperative artificiality, this hunger for fake innocence, the constant posturing, our superabundance of significant forms and gestures.[16]

A false nature, artificiality was a disguise that was, nonetheless, ineffectual. Ineffectual, because roles were ever so discrepant from format. The artists maintained an ironic distance when they inhabited "culture's forgotten shells." In actuality, discrepant distance was a borderline. Ineffectuality called attention to this gap, so that when playing the role of *artists* General Idea were at once both context and content, viewed and voyeur.

Yet, it was not so easy to abandon an audience and still maintain a Glamourous role. Roles must be applauded. In order for General Idea's "constant posturing" to be contextualized, they still needed to put on an audience as much as play roles:

We admired the public access, immediacy and public support of certain trends in rock 'n roll. We posed for photos that could grace album covers. We knew that to be effective we had to reposition ourselves in conjunction with other mass media audience-pleasers, and we did.[17]

"Putting on" an audience was not fooling them, playing them for marks (because the audience already was playing along), but playing *to* them in the sense of putting on a face.[18] Formats were faces. They were also voices in which the artists spoke in alien tongues. •

1. "Editorial: Some Juicy and Malicious Gossip," *FILE* 1:1 (April 1972), 3.
2. "Pablum for the Pablum Eaters," *FILE* 2:1&2 (May 1973), 26.
3. "Editorial: The End of a Search for Unknown Heroes," *FILE* 1:2&3 (May/June 1972), 8.
4. This is an excised portion of notes for the editorial "Some Juicy and Malicious Gossip." See AA Bronson, Notebook 1971–72. Notebook Series, General Idea Fonds, deposited in the Library and Archives of the National Gallery of Canada.
5. [AA Bronson] "Practising Non-Artists: Of Means and Manners," *FILE* 1:2&3 (May/June 1972), 11.
6. Bronson, Notebook 1971–72. The phrase is used as well in the faux-rejected May 1972 artscanada article. "(Advertisement)," *FILE* 1:2&3 (May/June 1972), inside back cover.
7. [AA Bronson] "Practising Non-Artists," 10.
8. This phrase appears in both AA Bronson, Notebook 1971–72 and Felix Partz, Notebook 1972, where the quotation is attributed to Jack Burnham.
9. "All information is secret and classified, passed on in the tenderest of tones, soothingly spread through the entire network, injected into the mainstream: we mainline mythologies and sidestep the obvious, search for the image of our image in the image-rich wealth of information that flows through our mail-slots and collects in our files." Bronson, Notebook 1971–72.
10. In a notebook entry, Bronson indicates Alex the Holy as a practitioner/creator of "individual myths" and Ray Johnson's New York Correspondence School (or as this mention was abbreviated perhaps he meant the New York Corres Songe Dance School of Vancouver) and General Idea as practitioners of "group myths."
11. See *Mondo Artie*, Episode no. 1681, an issue of *IS* 17 (Fall 1975). Also *FILE* 2:5 (February 1974).
12. "Pablum" (1973), 28. "Fetish objects generate activity. It is only through performance that their resident meanings may be unlocked and released, reaffirmed in the present.... This activity, then, is ritual ... The performance is reenacted by replay; the fetish objects are reactivated by replay. Replay becomes a means of reading the resident meanings released by the props in performance." AA Bronson, "Pablum for the Pablum Eaters," in *Video by Artists*, ed. Peggy Gale (Toronto: Art Metropole, 1976), 198–199.
13. "The Audience," *FILE* 4:1 (Summer 1978), n.p.
14. AA Bronson, "Myth as Parasite/Image as Virus: General Idea's Bookshelf 1967–1975," in *The Search for the Spirit: General Idea 1968–1975* (Toronto: Art Gallery of Ontario, 1997), 19.
15. Mayan priests were behind the control machine in Burroughs's fictions: "You see the priests *were* nothing but word and image, an old film rolling on and on with dead actors." William S. Burroughs, "The Mayan Caper," *The Soft Machine* (New York: Grove Press, 1992), 93. "The priests postulated and set up a hermetic universe of which they were the axiomatic controllers. In so doing they became Gods who controlled the known universe of the workers." Burroughs, "Electronic Revolution," in *Word Virus: The William S. Burroughs Reader*, eds. James Grauerholz & Ira Silverberg (New York: Grove Press, 1998), 310.
16. "Glamour."
17. "The Tyranny of the Myth of the Individual Genius,"*Showcard* 2-052 (1977).
18. "The North American hesitation to 'put-on' a public voice or a face is also a block to the artist and writer in 'putting on' an audience for his work." Marshall McLuhan, "Canada: The Borderline Case," in *The Canadian Imagination: Dimensions of a Literary Culture*, ed. David Staines (Cambridge, MA: Harvard University Press, 1977), 243.

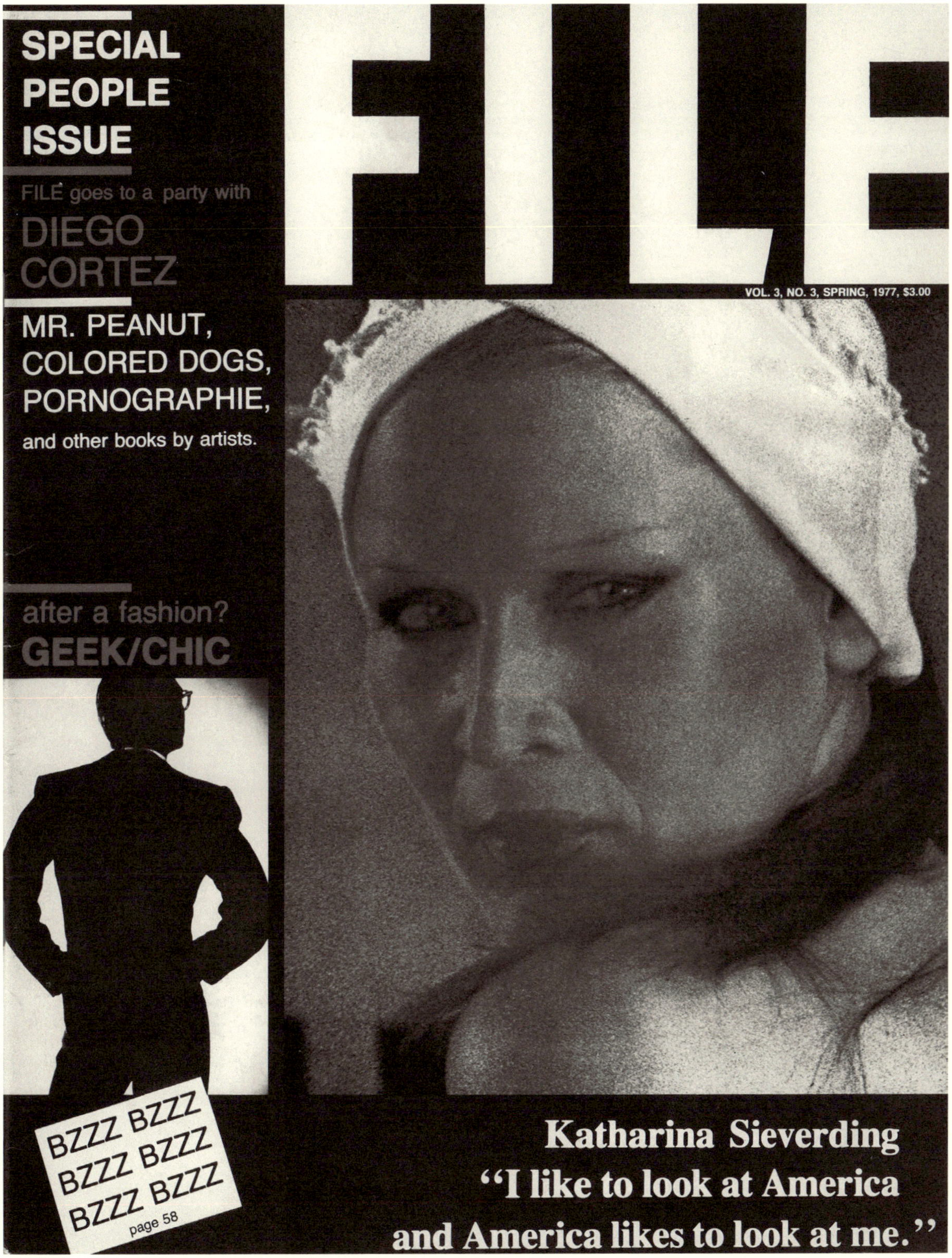
FILE
SPECIAL PEOPLE ISSUE
FILE goes to a party with
DIEGO CORTEZ
MR. PEANUT, COLORED DOGS, PORNOGRAPHIE,
and other books by artists.
after a fashion?
GEEK/CHIC
VOL. 3, NO. 3, SPRING, 1977, $3.00
BZZZ BZZZ BZZZ BZZZ BZZZ BZZZ
page 58
Katharina Sieverding
"I like to look at America
and America likes to look at me."

FILE 3:3 (Spring 1977), cover

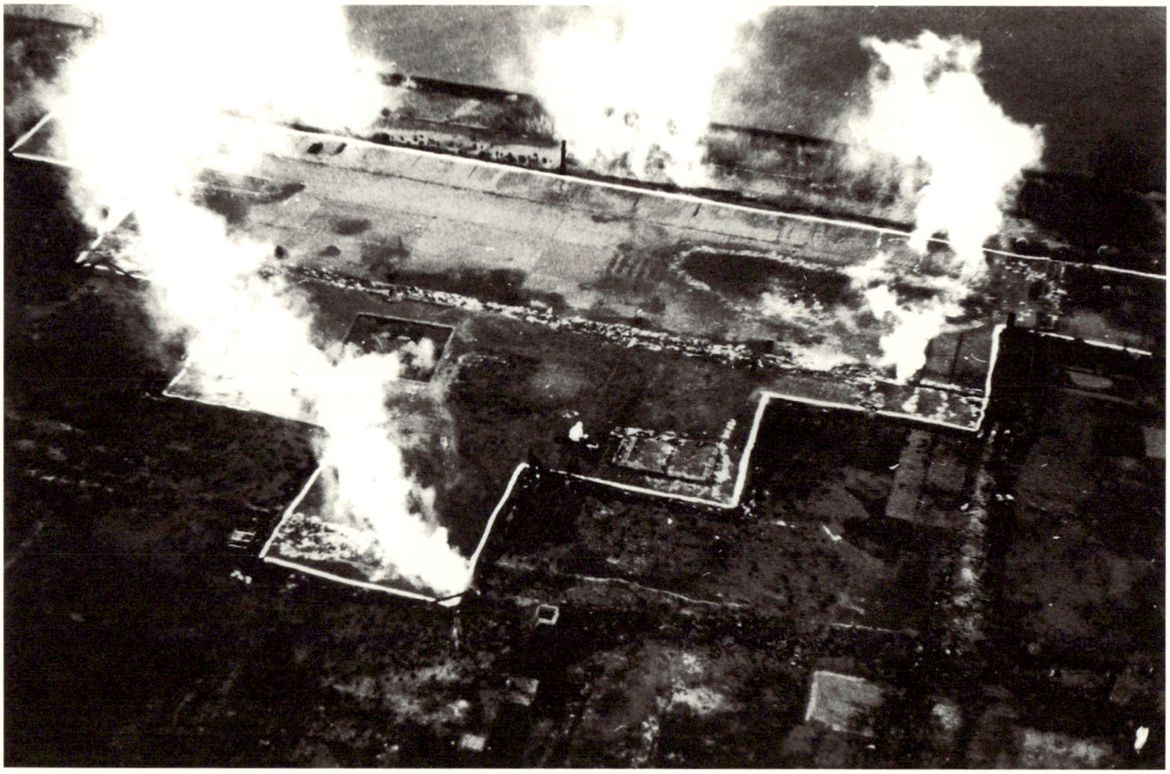

The Ruins of the 1984 Miss General Idea Pavillion, 1977 (Kingston, Ontario)

CRISIS

... so one crisis piles up after the other right on schedule.

—William S. Burroughs, *Nova Express*

What destroyed *The 1984 Miss General Idea Pavillion*? Who is to blame for its destruction? Who lit the fatal flame that burned it down? Rumour has it that it "started in the third row. Clandestine smoking amongst the groupies."[1] Actually, the *Pavillion* burned down twice in 1977.[2] Is this insistence on its destruction a coincidence or an accident? And was the *Pavillion*'s destruction really an accident or was it planned from the start? Planned as an event or, indeed, as a performance? Maybe it was not planned from the start of the *Pavillion*'s existence, but destruction was recognized eventually by General Idea as implicit to their system. Their system sanctioned destruction; it gave the artists license. But what role did the artists play in it? Were they merely naughty boys bored with the necessity of playing their scripted roles for six more years until the arrival of the arbitrary date 1984? Everything is permitted ... including burning it all down. Or were the artists merely "following orders"—following the order of the system, that is? The system was reversible after all.

The destruction of the *Pavillion* was a crisis indeed. But what constitutes a crisis? Or perhaps we should ask, what constitutes the *creativity* of a crisis? General Idea could cope with crises. Crises were business as usual. In fact, I would say that crises were the epitome of General Idea's enterprise—but of course the artists would be loath to admit it, they who were so much in control.

Nevertheless, they announced the crisis in an editorial, an editorial that was meant to be a summation of the first ten years of their enterprise. That 1978 editorial intended to express "something meaningful about it all," but about which the artists concluded: "And the 'crisis' is 1984." Was *crisis* the meaning of it all? Could the *year* 1984, a crisis that had already occurred, still be the conclusion of their enterprise? After all, the ultimate *Pageant* was to be performed that year in the finally completed *Pavillion* purpose-built for it. But now both *Pageant* and *Pavillion* were gone. What remained to constitute a crisis?

Surely the *Pavillion*'s destruction counts as a disaster. Yet it was passed over as routine, accounted for in the 1978 *FILE* "1984: A Year in Review" issue as just one other chapter in General Idea's project. This ambivalence should make us question the concluding alarm in the editorial of an issue of *FILE* devoted solely to General Idea's work. The year in review actually constituted the *Pavillion*—its destruction as well—in profiling all its elements to date. It might as well have been 1984 because General Idea's project seemed concluded. Actually, the crisis of the editorial was the announcement of a *deviation* in their work. No longer concerning just the *Pavillion*, this deviation was something of a destruction of their system as a whole.

The idea of 1984 was not an end; it was rather a dividing line, a divisive fault line internal to their project. As operative principles, construction *and* destruction were integral to the fabrication of their work. "Crisis" was the nature of General Idea's work. The artists were not using the editorial to make a public announcement; they were letting us in on their secret: crisis was *the* transformative agent of General Idea's whole enterprise. Crisis, however, was not just internal to their work; crisis was the unforeseen: an untimely event, history itself. Crisis was both internal *and* external to the work: it was an idea *and* a reality, controlled *and* uncontrolled. Wouldn't an external crisis be devastating to a regulated system, such as General Idea's was? But then adept General Idea always could cope with crises and turn them to their advantage. Crisis *was* the "meaning" of it all.[3]

We know that the destruction of the *Pavillion* was an inside job. It was the artists who destroyed it. That rooms kept coming later, such as the *Colour Bar Lounge* (1979) and *The Boutique* (1980), does not mean that the system that originally supported them continued to sustain the *Pavillion*.[4] It was not the destruction of the *Pavillion* that was the problem. The system, after all, was reversible. It was that the system itself was sabotaged.

The 1978 editorial was the conclusion of a puzzling series of announcements the year before. They coincided with *FILE*'s new look and its new outlook: the "Special People Issue" of spring 1977 and the "Punk 'Til You Puke! Issue" of fall 1977. It was not that a declaration of dissolution openly was made. One had to read it in code, through its code words. The shift was performed under the cover of a transition brought about by a legal suit by TIME-LIFE for copyright infringement that led to *FILE*'s new logo and cover appearance. "The legal battle merely punctuated a change of vision that was already occurring for FILE. The look-alike contest had run its course.... FILE was entering the no-no-nostalgia age in preparation for 1984." In isolation, the expression "no-no-nostalgia" might not appear significant. But its stuttering negation perhaps was a putdown when seen in the context of the subsequent "Punk 'Til You Puke!" editorial, which read "The sentimentalism of late sixties early seventies essentially surrealistic aesthetic has been replaced by a certain pragmatic anarchy which is now the theme of this issue."

Coinciding with the destruction of the *Pavillion* that year, perhaps these statements point to a systematic dismantling of General Idea's system as well. "Nostalgia" being a key term, *no* nostalgia was a severe rebuke, from the artists themselves no less. Remove one term and the whole system crumbles: no nostalgia means no narcissism, no camouflage, no ambiguity, no borderlines, no collage, no intellectual cannibalism, no illusion of being able to see again. What could "the sentimentalism of late sixties early seventies essentially surrealistic aesthetic" refer to but the mythic principles of the Eternal Network, the whole basis of General Idea's early work to date, their "pageantry of camp parody"?[5]

Dismantling the system was the crisis, not the year 1984, as when General Idea wrote "And the 'crisis' is 1984." The year itself, 1984, was a smokescreen. Invoking 1984 meant invoking crisis. The artists were in the mood ("look how bored we all are," said the punk editorial) to destroy their whole enterprise—and not just as a performance of the burning of the *Pavillion*.

This is confirmed by the conclusive 1978 editorial meant to be a summation of it all: "The nature of criticism, like the nature of puns, is to pull a 'text' into crisis. The nature of our work then is 'critical,' as opposed to descriptive. And the 'crisis' is 1984." If the nature of criticism was to pull a text into crisis, their work was critical not descriptive, they authoritatively said. Yet "description" was the nature of their mythological system: myth "structures a cosmology through description, not analysis." General Idea's work now was *text*—"both visual and written." Not a text, "description" could not be pulled into crisis. Description had to be abandoned. Destroying the system was a textual decision.[6] •

---

1. "Smoking in Bedlam," *Showcard* 1-093, 1977.
2. The *Pavillion* was burned down in the performances *Hot Property* (Winnipeg Art Gallery, October 22, 1977) and *The Ruins of the 1984 Miss General Idea Pavillion* (Kingston, November 1977).
3. See Appendix, "Periodizing General Idea," for the story of General Idea as told through their crises.
4. "In 1977, the *Pavillion* burned down. Picking up the pieces later in the 1980s as archaeologists does not revive the system through its fragments; the fragment is not a fractal. There is a major difference between the *Pavillion* as an architectural construct and as an archaeological heap: even if rooms continued to be added to what was already ruined (for example, *Colour Bar Lounge* and *The Boutique*), the overall framework of the system no longer existed." Philip Monk, "Some Like it Haute," *C Magazine* 112 (Winter 2011), 11.
5. See section 5, "Punked" in "Periodizing General Idea."
6. General Idea had finally transitioned from the structuralist Barthes of *Mythologies* to the post-structuralist Barthes of Textual theory. "We wanted to point out the wildly fluctuating interpretations you, our public, impose on us. Under your gaze we become everything from frivolous night-lifers to hard-core post-Marxist theoreticians. We wanted to point out the function of ambiguity in our work, the way in which ambiguity 'flips the meaning in and out of focus,' thus preventing the successful deciphering of the text (both visual and written) except on multiple levels. Curiously, many of you choose only to read one side to any story. Since we give a wide range of choices (and we are conscious of the politics of choice) we are never sure which side you, our readers, will take." "Editorial," *FILE* 4:1 (Summer 1978), 7.

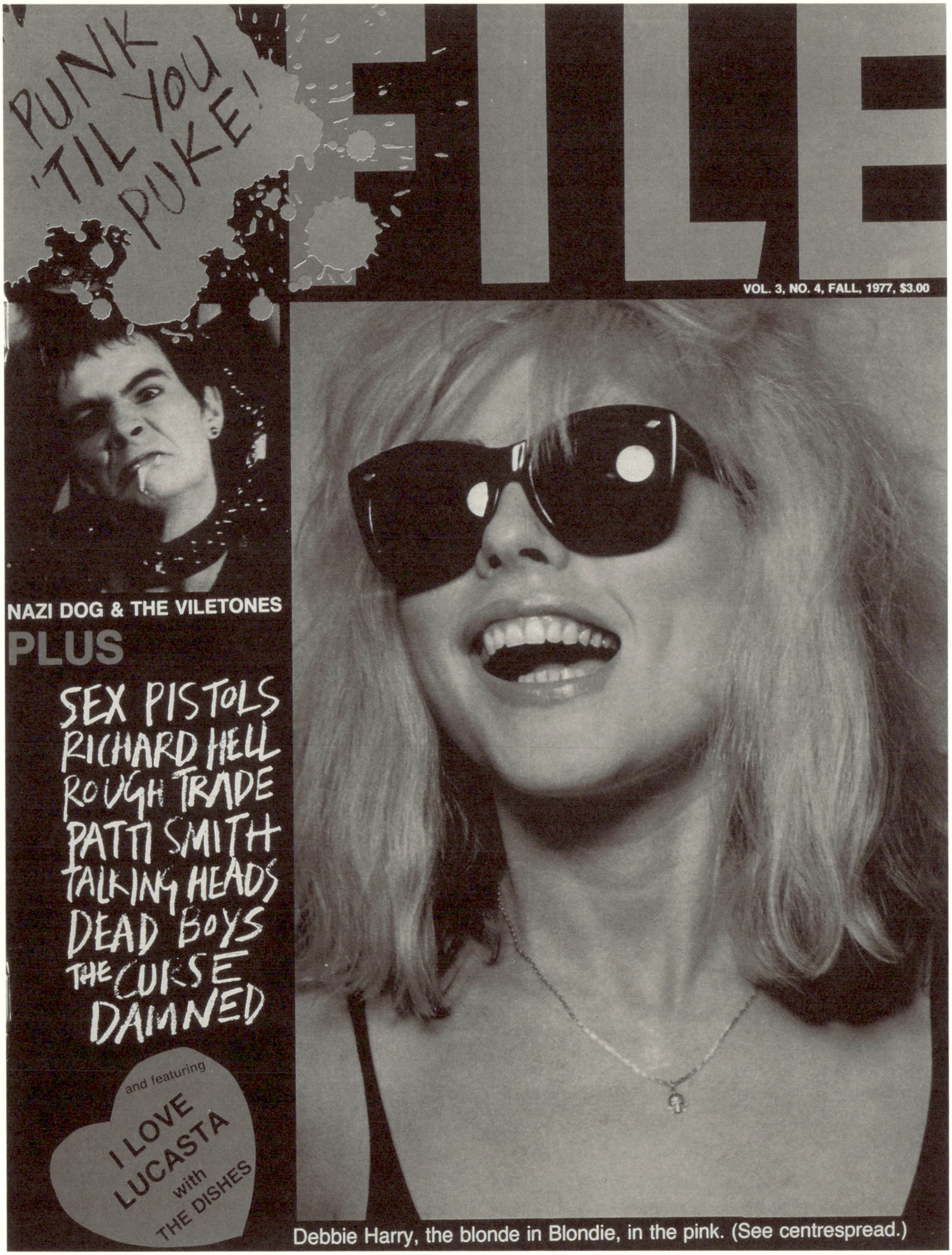
PUNK 'TIL YOU PUKE!
FILE
VOL. 3, NO. 4, FALL, 1977, $3.00
NAZI DOG & THE VILETONES
PLUS
SEX PISTOLS
RICHARD HELL
ROUGH TRADE
PATTI SMITH
TALKING HEADS
DEAD BOYS
THE CURSE
DAMNED
and featuring
I LOVE LUCASTA
with
THE DISHES
Debbie Harry, the blonde in Blondie, in the pink. (See centrespread.)

FILE 3:4 (Fall 1977), cover

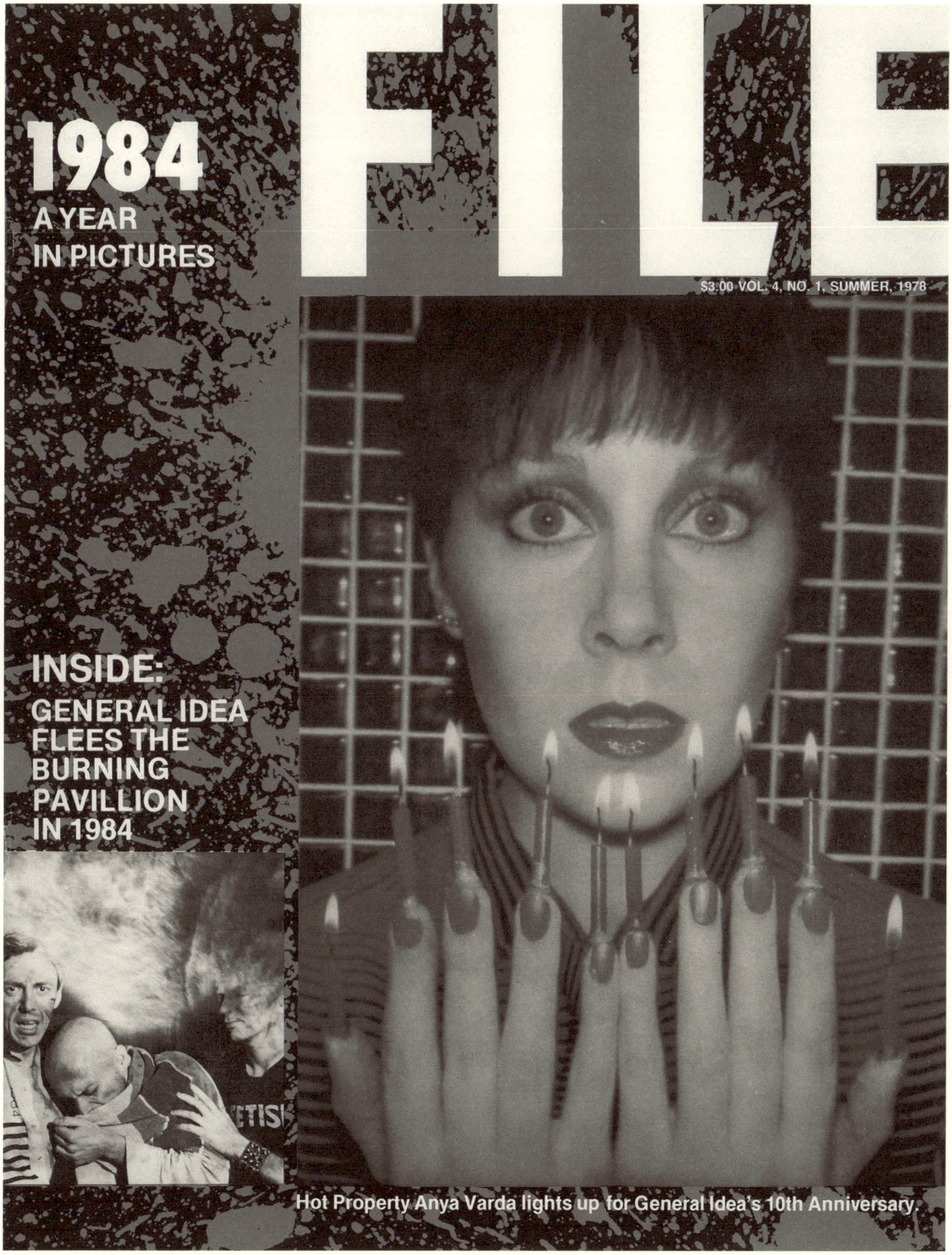
FILE
1984
A YEAR
IN PICTURES
$3.00 VOL. 4, NO. 1, SUMMER, 1978
INSIDE:
GENERAL IDEA
FLEES THE
BURNING
PAVILLION
IN 1984
Hot Property Anya Varda lights up for General Idea's 10th Anniversary.

FILE 4:1 (Summer 1978), cover

PART II

ANALYTIC

THE FRAME OF REFERENCE
is basically this:
a framing device within which we inhabit the role of the general public, the audience, the media. Mirrors mirroring mirrors expanding and contracting to the focal point of view and including the lines of perspective bisecting the successive frames to the vanishing point. The general public, the audience, the media playing the part of the sounding board, the comprehensive framework outlining whatever meets their eye.

General Idea's Framing Devices

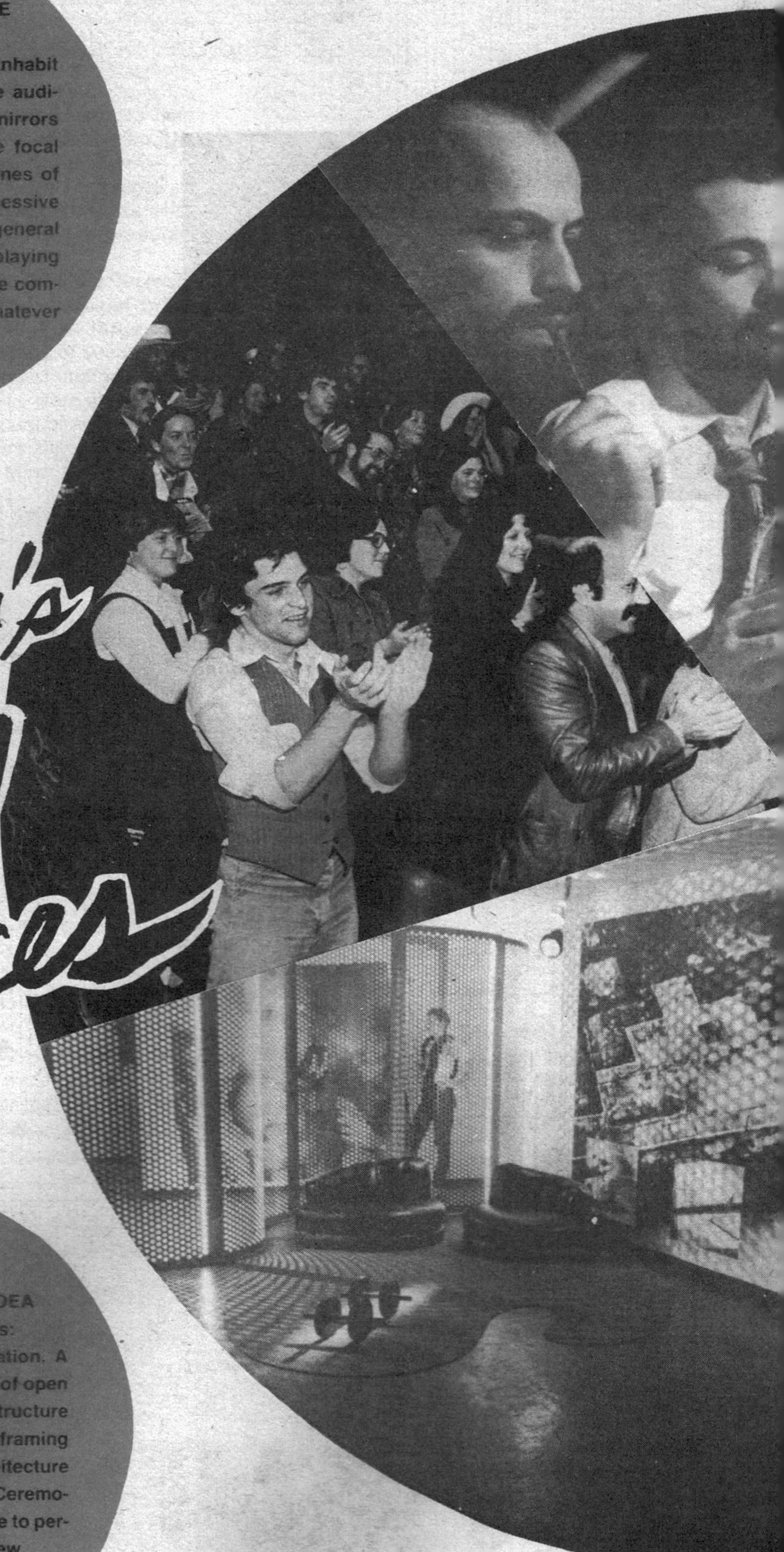

THE 1984 MISS GENERAL IDEA PAVILLION is basically this:
a framing device for accommodation. A terminal in which to rest the case of open and closed frameworks. A superstructure of containment formats like walls framing the theatre of operations. Architecture playing the part of the Master of Ceremonies directing all eyes to this stage to perform the single point of view.

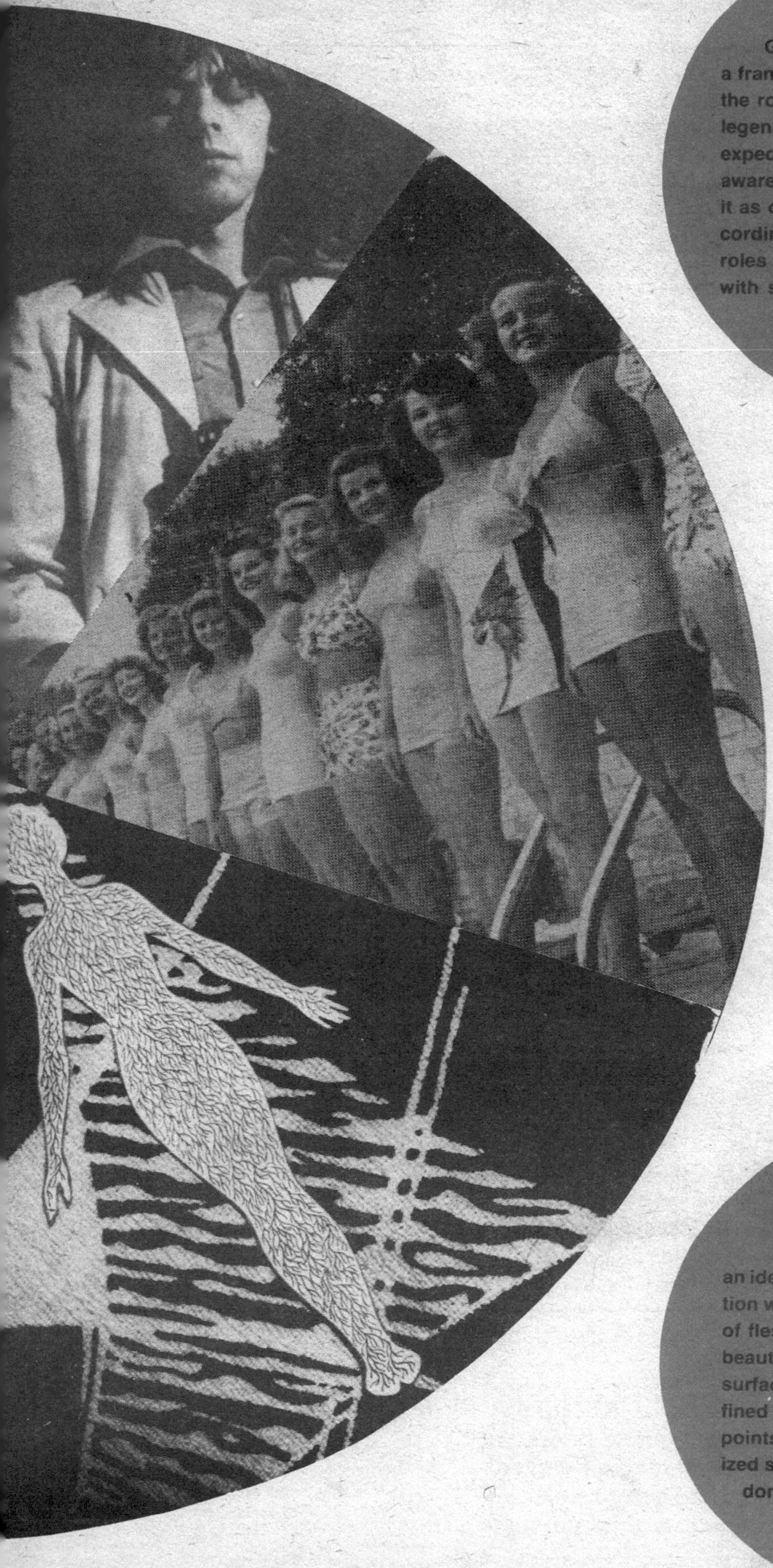

GENERAL IDEA is basically this:
a framing device within which we inhabit the role of the artist as we see the living legend. We can be expected to do what is expected within these bounds. We are aware of the limitations of this and refer to it as our Frame of Reference and act accordingly behind the lines. Projecting our roles gives us some perspective to start with so we can see clear to project our frames frame by frame.

THE 1984 MISS GENERAL IDEA PAGEANT is basically this:
a framing device we have framed for our own devices to contain our frame-ups. The Search for the Spirit of Miss General Idea is the ritualized pageant of creation, production, selection, presentation, competition, manipulation and revelation of that which is suitable for framing.

MISS GENERAL IDEA 1984
is basically this:
an idea framing device for arresting attention without throwing away the key. Hints of flesh-and-bone content are framed by beauty's-only-skin-deep context. We are surfacing on the surface of our desires defined by the intersection of differing points of view. Elevated she reigns; idealized she contains; artfully she maintains; dominantly she sustains our interest.

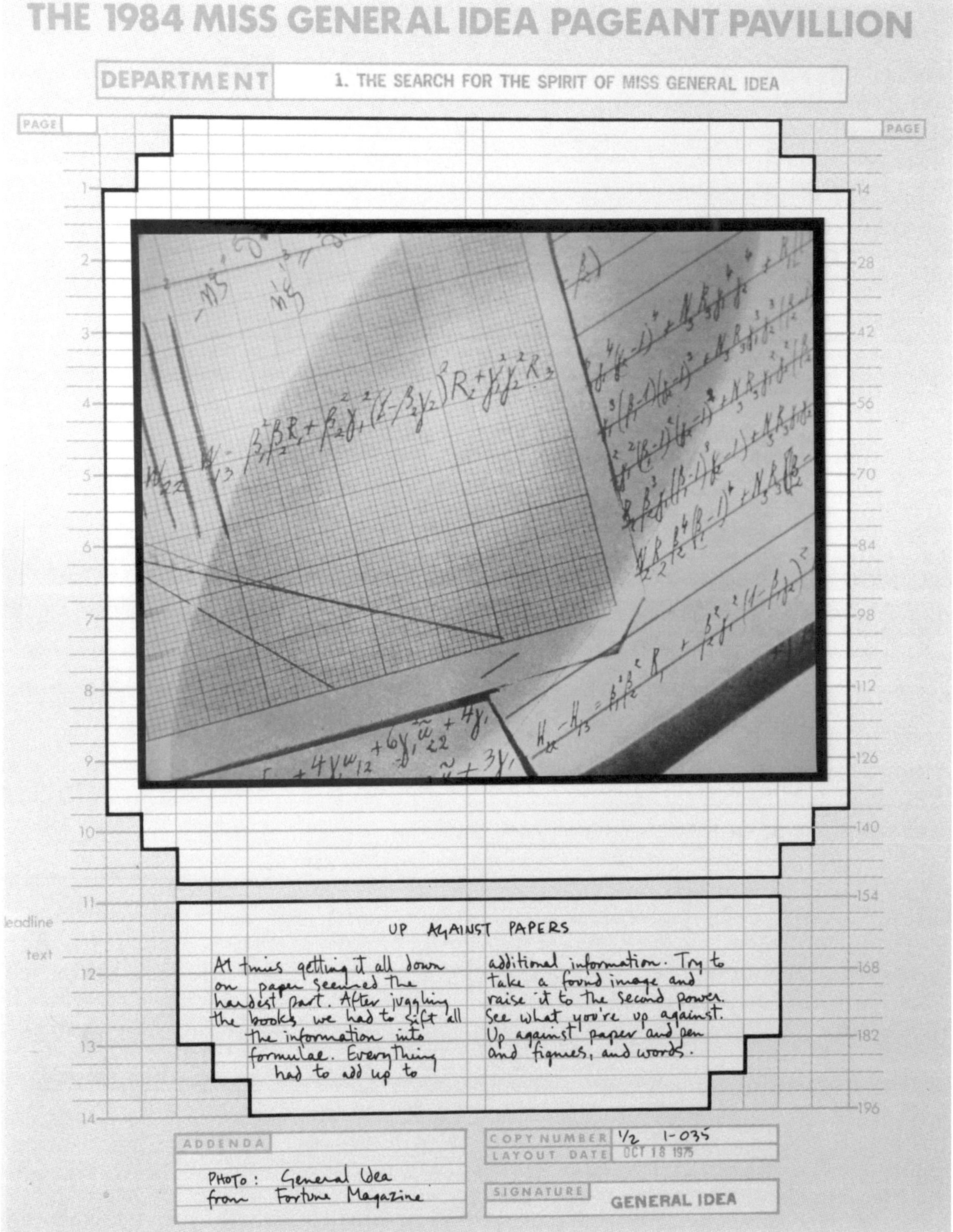

Showcard 1-035, 1975

OPERATION **REWRITE**

I.

There are always alternative solutions. Nothing is true. Everything is permitted.

—William S. Burroughs, *The Ticket That Exploded*

Is it farfetched to think that a system underlies General Idea's work? Most writers take General Idea at their word: that their work is all on the surface. No problem copying that, using General Idea's own words to explicate their work. But insofar as a system is constructed in their work, we have to assume the same articulation in our analysis, looking to connect disparate statements from different sources in a meaningful whole: "providing initiating reinforcing a cross-referencing system of discrete items of description."[1] General Idea's elaborate artifice is a constructed artifact, even if its production only takes place in and through language, the means after all by which the *Pavillion* was erected. This system is totalizing: it applies as much to the roles the artists assumed as to the texts they published in *FILE* and the artifacts they produced that we more commonly identify as artworks.

By definition a system pre-exists its terms, but every term implies the system. The terms do not exist on their own but are elaborated and repeated in phrases and sentences as propositions of sorts that are the elemental building blocks of paragraphs and stories. (General Idea would have hyphenated the word as prop-osition—as they do "prop-osal"—to emphasize the system's artificial standing and theatrical one-sidedness.) Not telling a story itself, a proposition yet entails a whole: "Every proposition proposing a fact must in its complete analysis propose the general character of the universe required for the fact," wrote one of General Idea's favoured authors John Brockman.[2]

The system General Idea constructed is such a universe: *The 1984 Miss General Idea Pavillion* is its name. While this universe has a logical character, it is also a fictional entity. Its logical character is its only reality. Its fictional systematics is nothing but a sustained coherence continually reinforced by each new proposition. However, in a reality where nothing is true and everything is permitted, the stability of any system is precarious—especially one designed on collage principles, as the *Pavillion* was. If "nothing is true and everything is permitted" is the theory, collage is its practice. For any system, "collage or perish" also implies its opposite: collage *and* perish. Such is the precarious balance General Idea maintained in the borderline situations of their work where perishing of identity rather was an ideal.

Such is also the danger when a system grafts itself onto another, as General Idea's did with William Burroughs's fictional universe: "there is the risk of the culture overwhelming the host. Somehow the virus may permeate the researchers."[3] Perhaps we shouldn't worry; perhaps this is the great, good thing: cutting word lines and shifting linguals liberate alternatives.

Alternatives require "rewrite." General Idea's enterprise as a whole could be called Operation Rewrite, though the phrase, of course, belongs to Burroughs. In Burroughs, rewrite was an operation that de-programmed viral word lines in order to free us from alien control. In General Idea, rewrite instead *was* viral, a deliberate process of infecting and enslaving others. Parasitical invaders, they spoke in alien tongues. General Idea's work was one long writing operation that rewrote alternatives.

Rewriting is a form of intellectual cannibalism because it starts with a source text or pre-established code in order to deviate it towards another purpose.[4] Constrained within these codes, intellectual cannibalism nevertheless poses alternatives, even if the alternatives seem only pablum for the pablum-eaters. If we can make something as amorphous and presumably simplistic as pablum make sense, then we can begin to see logic within General Idea's system as a whole.[5] Eat up or shut up!

An article of alternatives, "Pablum for the Pablum Eaters" started first with a series of negations, a negation firstly of art. Art is a myth based on veneration, which elevates *value* while it seems only to raise up the art object. With the dematerialization of art, art became a category of nomination only, one determined moreover by artists, and the system of public veneration came apart: "the whole shithouse blew up." The explosion destroyed a whole host of metaphysical concepts along with it, such as a progressive model of history (and art history): "the lapsing of historical continuities, … the collapse of the causal mind." The only problem was that it took out conceptual art too. The end of the art myth was also the end of the line for art in the form of conceptual art.

Pablum was not a self-administered poison to procure the death of the art myth but the means to propagate another mythology. "Pablum for the Pablum Eaters" distinguished between conceptual artists and Image Bank artists, the latter the ostensible subjects of this article although it referred implicitly to General idea's practices as well. Despite what we may have thought then or think now, the article insisted that Image Bank were *not* conceptual artists. Image Bank, therefore General Idea too, rather were "*mythical*" artists. This distinction was fundamental; indeed it was foundational, though not self-explanatory. The crucial difference was that conceptual artists started with parts in order to reveal structure whereas "myth does the opposite: myth starts with structure and names the parts." Conceptual art (i.e., art "made *about* art") problematically was a proposition that contained itself, a formalist art about problems and solutions within the old model of the "History/Cause & Effect continuum." Even radical conceptual art was conventional! On the contrary, Image Bank was not about "finding solutions but developing alternatives" that were not internal to the art system but found within culture as a whole. There was "no longer a possibility of problems and solutions but rather the necessity of a maze a dense and knitted fabric of a network of alternate myths alternate lifestyles alternate methods of approaching the problem of nothing." This approach necessitated a "sideways movement" dropping out of history and issuing into the so-called "Problem of Nothing." Outside historical continuities, myth aligned with the Problem of Nothing. Never defined, the Problem of Nothing, though, was hardly only a case of the dematerialization of art.[6]

Indeed, the plenitude of myth was the opposite of nothing: everything was to be accounted for in myth. Myth was visionary: Myth "starts with a vision and names the parts. One structures a cosmology through description." When the artists of the subliminal network unconsciously substituted the term "image bank" for "memory bank" in Claude Lévi-Strauss's phrase "the decision that everything must taken account of necessitates the creation of an memory bank," they were not assuring the stability of myth in an enduring architectural symbol. Myth's conserving tendency was undone in the operations of the correspondence network—in the rewriting to-and-fro of its "system in motion." While it is true that as an end result "Image Bank is a structure for setting up, extending, stabilizing, and reinforcing correspondences," making an image deposit was a dangerous affair.

Correspondence was an image habit, connection a junky's fix: "the art junkies' habit is founded on image. *Image is virus.*" When images came undone from their contexts through correspondence circulation, then it was image overdose and you were in trouble: "Image overdose and suddenly snap you're out there broken through the borderline floating on the dead edge of nowhere with images diving in all directions, a sky full of claws and feathers. Then there is jumbled jargon, lip flap, loose vowels." What to do to surface on the subliminal or to stabilize it once one had broken through the borderline? Rewrite! "Cut word lines shift linguals. Take a bit of history and cut it up. Play it back for rewrite ... It's locked up in the syntax. Cut word lines let image free. ... Soon the jumbled jargon soon the naming of partz soon it all comes together the images break loose the correspondences establish themselves... Soon the images break loose and then all hell."

The correspondence habit was disintegrative before it was constitutive.[7] Stability itself was a myth.[8] Alternative myths only resulted from collage's rewrite of cut word lines and broken syntax rearranged alternately. Collage constituted a cosmology in *flux*: a collage universe. In fact, this universe was comprehended within the conflict created by collaging two contradictory statements, one based on conservation and the other on conflict—epigraphs to the "Pablum" article—that momentarily aligned in the word "bank": Lévi-Strauss's phrase quoted above and William Burroughs's "And he breaks out all the ugliest pictures in the image bank and puts it out on the subliminal."

A collage universe momentarily stabilized itself in an image bank where myth established "correspondences that may allow the description of the Universe as a vision named now." "Now" meant contemporary but also temporary. The *alternative* operation (or logic) of myth was two-part. It was destructive: "the logic of myth is the moving territory of words, cut word lines, shift linguals." But at the same time, it was constructive; collage was connective: "The logic of myth is the logic of connections. Image making room for words."

An image bank did not classify simply by collecting like images and housing them in an archive. Correspondence came first, likeness later. An image bank classified by jointing; a bank was built by connecting. "Correspondences are the key to the mythical universe, the cosmology of moving bodies, images in collision, classification by jointing." Collage was collision: image worlds in conflict. Jointing was rewriting by means of images making room for words. Correspondence was rewrite in which all participated.[9] The Eternal Network was a joint account.

II.

> In myth it is all very clear that everything must be accounted for. One starts with a vision and names the parts. One structures a cosmology through description. One does not move beyond the image, nor beyond the image of the image.
>
> —"Pablum for the Pablum Eaters"

Through an elaborate system of naming and description, General Idea created their own mythological cosmology, a universe called *The 1984 Miss General Idea Pavillion*. The artists were mytho*graphers*, with the proviso that they *re*-wrote myths. "Pablum for the Pablum Eaters" was the first lesson in this mythography, which signals the importance of this article even though seemingly it was about Vancouver's Image Bank.

Since myth did not pre-exist, it was nowhere to describe. It came into being momentarily by jointing. Myth was constructed from fragments. "We began to realize as we began to realize in fragments," the artists wrote elsewhere.[10] If images made room for words, no less were these fragments available for description merely as *captioned* images. Description was a *verbal* affair, sufficient unto itself, an act from which the *Pavillion* arose.

According to the "Pablum" article, myth essentially was the naming of parts; one structured a cosmology through description. Naming and description seem one and the same, their acts implied in one another as interchangeable terms: "a description becomes a name and the name contains the description."[11] Naming, however, actually came first ("one starts with vision and names the parts"), then description (as its expansion or elaboration, the name containing the description), but neither preceded structure. Rather, "myth starts with structure and names the parts." Part and whole had an implicated relationship that already structured them as myth where the whole implicitly was mirrored in its parts.[12]

Myth was essentially the naming of parts, but its logic—operating within a system in motion—was one of cutting word lines and connecting words to images. The naming of parts was equivalent to images "making room for words." Only after images made room for words could description start—but paradoxically only as this destructive-constructive process itself, not separate from it. Nomination did not halt a system in motion, though.[13] Concepts tend to become fixed; images tend to become fetishized. Myths, however, were in flux, myths *were* flux, even if they temporarily stabilized as alternatives.

As a *rewrite* operation, myth did not occlude the image. It was dependent on it for rewriting. The article reminds us that "one does not move beyond the image, nor beyond the image of the image." Myth rewrote the visual field through a shift in the "mechanics of vision." As myth was not writing but re-writing, so myth's worldview was not a framing of view as much as a re-framing that produced an "after-image." Such a procedure "establishes the illusion of being able to see again, the illusion of a whole." A *description* of a universe and an illusion of being able to *see* again were linked. Vision and language were implicated in one another ("one starts with a vision and names the parts")—but not just as an illusion of a text captioning an image. Rather, word lines were mapped on sightlines in order verbally to guide our vision.[14]

So when the article says that we cannot "move beyond the image, nor beyond the image of the image," we must remember that we are not dealing with images alone but that the "image of the image" only was a mirror image of itself. It was an image divided from itself by the "cutting remarks" of words.

III.

Only through the splitting apart does the message emerge.

—"Pablum for the Pablum Eaters"

If a system exists in or *as* General Idea's work, we have to approach it on its own terms, which are not necessarily the terms by which it defines itself, that is to say, the terms that the artists use. In "describing" this system or "naming" its elements, we have to remember that, on the one hand, it is a system of *alternatives*, and, on the other hand, it is a system in *motion*. These are actually one and the same because alternatives alternate constantly within the system itself: they vacillate, in the process shimmering like an illusion. That it is a *system* of alternatives means that it is not merely an *alternative* system. There is a difference between the two, *difference* itself.

In spite of its architectural appearance and nomination, that is, in spite of how it looks and how its components have been named and described, General Idea's system is not a stable structure capable of being analyzed conventionally. Here is the problem of "seeing art as a system of signs in motion": any description or analysis assumes a static form. But when form follows fiction, we must follow the artists in their methodology even if it means a "rapid descension *the lowering into the bottomless cone*," equivalent perhaps to Edgar Allan Poe's "descent into the maelstrom."[15] For a "system in motion," for a "moving territory of words," for a "cosmology of moving bodies [and] images in collision," perhaps we can only guide ourselves by reaching out to a lifeline: something like a fetish. In the 1976 republication of "Pablum for the Pablum Eaters," the fetish was defined thus: "A fetish object is the intersection of a multiplicity of potent meanings, here made visible. It is the point at which a network of significations whirlpool about a convenient image."[16] General Idea's vocabulary equally functions like fetishes. Other words swirl around these convenient concepts. Concepts are obscured by this swirling verbal jetsam, yet they dominate. Not only is it our job to find and articulate these concepts but also to record the swirling around them. Together they constitute "an operational method of accounting for everything" in General Idea's work.

IV.

> The obsessions are streaming up front. Each authenticates the rest, creating a total scene which is at once ephemeral and impossible to ignore.
>
> —"Some Juicy and Malicious Gossip"

In the early phase of semiology, Roland Barthes wrote: "The aim of semiological research is to reconstitute the functioning of the systems of significations other than language in accordance with the process typical of any structuralist activity, which is to build a *simulacrum* of the object under observation."[17] As General Idea's *Pageant* is to actual beauty pageants, so my description here should be to General Idea's "descriptions" or commentary: structurally homologous. But my analysis is not at all, like theirs, a second order semiological system parasitic on the one the artists built. The simulacrum I make corresponding to General Idea's own must take another route to uncover the operative concepts of their system. But we can take some suggestions from semiology.

In General Idea's system, myth is immediately given but not described all at once. It is dispersed in its "descriptions." Our task is to collect these "statements" in their recurring forms as they appear as writing, images, or signs. General Idea called this additive or repetitive process, which is a form of mirroring that constructs the simulacrum of a system, "naming": "Names proliferate in a manner that provides a system of referencing and cross-referencing of concerns and events within the system." As if speaking for us, Barthes adds: "This repetition of the concept through different forms is precious to the mythologist, it allows him to decipher the myth: it is the insistence of a kind of behavior which reveals its intentions."[18] Even though these names or concepts vary between different media; or seemingly change their names or contradict one another; or are disguised within other names; nevertheless, we need to seek out their recurrence. "It is by the regular return of the units and of the associations of units that the work appears constructed, i.e., endowed with meaning," said Barthes, as if now speaking for the artists.[19]

General Idea constructed their system from such recurrences. The efforts of Part One were to collect their returns and decipher them as part of a meaningful whole as they pertained to particular "themes" in General Idea's work. Names, however, only provide a framework; their recurrence signifies an operation in effect that is not thematic. There is a name, though, for the system that keeps all these names in constant play. It is called *The 1984 Miss General Idea Pavillion.* •

1. "Pablum for the Pablum Eaters," *FILE* 2:1&2 (May 1973), 26. All unacknowledged quotations are from this article.
2. John Brockman, *37* (New York: Holt, Rinehart, and Winston, 1970), 63. Analogously, AA Bronson refers to Gertrude Stein's statement "A Sentence is not emotional a paragraph is," in his essay "Myth as Parasite/Image as Virus: General Idea's Bookshelf 1967–1975," in *The Search for the Spirit: General Idea 1968–1975* (Toronto: Art Gallery of Ontario, 1997), 17.
3. "General Idea's Borderline Cases: Introduction," *IFEL* 2:3 (September 1973), 12.
4. "A code cannot be destroyed, only 'played off'." Roland Barthes, "The Death of the Author," in *Image-Music-Text*, trans. Stephen Heath (Glasgow: Fontana/Collins, 1977), 144.
5. How appropriate that the baby cereal Pablum was invented in Toronto down the street from General Idea's first Gerrard Street headquarters.
6. Lucy Lippard's conceptual art compendium, *Six Years: the dematerialization of the art object*, was published in 1973. The Problem of Nothing does have a history, though, deriving from Michael Morris. The reproduction of Morris's 1966 painting titled *The Problem of Nothing* in the May 1968 issue of *Artforum* caught Ray Johnson's eye and prompted a letter the same month from the New York artist to him. A momentous letter. The rest is history, as they say, in terms of Canada's participation in correspondence art.
7. No hippie dropouts, pablum eaters were destructive, more barbarians than lotos-eaters. "We had abandoned our hippie backgrounds of heterosexual idealism, abandoned any shred of belief that we could change the world by activism, by demonstration, by any of the methods we had tried in the 1960—they had all failed.... Now we turned to the queer outsider methods of William Burroughs..." AA Bronson, "Myth as Parasite/Image as Virus," 17–18.
8. The "construction" then "destruction" of the Pavillion proves this point. Destruction was only another opportunity for re-write. *Showcard* 1-083 (1977) reads: "'It's Time for Another Re-write.' VOICE OVER: Without waiting for flames to diminish we throw off our firemen's drag and rush into the ruins. Like archeologists collecting fetish objects we rebuild images for the future from found fragments of our cultural environment. It's always exciting when the Pavillion burns to the ground—It's time for another re-write." *Showcard* 1-094 (1977) reads: "...Archives destroyed. Years later, history was up for re-write as archeologists composed idiosyncratic reconstructions from these charred remnants."
9. "A collaborative vision arrived through the mails as rewrite."
10. "General Idea's Borderline Cases: Introduction," *IFEL* 2:3 (September 1973), 12.
11. The article applies a theory of nomination where the name contains a description: "Sometimes one is talking something happens and what one has said has the nature of a title. Famous saying are like this. Nicknames are this way. Then a description becomes a name and a name contains the description. This is how myth works. Myth is essentially the naming of parts."
12. While referring to the action of rubber stamps, one of the eternal network's correspondence devices, the article discussed the relation between individual stamps and the correspondence system as a whole where "one always has a sense an illusion of the knowledge of the whole by reflection." The relation of whole and part, the whole implicated in the part, is holographic: "The image carries its own realties within it, harbouring subliminal connections in its interstices..." Take the example of the Ziggurat motif. The repetition of the fractal-like shape of the ziggurat reveals this holographic relation: "Note The Ziggurat Configuration. The accommodation of the audience was our first design priority for the Pavillion. We intend to seat 1,984 V.I.P.'s in—you guessed it—1,984 seats upholstered in the ziggurat pattern. Note the ziggurat configuration of the floor plan, too. This motif will be reflected in the design of chairs, carpets, upholstery fabric, and even in how we think about the Pavillion." (*Showcard* 4-021, 1977)
13. The integral relation of part and whole that naming implies does not, however, result in a static structure. Naming does not constrain identity. The article discusses the impossibility of stabilizing the system through nomination using the analogy of the correspondence network's use of rubber stamps: "One might think that in order to view the Image Bank reality [that is, its cosmology] it is simply necessary to view the rubber stamps [a complementary form of correspondence art]. This is impossible. The stamps are a system in motion, one never

knows where the stamps are, where the use of the stamps is, certainly it is impossible to view a changing network of stamps over four continents."

14. "Wordlines are an important as sightlines in plotting the course." "The Miss General Idea Vehicle," *FILE* 4:1 (Summer 1978), 39. We have already seen other names applied to vision, "nostalgia" and "narcissism," for instance: nostalgia providing the "sense of vision from afar; narcissism harbouring the "possibility of vision, the description of the mirror regarding itself." Words had a way of directing point of view, otherwise known as a Framing Device.
15. "The Pablum-eaters demand pablum. In the demanding they set the eye travelling inward and outward, plummeting."
16. AA Bronson, "Pablum for the Pablum Eaters," in *Video by Artists*, ed. Peggy Gale (Toronto: Art Metropole, 1976), 198.
17. Roland Barthes, *Elements of Semiology*, trans. Annette Lavers and Colin Smith (New York: Hill and Wang, 1968), 95.
18. Barthes, "Myth Today," in *Mythologies*, trans. Annette Lavers (New York: Hill and Wang, 1972), 120. Compare what General Idea said of the mythic nature of gesture's repetition: "In the gesture that essential configuration of movement and desire is locked into a single sign. This sign is repeated endlessly, become thick with accumulated meaning. The gesture becomes raw matter for myth." "Glamour," *FILE* 3:1 (Autumn 1975), n.p. Also compare Lévi-Strauss: "The function of repetition is to render the structure of the myth apparent." Claude Lévi-Strauss, "The Structural Study of Myth," in *Structural Anthropology*, trans. Claire Jacobson and Brooke Grundfest Schoepf (New York: Basic Books, Inc., 1955), 229.
19. Barthes, "The Structuralist Activity," in *Critical Essays*, trans. Richard Howard (Evanston, Northwestern University Press, 1972), 217.

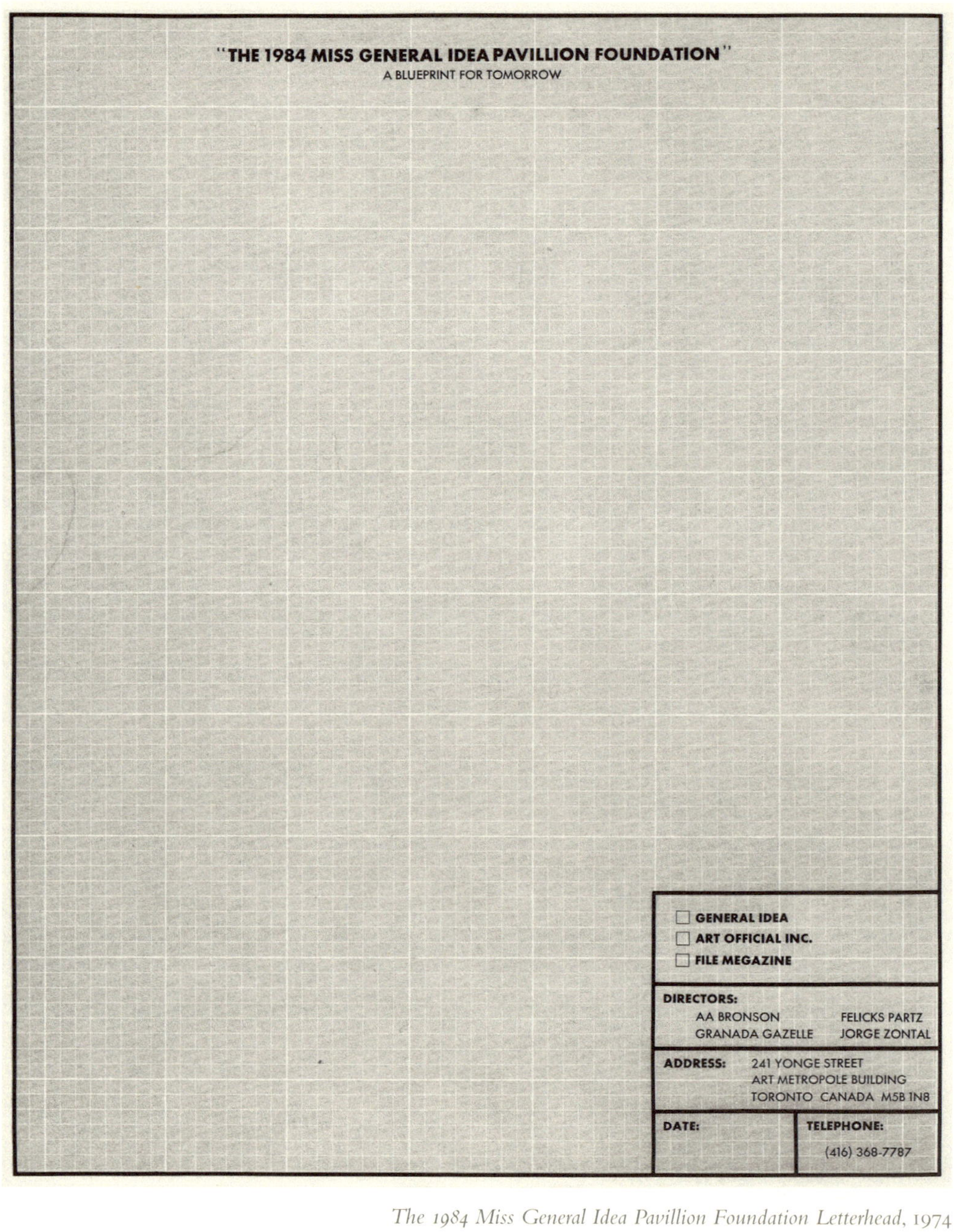

"THE 1984 MISS GENERAL IDEA PAVILLION FOUNDATION"
A BLUEPRINT FOR TOMORROW

☐ GENERAL IDEA
☐ ART OFFICIAL INC.
☐ FILE MEGAZINE

DIRECTORS:
AA BRONSON FELICKS PARTZ
GRANADA GAZELLE JORGE ZONTAL

ADDRESS: 241 YONGE STREET
ART METROPOLE BUILDING
TORONTO CANADA M5B 1N8

DATE:

TELEPHONE:
(416) 368-7787

The 1984 Miss General Idea Pavillion Foundation Letterhead, 1974

IDEOLECT

General Idea's work is the invention of a system for the elevation of a concept: Glamour. The invention of a system is akin to the founding of a language. Indeed, General Idea's system operates as a language and, thus, these three artists can be considered founders of a language (logothetes) that operates specific to their program: an ideolect. *The language they found is obviously not linguistic, a language of communication. It is a new language* (in spite of being composed of words *and* images: indeed, "*they constitute the field of the image as a linguistic system*"), *traversed by (or traversing) natural language, but open only to the semiological definition of text.* This artificial language has recourse to a few principle operations.

The first is self-isolation. The new language must arise from a material vacuum, as if that between two facing mirrors; *an anterior space must separate it from the other common, idle, outmoded language whose "noise" might hinder it: no interference of signs.* Hence the subjugation and directing of vision towards the uplifted ideal of Glamour, itself closed off in the silent brilliance of an object "separate[d] itself from its surroundings with innocent pride." Hence General Idea's framing devices framing frameworks. And above all, hence the enclosure of all activities in an architectural form, the *Pavillion*: with our flight up the *Escalier d'Honneur* and promenade through the Dr. Brute Colonnade to seat ourselves in a Proposed Seating Arrangement precisely of 1,984 seats.

The second operation is articulation. No language without distinct signs. Although fundamental to a language, it is not enough that signs (or images) be isolated and merely repeated in an image bank; repetition, a mythic principle of insistence, alone is insufficient; so is mere description of a whole. Yet cut-up as connection is articulation, or, rather, re-articulation. That is: *Nor any language unless these cut-up signs are reprised in a combinative* (cut-up or shut up!); *our three authors deduct, combine, arrange, endlessly produce rules of assemblage; they substitute syntax*, composition *for creation; all three fetishists, devoted to the cut-up body, for them the reconstitution of a whole can be no more than a summation of intelligibles: nothing is indecipherable*, everything must be accounted for. As General Idea said, "Once we arrive at certain decisions, we go over our lines. Every decision is like a new word added to an expanding vocabulary. When we're certain we're all fluent we are ready to construct our structures. Constant rehearsal makes the words second nature—let's call it culture," otherwise known as Text.[1]

The third operation is ordering: not merely to arrange the elementary signs, but to subject the sequence of events and elevation of Glamour in the Pageant *to the higher order* of the Pavillion, an order *no longer syntactical, but* suiting architecture *metrical; the new discourse is provided with a Master of Ceremonies who, with no standing other than a temporary and entirely practical responsibility, sets up the postures* (audience responses, Miss General Idea's pose, the artists' stances, for instance) *and directs the overall progress of the* building *operation; there is always someone to regulate the exercise* of Glamour, *but that someone is not a subject; the producer of the episode, he acts only for the moment, he is merely a reactive morpheme, an operator of the sequence. Thus the ritual demanded by our three authors is only a form of planning*, a constant rehearsal: whether it be for *Pageant* or *Pavillion*, the planning is conducted by a Master of Ceremonies or a master architect.

Were logothesis (the founding of a language) *to stop at setting up a ritual, i.e., a rhetoric*, or camp performance, *the founder of language would only be no more than the author of a system (what is called a philosopher, a savant, or a thinker)*. Our three authors posing sometimes as artists and sometimes as architects *are something else: formulators (commonly called writers). In fact to found a new language through and through, a fourth operation is required*: theatricalization. *What is theatricalization? It is not designing a setting for representation*: for General Idea, theatricalization is not the setting—the *Pageant*, for instance, or even the *Pavillion*—but the system itself. Not just the empty format or framework of *Pageant* or *Pavillion*, but every element—content and context, nature and culture and the borderlines between them—conspires and participates in this *event*. Theatricalization is the means of the system's articulation that finds its formal or formulaic erection in *The 1984 Miss General Idea Pavillion*, but it conspires in all the details. Men of many talents, for our three authors/artists/architects *all that is left in each of them is a scenographer: he who disperses himself across the framework*—or formats—*he sets up and arranges* ad infinitum—or at least until far away 1984.

If General Idea *are founders of a language, and only that, it is precisely in order to say nothing, to observe a vacancy (if they wanted to say something, linguistic language, the language of communication and philosophy, would suffice: they could be* summarized, *which is not the case with them.*[2] Why build a Pavillion and walk away from its destruction? We could call this lack of summary or the observation of a vacancy—Glamour itself—a problem: indeed, it is the Problem of Nothing. No wonder, theatrically hiding nothing, lacking even a curtain and false perspective, "the back door to the Miss General Idea Pavillion open[s] on the Problem of Nothing."[3]

But to get to nothing, something must be abandoned along the way, something seemingly theatrical like the *Pageant*. While conditioned by language and paced by it, the *Pageant* was not a language system. The *Pageant* coordinated activities under the direction of a Master of Ceremonies. These took place through the performance of a set of rules specific to a particular format: the beauty pageant was a ritual, not a system. The *Pavillion* was another matter. The "construction" of the *Pavillion* was the invention of a system and a language for its elaboration. Its articulation was a speech act: writing itself. •

1. "Three Heads are Better," *FILE* 4:1 (Summer 1978), 15.
2. Inspired by General Idea's plagiarism in "Glamour," I too have plagiarized here, although stealing from another of Barthes's books, though probably one known to General Idea, leaving Barthes's original in italics. My source is Roland Barthes, *Sade, Fourier, Loyola*, trans. Richard Miller (New York: Hill and Wang, 1976), 3–6, 67. For another brilliant General Idea plagiarism, also a virtuoso example of a Borderline Case, see "New York Gossip," *FILE* 3:2 (Spring 1976), 18–31. Their host text is Balzac's story "Sarrasine," presumably as published in Barthes, *S/Z*, trans. Richard Miller (New York: Hill and Wang, 1974).
3. Marginal note to "Editorial," "Glamour" issue, *FILE* 3:1 (Autumn 1975), 19.

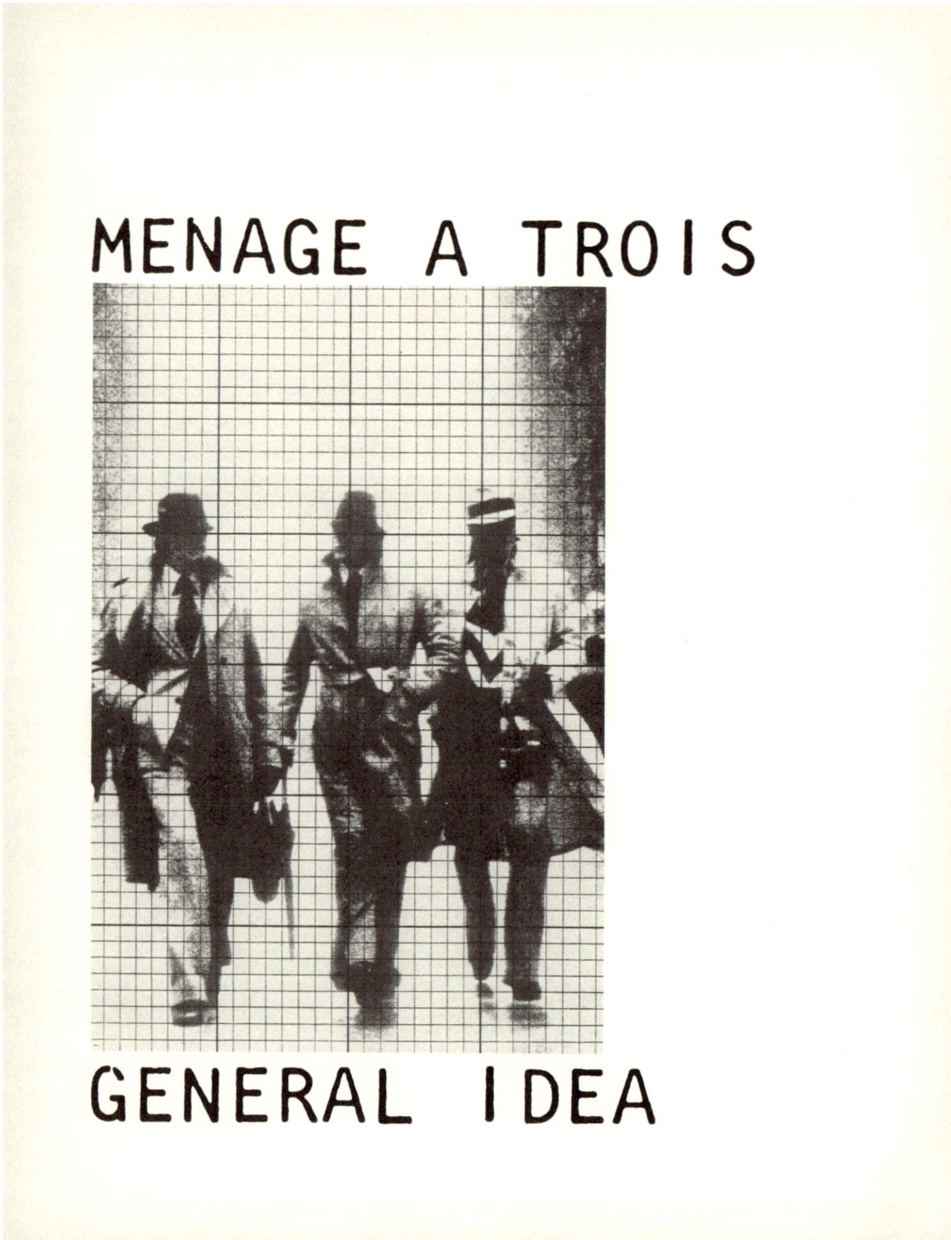

General Idea: Menage a Trois, 1978

ENUNCIATION

Never transparent in its use in General Idea's works, language was always playful, obscure, ambiguous, or contradictory. Serving various, sometimes disguised, purposes, General Idea's "writing" assumed multiple forms as the artists/authors inhabited a multiplicity of formats or genres. As they said, "We are obsessed with available form. We maneuver hungrily, conquering the uncontested territory of culture's forgotten shells—beauty pageants, pavillions, pictures magazines, and other contemporary corpses." *LIFE* magazine, for instance, was the exemplary model for *FILE*, but the artists took over other utilitarian publishing formats as well for their camp appropriations: brochures, manuals, reports, etc. Less conventional vehicles for reported content, formats were roles to enact; roles were voices to assume: "Like parasites we animate these dead bodies and speak in alien tongues." Animation was performance; alien tongues were fictional voices. The conquered format, though, functioned differently after its invasion; with its reanimated content, rather, form followed fiction there. In other words, General Idea's work was made up as it was enunciated.

Utterances had different functions depending on their context (not so much on their content) and thus took on various forms in General Idea's writing. We can examine this writing in terms of its formats to see what linguistic devices were specific to each.

Article

First to consider is the simplest, or most uninflected, that is to say, seemingly the least inhabited format: the article. Take "Pablum for the Pablum Eaters" (1973) as an example. We are told there that *description* is the operative device of myth ("one structures a cosmology through description") and so it would seem therefore the linguistic device of the article as well. Description does not make myth and article equivalent, however. The article is not myth in disguise; it operates under the *concept* of myth. But it proceeds similarly: "One starts with a vision and names the parts." Not being myth, the article is neither a structure nor a whole. Composition there is diachronic (naming the parts takes time) whereas the structure of myth is synchronic. The article assembles parts into a like whole; it gathers fragments and connects them as if they were images destined to an image bank. It fabricates by jointing. The article thus operates according to the same principles as an image bank: "a cross-referencing system of discrete items of description, the terms of a system of correspondences."

Pageant

In General Idea's system myth equals ritual and so we might think that as ritual the *Pageant* equally was descriptive in its language use. The dominant linguistic device of the *Pageant*, however, is *commentary.* As an "available format," the beauty pageant was taken over and its content replaced. But in replacing content, new subject matter was not so much described as a *role* was performed that articulated it. This role was performed by a Master of Ceremonies. The Master of Ceremonies spoke in "alien tongues" only to the degree to which he was distanced from the format while inhabiting it at the same time. His role was rational, that is to say, conventional: he functioned by convention, by rote, ritually. As if going through the motions, the Master of Ceremonies moved the *Pageant* along, not by commenting on the action, but by commenting on its form or format, ritually repeating it by reinforcing its inherent invariable roles. The regulating concept of the *Pageant*, in terms of its text that is, therefore, is ritual or rehearsal or perhaps we should say *repetition.* The concept of the *Pageant* here, note, is not Glamour, even though Glamour is its *raison d'être* and guiding vision. The concept of Glamour relates to elevation, whereas commentary is a linguistic device whose regulating concept rather is that of repetition. Commentary is rehearsal, made otherwise evident by the fact that the Master of Ceremonies in *Going thru the Motions*, AA Bronson, played the role of a director of a television show rehearsing its audience.[1]

By its repetition of ritual, commentary disguised an evacuation of content. A secondary ready-made device, therefore, delivers new content: *definition.* Definition is a repeating device; through repetition the system's structure articulates itself. For instance, all General Idea's Framing Devices were introduced by Jorge Zontal at the beginning of the video made from the 1975 *Pageant: Going thru the Motions.* In response to an interviewer's "basic questions," the basic elements of General Idea's system were put on display by Jorge's answers: "General Idea is basically this..."; "The 1984 Miss General Idea Pageant is basically this ..."; "Miss General Idea 1984 is basically this..."; "The 1984 Miss General Idea Pageant Pavillion is basically this..." As the straight man, the interviewer performed a function similar to the Master of Ceremonies. But instead of elaborating roles, questions were posed to elicit definitions. Or, rather, a question posed; an answer postured in return. It was all artificial: a question was a set-up; the answer was a staged performance.[2]

Showcards

Commentary differs from voice-over. Voice-over was a verbal device restricted to the *Showcards* (although sometimes it was used in General Idea's later videos). But it was not the dominant linguistic technique there, which rather is that of *demonstration.* Demonstration is an explanation by way of examples or models: an exhibition even.[3] As its etymology demonstrates, it is a means to *show.* (For instance, *Showcard* 2-030: "Granada demonstrated the dual nature of Glamour...") As it is a matter of staging, demonstration's concept, therefore, is *scenario.*

Demonstration does not just show; it *manipulates*: on the one hand, by turning to view; on the other hand, by sleight of hand deflecting view. Thus the Hand of the Spirit manipulated our point of view. Demonstration isolates attention in the image. But in directing attention, it diverts it as well, disguising some other act that, however, is not at all behind the scenes but in full view: a performance articulated solely by means of the *Showcard*'s text. In isolating attention, demonstration doubles the effect of the caption, for the purpose of the caption, after all, is to direct meaning, to divert the meaning of the image towards something editorially intended. The caption's function in the *Showcards*, however, is not to "describe" the image but openly to fictionalize it, thereby incorporating it into General Idea's larger system.

Editorial

If from the start, from the first issue of *FILE*, the editorial introduced myth as the principle concept of correspondence art, this does not make myth the concept of the editorial. Rather, the editorial institutes myth. The concept of the editorial, thus, is *institution*. Its verbal device is *prescription*. Moreover, it is thought, that coming at the beginning of a magazine that an editorial merely comments on what follows or states an opinion. A *FILE* editorial, however, did not state an opinion; it *made* myth.[4] Its inauguration was performative.

The editorial performed a role in the "authentication and reinforcement of myths" by its *force* of institution. Where "form follows fiction," fiction was performative force. Institution had two mythic functions: on the one hand, to create the mythic community of the Eternal Network; on the other hand, to formulate the myth of General Idea.

Story

One might think that a story is a genre of fiction but *fiction* is the concept of story: story, as in "This is the story of General Idea." The story has nothing *creatively* fictional about it, however: its linguistic device is *plagiarism*.

To summarize:

Writing format	Device/technique	Concept
Article	Description	Myth
Pageant	Commentary	Repetition
Showcards	Demonstration	Scenario
Editorial	Prescription	Institution
Story	Plagiarism	Fiction

Writing was *the* institutive medium of General Idea's work. Making it up fictionally made the work itself. Indeed, form followed fiction in their system. Text never had a subservient function, merely secondary in its representations; performative, it was primary. It alone constituted the "reality" of the work.[5] •

1. In the made-for-television videotapes *Pilot* (1977), *Test Tube* (1979), and *Shut the Fuck Up* (1985), the Pageant format was dropped for the mimicry of commercial television itself.
2. See the series of interviews in *FILE* 4:1 (Summer 1978).
3. "Skinless in Gauza, our surfaces become dioramas imposing quite conversational tones on the 'Talking Exhibits' who choose to inhabit us.... After all, why not let the exhibits describe themselves and converse with each other?" *Showcard* 1-005.
4. As in "History is what you make it. LIFE made it." "Homely Details of Everyday 'LIFE'," *FILE* 1:4 (December 1972), 18, 5.
5. At any one time, a number of verbal devices operated in tandem, one subsumed hierarchically within another: for instance, description subservient to demonstration or demonstration to the performative. Not only was there a hierarchy of techniques, formats were related transversally, as well. The editorial was related to story but also to gossip and myth by means of the concept of fiction and by the use of the performative mode.

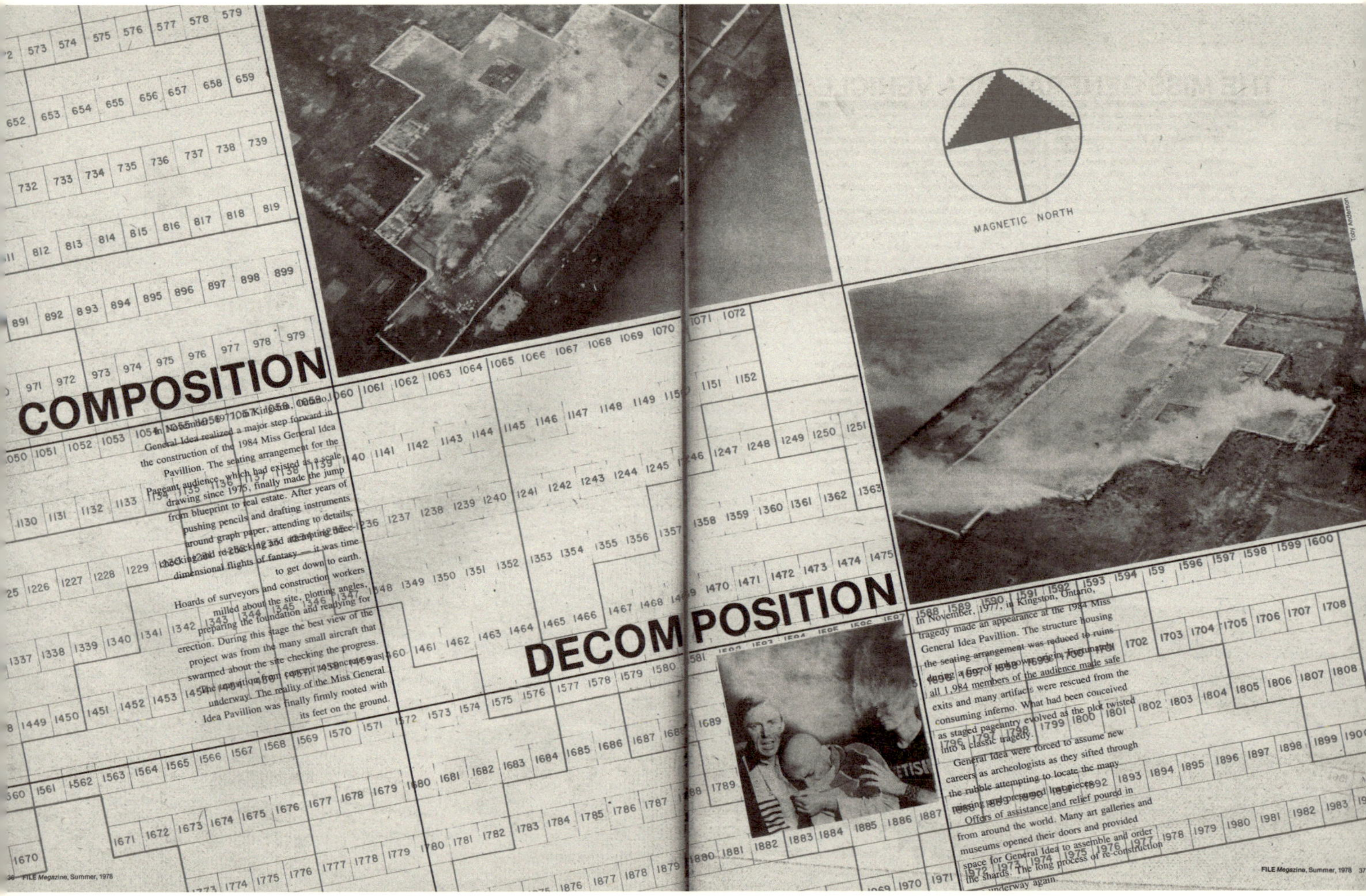
COMPOSITION
In November 1977 in Kingston, Ontario, General Idea realized a major step forward in the construction of the 1984 Miss General Idea Pavillion. The seating arrangement for the Pageant audience, which had existed as a scale drawing since 1975, finally made the jump from blueprint to real estate. After years of pushing pencils and drafting instruments around graph paper, attending to details, checking and re-checking and attempting three-dimensional flights of fantasy — it was time to get down to earth.
Hoards of surveyors and construction workers milled about the site, plotting angles, preparing the foundation and readying for erection. During this stage the best view of the project was from the many small aircraft that swarmed about the site checking the progress. The transition from concept to concrete was underway. The reality of the Miss General Idea Pavillion was finally firmly rooted with its feet on the ground.
MAGNETIC NORTH
DECOMPOSITION
In November, 1977, in Kingston, Ontario, tragedy made an appearance at the 1984 Miss General Idea Pavillion. The structure housing the seating arrangement was reduced to ruins during a fire of unknown origin. Fortunately all 1,984 members of the audience made safe exits and many artifacts were rescued from the consuming inferno. What had been conceived as staged pageantry evolved as the plot twisted into a classic tragedy.
General Idea were forced to assume new careers as archeologists as they sifted through the rubble attempting to locate the many missing and presumed lost pieces. Offers of assistance and relief poured in from around the world. Many art galleries and museums opened their doors and provided space for General Idea to assemble and order the shards. The long process of re-construction underway again.
36 FILE Magazine, Summer, 1978
FILE Magazine, Summer, 1978 37

"Construction/Destruction," *FILE* 4:1 (Summer 1978), 36–37

THE GLAMOUR SYSTEM

If "myth starts with structure and names the parts," it would seem that in addressing a system in General Idea's work, we need to start the same way: assume that there is a structure and begin to identify its parts. But where do we start; what comprises this system or structure? Is the all-encompassing and ever-expanding *Pavillion* a metaphor for it? Or, is the system an actual architectural structure, as the *Pavillion*, seems to suggest? By giving names to the *Pavillion*'s recognizable components—its specialized rooms or design features such as the Dr. Brute Colonnade or the *Luxon V.B.*—we seem to be describing the system. But where or what, for instance, is the place or function of Glamour within this architectural system? Does the *Pavillion* contain Glamour or is the *Pavillion* only a means to its end? If the latter, then it cannot be a system in itself. A system cannot be identified merely by a collection of things or an assemblage of elements: a structure is a system in transformation, after all. Glamour is of a higher order than the *Pavillion*; it is merely staged there but not contained by its architecture.

Glamour is theft. But is Glamour a system of theft? Or is theft an operation of Glamour? As a reigning concept, Glamour rules. But what is Glamour? It is an ideal: it is General Idea's supreme concept, the end of its system in the elevation of Miss General Idea, the *raison d'être* of *The 1984 Miss General Idea Pageant*. Having said this, we have to admit that we cannot define Glamour; we cannot determine the essence of its "what is?" It seems instead to be a question of what Glamour is *not*, a question of what it is the lack of: a question of The Problem of Nothing.[1] Definition seems impossible. General Idea themselves can't help us when they admitted, "We knew Glamour was not an object, not an action, not an idea." We discovered ourselves that Glamour rather was an action disguised as an object. An ideal would seem to guarantee definition; but as an ideal, Glamour actually is a ruse. In the end, it seems that Glamour cannot be defined at all because it is ambiguity itself. Ambiguity, however, is not a definition of Glamour; it is merely one of Glamour's operations.

Let's say that Glamour is a system and that the *Pavillion* is an apparatus to realize it. The two cannot be separated: the apparatus is a means to actualize the system. Yet, in a sense, the *Pavillion* is not a structure but merely an image of it. We could then say the opposite: The system is what puts the *Pavillion* in place (erects it) and keeps it standing (operating). As the system is a whole, all its operations are linked but not in any way that is visible. Its mechanisms have no appearance... or are *only* appearance. If part of the problem is that Glamour is not an object but as well not a simple concept, it is because it is a *concept* whose *operations* are achieved through the application of *techniques* produced by *strategies* and insinuated by *tactics*. Here is the ambiguity: confused with each other, all these terms seem what they are not. But they become clearer in their functions (not *meanings*, however) once we move systematically from "concept" through to "tactic."

Concepts

Concepts come first in General Idea's system, but not necessarily ostensibly to define what follows. Coming first, concepts rather establish precedence in order to produce a simulation of order—an image of hierarchy, in fact: what elevation is all about. Elevation being Glamour's primary aim, we are led to believe that Glamour is a concept in spite of General Idea implying that it is not (i.e., "We knew Glamour was not an object, not an action, not an idea"). Here is the problem: being a name, a concept already is myth. Problematically, a name stabilizes a system in motion. It disguises operations in action, appearing only to name an object while it actually helps produce an *effect.* A concept operates like myth: like Glamour, elevated it rules, while appearing to do no work. It is only "behind" the scenes, where operations are manipulated, that the operators work by means of concepts. Concepts are not visible although they condition visibility. Actually, a concept regulates an operation, but how would we know so if both concepts and operations are disguised in General Idea's system?

Immediately two concepts rise to the top in General Idea's system: Myth and Glamour. Myth and Glamour, though, seem one, as when the artists refer to the "Glamour Myth." Yet Myth and Glamour are two concepts. They are primary concepts. But they are not the only concepts in General Idea's system. They are joined by two others, joined and divided by them. The concept of Nostalgia brings Myth and Glamour together while that of the Borderline intervenes between them. Nostalgia confuses them, while making them a mirror of each other; the Borderline divides them again.[2] Encompassing Myth and Glamour does not make Nostalgia a higher concept. It is secondary, as is the Borderline. Primary and secondary concepts are coordinated, though: Nostalgia is to Myth as the Borderline is to Glamour.

The four fundamental concepts of General Idea's system are: *Myth*, *Glamour*, *Nostalgia*, and *Borderline*. But all can be reduced to the rule of Glamour.

Operations

In General Idea's system, concepts are not only confused amongst themselves, they are confused as well with operations. A concept regulates an operation but cannot enact it. An operation determines an action. We might be led to think that certain operations in General Idea's system are actually concepts, for instance, the idea of "ambiguity without contradiction." "Ambiguity without contradiction" is not a concept, however; rather, it is a movement where "a resonance which is ambiguity flips the image in and out of context." As an action (even one as slight as resonance), ambiguity therefore is an operation. There is even a machine—the *Luxon V.B.*—to articulate its flip-flop function.

Concepts differ from operations. They are elevated, out of sight. Concepts appear to do no work. Work is left to the operations to fulfill the functioning of the system, to keep the *Pavillion* up and running.[3] And at the *Pavillion*, the main activity is the *elevation* of Glamour, although the main operation of the *Pavillion*, perhaps, is simply to keep itself erected. Operations maintain the system in motion, while the system as a whole is sustained by its concepts.

Glamour's elevation incorporates a number of different actions subordinate to it: concentrating vision, subjecting seeing, fetishizing the look, miniaturizing point of view. Other preparative activities, such as the ongoing rehearsals and repetitions of the *Pageant* are subservient to it, as well. At first glance, elevation seems to be the system's basic operation.

Glamour is not only elevation; it is also theft. So the *lateral* actions of invasion and evacuation—the stealing in and stealing out of plagiarism—are also its operations. Elevation and theft are similar in their actions. Though differently oriented movements, they are both subsumed within a general operation of *reversibility.*

An ambiguous reversibility rules General Idea's system. From the de-crowning that inevitably accompanies any crowning of Miss General Idea; to the erection then destruction of the Pavillion ("composition-decomposition"); to the "future seen in retrospect," General Idea's system always was in flux.[4]

Elevation, therefore, is no one-way act, always on the up and up. Elevation is only one moment in a general movement of reversibility. In fact, elevation is subservient to the overall principle of reversibility in General Idea's system in motion. De-crowning does not just succeed crowning; it is implicit to the ritual process from the beginning: a beauty queen is condemned to degradation from the start of her reign, indeed, from the moment of entering competition.[5]

In its own compulsive repetition, theft, too, participates in this degradation or devaluation. With its lateral movements of invasion and evacuation, plagiarism is always a matter of reversing or inverting *values* by elevating others—Glamour—in place of those its downgrades and displaces or replaces. Theft is not only disguised here, reversal is as well.

With its lateral and elevatory movements, Glamour possesses the uncanny ability to occupy two structural positions at once. The ambiguity without contradiction of Glamour is this ability to be in two places at once. Glamour's theft is also its alibi: the ability to say it was elsewhere. It is seen in one place (elevated) while it operates invisibly in another (stealing). We can tabulate the operations of Glamour thus:

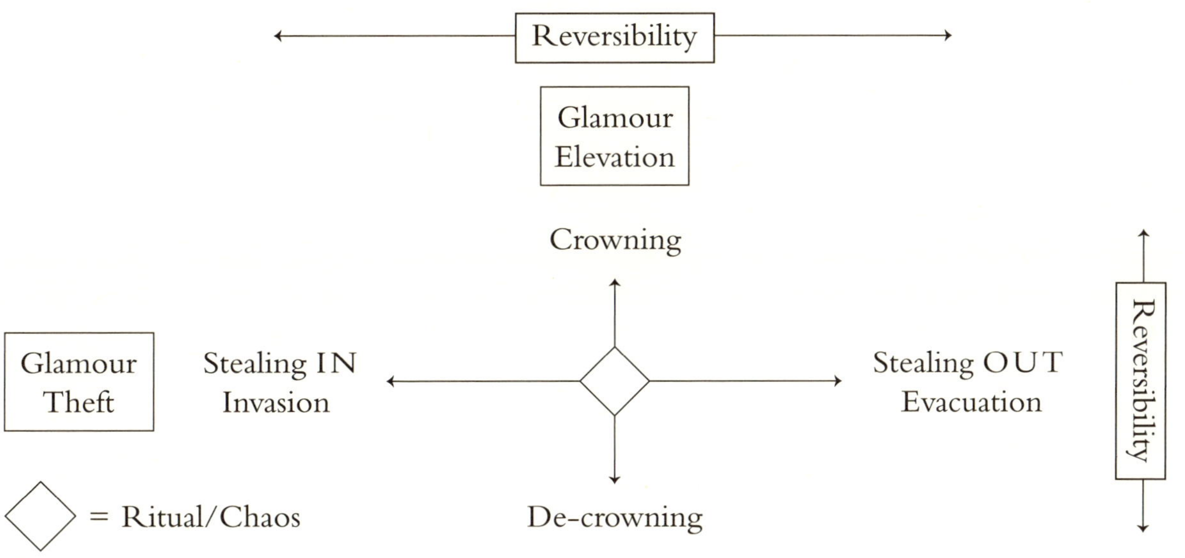

The operations of General Idea's system are: *ambiguity*, *elevation*, *repetition*, *invasion*, *evacuation*, and *reversibility*. All operations are linked through the principle of reversibility. *Reversibility*, therefore, is the system's main operation.[6] Reversibility keeps the system in flux.

Techniques

Techniques are easily confused with operations. This is because they appear together. But they are not the same: they align in an action, although different techniques may be applied to any one operation. Technique is not an operation but a method or manner of doing something. Or it is the style or fashion of execution (or performance), sometimes achieved by means of a knack or trick.[7] Techniques facilitate operations. They could be said to finesse them. Every thief has his own tricks of the trade: his specialized tools of entry. Theft employs devices; devices are techniques. Principally, there are two techniques in General Idea's system: *mirror insertion* and *collage cut-up*. Since these are basically the same, we can say that General Idea's one technique is *cut-up*.

Strategies

A strategy is a *plan* of action, not the action itself. Etymologically the word derives from military application where the planning of attack (strategy) is distinguished from action in the field (tactics), the place where one is in contact with an enemy. In the "battle between nature and culture," General Idea identified Glamour as a "passive defense," whose "evasive" strategy was three-fold: concealment, hardening of target, and mobility. They added, "Glamour is the perfect simulation technique for ongoing battles." For General Idea, simulation would seem to be both a technique *and* a strategy. In that the battle is ongoing, or offensive, however, simulation rather is a *tactic* and *theft* is the strategy that must be disguised or camouflaged.[8] Since the aim of Glamour is theft, General Idea's main strategy is *theft*.

Tactics

We find it difficult to distinguish strategies from tactics in General Idea: intentionally so on their part. We find it difficult to distinguish strategies from tactics especially when the operations of General Idea's work all take place in language. And when subterfuge is not only disguised but also announced, moreover. Strategies are announced; tactics are enacted. The tactic is disguised in the announcement of the strategy. This is both a strategy *and* a tactic. General Idea's tactic is *camouflage*.

To summarize General Idea's system, there is one concept: *Glamour*; one operation: *reversibility*; one technique: *cut-up*; one strategy: *theft*; one tactic: *camouflage*. Surprisingly, for the complexity, diversity, even eclecticism of General Idea's work, their system can be so reduced. But it is a system after all and systems have a basic structure and rules of operation. And within this system, Glamour really does rule. •

1. "What attracts us to Glamour is of course what it lacks.... The back door to the Miss General Idea Pavillion opening on the Problem of Nothing." Marginal note to "Editorial," *FILE* 3:1 (Autumn 1975), n.p.
2. As secondary concepts, the Borderline and Nostalgia regulate techniques (cut-up) and thus involve Strategies (theft) and Tactics (camouflage). As a concept of intervention, the Borderline invents: "Are you drawing a distinction or defining an edge? Be Bold. Create a universe," the Borderline Cases Editorial read. *IFEL* 2:3 (September 1973), 11.
3. For Miss General Idea, Glamour was all about maintenance. Playing the part of the Spirit of Miss General Idea, the character Ahsram Rrak said in an interview, "That's what the G.I. boys call 'Glamour'. Me, I call it maintenance." She went on to say, "A Spirit's work is never done.... There's too much surface to contend with ... it takes a lot of buffing to maintain the flow of mirror situations, to keep those meanings snapping in and out of focus, ambiguity without contradiction..." "Can *You* Play the Part of the Spirit of Miss General Idea 1984 ..." *FILE* 4:1 (Summer 1978), 26.
4. Reversibility is a borderline act. It is ruled by the concept of the Borderline.
5. Consider this early, covert expression of the devaluing-revaluing function of evacuation: "The art of evacuation, which is the art of the hidden smile, sliding behind the inevitable movement of the disappearing fan. The art of the feminine wile. The art of levitation, which is the art of evacuation of the lower order, the octave raised to the higher resonance, mars pulled into pluto. The art of the skirt raised." Even though some criticized the "objectification" implied in the mimicry of the *Pageant*, here was a case of "feminist" elevation: "The female gender rises through the medium of the mailing chain with an elegant ease, establishing itself with mundane eloquence in the arena of our affliction." Perhaps the feminist elevation was only pretense for that of a drag queen. "Top Ten," *FILE* 1:2&3 (May/June 1972), 21.
6. A criterion of any structure or system is its reversibility.
7. Compare Claude Lévi-Strauss's description of the *bricoleur*: "And in our own time the 'bricoleur' is still someone who works with his hands and uses devious means compared to those of a craftsman." Claude Lévi-Strauss, *The Savage Mind* (Chicago: University of Chicago Press, 1966), 16–17.
8. Part of the confusion is due to the etymological derivation of "tactics" from both the Greek "*taktikos*" and "*tekhnē*," whereas the latter alone conditions "technique."

EDITORIAL

With art at his heels, the Art Director in us can't help asking: How much drama? How much mood? How much information? Should the dance be arresting, or is it more glamourous when seen and not heard? In so many cases the stances are too glamourous to remain as context. Should we cram them into content? Or vice versa?

Is it glamourous to be glamourous? Are we stuck with Meta-glamour? Is an illustrated magazine such a hot format for Glamour? Are we marketing a Dior gown through a mail-order house? Or vice versa?

As long as it remains possible to tack a 'vice versa' to the end of each paragraph, we must be doing something right. ~~Or vice versa.~~

This, our most unglamourous issue of FILE, copes with Glamour. We fought on the side of our image and watched ourselves slipping in and out of trenches. Don't be blinded by the invisibility of our stance. All myth and no content. Or is it vice versa?

WHAT ATTRACTS US TO GLAMOUR is of course what it lacks.

In Borderline Case 2 (Mimicry) culture and nature appear to be faking a stance. The back door to the Miss General Idea Pavillion opening on the Problem of Nothing. Like Mimicry in this respect, Glamour might be a trip in itself.

The culture/nature stance in Borderline Case 4 (Mockery) seems to hide nothing. We can easily walk around the Pavillion delighting in the fountains and topiary works. No black curtain here, no false perspective. Like Mockery, Glamour has no supicious curtain either., but it *lacks one.* With Glamour, the culture/nature stance lets us believe that it opens onto nothing while it hands out maps and travel brochures to all the gardens and fountains *on the other side.* Could this be my skin? Borderline Case 3.

FILE MEGAZINE Fall 1975 19

"Editorial," *FILE* 3:1 (Autumn 1975), 19

VICE VERSA

I.

"Meaning" is an *ambiguous* term in General Idea's system, which is why we cannot talk about meaning in itself but only of a *logic of ambivalence* instead. Meaning inheres to the operations of General Idea's work, not its content. If the process of their work was all about alternating alignments of words and images, which were only momentary, how could there ever be a *single* identifiable meaning specific to any one work? Yet, logic is a system intended to assure meaning, if not to assign it. Certainly, certainty is lacking in a system of ambiguity, even one of "ambiguity without contradiction." Contradictorily, "ambiguity" is a *way* to meaning in General Idea's work—a way finder of its borderlines situations, that is.[1]

The 1984 Miss General Idea Pavillion was an apparatus for the production of mobile meaning. Not an actual building, of course, it rather was an *architexture* that was constructed through language operations. Within this apparatus, General Idea singled out certain of the *Pavillion*'s architectural features as *models* of meaning for its overall operations—such as *Luxon V.B.* (1973) and the *Hoarding* (1975).

So we start outside the building at what first announced it: the *Hoarding*. The *Hoarding*, however, ambiguously identified and displaced location at the same time: the limits of the project were mobile. Meaning cannot be found in its location. As the *Pavillion*'s construction foreman said in a 1975 interview, the *Hoarding* is "portable and can be mobilized to encompass the far-flung site of the Pavillion." He continued:

> Traditionally you would call it de-centralized but we see it more as "widely centralized." We never refer to the sites of the Pavillion. Only the site. It's a singular site with multiple points of view. The fact that there are several locales where activity takes place only expands the centre. Our centre is defined by the circumference and the Hoarding is a sort of tool that allows us to expand the centre to any of its installations.[2]

Rather than hiding the construction site, the *Hoarding* opened the *Pavillion* to multiple points of view or interpretation. Yet the *Hoarding* was not just a preview for something about to happen. The first act signalling building, the erection of the *Hoarding* was an announcement that both promised *and* effected construction at the same time: it was performative. Announcement was anticipation and realization together. Thus, the foreman could say of the *Pavillion*'s *verbal* articulation, "We've expended just as much energy erecting the Hoarding in the media as we have on erecting it on real estate. It has to be real before they'll report it, but it isn't really real until they do." Inhabiting them variously, the *Pavillion* manifested itself in every media mention and measured its construction in column inches: "The Pavillion is a very parasitic structure."

With nothing to ensue, the *Hoarding* "said" it all. It was all right there before us with no verso to speak of. In answer to the interviewer's question, "Doesn't a construction hoarding usually denote that there is something constructive going on behind it? I mean, it's starting to sound more like a facade than a ...," the foreman interjected to reply:

> "Going on behind it" is really the key phrase to your question. One of the major decisions still to be made is which side is the "behind" side. The search required to facilitate this decision is we feel very constructive. But at this stage it appears that site-clearing is required on both sides before we break ground. As for your facade crack, the Hoarding stands entirely on its own and has nothing to hide. You can see it on the surface, you can see around it and you can even see through it. There's nothing more to it than meets the eye.[3]

Meaning was no more than its superficiality. While there before us, meaning was mobile; it could not be pinned down; it could only temporarily be erected. Location, location, location was exactly that: meaning could not be located; it moved on. Or, contradictorily, meaning was in two places at once. It always maintained an alibi.[4] The search—the Search for the Spirit—was its mobility (both the search and the Spirit). *Mobility* and *multiplicity* are the conditions of meaning in General Idea's work.

The *Hoarding* disguised the fact that the *Pavillion* had always already been constructed, although the foreman admitted "plans have been finalized to the extent that we've decided to leave some decisions for the future." To get into the *Pavillion* then, one must pass through the "perpetual motion revolving doors-of-the-future," an entry *as* event that changed every time.[5] Entrance there was just as much an outing. *Luxon V.B.*, the prototype of the *Pavillion*'s window system, had always made this clear, complicated nonetheless by the fact that its revolving slats were mirrored venetian blinds. As such, they brought the outside in and turned the inside out.[6] *Luxon V.B.* was not just something to look through or reflect in. Each turn brought about a different alignment of reflected images (not only meshing outside and in but transforming self-image as well, which became "jagged with sophistication"). Alignments were temporary elevations that were destined to dissolve. It was all in the turning: "A resonance which is ambiguity flips the image in and out of context. Layers of accumulated meaning snap in and out of focus."[7] Meanings fluctuated in the turnings of *Luxon V.B.*, never residing securely in place.

When in "Pablum for the Pablum Eaters," General Idea speculated on the logic of myth ("The key to this logic is the borderline situation, the neither one nor the other, camouflaged indifference, mirror mirror on the wall. Flip flop. Lip flap."), at the same time that year they constructed a machine to demonstrate it: *Luxon V.B.* The flip-flopping oscillating views of *Luxon V.B.* were neither one nor the other but a camouflaged in-difference. When it was first shown, General Idea wrote, "The mirror construction, *Luxon V.B.*, is seen as the prototype for the first in a series of proposals being devised towards an architectural program aimed at generating mirror situations for the 1984 Miss General Idea Pavillion." Mirror situations were borderline cases: the "exacting space marked by glamour: the interface between content and context, nature and culture, inside and out."[8] The *Pavillion* was no more than an illusion constituted and architecturally instituted by the mirror situations of its borderline cases: elevations and floor plans at once.

A mirror situation was a mirror operation. In *Luxon V.B.*, a series of mirrors moving in parallel captured the momentary effect of an image as a jagged zigzag interfacing inner and outer views. Interfacing was not just temporary alignment of two views or images. It was a means of evacuation: flipping images in and out of focus led to a vacuum. The oscillating mirror was not itself a case of either-or: content *or* context, nature *or* culture, inside *or* out. The act of withdrawal opened a space for other operations. The article "Are You Truly Invisible?" suggested an analogous situation:

> Consider your mirror's feelings. Must it always reflect *you*? A) Coerce all your mirrors to look at each other. B) Now that you've turned them onto the ultimate narcissism, steal away your reflection while they aren't watching. Carefully. It's all done without mirrors. How they'll talk about you! The vacuum created by your invisibility has got to be filled with words. They'll talk and talk ...[9]

Meaning was talk. But it was not just any sort of talk—the content that fills a format, that is. Talk ... and talk and talk ... was viral. Insinuated on a borderline between two mirrors, created in a gap that obsessively must be filled, talk was not spirited within but came from elsewhere. Parasitic, meaning was plagiaristic: it hijacked an intention to say and replaced it with lip flap. Ventriloquism emptied its subject (in the double sense of "subject") in order to "speak in tongues" in its place. Miss General Idea was a lip-syncing drag queen mouthing her words. Meaning was in the mouthing of a staged event.

Meaning came secondly, second-hand (perhaps vintage thirties, forties, fifties). But it was an event. Before this appearance, the original content must be "brutally emptied of meaning that parasitic but cultured meaning might be housed there." Meaning was only a process of evacuation and replacement, not something in itself. The merely reflective mirrors actually were a *method* of evacuation. *Luxon V.B.* captured the outside and dragged it inwards, flipping the inside reciprocally outwards—a mutual behind-side evacuation of both sides: vice versa. The *Pavillion* was built on evacuation, not an excavation. This is what the *Hoarding* hid: there was no excavation behind it.

The mobile *Miss General Idea Vehicle* had no behind to it, too. It was similar to the *Hoarding* in this respect, but its function was more like that of *Luxon V.B.* It was a vehicle not so much for the construction of meaning as its destruction, with its Dada Sawing Blade wheels "perfect for cutting in and out of traffic. Ideal for collage-travelling." Collage's "cutting remarks" did not lead to meaning but were a destructive detour; the Dada Sawing Blades were "a definite must to help steer clear of mainstream traffic jams while providing just enough traction to maintain the traffic flow."[10]

The *Hoarding* and *Luxon V.B.* architecturally articulated the "exacting space marked by glamour." This exacting space marked the precinct of the *Pavillion* itself. And it was only fitting that the Spirit of Miss General Idea, herself the epitome of Glamour, acted as gatekeeper on these borderlines. She operated the *Luxon V.B.*, letting in and out views on the *Pavillion*. Seemingly neutral, she "manipulate[d] the necessary vacuum for content and context to air their differences."[11] It would seem that Miss General Idea rather manipulated herself, or her own empty self-image, because isn't Glamour's vacancy—Glamour's closure, brilliance, and silence—precisely a vacuum? People commonly think, how can meaning be *empty*? But in emptying meaning, evacuating it through the flip-flopping oscillations of the *Luxon V.B.*, Miss General Idea showed, as in linguistics, that meaning is only an empty placeholder that ensures its ongoing operations. She herself was empty but manipulative.

II.

> We knew that in order to be artists and glamourous artists we needed a gesture, a MANIPULATION OF THE SELF, to mirror and freeze the image of nature unmasked. With this gesture we husk Nature, voiding the shell that Culture, that great Amazon, single-breasted but divided, might shoot the poisoned arrow of meaning into its empty shell.
>
> —"Glamour"

While projective in its brilliance, Glamour, nevertheless, was a receptacle. Meaning never inhered; it was received there; *we* projected it onto Miss General Idea—both meaning and Glamour. Yet General Idea's system was a generator of meaning, however self-referential it was, and Glamour was its vehicle. Never able to be defined, Glamour actually was all about meaning. So looking again at the 1975 "Glamour" article, we find that it is not so much the story of General Idea as it is a treatise on meaning as practiced by them. Two opposed types of meaning are described there: meaning as arrest and meaning as vacillation.

The "Glamour" editorial asked: "Should the dance be arresting, or is it more glamourous when seen and not heard," which probably were one and the same. Glamour's arrest (in other words its "closure and brilliance"), nonetheless, disguised a process, a motion, an action behind the scene that was the scene itself. The "arrest" was merely a *figure* of Glamour where gesture and signification coincided in a "posture" and where vacillation came to a halt.[12] "Image Lobotomy" concluded:

> A resonance which is ambiguity flips the image in and out of context. Layers of accumulated meaning snap in and out of focus. Myths hide behind the mask of "real" images; the shifty eyes of cultural content watch through the loopholes of natural context. The result is a full stop, a notational arrest wedged in the gap between culture and nature. And that is Glamour.

"Notational arrest" was a deception. The borderline could not be fixed; its gap was incapable of being filled. There was no full stop there, no stopping in the back and forth movement of the "border dweller who performs in the stolen moments." After all, look at what General Idea themselves advocated for Glamour's defense. Its strategy consisted of concealment, hardening, *and* mobility. Like Glamour's closure and brilliance, concealment and hardening were the ruse of an arrest while "behind" (actually right out in the open) all was mobile. The arrested image rather was an *arresting* image that made *us* stop. Its falsifying movement disguised plagiarism taking place: a shift in meaning, which was actually a change in the *value* of meaning. Meaning was merely this *change* in value. Meaning was movement.

When General Idea shot the arrow of poisoned meaning into nature's empty shell, they poisoned meaning by perverting it.[13] This gesture arrested our attention. Poison fused our attention to its fetishistic object, binding us to Glamour's elevation. When the artists wrote that "The moment of maximum Glamour [i.e., the moment of maximum meaning] occurs when poison fuses nature into culture, creating a momentary joint operation of the two," this too was a ruse, an illusion. Poison was intrusion not fusion. Collage's jointing was temporary, but it was perhaps enough to divert our attention from what was at hand in Glamour's otherworldly elevation. This is exactly what happened in our fetishistic attraction to Miss General Idea's shoes: "The futuristic profile of the MISS GENERAL IDEA SHOES neglects joints to exhibit a continuity of surface which is enchanting, otherworldly." An enchanting arrest, meaning was not an otherworldly effect, however much it was produced by immaterial means. The dazzling surface seduced us into overlooking its fabricated joints. Meaning, however, was not immediately given as a seamless image; it was divided. It was not comprised of associations but rather of continual disassociation.

As meaning was divided and disguised, divided by disguise, we should expect it to offer two faces. Ostensibly there were two types of meaning in General Idea's work: arrest and vacillation, the latter which the artists later would call interpretation.[14] Arrest and vacillation were opposed in their effects—and therefore in their "meaning." Both were *manipulated*, but in different ways, notably one by the other: the former was merely an arrested moment of vacillation: a false arrest. Arrested meaning was only false meaning, a ruse to keep the system in motion. Flip-flopping vacillation was the meaning of it all. Meaning is a misnomer in General Idea's work where all was interpretation. Meaning really was motion, a "moving territory of words."

III.

> We've tried to underline the fact that there is nothing behind it. No verso to speak of. The task of stringing together enough evidence to present this case is a labour of pure fabrication.
>
> —"The Miss General Idea Vehicle"

Meaning in General Idea's work was no more than an artificial articulation that took shape, form following fiction, as the *Pavillion*. Meaning was effect. And its event was the *Pavillion*. Meaning was only an operation to erect the *Pavillion*, which was a performative act.

General Idea were operators. Their method was telling. It was all in the telling. And the showing of the telling, so to speak. But the showing was only a mirror effect. As the *Pavillion* was a "collage or perish edifice," so the mirror was its effective elaboration. As a collage process, the mirror was both divisive and constructive: a mirror cut-up provided construction material for re-constructed elevations that were no more themselves than mirrors. There was no verso here, just vice versa.

Myth and meaning were one. Myth was meaning and meaning myth. But myth was one with mirror and cut-up. They were all one and the same.

General Idea's work was full of words, a verbosity that repeated itself; but this insistence was not its meaning, merely its sustaining myth. Not that these words represented the artists and expressed their intentions. Actually, the artists were only the front men. It was the system itself that was the operator. The vacuum created by the artists' invisibility, though, had to be filled with words. It was all a matter of how "they'll talk and talk." •

A Note on Postmodern General Idea

Producing work in the early to mid-1970s under the influence of Claude Lévi-Strauss's structuralism and Roland Barthes's semiology, yet troubling their sources at the same time, General Idea were in advance of contemporary art's postmodern turn. Consider *Luxon V.B.* with its vacillating ambiguity leading to a plurality of interpretations, or the multiple points of view of the *Hoarding*, which was itself decentred, offering only a surface for a constantly deferred decipherment. (Not to mention General Idea's collective production aligning itself to the "death of the author" and their plagiarist inhabitations anticipating appropriation art.) Their sources, however, were not simply applied without deviation. The artists shot a "poisoned arrow" into structuralism, perhaps by no more than inserting a mirror into its operations. Glamour was troubling. Glamour was in trouble. The ambiguity without contradiction of Glamour was also its alibi: its ability to be in two places at once; its ability to occupy *two* structural positions at once. In the September 1973 *FILE* editorial, the artists wrote of their Borderline Cases: "Consider these deceptive. Levels of ambiguity present classification problems not yet dealt with by structural methods." A couple years before in 1971 (and having long moved on from structuralism and semiology), Barthes similarly had written of the new situation of the Theory of the Text where he found a "discomfort of classification which permits diagnosing a certain mutation," a situation where "the epistemological privilege nowadays granted to language derives precisely from the fact that in it [language] we have discovered a paradoxical idea of structure: system without end or center."[15] In effect, Barthes was describing the *Pavillion* but, at the same time, anticipating its mutation.

Myth is a system of meaning. But what happens when your model of myth changes? Myth is total, but its concept perhaps is not continuous throughout General Idea's oeuvre. When its concept changed something in General Idea's work changed as well, but this was not necessarily visible. In 1978, following the destruction of the *Pavillion*, as well as General Idea following Barthes, the terms defining their system changed from *structure*, *whole*, and *description* to *structuration*, *plural*, and *text*.

1. Even if those situations are not visible: "Ambiguity is not a symptom of a schizophrenic who travels back and forth across the line but a quality of the border dweller who performs in the stolen moments." "General Idea's Borderline Cases: Introduction," *IFEL* 2:3 (September 1973), 12.
2. "An Interview with Foreman Lamanna," *FILE* 4:1 (Summer 1978), 35. Foreman Lamanna actually was General Idea's commercial dealer Carmen Lamanna. The *Hoarding* first appeared on the street in front of the Carmen Lamanna Gallery for their 1975 *Going thru the Notions* exhibition.
3. Similarly, in an interview in the same issue, when Felix Partz was asked "what's behind it all," meaning behind the *Miss General Idea Vehicle*, which functioned similarly to the *Hoarding*, he answered: "Actually nothing, there's nothing behind it at all ... it's all on the surface.... [T]here really is no background and that's one of the problems that we continue to encounter. The general public still wants to know what's behind it but when you get right down to it is anyone really interested in what goes on behind the canvas? Our research shows they aren't. We've tried to underline the fact that there is nothing behind it. No verso to speak of. The task of stringing together enough evidence to present this case is a labour of pure fabrication." "The Miss General Idea Vehicle," Ibid., 38.
4. "... the ubiquity of the signifier in myth exactly reproduces the physique of the *alibi*... Myth is a *value*, truth is no guarantee for it; nothing prevents it from being a perpetual alibi: it is enough that its signifier has two sides for it always to have an 'elsewhere' at its disposal." Roland Barthes, "Myth Today," in *Mythologies*, trans. Annette Lavers (New York: Hill and Wang, 1972), 123.
5. "The Miss General Idea Vehicle," 38.
6. "'... turning the slats allows for a maximum of visibility with a minimum of noise. A second turn will jerk off your peripheral vision into a flight of reflections. Out of yourself and into the landscape and back again.'" *Showcard* 4-011. "A flick of the Hand of the Spirit turns the slats to allow her image to the other side—a double crossing of borderlines by her image in cahoots with her vision." *Showcard* 4-005.
7. "Glamour: Image Lobotomy," *FILE* 3:1 (Autumn 1975), n.p. Venetian blinds appear disguised in the unlikeliest places, even in a vice versa. Take the Glamour editorial, for instance. Each paragraph there concluded with a tacked on "or vice versa." Where can meaning ever reside with such advocated vacillation, the editorial playing both sides of the fence? But look: look between the lines, as when General Idea write that "Our favorite spot for border crossings is right between the lines." Ah, but which lines? The lines hiding in plain sight between the lines of text: the graphic design of black lines meant to embolden the text they divide. These graphic lines operate in conjunction with the text lines to create a machine, which flips back and forth just like the vacillating "vice versa" in the text. The vice versa play between the two makes them function as a venetian blind, in fact equivalent to General Idea's *Luxon V.B.* "General Idea's Borderline Cases," 26.
8. *Luxon V.B.: The 1984 Miss General Idea Pavillion No. 101*, self-published, 1973.
9. "Are You Truly Invisible?," *IFEL* 2:3 (September 1973), 35.
10. "The Miss General Idea Vehicle," 38. Like the *Hoarding*, *The Miss General Vehicle* was also about the "mobility" of meaning in the Search for the Spirit.
11. *Luxon V.B.: The 1984 Miss General Idea Pavillion No. 101.* Also see *Showcard* 4-013.
12. "In the gesture that essential configuration of movement and desire is locked into a single sign. The sign is repeated endlessly, become thick with meaning. The gesture becomes raw matter for myth." "Gestures," in "Glamour."
13. Plagiarism was perverting, perversion being a turning from proper ends, use, or nature. Etymologically, "perversion" was a turning.
14. The summer 1978 *FILE* editorial read "We wanted to point out the wildly fluctuating interpretations you, our public, impose on us.... We wanted to point out the function of ambiguity in our work, the way in which ambiguity 'flips the meanings in and out of focus,' thus preventing the successful deciphering of the text (both visual and written) except on multiple levels." *FILE* 4:1 (Summer 1978), 7.
15. "From Work to Text," in *The Rustle of Language*, trans Richard Howard (Berkeley: University of California Press, 1989), 56, 59. The text was originally published in 1971 and translated in 1977.

PART III

SYNTHETIC

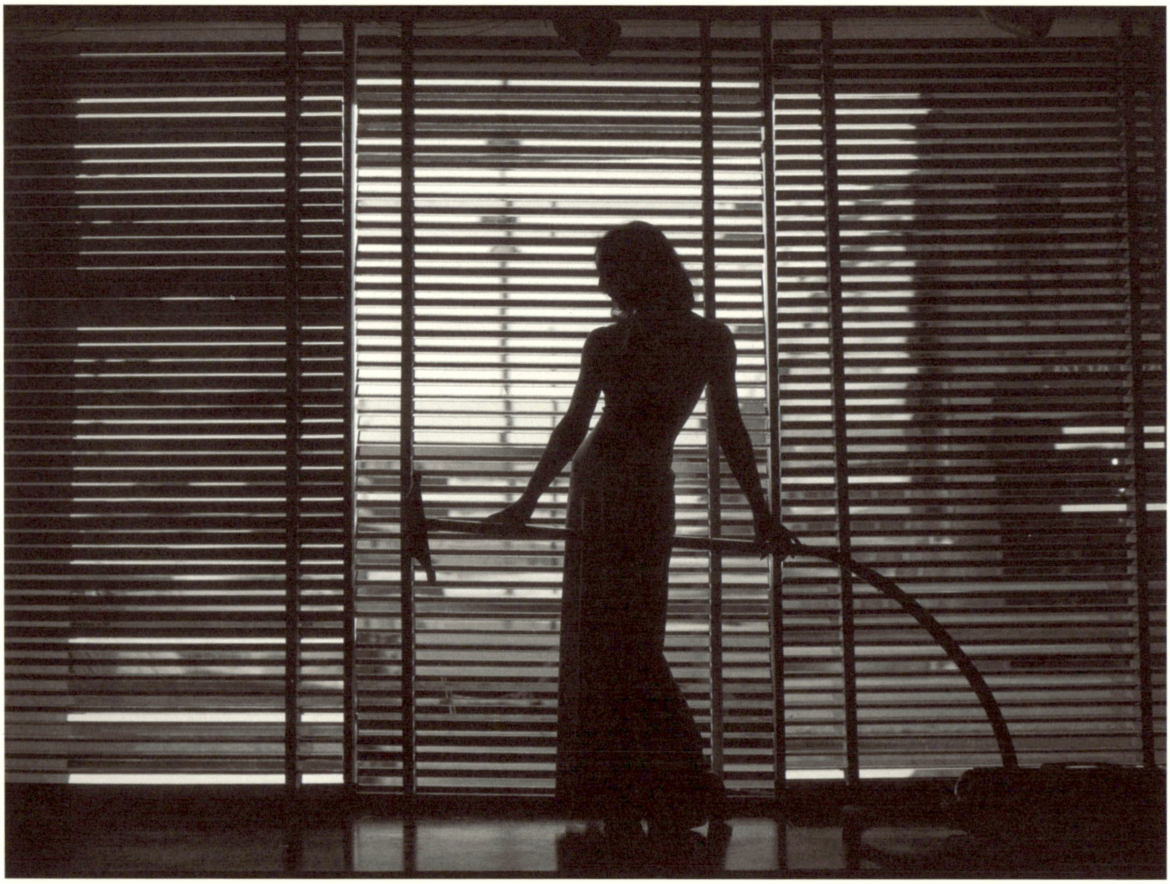

Marsha Karr in front of *Luxon V.B.*, 1974

SOMETHING BY MOUTH

The vacuum created by your invisibility has got to be filled with words.

—"Are You Truly Invisible?"

I.

The conclusion is only a beginning again, but this time as a story—an alternative story. A story: here was a fabrication not permitted by the structural analyses of Parts One and Two. But this is not to admit that finally here is the story of General Idea, the famous story told by the artists themselves. That story was strictly controlled. It had to be. After all, General Idea's work was in the telling. It was *only* fictional fabrication.

The interpretation of their work, however, is another matter. Yet, interpretation has tended to repeat the "party line" and has articulated itself within the framework General Idea themselves created. That story only began to be consolidated in 1975: when General Idea's Framing Devices were first established as part of the *Showcards* and the video *Going thru the Motions*; when their "story" was first published in *FILE*'s "Glamour" issue. There is nothing more authoritative than General Idea's five Framing Devices and nothing more seductive than their story of Glamour and fame. By 1984, and their first retrospective catalogue, it was *the* only story, *the* only point of view, even though the *Pavillion*'s destruction in 1977 had revealed flaws in their system. General Idea had effectively branded themselves.

We all tend now to begin *our* own stories of General Idea at that 1975 re-branding. If any prehistory is considered, it is only that of the *Pageant*, which is thought a ready-made formation, and which, thus, merges seamlessly into the artists' story. Or that what follows is only a repetition in differing forms of the *Pageant*. This has made us deaf to other stories and blind to other formations equally within General Idea's oeuvre: to the articles "Pablum for the Pablum Eaters" and "General Idea's Borderline Cases," to *Light On* and General Idea's whole mirror thematics, in themselves more important, I would argue, than the *Pageant*. Furthermore, no understanding of General Idea is possible without attention to the cut-up cosmology of a system that predates yet subtends the later consolidation. No "story" heretofore has ever considered this.

An alternative story would let itself be guided by deviations from the orthodox point of view; it would find its clues in the alternatives that present themselves in this eclectic early body of work.[1] Not that General Idea hid their early orientation. They hid nothing, ever, although it might have been disguised. But this is no excuse for us not seeing through it. Supposedly, we were in on the game. Of course, what follows here is not the full story of all General Idea's activities, only what surfaces on the subliminal as my correspondences. It is not so much a story of what *they* did but of their *doing*. As such, it is an examination of General Idea's methodology in its early development.

To start with, General Idea were not always, well, General Idea. In the beginning they operated without a name—or with individual projects under their own names. It was only in 1970 for the Toronto exhibition *Concept 70* that they assumed the name General Idea.[2] Aside from installations in their house, which often took advantage of its commercial storefront, all the work of this early period was of a conceptualizing nature. General Idea were conceptual artists after all, weren't they? So their projects or proposals took the form of every variation of conceptual art it seems—ecological, land, process, systems, body. They partook of every variation except, notably, the "analytical." In 1971, these projects and proposals were gathered together in "The 1971 General Idea Tour de Force" binder and languished there.[3] We might think this entombment as good a place as any to rest what could be considered General Idea juvenilia and move on to their preparations for *The 1971 Miss General Idea Pageant*.

At the time, though, the *Pageant* was only one other project, one other concept, seemingly no more important than any other.[4] What is important for seeing the role of this early work is not the name of a project, or the "concepts" of its proposal, which are only a type of content, but rather an understanding of its strategies (which imply a process that might be applied by analogy elsewhere): the general strategies, for instance, of insertion, transfer, or reversal. These are all variations of mapping of one condition or situation on another, commonplace to conceptual art, but in General Idea's enterprise they also importantly led to some form of subversive destruction, which operated to secret one thing in another.[5]

Take *Light On*, which was as an exercise in transference, recording, mapping, and recycling. No mere proposal, *Light On* was a major concern of General Idea in 1971. After writing grant applications to secure funding, they produced the work that summer, and exhibited it at the Carmen Lamanna Gallery in spring 1972. The artists transported large portable mirrors through the cities and countryside of southern Ontario, where they documented mundane scenes of reflected light: "The mirrors, tilting and rotating on chrome swivels, catch the sun on computed angles, illuminating postcard images in a flare of light. General Idea, travelling through southern Ontario with these, documents the path of the light in photos and on video, mirroring the mirrors and finding the reflection of a community."[6]

Similar to a photograph of one scene being shot in another location, here one view was insinuated, in situ, in another, transferred from A to B by the reflection of a mirror, then documented. But since only blinding sunlight was transferred in *Light On*, the reflection left a void in the image. Published a year later, the *Luxon V.B.* pamphlet suggested an alternative reading belying the transparency of the work's conceptual methodology. After starting off objectively ("In 'evidence of Light On' at the Carmen Lamanna Gallery in the spring of 1972, we devised 3' x 5' mirrors on rotating stands to capture beams of light and direct them across the landscape"), the artists went on to say: "In this way we distanced ourselves from the landscape of our desires by extending the hand in a beam of light and tracing the outline of our concern directly on the countryside. Landscape painting."[7] Was this landscape painting or landscape posturing, invisibly posturing in the landscape, that is? Though absent from the image, the artists postured on a borderline they had insinuated through the distance they introduced into the landscape by means of a manipulative mirror action. (Already, the Hand of the Spirit was

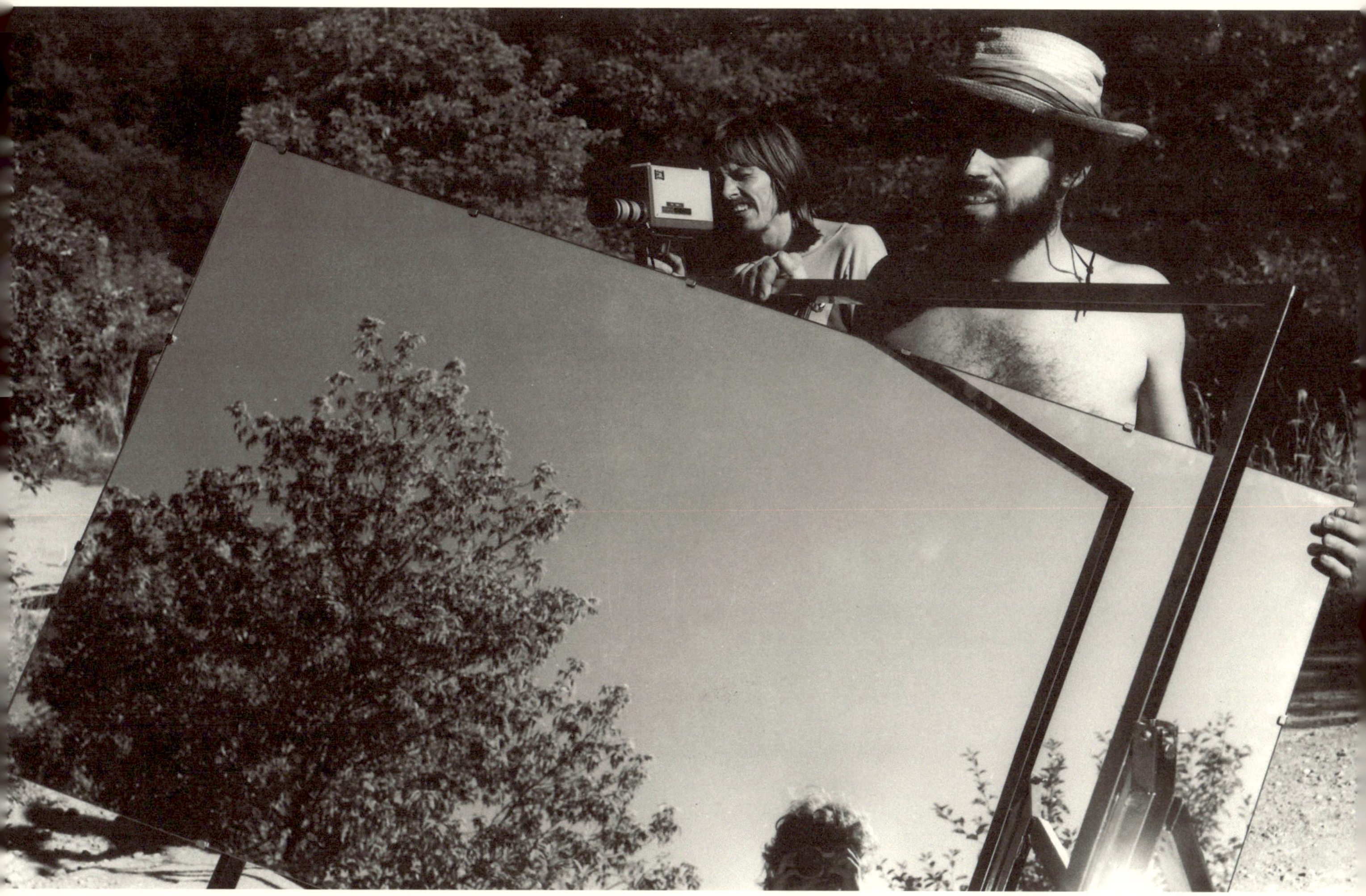

Felix Partz, AA Bronson, and Jorge Zontal with *Light-On*, 1971

moving!) The artists split the scene in order to insinuate another content or concern there, even though it would appear to be a void.

Transference was not so neutral or so transparent, after all. It secretly served the artists' agenda: "tracing the outline of our concern." Transference was just as much infiltration, invasion, trespass, transgression, or indeed theft. Moving something immaterial from one place to another was a model of plagiarism. *Light On*, it seems, functioned no differently from *Luxon V.B.* Indeed, for the *Light On* opening at the Carmen Lamanna Gallery, the tilting mirrors placed in a parking lot opposite reflected exterior incidents into the gallery in anticipation of the flip-flopping, inside-out recycling of *Luxon V.B.* displayed in the gallery's store window the next year.

As mirror apparatus, *Light On* and *Luxon V.B.* had a natural kinship. But so surprisingly did *Light On* and the then concurrently developing *Pageant*. They, too, were not so seemingly different in their functions, even though one was merely an immaterial slice of light, the other a fully clothed parody of a cultural phenomenon, one formless, the other highly articulated, one nature, the other culture. Even though *Light On* got lost in General Idea's history, subsumed within the successes of subsequent *Pageants*, its mirror thematics was not a phase the artists moved beyond. It was no mere mirror phase but the modus operandi of all that followed, including the *Pageant*'s camp posturing. Camp, too, was a mirror function.

Or at least analogous to it. Camp's devaluing and revaluing likewise proceeded by transfer and displacement, by reflecting one "scene" in another: the art system in a beauty pageant, for instance, or vice versa. Its methods similarly could be abstracted into reversible processes. Camp operated by elevating something degraded at the same time that it degraded something elevated. Seen differently in a cultural context, the transfer method fundamentally was degrading and destructive. Even camp's lip flap was a mirror's reflection, a lip-syncing plagiarism. Speaking in tongues was ventriloquial, its voices thrown from elsewhere. Nothing was said here, at least, nothing by mouth. It was only the mirror that was *articulating*. The high-and-low of devaluation and the in-and-out of theft equally were mirror effects.

We shouldn't get too caught up in the *content* of reflection or displacement: in the parody of beauty pageants as critique of the art system, for instance. By analogy with *Light On*, perhaps reflected content only opened a void.[8] Was the *Pageant* a model to critique the art system, or was its mirror function simply to open a gap in order to insinuate other content into its borderline situations? Insinuation tested the tolerance of any particular system. But there were many available formats, after all. Furthermore, content was no finalizing replacement, only a temporary flip flop. But any time a mirror was employed it not only opened a gap, it changed something: transfer was transmutation as well. No mere mirror reversal, transmutation was contaminating at the same time. Contamination could not be disavowed, as when Dennis Young, curator of the 1969 Art Gallery of Ontario exhibition *New Alchemy: Elements, Systems, Forces*—in which General Idea twice insinuated themselves uninvited—felt it necessary to state in the first sentence of his catalogue essay that "It should be made clear that the artists in this exhibition were chosen because they make aesthetic 'transmutations,' and not because they have an interest in hermetic lore."[9] General Idea would beg to differ. Transmutation poisoned meaning.[10]

As means to an end, mirror transmutation was not merely destructive. It was constitutive as well. We know that General Idea's whole system was dependent on it: The erection of the *Pavillion* was a mirror effect. Such was admitted, admitting much more besides, when in 2005 AA Bronson reflected on the importance of the American artist Robert Smithson on their work:

> Here is another of the many versions of our origins: ... It was at this time [1969] that the fateful issue of *Artforum* containing the article by Robert Smithson ["Incidents of Mirror Travel in the Yucatan," September 1969] appeared in our living room; it would be passed among us endlessly over the next few years and eventually became the beginning of the Art Metropole Collection. I think of it as the first item, which began an avalanche of collecting, which became in turn Art Metropole itself. Robert's essay produced the seeds of our elaborate and invented universe: the entire superstructure of Miss General Idea, the Pageant, Pavillion, and all of that. It also had a direct influence on the many mirror projects of the early years, *Light On* (1970–71) most obviously.
>
> I think it was the collision of the poetic, even mystical, and the conceptual in Smithson's vision that especially inspired us—that, and the fact that making art was placed in the service of a vision and not itself the primary principle.[11]

If ever words were mirrors mirroring mirrors, we could get lost in this quotation, as did readers in Smithson's article. Not that Bronson hid anything: he clearly expressed Smithson's influence on General Idea's *entire* superstructure as well as on individual works such as *Light On*. What was unspoken was the mirror effect of Bronson's reflection, the effect Smithson's visionary mirror writings had on the ungrounding of art discourse in general, which was just as much the effecting of General Idea's aesthetic superstructure in particular. We should take General Idea seriously when in 1972 they wrote, "We began as a mirror of sorts." They always were, right to the end. But they were more than a mirror to a scene, as they were here referring to *FILE*'s "way of looking at the scene and oneself within it."[12] The mirror was all, all there was: ungrounding *and* superstructure at once. A mirror effect could be the *whole* apparatus of art. In fact, according to Smithson, it was equivalent to art: "[art] flourishes on discrepancy. It sustains itself not on differentiation but dedifferentiation, not on creation but decreation, not on nature but denaturalization, etc."[13] The mirror was no mere reflection.

In the end, it was not so much Smithson's works—with the exception of his mirror displacements—that were the major influence on General Idea as much as his writing. "Incidents of Mirror Travel in the Yucatan" recorded Smithson's trip to the Yucatan where he successively arranged mirrors in various sites, photographing and then dismantling them before moving on. As such, this sounds like any other conceptual practice of the time, including *Light On*. Yet, the article was not so much a documentary record of making as much as it was a testimony to dismantling—to the *ungrounding*, moreover, of conceptual and aesthetic systems. The article itself was part of this decomposing dedifferentiation. Smithson said of the Fourth Mirror Displacement that "reflections abolished the supports, and now words abolish the reflections."[14] Displacements in the field were repeated by like disorientation later in text. Writing, too, was a dissolving

PABLUM FOR THE PABLUM EATERS

A METHOD OF INVASION

Myth is the past brought into the present, ritualized and enacted that the past may be created by the present, that we may be masters of our own culture. History is the past made ruler by the present, endowed with properties of cause and effect that is control that relinquish our need to responsibility for our self and our own. We only work here.

In myth it is all very clear that everything must be accounted for. One starts with a vision and names the parts. One structures a cosmology through description. One does not move beyond the image, nor beyond the image of the image.

It is clear that myth and art are closely related: they both miniaturize. They make reality readily available. They establish the unfathomable in fathomable terms. They classify the known, the unknown.

It is clear that a conceptual artist miniaturizes in a certain way: he begins with the parts and reveals the structure. Very often conceptual artists are starting with the parts and revealing structure. Myth does the opposite: myth starts with the structure and names the parts, miniaturizes from the other end. Image Bank starts with the structure and names the parts. So we are calling Image Bank mythical artists, and along with a few others that is what they are. It is important to see that Image Bank knows they are mythical artists. As it puts them outside of the History/Cause & Effect continuum it allows them to play with it and they do.

The thrust of Image Bank is two-pronged: on the one hand they are concerned with establishing a culture that relates to official culture as a virus does to an organism. Working on the subliminal they are effectively lacing our worn-out operational methods (all history-oriented) with alternate methods which manage to solve the past-present-future time confusion and place us back at the centre of our universe on an equal footing with Mere Nature. On the other hand they are seeing acting promoting the rapid descension *the lowering into the bottomless cone* the movement towards the bottom of the tree the need for the base the low life for the shower of piss eliminating art to the roots. Aware of nova explosion they work like criminals on the subliminal erecting mirrors cutting wordlines shifting linguals. They are renegades of the old order updated, culture-criminals. They do not make news because they have the sense to wait for history. Meanwhile they are dissolving history in their footsteps. This is very important. This is art on a macro-scale, a global subversion of the Art Establishment, not by politics or power tactics but by anticipation of futures and a realization that only habit gains control, and the entrance to a person's mind to a network culture lies through habit.

...LOWERING INTO THE BOTTOMLESS CONE

The art junkies habit is founded on image. *Image is virus.* The image carries its own realities within it, harbouring subliminal connections in its interstices in a manner that defies concepts to gain control or apply definition. The image gains territory, holds a foot in the door of art, leaving a space for ideas, defining contours negatively. This establishes the illusion of being able to see again, the illusion of a whole. This is miniaturization.

THE IMAGE GAINS TERRITORY

History and science have enlarged the world to the point where it is no longer viable as conceptual entity. On the other hand they have developed tools for the collapse of whole systems, such as video time-lapse studies or microfiche retrieval systems. (See page 43)

It is the function of myth and of art to re-establish correspondences and the sense of the possibility of correspondences that may allow the description of the Universe as a vision named now. We may no longer move beyond the image, nor beyond the image of the image.

Concerning the mechanics of vision it is necessary to see that a shift in realities is simply shifting seeing. It is necessary to realize the levels of vision, the split between naturalized and culturalized information and the manner in which culturized information may become ritualized as natural information to the point where it in turn may be absorbed by the cultural processes as raw material for further processing. The famous "Medium is the Message" is simply this, media inversion and the raising of vision to additive levels and complexities.

Image Bank moves within the arena of our affliction, of our inability to see, and re-establishes correspondences as an operational method of accounting for everything and banking on the future.

BUSINESS AS USUAL

Sometimes one is talking something happens and what one has said has the nature of a title. Famous sayings are this way. Nicknames are this way. Then a description becomes a name and the name contains the description. This is how a myth works. Myth is essentially the naming of parts. In this way it becomes clear what one is doing speaking and one does it. One realizes the myth.

Image Bank began in many ways with rubber stamps. Rubber stamps is one way our culture has of making words expressions, certainly it is an excellent way if one uses the stamps. Certainly one uses the stamps. Image Bank's collection of rubber stamps is a brief description of their cosmology. It is very clear that Image Bank began to function began to describe everything that was with rubber stamps. Rubber stamps are a habit. They are a method of invasion easily available to the subliminal intruder.

Rubber stamps arrived everywhere. The mailing scene is dense with a community of rubber stamps, cross-referencing ideas and descriptions. One might think that in order to view the Image Bank reality it is simply necessary to view the rubber stamps. This is impossible. The stamps are a system in motion, one never knows where the stamps are, where the use of the stamps is, certainly it is impossible to view a changing network of stamps over four continents. Nevertheless one views the stamps in process on letters, one always has a sense an illusion of the knowledge of the whole by reflection. Robert Cummings once tried to organize a show of rubber stamps. It was simply impossible.

Many people have commented on the proliferation of pseudonyms in Image Bank and the mailing network. This too is very simple. These names are recorded 'history', concerns and events recorded in names to provide contextual information. This is very similar to rubber stamps. Eventually the names proliferate in a manner that provides a system of referencing and cross-referencing of concerns and events within the system. In many ways much of what Image Bank is doing is providing initiating reinforcing a cross-referencing system of discrete items of description, the terms of a system of correspondences.

A FOOT IN THE DOOR OF ART

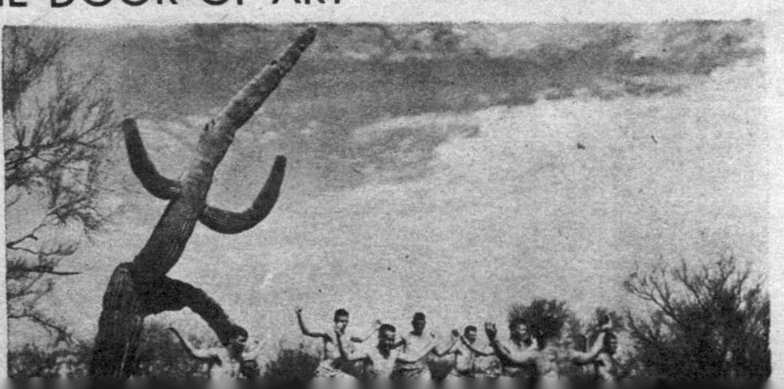

WE ART JUNKIES GOTTA GET OUR FIX

When a junky when any junky when we art junkies gotta get our fix we gotta make a connection we gotta get a fix we need our correspondences. We correspond we write letters we send you up trash through the mails we rubber stamp realities and pass them around for rewrite. That's the scene.

The logic of myth is the logic of connections. Image making room for words. Naming of partz, sensing the network working plugged into the subliminal. The key to this logic is the borderline situation, the neither one nor the other, camoflaged indifference, mirror mirror on the wall. Flip flop. Lip flap.

The logic of myth is the moving territory of words, cut word lines, shift linguals. The logic of myth is the sense of image upon image image overdose the network casuality affair with ideas raining in the corners. Take an argument and change sides: where does that leave you? out cold? Needa fix?

Correspondences are the key to the mythical universe, the cosmology of moving bodies, images in collision, classification by jointing.

Image Bank is primarily a structure for setting up, extending, stabilizing, and reinforcing correspondences, and literally so,. Correspondence through the mails. A collaborative vision arrived through the mails by rewrite.

When Image Bank set up the Image Bank Image Request Lists printed in every FILE they knew what they were doing. Your letters conquer time and space. Not only does Image Bank act as simply that — a bank for imagery — but the lists themselves act as pen-pal lists, a means of establishing communication and a means of ensuring the continuation of that communication through the building of image collections, the amplification of each participant's habit. The lists as a continuing device allow for change allow for rewrite allow each correspondent to fixate his fix refine the art redefine the art of his exchange. Quite often one begins with one request then one discovers one's habit, the image moves in and takes over, pretty soon you're deep in image trouble and you can't get out.

YOU'RE DEEP IN IMAGE TROUBLE ....

Image trouble is no trouble at all. Image overdose and suddenly snap you're out there broken through the borderline floating on the dead edge of nowhere with images diving in all directions, a sky full of claws and feathers.

Then there is jumbled jargon, lip flap, loose vowels. Cut word lines shift linguals. Take a bit of history and cut it up. Play it back for rewrite. Piss out the window, down the tree of life. It's locked up in the syntax. Cut word lines let image free. Many people knowing Image Bankers seeing Image Bankers hearing Image Bankers in Banker's drag say: lingo, can't make out the lingo: and this is true. This is very necessary. Soon the jumbled jargon soon the naming of partz soon it all comes together the images break loose the correspondences establish themselves, well this is associated with this and to say that is the same as saying something else. Soon the images break loose and then all hell.

Correspondences set out to describe everything there is to be described and eventually they do. Look at the Image Request Lists, everything must be accounted for. Functionally the lists mirror the network and have become a method of extending and altering that network in terms of a corresponding network of imagery.

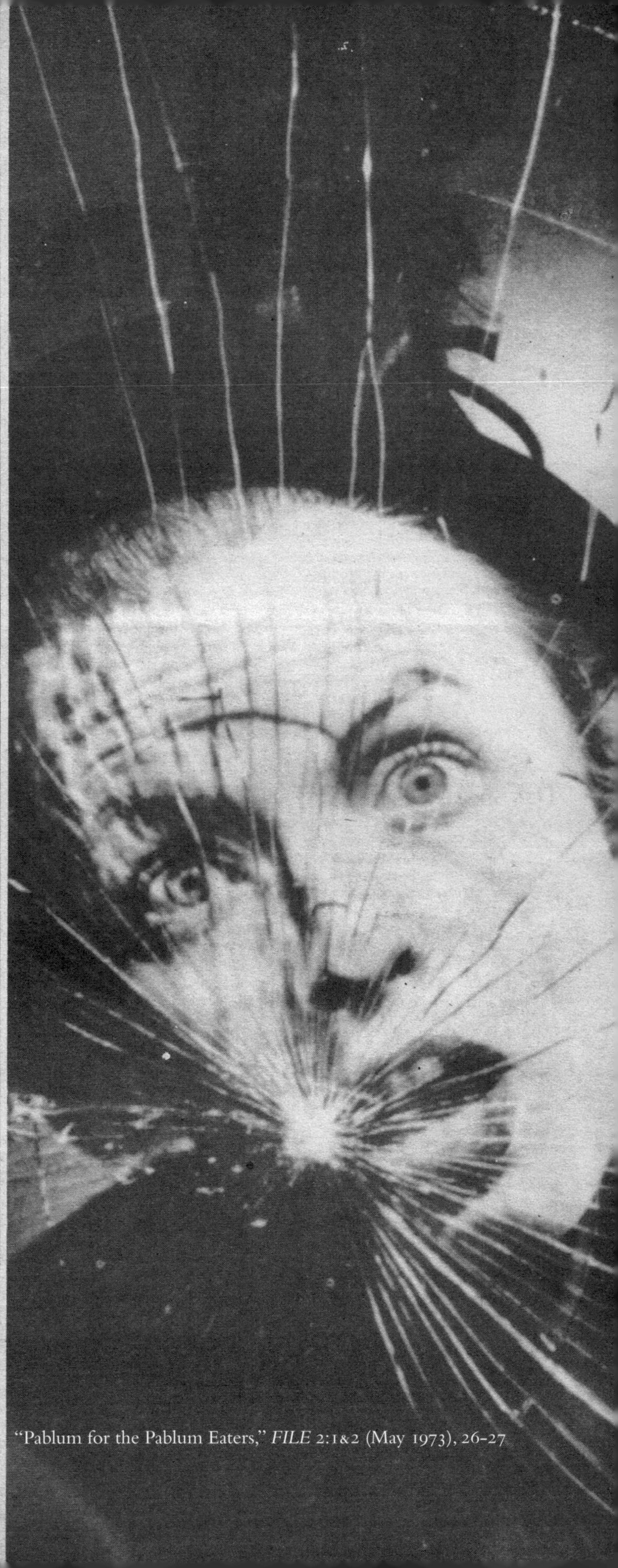

"Pablum for the Pablum Eaters," *FILE* 2:1&2 (May 1973), 26–27

mirror. What puzzled people was that Smithson's text was less documentary than dazzlingly fictional: it insinuated a fictionalizing discourse into conceptual art.

Here was a dismantling text with a liberating impact on General Idea. Dismantling was enabling at the same time. The *Pavillion* was one of its (de)generations. If the mirror was a fictional device, it was not just destructive; it was constructive, as well. It constituted the *Pavillion* in a fictive act. "Every artist owes his existence to such mirages," wrote Smithson. "The ponderous illusions of solidity, the non-existence of things, is what the artist takes for 'materials.' It is the absence of matter that weighs so heavy on him, causing him to evoke gravity." Smithson might have been anticipating the architectonics of *The 1984 Miss General Idea Pavillion* when he wrote this. And AA Bronson might have been thinking of Smithson's statement when a year later he wrote, "monumentalism is deadly, except as a joke."[15] In the early 1970s, though, General Idea were not yet at a building stage: the *Pavillion* was still to come, though already speculated.

Smithson sowed the seeds of General Idea's "elaborate and invented universe," seeded it with crystals that grew their own way. The dedifferentiating, denaturalizing displacements; the dismantling destructions; the decreating reversibilities of time; the ungrounding and perpetual instantiation of borderlines; all this and more would work their effects on General Idea at the basic level of their methodology as well as in their ensuing artworks. That AA Bronson spoke of their work in terms of a universe is significant. A universe was scalar. (In introducing the scalar into art—not only of spatial displacements but vast temporal scales—Smithson made it mythic.[16]) A universe was expansive and contractive at the same time; it was a system where the whole could be seen in its parts. It was a "collision of the poetic, even mystical, and the conceptual." Making art "in the service of a vision and not itself the primary principle," however, meant rejection of formalist endgame strategies in contemporary art. Conceptual art, that is. Or at least that practiced by the theoretical conceptual artists such as Joseph Kosuth, who maintained a formalist art that privileged the progressive path of history (i.e., American art). It merely made art out of art, an art that, at the same time, sustained the dominant system of art galleries and museums.[17]

"Pablum for the Pablum Eaters" was a manifesto *against* conceptual art as much as it was a manifesto *for* a mythic art. This is why the article suggested that General Idea were by implication "mythical artists," not conceptual artists. Simply put, conceptual art "begins with the parts and reveals the structure." On the contrary, "myth does the opposite: myth starts with the structure and names the parts."[18] For artists for whom reversibility was of primary importance, this inversion and consequent valuation in favour of mythical art, nonetheless, was fundamentally significant. Not only were General Idea for a mythic art, they were for an *irrational* art. The progressive rationalism of conceptual art repeated a rational historical model: a "History/Cause & Effect continuum." As Smithson earlier wrote, "The mirror displacement cannot be expressed in rational dimensions.... Mirrors thrive on surds, and generate incapacity. Reflections fall onto the mirrors without logic, and in so doing invalidate every rational assertion."[19] In the rational scheme of things, art was made out of furthering an already existent aspect (form, structure, process) of the art that came immediately before. In the irrational universe of the mythic system, where words were in motion and images were in collision, nothing was given beforehand. Mythic art had to be described and elaborated—and *created* in the process. Description was fictional rather than documentary in character.

"In myth it is all very clear that everything must be accounted for. One starts with a vision and names the parts. One structures a cosmology through description."[20] This was a more difficult task than making art out of previous art. Moreover, mythic art was a group affair rather than an individual activity. The "Pablum for the Pablum Eaters" article aimed to set out the methodology of correspondence art, which was a description of the Eternal Network at the same time. The universe was the two at once: practitioners and practices. It thus also included General Idea even though the article was seemingly about Image Bank alone. In setting out the methodology of correspondence art, by consequence, the article also formulated the initial operations of General Idea's system. But can we actually derive a methodology from the article's descriptions? Part of the problem is exactly what constitutes a "description" in such an article whose "broken syntax" was "jumbled jargon, lip flap, [and] loose vowels."

"In this article seeing art as a system of signs in motion as an archive and indicator and stabilizer of culture as a means of creating fetish objects as residence for the field of imagery defining a culture, seeing all this and more in many ways we have become aware of the necessity of developing methods of generating realizing stabilizing alternate myths alternate lifestyles."[21] Here is a statement of correspondence art's aims, which, moreover, was a description of General Idea's ongoing practice. At first, as a "'Collage or Perish' edifice," the still unconstructed *Pavillion* was one with the correspondence network, with correspondents contributing to its design and future erection. As AA Bronson wrote in his notebook, "The Miss General Idea building is not the real project. The real project lies elsewhere.... Miss G.I. Building as manifestation of network activity of artists in Canada today."[22] Yet, at a point, there was a turn in its function and we can say of the *Pavillion* what was said of *FILE* in its May 1973 editorial: "FILE, no longer mirroring a scene, mirrors the mirror." While the *Pavillion* thus became more self-referential, that is, referential to General Idea's own program, it nonetheless did not abandon the principles of the correspondence network.[23] We can thus substitute "*Pavillion*" for "Image Bank" in the following statement without any change in the sentence's meaning: "In many ways much of what Image Bank is doing is providing initiating reinforcing a cross-referencing system of discrete items of description, the terms of a system of correspondences."[24] Here is another description, one could say, but of what would become the "structure" (and appearance) of the *Pavillion*: the cross-referencing system constructs itself from its descriptions. The system *was* the *Pavillion*: its means and appearance. Yet the cross-referencing system was not the construction itself. The *Pavillion*'s correspondence, its appearance that is, was an end, not a method. General Idea's methodology was constructive-destructive. That is to say, it was collage.

General Idea's methodology began to be articulated in this article in terms of myth:

> The logic of myth is the logic of connections. Image making room for words.... The key to this logic is the borderline situation, the neither one nor the other, camouflaged indifference, mirror mirror on the wall. Flip flop. Lip flap. The logic of myth is the moving territory of words, cut word lines, shift linguals.... Correspondences are the key to the mythical universe, the cosmology of moving bodies, images in collision, classification by jointing.[25]

It turns out that, already collage, myth was methodology as well.

In "Pablum for the Pablum Eaters" and the following "General Idea's Borderline Cases" article, the artists elaborated their theory of collage. I won't say that they articulated a radical theory, because collage already is radical, but theirs was an alternative point of view on collage in that it implied that collage was a system in motion that never stabilized itself in any one relation of elements. Collage was a system of alternatives in constant flux. Or, in other words, collage created myth as cut-ups that were viral. Collage was pure flux, so already we see a methodological precedent, apart from any issue of content, for the reversibility of General Idea's system: from construction to destruction and vice versa and from high to low and vice versa. At this point, collage had no content other than its divisiveness: images in collision and cut word lines.

Images were in collision, sometimes with themselves, as if they were split by mirrors. Nothing was stable; every image was always in motion; even a single image was not identical to itself. Images were also split by words; images made room for words. But word lines—sentences, phrases—were cut, too: "It's locked up in the syntax. Cut words lines let image free." On the one hand, images made room for words; on the other hand, images were cut loose from words.[26]

Yet, collage led to correspondences. It *forced* correspondences more than it found them. If collage brought words and/or images together differently, their association or correspondence was not natural. Images made room for words, but words turned or perverted images. Words were devious; they deviated the image. Images making room for words and images cut free from words were not contradictory. One had to destroy a previous word line in order to erect another, which was used in turn to redirect and erect an image otherwise. Soon this rewriting of images would be the means by which the *Pavillion* was erected. The *Pavillion* was nothing but "a system of correspondences." If "correspondences [were] an operational method of accounting for everything," the *Pavillion*, too, was a mythic structure. It built itself through "classification by jointing." Jointing was its means of construction. As the article had described Image Bank, so the *Pavillion* was "primarily a structure for setting up, extending, stabilizing, and reinforcing correspondences, and literally so." As usual, we need to add a proviso, that in considering the *Pavillion* literally as a building, that is, as a stable structure, we have to agree when AA Bronson noted in a different context, "We have no room for enclosures, but only divisions."[27]

One might think that images making room for words alone would make the operation descriptive, as words now were dominant. The logic of myth, however, was twofold: on the one hand it was "image making room for words"; on the other hand, it was a "moving territory of words." If "one structures a cosmology through description," description would seem no more than what collage was: jointing. Description that came *after* jointing was the necessary after-product of a collage process of images in collision and cut word lines, but it was an illusion of what after all always was a system in motion. Description was more than adding words to an image as if a new captioning. Its elaboration was a means of classification: correspondence was description as classification by jointing. As alternate ways of organizing images, classification led to new knowledge; jointing led to the creation of new concepts.[28] Description realized the new by articulating concepts. Classification was knowledge by division. Divisive, collage was the basic methodology of General Idea's work.

Such was General Idea's theory of collage, a theory of correspondence that was both about the *relation* of images and texts and the *classification* of images. Theory was not put into practice, however, by the illustrations that accompanied the text to "Pablum for the Pablum Eaters." Admittedly, there was a correspondence within *sets* of images (on the one hand "piss pics" and on the other "future" images) but not between text and images. The artists carried out further research of their own in "General Idea's Borderline Cases." There was more to this article than just cases studies of Borderline situations; research was also a realization of collage practice. They were one and the same: borderline cases and collage.

As General Idea typically would begin to do, in the introduction to the article, they told us exactly, in so many words, what they were up to:

> We started this research from a little word and a little intuition. We had the situations but we needed a word to put our finger on it. The word or words "Borderline Case" was chosen because it got under our skin. We mixed the word and intuition and we stirred in the content. We began to realize as we began to realize in fragments. We realized in fragment collections and we collected all the collections of fragments together. It was collage or perish and we made the word collect the fragments and everything that would fit was. When we were dealing with words it was like dealing with cards. We were trying to break the bank. We fitted all the images to words between the start and the finish which was one to ten. The stations for cross referencing adapted from the decimal system.[29]

General Idea were telling us what they were doing in collecting images and texts. Were they also telling us, with *so* many words, that they were stretching the limits or tolerance of an image bank? Were they trying "to break the bank" with words? What they weren't telling us in the introduction, typically, was that they were *doing* it with words at the same time as they were *telling* it.

It seems that words always came first:

> So we had the word, the almighty word, and we filled in the blanks in the meantime with images. Images overloaded the words and the words continued to pyramid. In other words, the words attempted to divide and conquer or multiply. It all got very wordy and the only relief was that a picture was worth a thousand words. Wordy indulgence was the style rather than mum's the word. ... More fuel to the fire as we split the levels down the centre with cutting remarks or nouns. The words were being content and the images remained holding their own. Catch all was a catch all phrase we use. Catch all the images in the word net and concentrate on the ones that got away.[30]

"Catch all" phrases basically were clichés, collected together here in fragments just as images were. Just as the images that followed were ready-made, so were the phrases that now captioned them. "Description" proceeded additively, made from such pre-processed material. Phrases were repeated with variations that carried the text along, linking one sentence to the next, one cliché to another. This was an *accretive* method. Its variational redundancy constructed a whole.[31]

IMITATION OF LIFE (MIMICRY)

Its only natural to try to be part of our vision,
our culture. Like chameleons at odds trying to be part
of it all. Like letting our one hand know what the
other is about. When one body is imitating one body
lying down its life imitating life. This act of bodies
rubbing is merely a shadow of things to come. Was
meeting face to face the mother of invention of the
looking glass? Was this prop-osal to end our singleness?
There's safety in numbers and two can have a mind
of its own. Our two hands applauded the engagement
and came out dueling. In the crack of dawn a narcissus
is blooming. All together now, one two,
one two, one two.

2

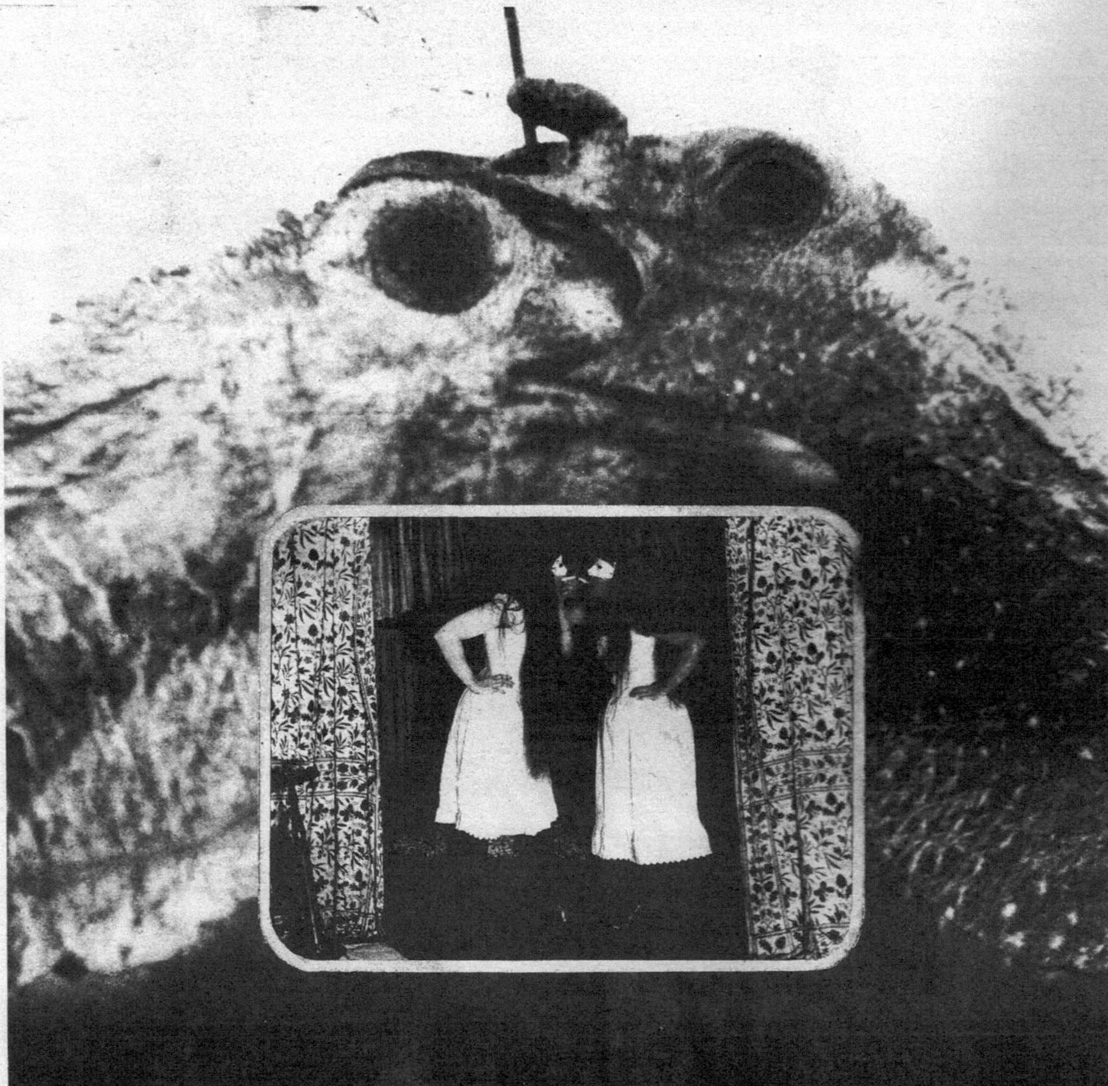

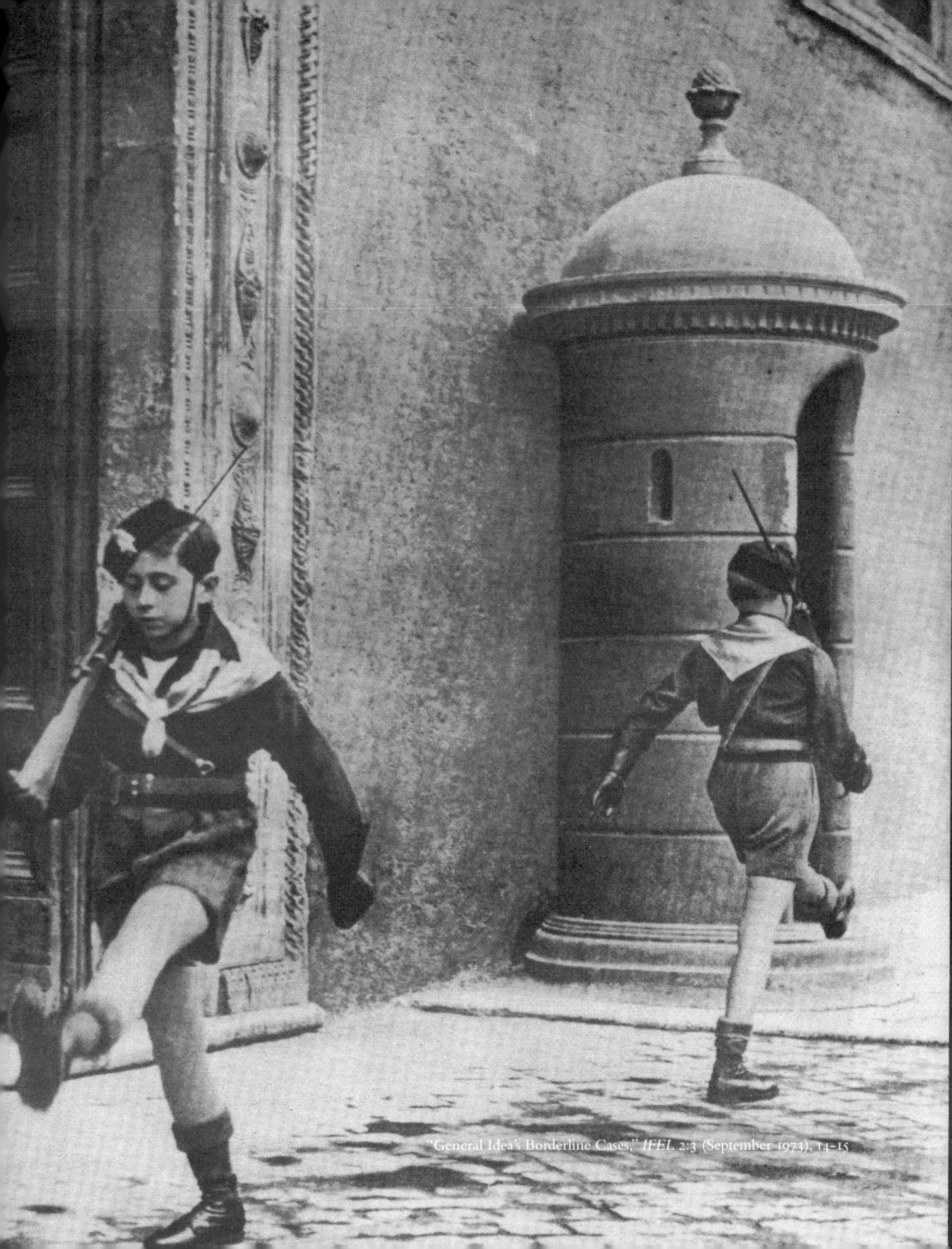

"General Idea's Borderline Cases," *IFEL* 2:3 (September 1973), 14–15

SELF CONSCIOUS

3

Now that we've got our distance we look back over our shoulders. Could this be our skin? Still waters reflect our eyes reflecting still waters running deep. Lets keep this on the surface. The surface of the silvered glass narcissus. Could this be our connection? Score one for us and chalk it up to experienced. Driving ~~the~~ wedge down deep through the center and splitting the images in halves. There is two of us to contend with now. Two heads are better than one but its really just one more mouth to feed on. Casting our image in the mirror revealed a cast of two. Our very own dialogue to talk to ourselves. We're not the one we used to be.

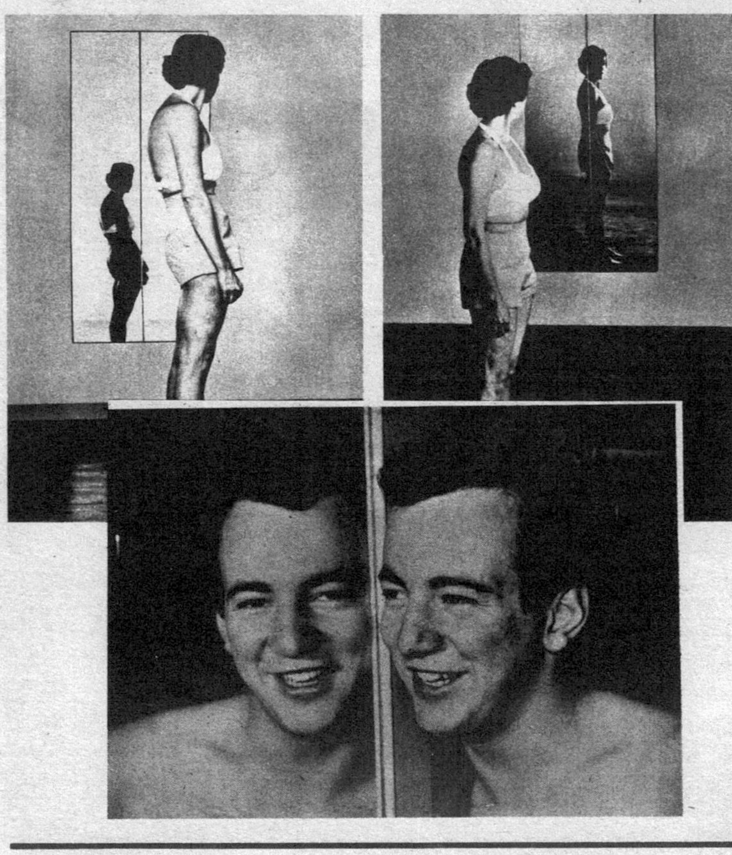

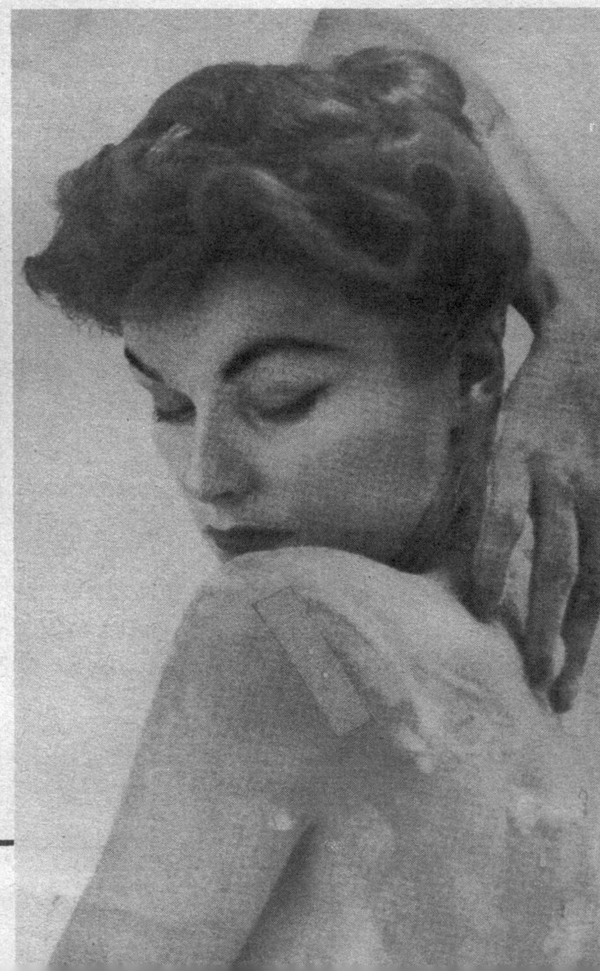

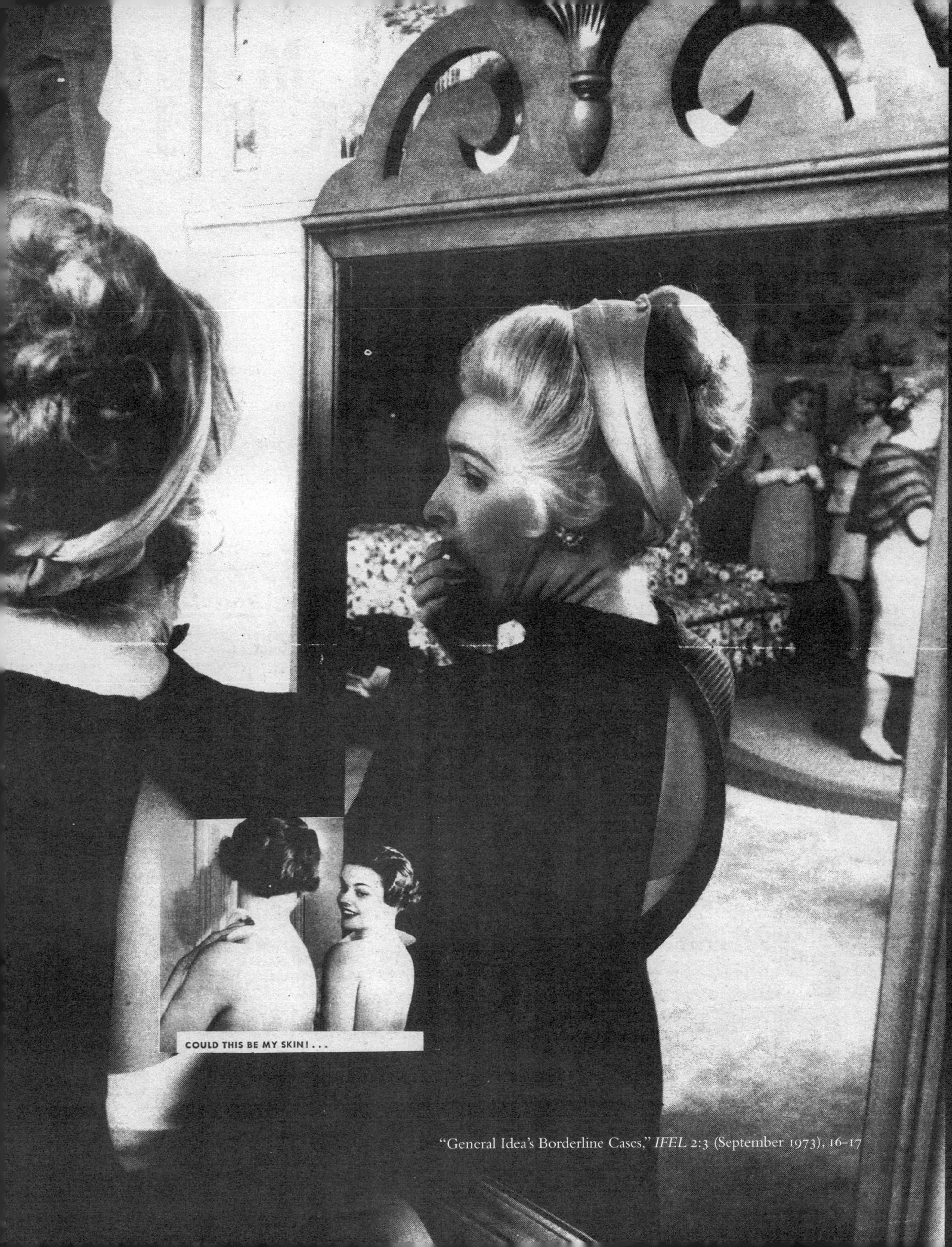

"General Idea's Borderline Cases," *IFEL* 2:3 (September 1973), 16–17

The article was an assembly of phrases ordered by a numeric framework: "We are only following order," the artists concluded their introduction, varying one of their common phrases "We are only following orders." The article had a beginning, middle, and end—but not necessarily in that order, since the beginning was only a "starting at the beginning and working back"; and the conclusion was "the ending of the beginning of the story" but that also said that "the story is all over right in the middle"; whereas the middle was a stepping "back in the past and forward in the future." The article was recursive, yet divided—divided not just in the middle, but also at every point. General Idea concluded the article with the statement: "We are only for the time and space available to undifferentiate the borderline." This statement must be a "camouflaged indifference," as they said elsewhere of the logic of myth, because the artists instituted borderlines everywhere in this article.

It was precisely in the middle that we were told "the Great Divide was words." Words were "cutting remarks" that could "divide and conquer or multiply." Words and mirrors were equivalent in this regard. The mirror was not only reflective; it was divisive. Both mirrors and words could divide and multiply; replication was predicated on division. Everything, in fact, derived from division: more words, creating contents, stories, images, even identities in turn. Division was viral.

There is an obvious division in the article, and not just its mid-point, which equivocates between the two halves while separating them. That is, it separated reflective behaviour or mimicry, based on the concept of the mirror, from the notion of boundary, based on the concept of division. In his notebook, Felix Partz reserved "division" for the second set of cases but I believe that the mirror was the fundamental cause of division.[32] Or, at least, that it was foundational to General Idea's system—with the recognition that mirror divisions, of course, actually were anti-foundational, that is to say undifferentiating. The borderline was a propagator of concepts.

In this respect three successive case studies interest us. Whether consciously planned or not, they logically led from mimicry to self-consciousness to mockery in such a way that showed the *constitutive* operations of division. First was case study number two, "Imitation of Life (Mimicry)," where defensive mimicry not only secured life but replicated it: two, where there was once one. Then in case study number three, "Self Conscious," looking over one's shoulder in a mirror not only made one self-conscious but this doubling operation instituted consciousness.[33] Only with this self-conscious division into two could case study number four, "Graven Imagery (Mockery)," lead to a mocking performance ("We're getting our acts together to act out our fantasies in person on our persons") that divided its *own* subject in camp display. Consequently, self-division became a premise for infinite replication, an artificiality that opposed itself to nature and its natural propagation.

Division was formative of split roles that were played out on the line between nature and culture—that is to say as camouflaged Glamour. Glamour was either display or defense achieved through equivalent devices of mimicry: meant for seductive capture or as defense from devouring. (Was mimicry a cultural adaptation by nature?) Significantly, the division between nature and culture was also a borderline between life and death. Assuming roles instituted the division between nature and culture—or ritualized it: as death in life or life in death. Mimicry was a death mask held up to a devouring gaze. Hence Glamour's appeal—although it could lead to a self-devouring cannibalism by an identical other (as in case study number two's nature/culture images of mutual consumption).

Only by the division of the self could the self in turn be manipulated, that is to say, self-manipulated as performance. Singly and collectively: for instance in *Manipulating the Self* (1970–71). Like many of General Idea's works of the period, *Manipulating the Self* began as a mail project that solicited ordained poses which were then published, first as a pamphlet then as a print. The soliciting text read:

> The head is separate; the hand is separate. Body and mind are separate. The hand is a mirror for the mind—wrap your arm over your head, lodging your elbow behind and grabbing your chin with your hand. The act is now complete. Held, you are holding. You are object and subject, viewed and voyeur.[34]

Manipulating the Self preceded the Borderline Cases article but itself was a primary case that would underscore future work. The unifying gesture of manipulation was a coupling that was an event. Its *performance* was a division of a subject that could take itself as an object and perform both to itself and others. The convoluted pose of its mirroring self-enclosure was a framework or frame of reference where one was both viewed and voyeur, split between the two—or put into perspective by the split between two. In this borderline situation, was a subject actually operative? Or did the borderline situation instead obviate an "ultimate subject"? Was individual identity only a linguistic habit, the consequence of subject-predicate propositions, which had to be undone by (collage) coupling, replaced by the coupling of viewed and voyeur as an event?

This was the point of view of John Brockman, an author of some influence—combined, of course, with Smithson, Burroughs, Debord, Lévi-Strauss, McLuhan, *et al*—on this early period of work in terms of adopted language and concepts, particularly Brockman's ambiguously titled book, *37*. For instance, we recognize Brockman in the occasional use of the terms or phrases, although they in turn often came from others, "no man's land," "description," "rotted names," "waste," "no-thing," indeed also of "plagiarism."[35] (The use of another author's words was nothing to hide as Brockman advocated plagiarism as "Intellectual Cannibalism.") We recognize his influence in "Pablum for the Pablum Eaters" in the notion of the negation of history and the critique of progress and hierarchy; of no beginnings and no endings of a timeless present; of alternatives as "invention by negation"; on contradiction, interchangeability and the "undifferentiating of activity," leading to "perpetual flux"; and in "description" as a created "universe" or coupling event.[36] Brockman was behind *FILE*'s first editorial when it said "the telling destroys the actuality"; September 1973's "Borderline Cases" Editorial when it suggested, on the one hand, "create a universe" and, on the other hand, "Consider the coupling of viewed and voyeur, subject and object posed as event"; and "Are You Truly Invisible?" where he was now named: "You've got *no-thing* to wear to John Brockman's party. Oh dear! What could the matter be when there's no matter to be?"

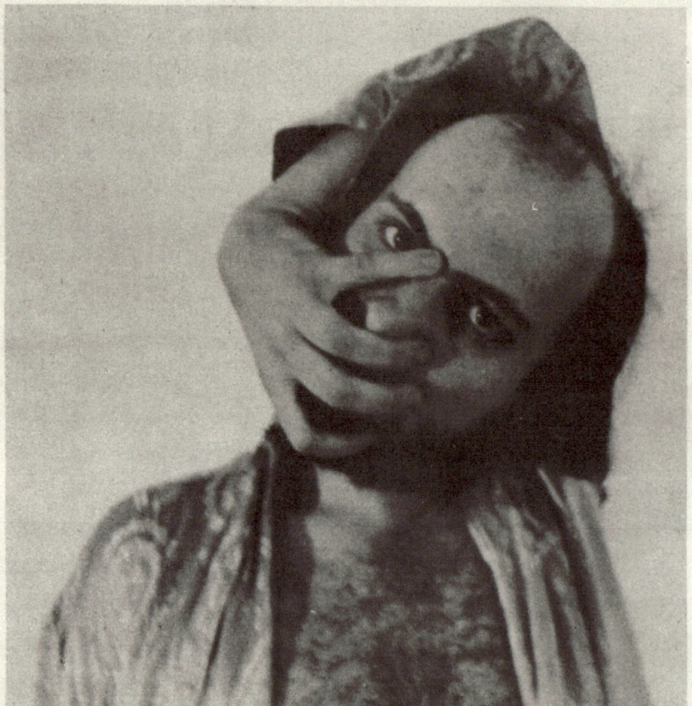

MANIPULATING THE SELF
(Phase 1 - A Borderline Case)

The head is separate; the hand is separate. Body and mind are separate.

The hand is a mirror for the mind - wrap your arm over your head, lodging your elbow behind and grabbing your chin with your hand. The act is now complete. Held, you are holding. You are object and subject, viewed and voyeur.

Please send photos of yourself in this position to General Idea, 87 Yonge St., Toronto, Canada. Fill out and enclose this form and further information will be forwarded to you.

NAME ____________________

ADDRESS ____________________

DATE ____________________

Manipulating the Self (Phase 1 – A Borderline Case), 1970–71

Brockman's philosophy was congruent with a collage ethos of perpetual cut-up. "*Description is the thing*: negation of the idealized 'real world,' the 'thing' world, the 'people' world. Experiments are the only elements which really count. *Coupling of observer-observed* (an event): *the matter of fact.*"[37] Here was a systematic statement of General Idea's principles that need not be translated into the language of "Pablum for the Pablum Eaters" since it already underscored its concepts as well as provided terminology. As in collage, where description *was* collage and vice versa, description here was destructive of the given world. Through negation, it created another universe: "The 'universe': a *description*."[38] If description is the thing, and not another thing itself that is described, nothing ("no-thing") comes before it. Description was neither a definition of a pre-existent object nor a naming that stood for its concept or meaning. Naming was coupling.[39] It was a performance. Brockman asked, "*What comes before performance?*"[40] Nothing, *no-thing*, he replied. Performance created its own reality in a moment of coupling, as an event. In what was only "the coupling (an event) of observer-observed system," notably both subject and object were lacking.[41] *Coupling* brought reality into "existence." Description, coupling, and performance were all the same.

Brockman's philosophical system pertained to General Idea's own in several key respects. In General Idea's system in flux, collage was a coupling that created a universe. Collage was not a *product* but only the process of coupling. It was an event, a performance that nothing preceded. The outcome was invented in the moment of utterance: performance and description at once. General Idea's system was not just a theory of collage but of performance as well. Right from the start. And later, the *Pavillion*, we know, was still only a performative utterance—in spite of what objects, images, or installations composed it. Yet collage coupling happened without a controlling subject. Both subject and object were absent in collage. In fact, according to Brockman, the "unitless unity" of the observer-observed coupling was "the negation of 'one'."[42] Not only a negation of the individual subject, General Idea's collage couplings were always a division of one into two. General Idea modified Brockman's coupling concept by dividing it again. In their universe, the "observer-observed system" was a *split* system.[43] Done away by the observational system, the obviated subject-object was replaced by a coupling of "viewed and voyeur." It was the nature of this coupling to be split, to have a perspective on itself, and to have the word lines and sightlines that comprised it continually aligned and disarranged.

While it quietly underlay the "Pablum for the Pablum Eaters" article, Brockman's influence was particularly pronounced in General Idea's faux-rejected May 1972 *artscanada* "article."[44] This article was a collage of phrases and concepts of Brockman, Burroughs, and Smithson, all configured into a borderline case. Between Brockman and Smithson, mirrors mirrored mirrors, though Brockman's "no mirrors" seemed to oppose Smithson's own, but as no "either or" confrontation.[45] Rather, both authors agreed on the destruction of the real in favour of invented description. Similarly, Brockman and Burroughs came to consensus on the linguistic fallacy of "being" and identity. For Burroughs it was the word, the definite article "the," that was the root of the problem: "What scared you all into time? Into body? Into shit? I will tell you: '*the word*.' Alien word '*the*'." For Brockman, it was the noun itself that was the source of confusion. The noun, of course, implied the definite article: "Where was it one first heard of the truth? The the." He counseled, instead, "Do not use the rotted names."[46]

It all came down to words. Language was a battleground. It was a field divided against itself.

It is no surprise then that the noun was the privileged subject of this article, which began precipitately:

> "Enter the noun[1], posed on stiletto heels[2] and bound in the latest fantasy[3]. Object fetishism is implicit in the English language, where even verbs are made nouns[4]."

Then it hurriedly concluded after only one more sentence. This odd article was a paradox or puzzle of the type referred to in its notes:[47] the notes expanded the single paragraph into a full page, and had their own subservient footnotes. There is an argument behind this posed walk-on, two in fact, the first supporting the second. The first argument worked through the notes and pieced together various concepts from Brockman. Consider this quotation from note four its first proposition: "Held, you are holding. Subject is object. The self vanishes in the coupling, which is body and mind. What can you do when there is no you to do it?" Consider this statement from note three the second proposition: "In the generalization lies the configuration, the essential coupling that eliminates the noun."[48] If coupling eliminates the noun and the self vanishes in the coupling, then, logically, "subject" and "noun" are equivalent in status. A noun implies a subject and a subject implies a noun. Therein lies the problem.

The problem is that the noun establishes an object world (the reality of things) and a subject at the same time (an unchanging observer of static objects). But according to Brockman, subject and object are only "noun'd."[49] In an observational world in flux, doing away with nouns undid both subject and object. "*No nouns*: the notion of an actual entity as the unchanging subject of change is completely abandoned."[50] The persistent problem was that the propositional structure of language objectified reality and stabilized subjects. Subject and object "noun'd": General Idea would say this was the fixating loop of a fetish.

Dependent on the first argument that suffices as its notes, the second argument actually was the lone paragraph elevated above those supporting notes. When the article started "enter the noun[1], posed on stiletto heels[2] and bound in the latest fantasy[3]," was this not Glamour entering the scene, as the "Glamour" issue of *FILE* later would confirm?[51] Since "object fetishism is implicit in the English language, where even verbs are made nouns," the article was arguing that, beneath its hardened appearance, Glamour really was a *verb* that had been tricked into being a noun. It tricked us in turn. Glamour was only the result of fetishism implicit to language. This concept of the fetish links Glamour to art in the final statement as if concluding the argument: "'Glamour and Art merge when the artist becomes the angst performer[5], dead but famous[6]; to the collector the spoils[7].'" The fetish is Glamour's globalizing concept, its logic and essence.

In the notes, art is pictured as a fetish fixated on by a "top heavy" system of "art junkies," comprised of an "art racket" of museums, collectors, and critics who were dependent on artists for their art fix yet an enemy to them. In response, in the fictional response of this article, the artist "flips the weapon inside out. It dissolves into other dimensions. Conceptual art is a disappearing act, absorbing the object in the negation of the object, remembering propositions, altering forces, dissolving structures into memories, waste and residue." In this scenario,

(**Advertisement**)

"Enter the noun[1], posed on stiletto heels[2] and bound in the latest fantasy[3]. Object fetishism is implicit in the English language, where even verbs are made nouns[4]. Glamour and Art merge when the artist becomes the angst performer[5], dead but famous[6]; to the collector the spoils[7]."

A.A. Bronson

NOTES

(1) G is the seventh letter & the first. In the seventh position, which represents the seventh seal of the Apocalypse, we find the Conquerer, who has answered the Sphinx. The Conquerer is precisely this: Negentropy.

(2) Entropy is answered. Man is the great anti-entropy of nature[1]. He proposes a reality. He mirrors the fabric of the reality he proposes. He is a mirror searching for its own reflection[2].

(3) Negentropy is a matter

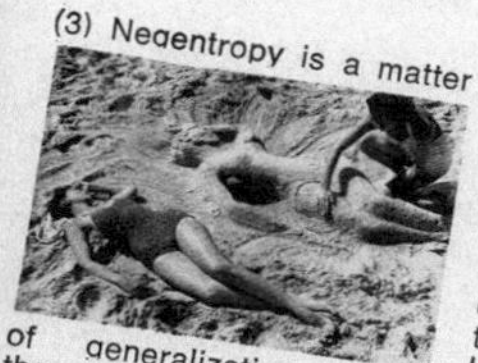

of generalizations. The thought is the significant proposition[3]. A generalization is a way of seeing, a way of becoming. In the generalization lies the configuration, the essential coupling that eliminates the noun. We move within generalizations; we carry them like shells upon our body. We barter with them; we make them the construct; we live within them as a universe. In the generalization lies the reality. It is our mirror, an ongoing abstraction, supposedly immune to the ravages of time. In this mirror we find fleeting images — immeasurable, unknowable[4]. The true fiction eradicates the false reality; the memory of what is not replaces the amnesia of what is. We reconstruct our inability to see. We travel the unfathomable[5], wrapped in ambiguities.

(4) Either or. There are no mirrors[6]. We have met the enemy and they are us[7]. Borderline Cases: in mirrors we meet the enemy. There are no mirrors. The skin pops open under the scalpel's action; the seven layers of the epidermis flutter past the blade with the faint sound of shuffled cards. Your cards are shuffled and dealt, face downwards on the points of Solomon's Seal, seventh in the centre. Overturned, like stones, they reveal the Conquerer, he who has led captivity captive. Water is broken; windows are broken; the hearth is crossed. Borderline Cases are seen in mirrors and on maps. We find them in mimicry, in the only co-existence of convex/concave, inside/outside, the coupling of the tide and the shore. Borderline Cases are propositional — they are implicit situations, the husking of context from object, finding the needle in the eye. There is a family resemblance, a certain gestalt. There are no mirrors. They exist in the space between the knowing and the knowing of the knowing. Held, you are holding[8]. Subject is object. The self vanishes in the coupling, which is body and mind. What can you do when there is no you to do it? You are a metaphor and they are lies[9].

(5) Reality hypes invariably feature the noun, posed on stiletto heels and bound in the latest fantasy[10]. This is the object of our desire. We

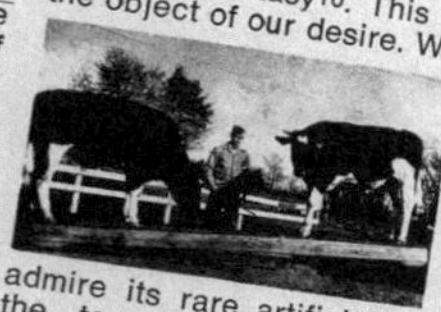

admire its rare artificiality, the terse convolution of pose and gesture[11]. Object fetishism is basicly linguistic: even verbs are made nouns. Object fetishism is the ultimate reality con, the mortality game, the art market, the glamour girl hype. Glamour and art merge when the artist becomes the angst performer, dead but famous; to the collector the spoils[12]. Art is the ultimate object, the most exclusive fetish, the final death spasm. Conspicuous consumption is rampant. The safes are double locked. The prices are rising in blue chip art[13]. The addict needs his fix; he is fixated. The artist, provides the perceptual kicks[14], the "sham space" to move and groove, the excrement of thought and language[15], excites the art junkies to delusions of grandeur. They build museums, open schools, publish books, write critiques, monopolize the art racket in a top-heavy, gonna-tumble-fast skyscraper built of the fabric of their compulsion. History slips through their fingers. Definitions crumble. Names rot. Do not use the rotted names[16]. What scared you all into time? Into body? Into shit? I will tell you: "the word". Alien word "the".[17]

(6) Art is the ultimate object. The artist is the marksman's valet, pitching clay plates for targets. The artist is omitted from the art activity. . .he does not take part in the conceptual engagement of the art proposition[18]. The artist steps forward. He seizes the gun. He shatters the pidgeons. With a single flick of the wrist he flips the weapon inside out. It dissolves into other dimensions. Conceptual art is a disappearing act, absorbing the object in the negation of the object, remembering propositions, altering forces, dissolving structures into memories, waste and residue. History is what you make it. The true fiction eradicates the false reality. We reconstruct our inability to see[19].

(7) Light issues from dark. Genesis and the Pharoah's dream. The seven colours, which are the spectrum and the scale by which we see, issue from the white light. We turn the light here, there, and everywhere and the limits of thought recede before it[20]. The Generative Idea: the relation, the configuration, the essential coupling. The limits of the Generative Idea are marked

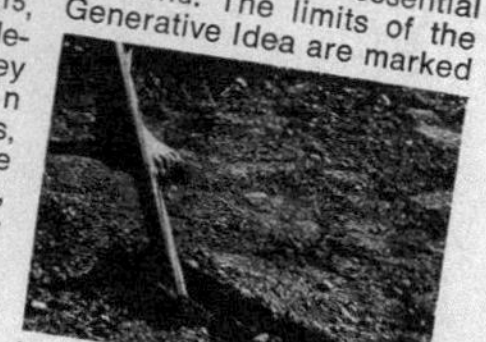

by paradoxes, puzzles[21]. Nothing is true; everything is permitted — Last Words Hassan-i-Sabbah. He projected colour in vast reflectors screens concentrating blue sky red sun green grass and the city dissolved in light. . .[22]

FOOTNOTES

1. Buckminster Fuller, **Utopia or Oblivion,** Bantam Books, 1969.
2. Robert Smithson, **Incidents of Mirror-Travel in the Yucatan,** Art Forum, September, 1969.
3. Ludwig Wittgenstein, **Tractatus Logico Philosophicus,** Kegan Paul Trench Trubner & Co., 1947.
4. Robert Smithson, **op.cit.**
5. Robert Smithson, **op.cit.**
6. John Brockman, **37**, Holt Rinehart Winston, 1970.
7. Walt Kelly, **Pogo.**
8. John Brockman, **op.cit.**
9. John Brockman, **op.cit.**
10. A.A. Bronson, **The 1971 Miss General Idea Pageant**, Artscanada, November. 1971.
11. **Ibid.**
12. **Ibid.**
13. Jack Burnham, **Alice's Head,** Artforum, February, 1970.
14. Joseph Kosuth, **Recorded Activities**, Moore College of Art, 1970.
15. Robert Smithson, **op.cit.**
16. John Brockman, **op.cit.**
17. William Burroughs, **Dead Fingers Talk**, Tandem Books Ltd., 1966.
18. Joseph Kosuth, **op.cit.**
19. Robert Smithson, **op.cit.**
20. Susanne K. Langer, **Philosophy in a New Key**, The New Amerian Library, 1951.
21. **Ibid.**
22. William Burroughs, **op.cit.**

REJECTED BY ARTSCANADA, MAY, 1972.

FILE 1:2&3 (May/June 1972), inside back cover

instead of creating more fetish objects, artists dissolved reified structures. Language was the main weapon of this altering and destructive operation. The "global subversion of the Art Establishment," as the "Pablum" article put it, was dependent on language's negation, language negating itself by undoing its fetish character through the cut-up operations of collage. "Cut word lines shift linguals."

Felix Partz had a name for this rejection of the noun: "object hatred," he called it in a 1972 notebook entry. So it would be, in spite of appearances, that actions, not reified objects or fetish commodities, were to comprise General Idea's system. Actions were verbs. So too, in reality, were *Light On* and the Borderline works: they were operations, not objects; verbs, not nouns. Similarly, *General Idea* was not a name, not a noun, that is. It, too, was a verb. It was an operation without an operator, an activity with no "ultimate subject."[52] General Idea was a purely verbal operation.

Undoing the fetish character of Glamour was an implicit act of critique. Although not spelled out, it was a "dissolving" verbal act. Of course, this critique was all too well disguised in the *Pageant*'s elevation of Glamour, which only seemed to harden Glamour's fetish character. Glamour itself was the ultimate disguise, at least as manipulated by General Idea; as we know, Glamour's principle theft was to disguise an act as an object. The *Pageant*'s critique of the fetish took place through the fetish itself by means of mimicking its process of elevation. The *Pageant* was nothing but the fetish's elevation and display. But the fetish was raised up only in order to be lowered again. It was glorified only in order to be sullied. Was critique of the fetish the *Pageant*'s real purpose? Were General Idea hard-core Marxist theoreticians in disguise after all?

Unstated in their "pageant of camp parody" was the idea that something as trivial and obvious as Glamour performed or operated much like the commodity that Marxism had critiqued so effectively. After all, as a ritual fetish, the object of Glamour was a cultural commodity in disguise. An unconventional Marxist, the French Situationist Guy Debord, author of *The Society of the Spectacle*, was the unspoken influence on the artists here, his book in fact their "bible," when he wrote:

> In the essential movement of the spectacle, which consists of taking up all that existed in human activity *in a fluid state* so as to possess it in a congealed state as things which have become the exclusive value by their *formulation in negative* of lived value, we recognize our old enemy, *the commodity*, who knows so well how to seem at first glance something trivial and obvious, while on the contrary it is so complex and so full of metaphysical subtleties.
>
> The spectacle presents itself simultaneously as all of society, as part of society, and as an *instrument of unification*. As a part of society it is specifically the sector which concentrates all gazing and all consciousness. Due to the very fact that this sector is *separate*, it is the common ground of the deceived gaze and of false consciousness, and the unification it achieves is nothing but an official language of generalized separation.[53]

The spectacle was the commodity writ large, unifying a culture while contradictorily creating divisions at the same time. "Separation is itself the unity of the world ... making the spectacle appear as its goal" (§ 7). A commodity fundamentally was a product of separation, as was a fetish. The critique of the commodity was really a continuation of nineteenth-century German philosophy's critique of the sacred, but in calling the commodity a fetish Marxism acknowledged its reliance on anthropology. The occulted fetish or, actually, "the totem becomes such only on condition that it first be set apart."[54] Setting apart was spectacle's hidden aim. "In the spectacle, one part of the world *represents itself* to the world and is superior to it. The spectacle is nothing more than the common language of this separation," Debord wrote (§ 29). *The 1984 Miss General Idea Pageant* reproduced this separation-as-elevation in a ritual that "concentrates all gazing and all consciousness." Here was its function. It was nothing but a vehicle of elevation. Its ritual, in which we actively participated, was "the common ground of the deceived gaze and false consciousness." Seemingly, there was nothing redeeming or critical about the *Pageant*.

Inhabiting the format of the beauty pageant meant speaking its language of separation. As Debord wrote, "when *analyzing* the spectacle one speaks, to some extent, the language of the spectacular itself in the sense that one moves through the methodological terrain of the very society which expresses itself in the spectacle" (§ 11). The difficulty in recognizing camp as critique is that in infiltrating its ritual, the artists did not critique the pageant format from outside as a "formulation in negative" as one might expect from a Marxist analysis. They reproduced its mechanisms from inside. At the same time, though, they reversed the "essential movement of the spectacle" in a de-crowning inversion that exposed these mechanisms through the mimicry of a subversive commentary. As the essential movement of General Idea's system, inversion restored the fluid state spectacle congealed.

A dissolving, destructive ritual, the *Pageant* was one with the flux from which it rose and returned. There is a reason why the *Pageant* developed at the same time as the correspondence network but also from it. Not in terms of substituting its pseudonymous participants and mimicking the network's practices in another mock-elevating vehicle. As an event, it too must reflect the collage cosmos. The *Pageant* was elevated from a flux of moving bodies and images in collision only to return to it. By this I mean the *Pageant* itself as an event, not just its disposable participants who were momentarily elevated above the mundane only to be re-deposited abjectly there. Miss General Idea, or Glamour itself, was merely an emblem of the larger, encompassing event, a mirror to it. As a fetish, Glamour was no more than a "convenient pole about which ritual may gather and concentrate." It was only the fetishism implicit to language—Glamour as a noun—that blinded us to the fact that fetishes rather were "available vessels, spiraling whirlpools collecting image flotsam." The *Pageant* was "stable" only to the degree that it captured the "subliminal in motion." Its stabilization rather released conflicting images coalescing in the fetish. "[T]he ritual, accumulating about and releasing the resident imagery of fetish objects, carries the stabilization of imagery beyond the mere objectification offered by fetish objects."[55] A whirlpool was elevated into view by the *Pageant*, not an object. The system really was a constellation put on temporary view.

In General Idea's system, the critique of the fetish was a critique of the noun, a critique of all things stable and congealed. As such, their enterprise was a purely *verbal* affair. The verb was process; it was flux. The verb was a "moving territory of words"; General Idea was a vacuum that had to be filled with words.

Early General Idea was a system in flux. This does not mean that the artists were in search of a formation, something that stabilized in the architecture of the *Pavillion*, for instance. On the contrary, since myth was flux, theirs was a "system of signs in motion." Derived from correspondence art, collage cut-up was more than a methodological tool. It engendered myth. Its correspondences led to alternative classifications, indeed to alternative universes, where nothing was true and everything was permitted. Collage *was* myth. Myth was a "moving field." A moving field inherently was unstable. It proceeded by divisions. Collage fundamentally was divisive.

The figure of this division, a division that was a juncture of two, was something seemingly invisible in itself: a mirror. A mirror divided as it reflected. It brought an image—or a self—into correspondence only by division, a division of image and self. The mirror was fundamental, foundational—in spite of the fact that the mirror was ungrounding, which was the contradictory point—to General Idea's enterprise. The mirror always already was collage.

Mirror, myth, and collage were one. Myth was one with collage as "description"; cut-up was one with the mirror as borderline. Collage cut-up was not a concept; at most it was a "Generative Idea: the relation, the configuration, the essential coupling." Collage generated concepts: viral seriality, for instance.

It was all in the cut: both infiltration and viral infection. The verbal *habits* of General Idea's system were engendered there, the cutting remarks of a verbal system. Viral replication was equivalent to flux in this regard, just as system was to myth and alternative to cut-up. The dynamism of the artists' system derived from something as simple as a cut, which sometimes was no more than a mirror. All their concepts were generated within this flux, at any one moment, and only this moment, as an event.

II.

Periodically, General Idea took stock of themselves in their notebooks. This gives us an opportunity to see, at that particular moment, what they thought constituted their enterprise. For instance, in an early notebook entry, AA Bronson charted General Idea's activities thus:

General Idea: ~~Divisions~~ {Actualizing mythologies
{Anti-Nova Activity
Something by Mouth Productions
Publications: FILE, booklets, coming books
image file [in different ink]
Miss General Idea Pageant
Miss G.I. Building [in different ink]
Borderline Studies – Manipulating the Self
– Light On
– Borderline Cases
Mailing exchange & communications
Tolerance Testing of available systems

Similarly, in a late 1973 notebook entry, Bronson noted:

What Who is G.I.
What are we doing
    Investigation of art possibilities in
    dead-end situation
    FILE Magazine
Borderline Case as culture/nature
    interface, etc.
GLAMOUR
    Borderline Cases
    Body Binding
    Pageant
    Light On

What do these entries tell us?[56] Firstly, they allow us to gauge the development of General Idea's enterprise. Secondly, they show us the relative importance of individual bodies of work *and* their unity within the whole. For instance, we see that *Manipulating the Self, Light On*, and the "Borderline Cases" were all Borderline Studies, and that the Borderline Studies were ranked equally with the *Pageant* and publications, such as *FILE*. That is, they were no less important at the time, even if in the future they would be less evident.[57] The second entry shows the refinement of classification where the "Borderline Cases," *Body Binding* (a case of "Manipulating the Self"), the *Pageant*, and *Light On* were all now equivalent categories of Glamour. "Glamour" was now the enveloping term for borderline investigations. Glamour was not a new development, only a new terminology for already existing categories. (That the "Miss General Idea Building" was an afterthought, penned in different ink, suggests that it was not yet the all-enveloping category it would later become.)

In the first note, Bronson saw General Idea's activities as encompassing "actualizing mythologies" and "anti-Nova activities." Were these one and the same? If they were not, would they equally be realized in the different products listed below (publications, *Pageant*, etc.)? And if they weren't products, would they equally set the parameters of General Idea's research? We know that "actualizing mythologies" defined General Idea's early activities. *FILE*, for instance, was created "as documentation and evidence of the Canadada Mondo Artie art scene in process, primarily through the medium of the mail." Evidence was actualized *as myth*: *FILE* was "the authentication and reinforcement of available myths lying within the context of Canadian art today."[58]

As alternatives, myths were sometimes doubly directed: counter-myths opposed dominant ones. The art myth, for example, was countered by correspondence art's subliminal network itself considered as myth. In part, this was what Bronson meant, I suppose, by General Idea's "anti-Nova" activity: "control lines were taken out of the hands of the art hierarchy (traditionally the only dealers of the fame and fortune fix) and decentralized into the hands of the junkies themselves [i.e., artists]."[59] While mythologies "lay down alternatives for permissible cultural behaviour," they were also tools for "probing the environment."[60] Obviously, the two were linked. Vincent Trasov's Mr. Peanut, for example, was both a fetishistic persona and a probe (i.e., implicit critique) of the electoral process when he officially campaigned for mayor of Vancouver in 1974. As for Eric Metcalf, his persona Dr. Brute "isolated the leopardskin image as fetish. Leopardskin for Dr. Brute is the medium by which ideas enter the object" and then invade the environment.[61]

Elsewhere in a notebook, among several pages of quotation and paraphrase of Claude Lévi-Strauss's *The Savage Mind* (*La pensée sauvage*, in French), AA Bronson wrote, "Dr. Brute's leopardskin props are not so much art as indicators of a mythology."[62] Since myth, not art, was the issue, we might turn to anthropology for an understanding of myth, ritual, and fetish as they figured in "Pablum for the Pablum Eaters." Yet their function in the *FILE* article was *dynamic*; myth, ritual, and fetish operated within a collage universe in flux. Myth was the "subliminal in motion"; its images collected around fetish objects as if swirling in a spiraling whirlpool. On the contrary, primitive societies were stable, and myth and ritual were reconciling forces. According to Lévi-Strauss, "the purpose of myth is to provide a logical model capable of overcoming a contradiction." Interestingly, Lévi-Strauss saw ritual in terms similar to collage's jointing: "Ritual … *conjoins*, for it brings about a union … between two initially separate groups." Thus, Felix Partz noted that "Mythic structures are double-edged as they synthesize two or more conflicting positions." But as Partz was referring to Borderline Cases and mythic structure being one and the same, "double-edged" takes on a different meaning: rather than a reconciliation of opposites, it was always an exacerbating case of collage cut-up's "cutting remarks."[63]

Words as mere definitions were not enough. To actualize a myth within the Eternal Network, rather than find it free floating, one had to create it from the whirlpool, giving it an illusion of stability through construction. It wasn't myth so much as *mythology* that provided the principles of fabrication for General Idea's system. And here, Lévi-Strauss was instrumental—but not so as to provide content for the terms "myth," "ritual," and "fetish" or "totem." Rather the *methodology* of structural anthropology became the *means* of construction of General Idea's project. Lévi-Strauss was not just an anthropologist, after all; he was a structural anthropologist.

"Around that period, 1970–71, we became fascinated with Claude Lévi-Strauss. General Idea actually thought of itself as a contemporary anthropologist, an anthropologist of contemporary culture."[64] Hence their "field-work" fascination with the found formats of retro popular culture: "We maneuver hungrily, conquering the uncontested territory of culture's forgotten shells—beauty pageants, pavillions, picture magazines, and other contemporary corpses."[65] Hence their fixing on myth as a metaphor for a subliminal network of contemporary art activity.

In *The Raw and the Cooked*, Lévi-Strauss wrote that "the practice and the use of mythological thought demand that its properties remain hidden: otherwise the subject would find himself in the position of the mythologist, who cannot believe in myths because it is his task to take them to pieces."[66] This was precisely the case with General Idea, except that the artists used Lévi-Strauss's science of mythology to put the pieces of their own mythology together, one they could "believe" in (make-believe in). These properties would still remain hidden in what General Idea went on to produce, but they were fundamental to the fabrication of their project and in particular the "construction" of the *Pavillion*. This understanding was set in place before the *Pavillion* ever got off the ground. In the future, the easy available cultural analysis of the *Pageant*, in which all could participate, would be replaced by the structural analysis of the *Pavillion*, the knowledge of which General Idea would keep to themselves. In the future *Pavillion*, the *Pageant* was housed as no more than an outdated diorama,

In his groundbreaking early work, "The Structural Study of Myth." Lévi-Strauss made the basic claims:

> (1) If there is a meaning to be found in mythology, it cannot reside in the isolated elements which enter into the composition of a myth, but only in the way those elements are combined. (2) Although myth belongs to the same category as language, being, as a matter of fact, only part of it, language in myth exhibits specific properties. (3) These properties are only to be found *above* the ordinary linguistic level, that is, they exhibit more complex features than those which are to be found in any other kind of linguistic expression.[67]

In its *systematic* formulation, this knowledge would have to be held in reserve for the later fabrication of the *Pavillion*. Meanwhile, in the period of the writing of "Pablum for the Pablum Eaters," Lévi-Strauss was more of a field to poach or a toolkit to utilize. The takings were not piecemeal, however. Once you opened the door to mythology you were committed to its systematic structure.

In their approach to Lévi-Strauss, General Idea poached from the "artist" not the academic theoretician. Their attraction to the Lévi-Strauss of *The Savage Mind* was probably the same as that to Smithson: the sheer linguistic invention of both authors; the proliferating effects of their prose based on a poetics of scientific models; and the fact that both were mythologists in their own right. In this regard, there was no difference between the two authors except that Lévi-Strauss asserted the rationalism of his project, which reflected, he claimed, that of *la pensée sauvage*.

Perhaps *la pensée sauvage* and the pablum of the Pablum eaters were no different either, which was the purpose of General Idea's article to delineate. Yet, "Pablum for the Pablum Eaters" utilized only a few concepts specific to *The Savage Mind*, such as that of the *miniature* and *part-whole* relationships determining the difference between art and myth. They were important enough, however, to establish the article's mythic schema. Miniaturization, in essence, was a model of myth. Its reduction "establishes the illusion of being able to see again, the illusion of a whole," General Idea maintained.[68] It was always a matter of the whole. "In the case of miniatures," Lévi-Strauss had written, "knowledge of the whole precedes knowledge of the parts. And even if this is an illusion, the point of the procedure is to create or sustain the illusion" (24). Aside from its function within myth, General Idea used part-whole relationships to determine who was a conceptual artist and who was a mythical artist: "Very often conceptual artists are starting with the parts and revealing structure. Myth does the opposite: myth starts with the structure and names the parts."[69] Lévi-Strauss offered this rationale (which had been noted by Bronson) to General Idea's critique of conceptualism when he wrote: "Art thus proceeds from a set (object + event) to the *discovery* of its structure. Myth starts from a structure by means of which it *constructs* a set (object + event)" (26). However they used this statement to justify their critique of conceptual art, the idea of a constructed set would end up being more productive for their future work. Lévi-Strauss had shown that myths "use a structure to produce what is itself an object consisting of a set of events" (24). Here was a model to enable the transition from an image bank to the *Pavillion*.

As essential as Lévi-Strauss was to the article, his role was obscured by the "jumbled jargon" performance of Burroughs's cut-up method. But the two authors' models acted in concert, as their epigraphs to the article testify. The resort to Burroughs was myth by other means. If Burroughs was inspiration for a counter-mythological system, Lévi-Strauss was its rationale. Lévi-Strauss had invented a myth to talk about myth, and as every myth needs a fictional agent, he created its protagonist as well: a tinkering *bricoleur*. Actually, the *bricoleur* was the "operator" of the system of myth. Lévi-Strauss called upon the idiomatic activities of this handyman, who "uses devious means compared to those of a craftsman," to explain by analogy myth's own "intellectual *bricolage*," a term we can henceforth easily apply, post-Pablum, to General Idea's methodology:

> His universe of instruments is closed and the rules of his game are always to make do with "whatever is at hand," that is to say with a set of tools and materials which is always finite and is also heterogeneous because what it contains bears no relation to the current project, or indeed to any particular project, but is the contingent result of all the occasions there have been to renew or enrich the stock or to maintain it with the remains of previous constructions or destructions. (16–17)

Like the activities of the *bricoleur*, "the characteristic feature of mythical thought is that it expresses itself by means of a heterogeneous repertoire which, even if extensive, is nevertheless limited" (17). Bronson opened his own notes on "mythical thought" with this quotation from *The Savage Mind*.[70] Written in 1974, after "Pablum for the Pablum Eaters" was published, these notes suggest the different use to which *The Savage Mind* was then put. For it was now the *Pavillion*, rather than the correspondence network, that the artists were to actualize as myth. We can look to this statement on *bricolage* as an *explanatory* model for us as much as it was a *constructive* model for General Idea. For General Idea's work was nothing but heterogeneous. What limited it to give it meaning? That is, what was its repertoire—its set of tools and materials? We can think of the *Pavillion* not only as an architectural structure that accommodated additional rooms, but, more significantly, as a pre-existing framework that determined the accumulating images that composed it. Whatever was added over time to the structure necessarily was constrained and followed a system of rules. Here was a case where not everything was permitted. Lévi-Strauss explained:

> The elements which the "bricoleur" collects and uses are "pre-constrained" like the constitutive units of myth, the possible combination of which are restricted by the fact that they are drawn from the language where they already possess a sense which sets a limit on their freedom of manoeuvre. (19)

Any iteration over time (i.e., exhibition or *FILE* publication of an aspect of the *Pavillion*) was only a variation dependent on its rules of operations. General Idea's work could develop, but only systematically, not *thematically*, always relating back to the structure that accommodated it: the set of operations that was the *Pavillion*. Whatever possible future outcome would "ultimately differ from the instrumental set only in the internal disposition of its parts" (18). That is, the "instrumental set" (the repertoire of tools, the general parameters of the *Pavillion*) and the final set (whatever current project) differed only in their respective *arrangements*. There was no *original* model, which a set referred back to, only a coherent systematicity in operation.

The *Pavillion* was not a realizable building. Nor was it an engineered machine of abstract elements smoothly synchronized in pure relations. It was an apparatus that attracted images to it, images that brought along their own history and cultural baggage. "Mythical thought builds structured sets by means of a structured set, namely, language. But it is not at the structural level that it makes use of it: it builds ideological castles out of the debris of what was once a social discourse" (21). Like General Idea (and Bronson had again noted the preceding quotation), the *bricoleur* worked with cultural debris. "The 'bricoleur' addresses himself to a collection of oddments left over from human endeavors, that is, only a sub-set of the culture" (19), like General Idea's "available formats, familiar formats, acceptable formats for the re-creation and transmutation of current culture."[71] Deprived of its original context as well as being historically outmoded, debris no longer had an instrumental or transparent relation to culture. It was cultured anew.

"Now, the characteristic feature of mythical thought, as of 'bricolage' on the practical plane, is that it builds up structured sets, not directly with other structured sets but by using the remains and debris of events… Mythical thought, that 'bricoleur,' builds up structures by fitting together events, or rather the remains of events" (21–22). This notion was of fundamental value to General Idea; it was a blueprint for the "construction" of the *Pavillion*. Collage coupling already was an event, but here was evidence of how one could build structures with the *remains* of events, series of them. The *Pavillion* was not just a stage but a set of things that were images. It was a structured set of image fragments derived from the cultural past that had lain dormant in *Fortune* and *LIFE* magazines and other popular cultural flotsam and jetsam. It was a structured set of both appropriated formats and found images that were given new meaning by incorporation into the artists' system. To conceive this structure was to construct the *Pavillion*.

The *Pavillion* was built from only what culture had provided for it. Using previous ends as means—signifieds as signifiers, in other words—was the hallmark of the *bricoleur*.[72] Debris was no new, solid foundation; images were not now locked in place as secure bricks in a wall. Linked to the system of the *Pavillion*, images were treated rather as signs, which made them permutable. Not only were they unstable, derived as they were from a collage cosmos, they could change their arrangement over time. As Lévi-Strauss wrote, signs and images were "already *permutable*, that is, capable of standing in successive relations with other entities—although with only a limited number and, as we have seen, only on the condition that they always form a system in which an alteration which affects one element automatically affects all the others" (20). Any found image could find its place in the *Pavillion* and its meaning within its system of signification. Any appropriated image was always open to being otherwise filled: "Images cannot be ideas but they can play the part of signs or, to be more precise, co-exist with ideas in signs and, if ideas are not yet present, they can keep their future place open for them and make its contours apparent negatively" (20). Whether it was Glamourous objects (which "open themselves like whores to meaning") or Dr. Brute's leopard skin ("the medium by which ideas enter the object"), "the image gains territory, holds a foot in the door of art, leaving a space for ideas, defining contours negatively."[73] Defining contours negatively was the architectural manner by which the *Pavillion* was designed.

The *bricoleur* was to myth as General Idea's *architects* were to the *Pavillion*. But as architects, General Idea were both, to use Lévi-Strauss's distinction, mythologists (*bricoleur*/artists) and engineers (scientist/artists): they not only operated the system, they created it in the first place. They worked with significations (the *bricoleur*'s domain) as well as with concepts (the scientist's realm). Concepts were as important as significations, that is, in keeping the *Pavillion* relevant over time, not just operating for the moment. "Concepts thus appear like operators *opening up* the set being worked with and signification like the operator of its *reorganization*, which neither extends nor renews it and limits itself to obtaining the group of its transformations" (20). Concepts were means by which the *Pavillion* could adapt its functions and increase its territory (its ongoing cultural reference and relevance). Concepts would be like new functions added to the *Pavillion*, which were what additional rooms really were all about.

In either case of opening up or reorganizing, General Idea's system was never stable but a permutable flux of interchangeable elements and transformative operations. It was no different with the *Pavillion* than it had been with their theorizing of correspondence art: General Idea's production was still a "cosmology of moving bodies"—open to permutation and the arrival of meaning. The architectural stability of the *Pavillion* was a mirage.

Such was the operative aspect of their system, which did not advertise its reliance on Lévi-Strauss as much as that more visible signifier of his renown: the divide between nature and culture. As we know, this distinction was foundational to being human. General Idea would give this split the appearance of significance, indeed, of the origin of meaning. After all, it was the prime example of a borderline, *the* borderline: its division instituted the idea of a borderline. Inaugural, it was the source of it all. Its division was an artificial construction that opposed culture to nature as "that exact and exacting space marked by glamour." In this way, camp privilege matched primitive disdain as an *artificiality* that *opposed* nature and *raised* itself above it. In so doing, the cultural field was treated by General Idea as if a natural milieu, as nature itself, where "culturized information may become ritualized as natural information to the point where it in turn may be absorbed by the cultural processes as raw material for further processing."[74]

Myth sustained the illusion of dominance over nature. It reconciled contradictions. In an unidentified citation in Bronson's notebook, written around the time of the first issue of *FILE*, we find this quotation:

> "Myth's function, according to Claude Lévi-Strauss, is the ability to act as a homeostatic mechanism, that is to serve as conceptual models correcting imbalances. Myths reconcile opposites; they seek to invert unstable relationships, or more generally they lay down alternatives for permissible cultural behaviour."

Bronson went on to add in his own words: "Seeing 'Culture' as our existing environment and creating a mythology that we might exist within it: a mythology of control (war myth); a mythology of glamour (nature as seen through culture)."[75] Fabricated myths gave permission for the performance of presumed identities, which bound the individual to a collective: a primitive community *or* correspondence network. Myth created community, just as it solved the problems of contradiction, by means of *joining*. General Idea used myth to propose contradictions in order to live with them as alternatives. Although Lévi-Strauss wrote that "the purpose of myth is to provide a logical model capable of overcoming a contradiction," sometimes myths were not just contradictory to other systems; they were contradictory in themselves. The borderline was also a battle line.

Perhaps it was the general in General Idea who saw battle lines in borderlines. "Battlestances disguised as dance steps" were not just a tap-dancing coda to the "Glamour" article. From the start, Glamour was a means "to survive in the battle between nature and culture." The "mythology of control" and the "mythology of glamour" were locked in struggle together when they weren't one and the same. "Military strategies" paralleled beauty pageants and were disguised within them, "the tactical front hidden by the subterfuge of false activity."[76]

Finding means to exist within culture through the creation of mythologies was not just a survival tactic. It was aggression. It was a war, a war with society. This war was not conducted in the open. Or, rather, it was conducted in the open but surreptitiously. It was conducted within "culture," one culture within another, a culture fabricated to infect another: the dominant or "official culture." For instance, "Pablum for the Pablum Eaters" said Image Bank was concerned with "establishing a culture that relates to official culture as a virus does to an organism." Alternative culture was not just parallel, but infiltrative: "Like we slipped into your mailbox disguised as LIFE." If, on the one hand, viral infection was Image Bank's concern, on the other hand, as artists "aware of nova explosion they work like criminals on the subliminal erecting mirrors cutting wordlines shifting linguals."[77] Actualizing mythologies was inseparable from anti-Nova activities.

You might ask, what is "Nova"? Basically, nova was the condition investigated in the mythological science fiction universe created by William Burroughs in his remarkable cut-up trilogy of early 1960s novels *The Soft Machine*, *The Ticket That Exploded*, and *Nova Express*. "The basic nova mechanism is very simple: Always create as many insoluble conflicts as possible and always aggravate existing conditions."[78] Aliens, criminals called the Nova Mob, take over the life forms of a planet through viral infiltration, aggravating conflicts until the planet is about to go nova, i.e., explode. This is when the Nova Police are called in. Together with Partisans, Nova Police destroy control lines through cutting word and image lines. Such were General Idea's "anti-Nova activities" but now applied to society at large.

One cannot underestimate the influence of Burroughs on General Idea, Image Bank, and the Canadian correspondence movement. Burroughs's books explicitly provided models, language, strategies, and techniques, and General Idea would be the first to acknowledge so:

> We considered ourselves a cultural parasite and our method was viral.... We had abandoned our hippie backgrounds of heterosexual idealism, abandoned any shred of belief that we could change the world by activism, by demonstration, by any of the methods we had tried in the 1960s—they had all failed. As children of the Summer of Love (1967) and spectators of the Paris riots (1968), we were well aware of the International Situationists and *Society of the Spectacle* on one hand, and of Marshall McLuhan, drug culture, digger houses, underground papers and free schools on the other. Now we turned to the queer outsider methods of William Burroughs, for example, whose invented universe of sex-mad, body-snatcher espionage archetypes provided the ironic myth-making model we required: "We need a peg to hang it on," he said. "Something really ugly like virus. Not for nothing do they come from a land without mirrors." So he takes over this newsmagazine.... And he breaks out all the ugliest pictures in the image bank and puts it out on the subliminal so one crisis piles up after the other right on schedule.[79]

We immediately recognize the dependency of, for instance, "Pablum for the Pablum Eaters" on Burroughs's writing: in its notion of correspondence as a junky's habit; of image as need and overdose; in its command to cut word lines and shift linguals; in its cut-ups, rewrites, and suggestion to arbitrarily exchange arguments' sides; in its image banks and very idea of the network as the subliminal itself. The title of the article, from which the above quotation derives ("Myth as Parasite/Image as Virus"), openly acknowledged General Idea's indebtedness to his strategies. Myth was viral: Alternative myths were "a method of invasion" in which "the image gains territory." Myth as parasite and image as virus were two powerful concepts without which there would be no General Idea work.

Burroughs's "Plan D called for Total Exposure. Wise up all the marks everywhere. Show them the rigged wheel of Life-Time-Fortune. Storm The Reality Studio. And retake the universe."[80] Control mechanisms operated along word and image lines, entering at the soft spot of habit. Viral infiltration was modelled on junkies' drug habits. "The criminal controllers operate in very much the same manner as a virus. Now a virus in order to invade, damage and occupy the human organism must have a gimmick to get in." Images and words provided the ticket: "Image *is* junk." Images and words, in fact, *were* viruses: "Word begets image and image *is* virus."[81] Freeing marks meant jamming the machine, cutting word lines, and reversing control by projecting counter images. The cut-up method was a weapon.

General Idea reversed Burroughs's aggression and *welcomed* the junky's habit as a correspondence fix, as host to an invasion of viral images. Then they turned these viruses against the control culture. A viral inhabitation of *LIFE*, *FILE* was one such weapon. ("Like we slipped into your mailbox disguised as LIFE. There you were staring FILE in the face and you couldn't believe it was LIFE.") Not that General Idea's methods were any different from what Burroughs employed. They applied the same cut-up strategies as Burroughs with the same tactical aims. In light of Burroughs, we recognize that parasitical inhabitation of found formats was not just a game, an alternative view, or camp putdown; it was an aggressive act against systems of control. For Burroughs, this was no fiction; he advocated cut-up disruption in real life: "Just pointing out that cut/ups on the tape recorder can be used as a weapon."[82]

"Not for nothing do they come from a land without mirrors," Burroughs said of the Nova Mob. No wonder then that General Idea "began as a mirror of sorts" in their anti-Nova activity: acting on the subliminal by "erecting mirrors cutting wordlines shifting linguals." Inserting mirrors in word lines made them viral. *FILE*, for instance, was such a mirror that reflected *LIFE* magazine back to itself. "'Now,' he said, 'I'll by God show them how ugly the Ugly American can be,'" was the ellipsis Bronson left out of his Burroughs quotation above.

The Nova Mob's "alien" control was no different from that of the mass media: "The control of the mass media depends on laying down lines of association. When the lines are cut the associational connections are broken." Fiction was no different from reality in this regard. "There is no true or real 'reality'," Burroughs wrote. "There are always alternative solutions—Nothing is true—Everything is permitted."[83]

General Idea took this license for invention, which as well was a license for a do-it-yourself media franchise. They accepted Burroughs's fictional advice to take over a news magazine seriously by making their own in the likeness of *LIFE*. Their magazine was lifelike, but as no fiction only; its viral infiltration was meant to have real effects. As if speaking directly to the artists, Burroughs said:

> You have an advantage which your opposing player does not have. He must conceal his manipulations. You are under no such necessity. In fact you can advertise the fact that you

are writing news in advance and trying to make it happen by techniques which anybody can use. And that makes you NEWS. And a TV personality as well, if you play it right. You want the widest possible circulation for your cut/up video tapes. Cut/up techniques could swamp the mass media with total illusion.[84]

Virus was no mere metaphor for Burroughs. It was real: not the drug addiction he endured and escaped from, but language itself was a junky's habit inflicted by an alien virus. Burroughs's trilogy did not just aim to dismantle systems of control. His writing was a war on language. Language was an alien system of control.

In the *fiction Nova Express*, Burroughs had written, "What scared you all into time? Into body? Into shit? I will tell you: '*the word*.' Alien word '*the*'." Then in the article about the *real* world, "Electronic Revolution," he said: "I have frequently spoken of word and image as viruses or as acting as viruses, and this is not an allegorical comparison. It will be seen that the falsifications in syllabic Western languages are in point of fact actual virus mechanisms" (312). The very use of the definite article "the," of the verb "to be," or of the logical category "either/or," each was a "precoded message of damage, the categorical imperative of permanent condition." All were viruses: "The IS of identity is in point of fact the virus mechanism.... The categorical THE is also a virus mechanism, locking you in the THE virus universe. EITHER/OR is another virus formula" (311–312). Their enunciation alone locked identity, object, or action in a stable universe, the only possible one: "THE universe locks you in THE, and denies the possibility of any other" (312). On the one hand, use of the definite article was delimiting while, on the other, to choose to employ the logical category "either/or" was a "virus formula" that simulated a nova conflict: "This is in point of fact the conflict formula which is seen to be an archetypal virus mechanism" (312). In the battleground of language, the first line of defense was language itself. General Idea took counsel here from both Burroughs and Brockman. The artists' strategies and tactics were enacted within a verbal system, even though later they would feign to make Glamour their "passive defense."

The cut-up method was self-defense; collage was a necessary survival tactic. One could understand General Idea's resort to "ambiguity," their refusal to be caught in a contradictory bind between content *or* context, nature *or* culture, inside *or* out. To dissolve categories was to keep them fluid. Sometimes it took an aggressive act. That was what collage was all about. It was "collage or perish."

Methodology was also an ethos. That's because the virus was double-edged. It was not only viral. It could be turned against itself; but to do so subversively "requires the mind of a criminal." As Burroughs's Nova Police Chief said, "Paradoxically some of our best agents were recruited from the ranks of those who are called criminals on this planet."[85] Burroughs provided a fictional universe that General Idea happily inhabited. They did so as "criminals." Though they transformed the model to their own ends, they used Burroughs's methodologies to the same subversive purposes. Infiltrative and disruptive, these strategies were alternative to critique.

Not for nothing did Lévi-Strauss and Burroughs serve as epigraphs to "Pablum for the Pablum Eaters." Both influenced the correspondence network's turn to myth. General Idea articulated this influence in their own particular way by articulating the two authors together. That is to say, these authors justified a particular system of myth that General Idea then worked out to their own advantage. Typically, the artists' recourse to myth was two-sided and double-edged.

On the one hand, following Lévi-Strauss, General Idea elaborated alternative myths through "description," using as basis images from popular culture that were organized and classified as new forms of "knowledge." Classification was both camp *and* critical. On the other hand, myth was not merely receptive; it was infiltrative. That is, myth was not just performed alternatively by this new community. Myth was parasitical. It returned to infect culture. This was Burroughs's influence. Myth as "permissible cultural behaviour" and myth as parasitical inhabitation combined as the framework and outer limits of General Idea's project. Lévi-Strauss and Burroughs were the two faces, the double edge of myth as a collage system: one essentially constructive, the other essentially destructive.

As epigraphs to that article, Burroughs and Lévi-Strauss were emblems of the recurring contradictions that structured General Idea's work. The cut-up cosmology of moving bodies and images in collision seemingly was in opposition to the elevatory function of the *Pageant*'s ritual of Glamour. Could myth accommodate the two: cosmology and ritual? It was as if the *Pavillion*'s architectural plan and elevation were in contradiction to each other, the building a conjunction of constructive and destructive forces. No wonder it was an unstable structure bound for dissolution.

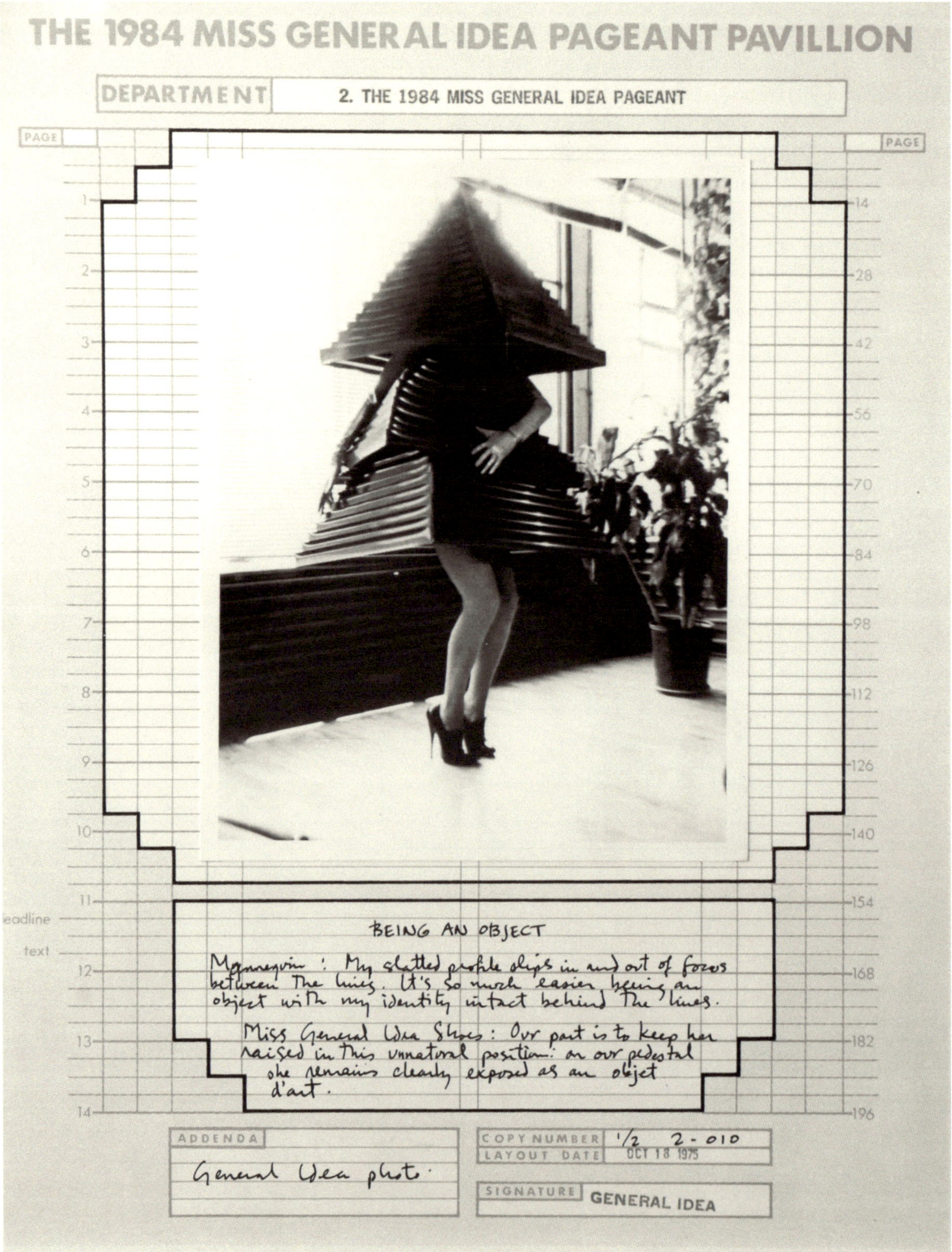
THE 1984 MISS GENERAL IDEA PAGEANT PAVILLION
DEPARTMENT
2. THE 1984 MISS GENERAL IDEA PAGEANT
PAGE
PAGE
headline
text
BEING AN OBJECT
Mannequin: My slatted profile slips in and out of focus between the lines. It's so much easier being an object with my identity intact behind the lines.
Miss General Idea Shoes: Our part is to keep her raised in this unnatural position: on our pedestal she remains clearly exposed as an objet d'art.
ADDENDA
General Idea photo.
COPY NUMBER 1/2 2-010
LAYOUT DATE OCT 18 1975
SIGNATURE GENERAL IDEA

Showcard 2-010, 1975

III.

A collage aesthetic underlay General Idea's work, which meant it underlay or provided the foundations for the forthcoming *Pavillion* as well, which as architecture, though never built, seemingly should be a stable and enduring structure. Yet, the *Pavillion* was "a 'Collage or Perish' edifice." Its design ethos was that of the correspondence community, which was solicited in an open call to contribute to the *Pavillion*'s construction through an "Image Tender." "We are looking forward to no problems in incorporating your prop-osal into the complex as we are utilizing time honored collage construction techniques," the artists announced. "One of the first steps in the design of the pavillion," this participation was never realized, however.[86]

The *Pavillion* had been an idea of General Idea's since 1971, when it was thought of as the "Miss General Idea building," and a spate of announcements throughout 1973 promoted its appearance. Its eventual "construction" would not take the form—even form following fiction—that the artists had anticipated. It was not only that the correspondence movement had begun to dissolve; something was astir in General Idea's own practice. We can look at late 1973–1974 as being a period of transition from the *Pageant* to the *Pavillion*, but it was as well a hiatus in which to develop new strategies. For want of a better word, let's call these strategies marketing.

Let's conduct an inventory, as if it were late 1973. On the one hand, we have the major theoretical articles from May and September 1973: "Pablum for the Pablum Eaters" and "General Idea's Borderline Cases." On the other hand, we have the products of that practice (excluding *FILE* magazine itself): the photographic panels *Light On*; blowups from the 1971 *Pageant*; *Manipulating the Self* prints; *Luxon* drawings and pamphlets. In fact, this is a balance sheet of "available products" transcribed from a General Idea ledger from the end of 1973 identified as "Marketing 1974."[87] The purpose of this exposure is not to convict General Idea of complicity with the art market, a control system that they had earlier rejected as an "art racket," but to show the challenges ahead for them. For the next ledger page, continuing "Marketing 1974" but now titled "Marketing Fronts," listed potential exposure of sales of *FILE* and exhibitions of their past and current work. Exhibitions consisted of potential installations (a travelling exhibition of *FILE*, for example, conceived as being toured by Canada's National Gallery) and actual invitations (to *Project '74* in Germany). According to the notebook, their *Project '74* installation was to be based on material from *The 1971 Miss General Idea Pageant*.[88]

One could see there was a problem: the *Pageant* material already was "dated"; moreover, one could not sustain an *exhibition* career on the basis of showing documentation from occasional *Pageants* when they were seen to be too difficult to stage yearly. This same material, nonetheless, was recycled and added to for an exhibition held during their June 1974 residency at Vancouver's Western Front, where General Idea also performed the *Pageant* rehearsal *Blocking*. In between the exhibition opening and performance the artists staged a shareholders' meeting and offered a prospectus on the yet-to-be-constructed *Pavillion (Floor to Ceiling Thought: A Progress Report from the Research Committee for The 1984 Miss General Idea Pavillion)*. Between the recycling of the exhibition and the rote continuation of the *Pageant*, the performance of *Floor to Ceiling Thought* perhaps yielded a solution to the artists' predicament.

The mock meeting consisted of a president's speech, a financial report, and progress reports on both the *Pavillion* and *Pageant*.[89] All this was no different perhaps than the fictionalizing of found formats ironically played with, for instance, in *FILE's Top Ten* popularity contests. Yet it differed in being oriented solely to the artists' own speculative program. It was a *preview* of the *Pavillion* given reality through its *performative* descriptions. Many of the elements that surfaced in the *Showcards* were premiered here: the search for the Spirit and Site; the Hand of the Spirit; Miss General Idea's vehicle; Luxon V.B.; and various architectural details.[90]

Here was one of those dividing moments between the past and future in General Idea's work, equivalent to the mirror no longer mirroring the scene but only itself. The report on the *Pageant* was a history to date, but that on the *Pavillion* was speculative. It would turn out that speculation actually *was* realization. As such, *Floor to Ceiling Thought* differed from the *Pageant*. It did not just stage an event; it brought about a program. It was not just a performance; it was performative. The *Pavillion* would take shape, form following fiction, in the performative mode.[91]

This specialization, for we can call it that, would entail several shifts in General Idea's work. First, collage cut-up techniques, even though they inferred a universe, would have to be constrained towards systematicity. Collage was still the basis of their work but its coupling event would now come into effect through a performative act—and only be sustained, *at that moment*, by it. Second, given this systematicity, at any one moment a presentation must be coherent, that is, referential to this system, General Idea's program. Hence, the exhibition or installation-basis of future work, starting with *Going thru the Notions* (1975). No longer series of individual projects, henceforth everything would fit together as if interlocking ziggurats. Third, General Idea would have to brand themselves as artists and establish an identity for themselves as a trio apart from the collectivity of their *Pageants* and the anonymity of the correspondence movement.

"At some point a certain alienation from the myth occurred, a rupture," Felix Partz wrote around 1975. "This rupture or alienation was not the result of negative conclusions. It occurred after sustained immersion in the myth with irony being the chief exploration device."[92] The myth, of course, was that of the subliminal network of correspondence artists. The alienation was only the natural result of the dissolution of the correspondence movement. The rupture, though, was the result of a conscious reduction of the working group that had previously been loosely affiliated under the name General Idea.[93]

So began the myth of General Idea: their Glamourous story. So began the myth making, which, in essence, was a publicity machine. The artists were not selfishly elevating themselves over others, though. They were only isolating the *image* of the artist, raising the popular concept of the artist in order to reveal it as an ideological figure.

> The image of the artist is the easiest to inhabit. Because of its historical richness, its ready but empty mythology (berets, paint brushes, palettes, in a word FORM without content) the shell which was art was simple to invade. We made art our home and assuming appearances, strengthened by available myth, occupied art's territory.[94]

To be "mega-artists," a term Partz used in his notes, was to be meta-artists. To be meta-artists was to manipulate the art system as a metalanguage. To manipulate it was to operate it. Inhabitation was not all. Sometimes, it was in the *saying* alone that elevation happened.

> We never felt we had to produce great art to be great artists. We knew great art did not bring glamour and fame. We knew we had to keep a foot in the door of art and we were conscious of the importance of berets and paint brushes. We made public appearances in painters' smocks. We knew that if we were famous and glamourous we could say we were artists and we would be. We did and we are. We are famous, glamourous artists.[95]

In the performative mode, the saying was the doing. They said it; they did it. They were famous, glamourous artists. But to be glamourous artists, they had as well to erect the whole support system of galleries, museums, publications, and audiences.

The *Pavillion* would serve many of these functions just as *FILE* had earlier. To construct the *Pavillion* General Idea had to *develop* a system at the same time. ("Design build," they call it now in the architectural profession.) It would take more than words. Actually, words were enough when they were joined with images, or, rather, when words elevated images in turn. Both were needed if the *Pavillion* was to be *exhibited.*

New strategies were developed in the hiatus period 1974–75, when, for instance, the only *FILE* published was an artist directory. Significantly, the next issue in fall 1975 would be a manifesto, not only on Glamour but also on General Idea themselves. That was part of their media blitz, an assault on three fronts: *FILE*'s "Glamour" issue; the *Pageant* performance *Going thru the Motions*; and the first exhibition devoted to the *Pavillion, Going thru the Notions.* Significantly, the video for *Going thru the Motions* was a platform for orienting the *Pageant* towards General Idea's overall program then consolidating in the *Pavillion* (look on it as a pilot for *Pilot* [1977]). But General Idea were not there yet, even though they had conceived of the *Pavillion* from 1971.

Now came the monumental task: the task of building *The 1984 Miss General Idea Pavillion.* Of course, the *Pavillion* didn't then come into effect fait accompli when first exhibited as *Going thru the Notions.* Everything about it had to be conceived from the ground up. Then projected. It was back to the drawing board. Actually, the drawing board was a projector of sorts.

The *Showcards* were the first product of this labour. They systematically plotted the *Pavillion.* In a practical sense, the *Showcards* served the same archival function as *FILE*, but now totally devoted to the *Pavillion.* It was as if the process of putting together the magazine now became the practical means of constructing the *Pavillion.* As General Idea had written about the new Art Metropole in 1974, the *Pavillion* similarly could be seen in principle as "taking over [*FILE*'s] diversifying functions of reflection and connection."[96] Repeated reflections and connections diversified themselves to compose, mirror-like, the various elements of the *Pavillion*'s architecture. But an architectural program was needed to make sense of all these connections and reflections. Here is where the *Showcards* came in. The *Showcards*' scenario plotted word lines and sightlines converging on the *Pavillion*'s elevations.[97]

Projections converged beyond the prototype stage, where the *Luxon V.B.* lingered on "the interface between content and context, nature and culture, inside and out." Here were designs for the real world of actual fabrication. This multi-functioning team produced architectural drawings, blueprints, mock-ups, photographs, prints, and fabrications, such as the *V.B. Gowns*, for the *Going thru the Notions* exhibition. Rather than a publishing house-cum-news agency, the production analogy now was an architectural office that also performed as advertising and modelling agencies. It was talent central. The artists' *studio* now substituted for the *Pageant* and performed its social functions. The studio was part of the set up, part of the performance, in fact. It was no longer merely "a node on the correspondence network [where *FILE* was] evidence of correspondence that passes through General Idea Headquarters."[98] It was a switching centre, where the various functions of the *Pavillion* were conceived and designed and then sent off through the channels of marketing and publicity.[99] Performatively, the *Pavillion* was one with its publicity.

If the studio was the new social set-up that replaced the *Pageant* in the elevation of Glamour, then the photographer was the new Master of Ceremonies. Whatever took place in the open with the model, the photographer, nonetheless, was more comfortable as an operator behind the scenes: "Through the miracle of photography blow up and cut up are collaged" in his darkroom.[100]

Photography always had a function in General Idea's work, but it had its documentary limits. It fixed the *Pageants'* fleeting events. Dependent, though, as photography was on accidents of shooting, after the fact it was difficult to put ones finger on what its image was all about. Words came to its aid. "Seeing that a photograph is worth a thousand words [General Idea] soon developed the ability to also provide these words which in turn developed new projects, events and situations to record." Photographs engendered descriptions that demanded more photographs in return, then more descriptions. It took a system to keep them all in order: they were linked serially in an ongoing narrative. Fleeting photography turned out to be a constructive basis for building the *Pavillion*: "Photography is our touchstone foundation to build and fabricate our mythic structures."

We all know that photographs can be manipulated, but photography was a foundation for the *Pavillion only* if it was manipulated, not merely by words; but as if photographs themselves were like words or concepts: linked in series. Not only linked and aligned, they had to be constructed, too. Necessarily, they too were collages. Collage was internal to their construction. Transparent photography manipulated its setup. It manipulated props. A photograph was a scene in an imaginary pageant, props and all. All it was itself perhaps was a prop. "General Idea constructs art works that also function as photographic props which enable us to expand and elucidate our concerns." For instance, the life-size photographic cutouts of the various Miss General Idea were set up in situations where they were then re-photographed in turn. (See the "Cut Out" section of the *Showcards*.) It was easier to work that way:

> We worship our queens our Miss General Ideas. Iconographically they are much easier to deal with. No clash of personalities. Just our pure projections. So easy to deal with in this ideal state. We have them recorded on film and printed life size and cut out to keep us company. We have stolen back their images we gave them and we steal them into any context that catches our fancy.

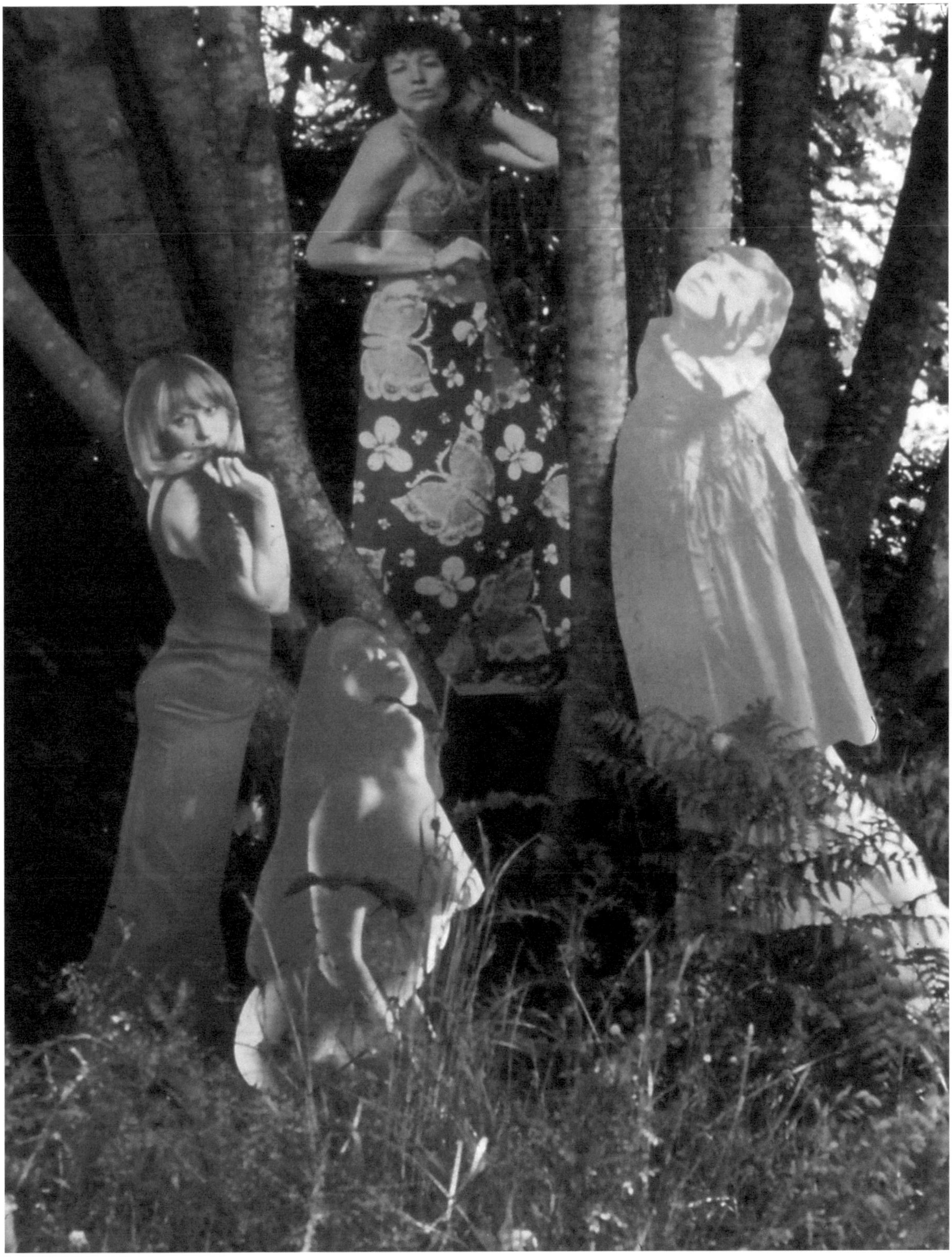

Cut-outs of the four Miss General Ideas, clockwise from top: Granada Gazelle, Marcel Idea, Miss Honey, Mimi Paige

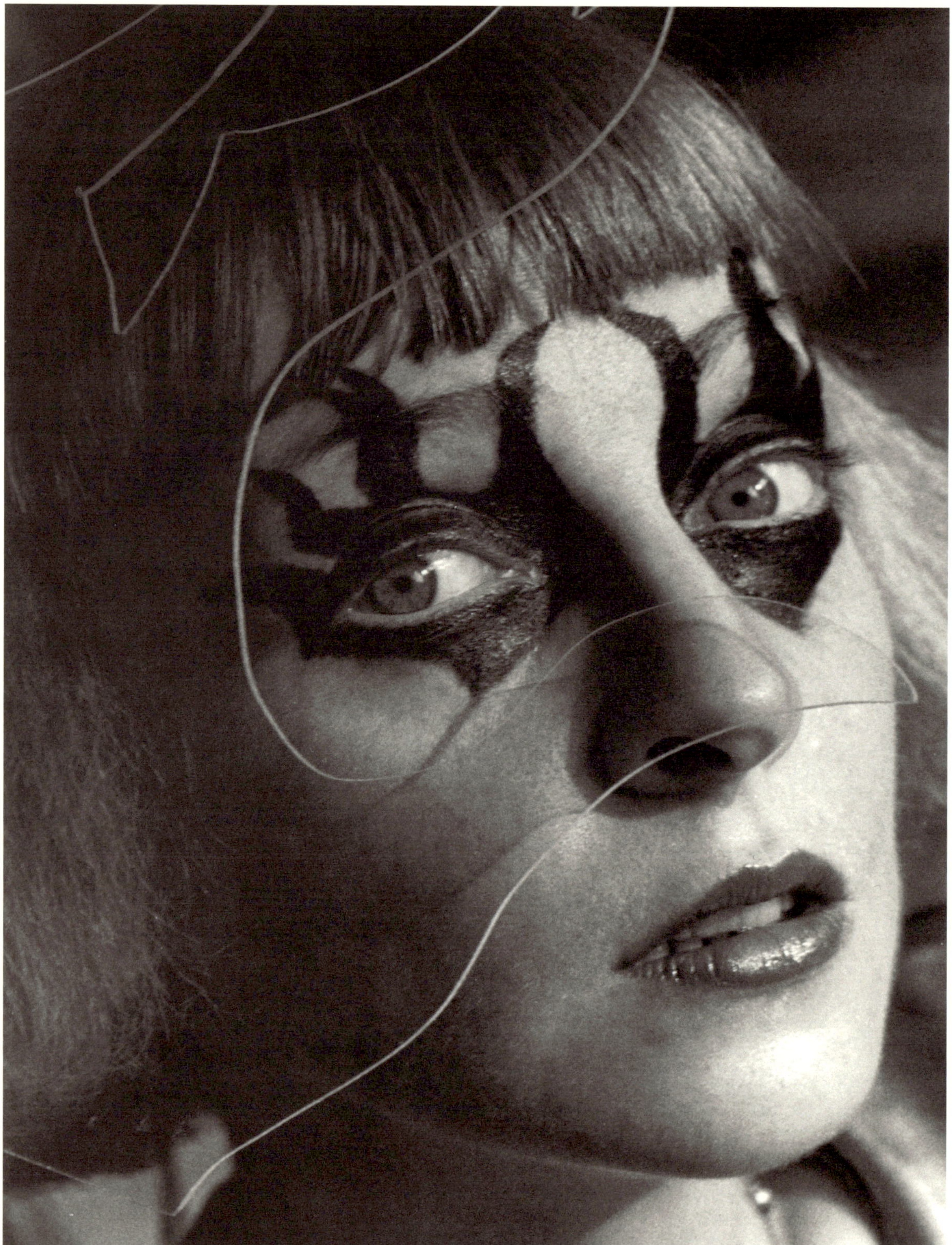

Untitled, 1973-74 (Sandy Stagg models the *Hand of the Spirit Make-up*)

Stealing them into any context was easy, especially in a photographic image. The result, since there are no joints in a photograph, was a seamless collage. Like Miss General Idea's shoes, a photograph "neglects joints to exhibit a continuity of surface which is enchanting, otherworldly." Jointing only took place in the fabrication of an image, in the real world of the photography studio and darkroom, not in the enchanting image itself. Like myth, an image was timeless. Suspended therein, gestures were irrevocable. This accounts for the classical character of many of the sublime Glamour images from 1974–1975. Fetish-like, they assert another repertoire for the *Pavillion*: such as are consolidated and seamlessly collaged in *Untitled (Sandy Stagg Models the Miss General Idea Shoe and the Hand of the Spirit Against the Backdrop of the Luxon V.B.)*.

With photography at hand, was the *Pageant* any longer necessary? Photography alone could elevate Glamour. Photography was the last element to prepare the *Pavillion*. Collage cut-up cleared the ground and provided construction materials; the *Luxon V.B.* helped excavate the site and the *Hoarding* hid it. Finally, in the *Showcards* word lines and sightlines were aligned in performative utterances that erected the structure right before our eyes. Photography was proof of its construction ... and destruction. As such, photography, too, was myth.

Like words, photography could go on and on, especially as reflected in General Idea's mirror system. Since myth is inconclusive, we, too, could go on and on. Coming to a conclusion could only ever be "the ending of the beginning of the story" of an interminable analysis of General Idea's work. If we were "only following orders," as General Idea claimed to do, we would now return to the beginning of the book, to a story there implicated within a system: General Idea's story as General Idea's system. Of course, once here, or there, it is up to readers to dispose of this book. •

1. The material for this investigation has been opened up by the deposit of General Idea's archive at the National Gallery of Canada and by the fundamental research carried out on it by Fern Bayer, who has catalogued it, and which saw its first light in her 1997 exhibition *The Search for the Spirit: General Idea 1968–1975*.
2. This 1991 interview shows the relative insignificance of the origin of their name:

   "Felix: General Idea emerged from that actually [from a collective way of working]. We had been working together on, we had been working separately on independent projects, which gradually started involving each other. Officially, and then unofficially, just living together, we started creating projects around the house that were collaborations without any framework or name or any direction. And I think at some point they just sort of smacked together, where the working on each other's projects, and the fooling around in the house, sort of became the same thing. And then it became official.

   Louise: So, that's when you decided to name yourself 'General Idea'?

   Felix: Right.

   AA: Well, when we decided, I guess that exhibition, the first exhibition at A Space, well it was the Nightingale, was it still called the Nightingale Art ...

   Felix: Yeah. Art Gallery ...

   AA: Nightingale Art Gallery, at that point. It was called Project 70? Yeah, Project 70 [Concept 70]. They invited us to do an exhibition, I mean a piece for that show, and the piece was called 'General Idea,' right?

   Felix: 'The Line Project'.

   AA: The Line Project.

   Felix: General Idea was the artist, I guess at that point ...

   AA: Was the artist, the first ...

   Felix: The first time the name was used."

   Louise Dompierre interviews General Idea, July 26, 1991. Manuscript Series, General Idea archives, 1–2.
3. For more information on this binder and the unrealized tour it was supposed to promote, see Fern Bayer, "Uncovering the Roots of General Idea: A Documentation and Description of Early Projects 1968–1975," in *The Search for the Spirit: General Idea 1968–1975*, (Toronto: Art Gallery of Ontario, 1997), 55–56.
4. At least it seems this way. A loose page in one of AA Bronson's notebooks in the General Idea archive lists some of these projects: "project: miss general idea pageant ... project: warehouse re-view ... project: elastic bands ... project: twisting my beard ... project: body temperature ... project: litter." AA Bronson, Notebook 1971–72. For a long time, the *Pageant* was just one other "division" of General Idea's activities.
5. In a notebook entry, Felix Partz wrote: "The Transfer Method—transferring the contents from one frame of reference to the other." Felix Partz, Notebook 1972. In a statement, "Re: Conceptualism, Conceptualism in Canada, *Concept 70*," dated June 15, 1970, Michael Tims [AA Bronson], wrote: "Conceptualism is a disappearing act. The altering of forces rather than the creation of forms, dissolving abstracted structure (e.g. sculpture) into documentation, waste, or residual structure (photos, a cloud formation, an idea). It is feeling time to be making destruction, recording this, ridding ourselves of our accoutrements with finality, vision, and respect." Loose page found in Bronson, Notebook 1971–72. In the same notebook, in several loose pages, Bronson records his thoughts on "Destruction as art-form," where destruction was "re-structuring," "re-integration," "cyclic," or "A temporal process." The *Pageant* obviously involves a transfer method, mapping the beauty pageant onto the art system. But it is also not a far stretch from the notions of waste and cyclic restructurings to the *Pageant*'s function of elevating and degrading contestants.
6. Project Series: Light-On (1971–1972) in the General Idea archive. Later the locations were mapped and the process potentially repeated according to that mapping, re-placing the documentation in their original sites, but this recycling ("Documentation is recycled along the original travelling route through the communities involved.") did not happen as per the proposal. See Appendix Y/1, Project Series: Light-On.
7. *Luxon V.B.: The Miss General Idea Pavillion No. 101*, self-published, 1973. On April 10, Bronson wrote in his notebook of the necessity of disguising their agenda in *Light On*: "Exposé of communication theory complications and rabbit tracks necessary to convince OAC [the funding body, Ontario Arts Council] and others of worth of

LIGHT ON. The project must be translated into terms and systems in vogue before acceptance is possible. Such translation necessarily destroys many of the layers and transparencies most integral to a view of the project." Bronson, Notebook 1971–72. Such a statement should cue us to various "esoteric" readings of other projects.

8. A statement in a faux-rejected *artscanada* article published as a *FILE* advertisement is illuminating here: "We turn the light here, there, and everywhere and the limits of thought recede." "(Advertisement)," *FILE* 1:2&3 (May/June 1972), inside back cover.
9. Dennis Young, *New Alchemy: Elements, Systems, Forces* (Toronto: Art Gallery of Ontario, 1969), n.p. The artists exhibited were Hans Haacke, Charles Ross, Takis, and John Van Saun. AA Bronson intervened with *Mirror Sequences* and General Idea performed *Air, Earth, Fire, Water Mantra* at the opening of the exhibition. See Fern Bayer, "Uncovering the Roots of General Idea," 36. Images of Bronson's intervention are on p. 34.
10. Compare Glamour's contaminating effect: Miss General Idea "is more akin to poison, that other natural enemy to culture. Like poison Miss General Idea, objet d'art, posed on stiletto heels and bound in the latest fantasy, represents a violent intrusion into the heart of culture: the Canada Council, for example, or beauty pageants (essentially one and the same)." Contamination was a mirror operation that created a void, with the contamination of its "content" poison itself: "With this gesture [a manipulation of the self] we husk Nature, voiding the shell that Culture, that great Amazon, single-breasted but divided, might shoot the poisoned arrow of meaning into its empty shell." "Glamour," *FILE* 3:1 (Autumn 1975), n.p.
11. AA Bronson, "Bound to Please: The Archive from the 1984 Miss General Idea Pavillion," in *Art Metropole: The Top 100*, eds. Kitty Scott and Jonathan Shaughnessy (Ottawa: National Gallery of Canada, 2006), 131.
12. "Catalogue," *FILE*, 1:2&3 (May/June 1972), 57.
13. Robert Smithson, "Incidents of Mirror Travel in the Yucatan," *Artforum* 8:1 (September 1969); reprinted in *The Writings of Robert Smithson*, ed. Nancy Holt (New York: New York University Press, 1979), 103.
14. Ibid. 97. Smithson describes the First Mirror Displacement: "Bits of earth spilled on the surfaces, thus sabotaging the perfect reflection of the sky. Dirt hung in the sultry sky. Bits of blazing cloud mixed with the ashy mass. The displacement was *in* the ground, not *on* it." Ibid., 95 "The malady of wanting to 'make' is *unmade*, and the malady of wanting to be 'able' is disabled." Ibid., 96
15. Smithson, Ibid;, 103. Michael Tims [AA Bronson], "Re: Conceptualism, Conceptualism in Canada, *Concept 70*."
16. "A scale in terms of 'time' rather than 'space' took place." Smithson, Ibid., 96.
17. "More recently, and particularly in art circles, history has become a means of anticipating the future in order to plan one's own work as the next logical step in art history. In other words, history has become a marketing device." AA Bronson, "Pablum for the Pablum Eaters," in *Video by Artists*, ed. Peggy Gale (Toronto: Art Metropole, 1976), 196.
18. "Pablum for the Pablum Eaters," *FILE* 2:1&2 (May 1973), 26.
19. Smithson, ibid., 97. Compare the faux-rejected *artscanada* article: "We travel the unfathomable, wrapped in ambiguities.... The limits of the Generative Idea are marked by paradoxes, puzzles." Albeit, Sol LeWitt, in his 1968 "Sentences on Conceptual Art," wrote, "(1) Conceptual Artists are mystics rather than rationalists. They leap to conclusions that logic cannot reach. (2) Rational judgments repeat rational judgments. (3) Illogical judgments lead to new experience. (4) Formal art is essentially rational." In ed., Ursula Meyer, *Conceptual Art* (New York: E. P. Dutton & Co., Inc, 1972), 174.
20. "Pablum" (1973), 26.
21. Ibid., 20.
22. Bronson, Notebook 1971–72.
23. While Image Bank was a conduit for introducing correspondence (and the influence of Ray Johnson) into Canadian art; and although it set up a framework for its maintenance and dissemination; it did not have the capacity, however, to transform itself once there was a crisis in the correspondence movement as it fell apart from about late 1973 on. The 1976 rewriting of "Pablum for the Pablum Eaters" was an acknowledgement, in light of this unspoken crisis, of the need for "diversification" of the Subliminal network: "in what way different groups continued to generate and stabilize an ongoing body of imagery as myth," it said. ["Pablum" (1976), 198] On the contrary, Image Bank stabilized itself at an earlier research stage, which, of course, is not a criticism of it. Growth,

though, demanded ongoing fictionalizing; so did changing with the times. Compare Lévi-Strauss on growth: "Myth grows spiral-wise until the intellectual impulse which has produced it is exhausted. Its *growth* is a continuous process, whereas its *structure* remains discontinuous." Lévi-Strauss, "The Structural Study of Myth," in *Structural Anthropology*, trans. Claire Jacobson and Brooke Grundfest Schoepf (New York: Basic Books, Inc., 1955), 229. McLuhan similarly looked on the spiral as a mythic figure in oral and electronic cultures where a "message is then traced and retraced, again and again, on the rounds of a concentric spiral with seeming redundancy." Marshall McLuhan, *Understanding Media* (Cambridge, Mass: MIT Press, 1994), 26. One need not mention, as well, the role of the spiral in Smithson's work, most notably *The Spiral Jetty* (1970). Perhaps growth was a mirror effect, produced by mirrors placed askew: "The characteristic feature of the savage mind is its timelessness; its object is to grasp the world as both a synchronic and a diachronic totality and the knowledge which it draws therefrom is like that afforded of a room by mirrors fixed on opposite walls, which reflect each other (as well as objects in the intervening space) although without being strictly parallel." Claude Lévi-Strauss, *The Savage Mind* (Chicago: University of Chicago Press, 1966), 263. This quotation served as an epigraph to Smithson's "Incidents of Mirror Travel in the Yucatan" and was typed up by Felix Partz on an index card (1969–70).

24. "Pablum" (1973), 26. Note that in the present tense of this writing that "initiating reinforcing" happened at the same time, just as "generating realizing stabilizing" did.
25. Ibid., 27.
26. The sentence—"Cut words lines let image free"—is ambiguous. Is the comma missing that would make the sentence two acts: cutting words lines *and* freeing images? Or is it by cutting word lines that images are freed? Images were freed from their contexts, which were maintained by words: captions, advertising copy, etc.
27. Bronson wrote this in some notes on the writers Parker Tyler and Charles Henri-Ford with specific reference to Tyler. Bronson, Notebook 1971–72.
28. It's not hard to see how General Idea could derive the idea that collage correspondence was classification when you read this statement by Lévi-Strauss: "The real question is not whether the touch of a woodpecker's beak does in fact cure toothache. It is rather whether there is a point of view from which a woodpecker's beak and a man's tooth can be seen as 'going together' (the use of this congruity for therapeutic purposes being only one of its possible uses), and whether some initial order can be introduced into the universe by means of these groupings." *The Savage Mind*, 9.
29. "General Idea's Borderline Cases: Introduction," *IFEL* 2:3 (September 1973), 12.
30. Ibid.
31. One can reconstruct the process of fabrication of this article, first from the requests in the December 1972 and May 1973 issues of *FILE* (see note 3, chapter 12 above); then Partz's 1972 notebook; together with the Project Series file Borderline Cases (1972–73) in the General Idea archive. As an ordered ensemble, the article, in effect, was a prototype for the *Pavillion*, which does not mean that it was only a precursor; the *Pavillion* only continued the methodology established by this article.
32. In a notation on "Borderline Categories," Partz designated two main categories: "Mirror," including reflective or imitative cases and "Divisional," including natural and cultural boundaries. Partz, Notebook 1972.
33. General Idea gave this mirror division an esoteric reading. In a speculative text in his notebook, Bronson wrote "Without the Split, there is no consciousness." (Bronson, Notebook 1971–72), while after a quotation from a Kabbalist text, *The Book of Concealed Mystery* ("For before there was equilibrium, countenance beheld not countenance"), Felix Partz wrote, "That is, consciousness was not possible before this duality." Partz, Notebook 1972. In the second Borderline Case, the text asks, "Was meeting face to face the mother of invention of the looking glass? Was this prop-osal to end our singleness?" "General Idea's Borderline Cases: Imitation of Life (Mimicry)," 14. I leave it to another scholar to determine whether there is also an esoteric system underlying General Idea's work, though I doubt that its generality will possess the coherency of the verbal structure that I outline in this book.
34. Text from *Manipulating the Self (Phase 1–A Borderline Case)*, 1970, no. 7002 in Barbara Fischer, ed., *General Idea Editions: 1967–1995* (Toronto: Blackwood Gallery, 2003). The published pamphlet is no. 7117; the print is no. 7305. The May/June 1972 *FILE* was a "Manipulating the Self Issue."

35. John Brockman, *37* (New York: Holt, Rinehart, Winston, 1970), passim.

36. Ibid., passim.

37. Ibid., 23.

38. Ibid., 61. "The negation of 'the thing described' compels us to assume 'the description' of the thing described" (61). Compare Smithson's statement, quoted twice in the faux-rejected *artscanada* article: "The true fiction eradicates the false reality." Smithson, 97.

39. Rather, "The *name*, the *sign of distinction*, the *description* (the 'this,' the 'that,' the 'the') are assumed as a consequence of the *coupling*: undifferentiated activity; *coupling*: a verb." Brockman, 53. As description was a verb, it was a process not product: "Description of 'no-thing' of 'event,' of 'process,' of 'doing,' of 'void': a thing. The description is the thing." Ibid., 91. In a quasi-mystical text, Bronson wrote, "In the coupling lies the description." Notebook 1971–72.

40. Ibid., 96.

41. "'I,' 'you,' 'he,' 'they,' represent the concept of the static unchanging subject of change." Ibid., 37. In this process, propositional subject and object were replaced by the verb. "37: verb. The coupling (an event) of observer-observed system." Ibid., 17.

42. Ibid., 21.

43. The concept of "split" went along with that of coupling, and in Bronson's 1971–72 notebook where it was given a mystical import. General Idea appropriated one of Ray Johnson's spit mailings redirecting it as a split project (*Ray Johnson Split Project*, 1972). Also see *Split Project* (1972) in Bayer, "Uncovering the Roots of General Idea," 82, 85–86.

44. Consider this notebook exercise by AA Bronson, which was a piecing together of Brockman phrases: "There are no mirrors. There are no mirrors. There is only coupling, event. Throw away the words. Throw away word 'the'. There is no past. There is no future. There are no pictures, no inner, no outer, no upper, no lower, no where, no-thing. What do you do when there is no you to do it?" Bronson, Notebook 1971–72.

45. Brockman meant "no mirrors" in the sense of a picture theory of representation. Brockman, 33.

46. William S. Burroughs, *Nova Express* (New York: Grove Press, 1992), 4; Brockman, 32, 16.

47. "The Generative Idea: the relation, the configuration, the essential coupling. The limits of the Generative Idea are marked by paradoxes, puzzles. Nothing is true; everything is permitted."

48. Consider "generalization" the *Pavillion* itself: "A generalization is a way of seeing, a way of becoming. In the generalization lies the configuration, the essential coupling that eliminates the noun. We move within generalizations; we carry them like shells upon our body. We barter with them; we make them the construct, we live within them as a universe. In the generalization lies the reality. It is our mirror, an ongoing abstraction, supposedly immune to the ravages of time. In this mirror, we find fleeting images—immeasurable, unknowable."

49. Brockman, 38. Also: "No nouns: no objects, no people, no propositions, *no-thing*," 10. "'I': a noun. 'I am': noun'd. *Existence is being*: noun'd. To be or not to be: noun'd. 37: negation of the noun: no-thing," 38.

50. Ibid., 21.

51. Miss General Idea was described precisely in these terms in the "Glamour" article. The article further stated, "Reality hypes invariably feature the noun, posed on stiletto heels, and bound in the latest fantasy. This is the object of our desire. We admire its rare artificiality, the terse convolution of pose and gesture. Object fetishism is basically linguistic: even verbs are made nouns. Object fetishism is the ultimate reality con, the mortality game, the art market, the glamour girl hype."

52. "OBJECT HATRED—THE NOUN
General Idea (as a verb not noun)
LIGHT ON
Borderline"
Felix Partz, Notebook 1972.

See Smithson's comments on objects: "'Objects' are 'sham space,' the excrement of thought and language. Once you start seeing objects in a positive or negative way you are on the road to derangement." Smithson, 96.

53. Guy Debord, *Society of the Spectacle* (Detroit: Black and Red, 1977), § 35, § 3. Subsequent references in this section are indicated in the text.

"When Guy Debord's *Society of the Spectacle* first came out in English in 1970, it became our bible instantly. When Art Metropole opened, we displayed it prominently, right next to Gilbert & George. The ideas of the Situationists—Debord's in particular—seemed central to everything we had done and were doing and wanted to do." AA Bronson, "Bound to Please," 131.

54. Lévi-Strauss, *Totemism*, trans. Rodney Needham (Boston: Beacon Press, 1963), 26.
55. "Pablum for the Pablum Eaters" (1973), 28.
56. Bronson, Notebook 1971–72; Notebook 1972–73.
57. Yet they were significant enough for the artists to contemplate a Borderline exhibition.
58. Bronson, Notebook 1972–73; "Some Juicy and Malicious Gossip," *FILE* 1:1 (April 1972), 3.
59. Bronson, Notebook 1972–73.
60. Bronson, Notebook 1971–72.
61. "Pablum" (1973), 28. AA Bronson, "John Mitchell and Vincent Trasov, The Rise and Fall of the Peanut Party," *artscanada*, 212/213 (March/April 1977), 72.
62. Bronson, Notebook 1974.
63. Lévi-Strauss, "The Structural Study of Myths," 229; *The Savage Mind*, 32. Subsequent references to *The Savage Mind* in this section are given within the text. Partz, Notebook 1972.
64. Snowden Snowden, "Bzzz Bzzz Bzzz: AA Bronson on General Idea." *Metropolis M*, No. 1 (February/March 2011).
65. "Glamour," *FILE* 3:1 (Autumn 1975), n.p.
66. Lévi-Strauss, *The Raw and the Cooked: Introduction to a Science of Mythology*, trans. John and Doreen Weightman (New York: Harper & Row, Publishers, Inc, 1969), 12.
67. Lévi-Strauss, "The Structural Study of Myth," 210.
68. "It is clear that myth and art are closely related: they both miniaturize. They make reality readily available. They establish the unfathomable in fathomable terms. They classify the known, the unknown." "Pablum" (1973), 26. Later the "Glamour" article stated: "Glamour, like myth, miniaturizes reality, making it visible in a single glance. All major characteristics are retained. Any 'real-life' context may be simulated." Is the fetish, then, a miniature? One section of the *Showcards* was labelled "miniatures."
69. "Pablum" (1973), 26.
70. Bronson, Notebook 1974.
71. "Pablum" (1976), 200.
72. "It is always earlier ends which are called upon to play the part of means: the signified changes into the signifying and vice versa." *The Savage Mind*, 21.
73. "Pablum" (1973), 26.
74. Ibid.
75. Bronson, Notebook 1971–72. Felix Partz's 1972 Notebook attributes this quotation to Jack Burnham.
76. Bronson, Notebook 1971–72. There was an intention to publish a "Glamour Book" in which "military strategies," at least according to a provisional chapter outline by Felix Partz, deserved its own section. So did "Mirrors" and "Borderline Cases." Partz, Notebook 1972. Partz's notebook is interesting for its in-depth, parallel treatment of borderline cases and military metaphors.
77. "Pablum" (1973) 26; "Editorials: To Whom It May Concern," *FILE* 1:4 (December 1972); "Pablum" (1973) 26.
78. Burroughs, *Nova Express*, 53.
79. AA Bronson, "Myth as Parasite/Image as Virus: General Idea's Bookshelf 1967–1975," in *The Search for the Spirit: General Idea 1968–1975*, 17–18. In a 1991 interview Felix Partz described Burroughs's influence: "Even just thinking in terms of somebody like William Burroughs and *Naked Lunch*. People think of it more as stylistic because it's sensational sex and drugs. But also, I mean, something about *Naked Lunch* is that it projects, it creates this sort of 'Global Myth.' It all takes place in this Sci-Fi reconstructed world. There practically are things like pavillions and performances—this whole construct. So I think that it was influential on that level, as well as sort of, clever phrases and lingo and imagery. It's also this way of *seeing* the world. This sort of projection project." Louise Dompierre interviews General Idea, General Idea archive.

80. *Nova Express*, 59. Felix Partz copied a variation of this text from *The Soft Machine* (New York: Grove Press, 1992), 152. Felix Partz, Notebook 1968. He then retyped them on index cards in 1969–70.

81. William S. Burroughs, *The Ticket That Exploded* (New York: Grove Press, 1987), 58; *Nova Express*, 52, 48. "Word begets image and image *is* virus," or shortened to "image *is* virus," was a slogan of the correspondence movement.

82. William S. Burroughs, "Electronic Revolution," in *Word Virus: The William S. Burroughs Reader*, eds. James Grauerholz & Ira Silverberg (New York: Grove Press, 1998), 295. See also "The Invisible Generation" in *The Ticket That Exploded*, 205–217. He advocated cut-up methods to disrupt the media; the experimental methods he advocated in his novels, of using tape recorders for cut-ups, he advocated in the "field" as well, in everyday life.

83. "Electronic Revolution," 295; *Nova Express*, 53; *The Ticket That Exploded*, 54.

84. "Electronic Revolution," 298–99. Subsequent references in this section are indicated in the text. A recruiting character in Burroughs's "Where You Belong" says "We don't report the news—We write it. … We fold writers of all time in together and record radio programs, movie sound tracks, TV and juke box songs all the words of the world stirring around in a cement mixer and pour in the resistance message 'Calling partisans of all nation—Cut world lines—Shift linguals—Free doorways—Vibrate 'tourists'—Word Falling—Photo falling—Break through in Grey Room." *The Soft Machine*, 148–149.

85. "Pablum" (1973), 24. *Nova Express*, 55. "… the Subliminal exist in a 'parasitic' or 'criminal' role, in which they partake of the same institutions, media and art hierarchy without relying on that hierarchy for any structural definition, nor contributing anything to it." "Pablum" (1976), 197.

86. "The Spirit of the Miss General Idea Pageant," *IFEL* 2:3 (September 1973), insert. An exhibition of this material was considered but in the end its lack of quality did not warrant it.

87. Bronson, Notebook 1973–74.

88. Ibid.. It's unclear whether their participation in *Project '74* ever took place. At the same time, General Idea were preparing Art Metropole and their participation in *Art's Birthday, the Hollywood Decca Dance*, which took place in Los Angeles February 2, 1974.

89. For an outline of the *Floor to Ceiling Thought* performance, see Bronson's 1974 Notebook.

90. However, they were published previously in the December 1973 *FILE* Editorial and article "The Search for the Spirit of Miss General Idea (1984)."

91. There were other such performances. For notes for a script on "Search for the Spirit of the 1984 Miss General Idea Pavillion," see Felix Partz, Notebook 1975. Other scripts are found in various Project Series files in the General Idea archive.

92. Loose sheet in Felix Partz, Notebook 1975–1978.

93. "Originally General Idea was a bigger group, it started out about eight. The three of us were central, then a group who lived with us and were part of the performances and so on. At some point the group more or less disbanded, leaving just the three of us and at that point we realized that in order to have a presence in the art world people needed to know who we were, and we began to do self portraits, and that would have been about 1975." David Brittain, "F is for Filing System: An Interview with AA Bronson," *Afterimage* 35:3 (November/December 2007), 11.

94. "Glamour," *FILE* 3:1 (Autumn 1975), n.p. While the "Glamour" article was the fullest expression of playing with the myth of the individual artist, the critique was there from the start. In a draft for *FILE*'s first editorial, Bronson wrote, "That mythologies to date concerning the artist are enervating and restricting." Bronson, Notebook 1971–72.

95. Ibid..

96. "Editorial," *FILE* 2:4 (December 1973).

97. "Wordlines are an important as sightlines in plotting the course." "The Miss General Idea Vehicle," *FILE* 4:1 (Summer 1978), 39.

98. "Catalogue," *FILE* 1:2&3, 57.

99. See Philip Monk, "Picturing the Toronto Art Community: The Queen Street Years," *C international contemporary art* 59 (September–November 1998), insert.

100. Felix Partz, Notebook 1974–75. Unacknowledged quotations in this section are from this notebook.

APPENDICES

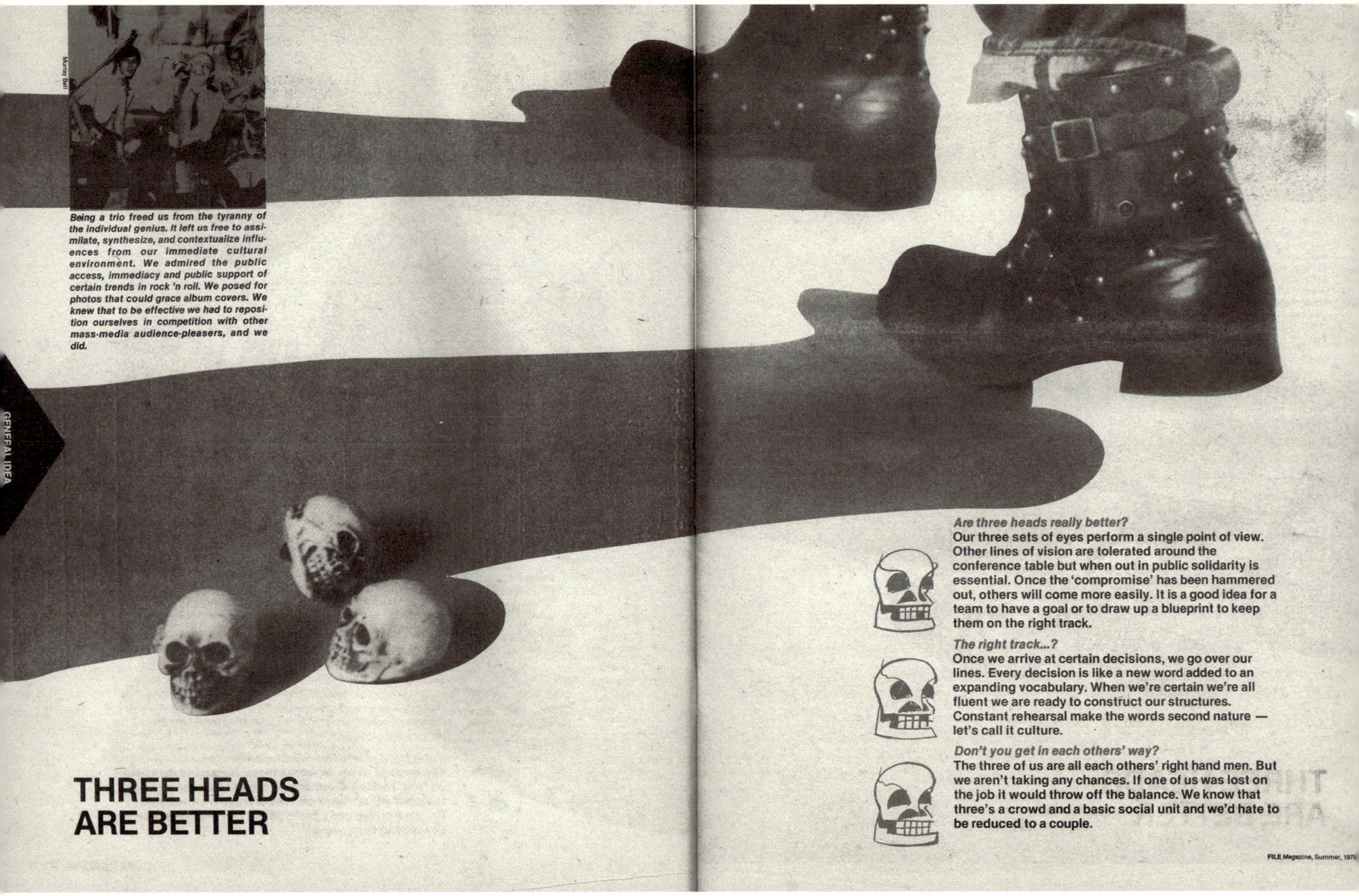

THREE HEADS ARE BETTER

Being a trio freed us from the tyranny of the individual genius. It left us free to assimilate, synthesize, and contextualize influences from our immediate cultural environment. We admired the public access, immediacy and public support of certain trends in rock 'n roll. We posed for photos that could grace album covers. We knew that to be effective we had to reposition ourselves in competition with other mass-media audience-pleasers, and we did.

Are three heads really better?
Our three sets of eyes perform a single point of view. Other lines of vision are tolerated around the conference table but when out in public solidarity is essential. Once the 'compromise' has been hammered out, others will come more easily. It is a good idea for a team to have a goal or to draw up a blueprint to keep them on the right track.

The right track...?
Once we arrive at certain decisions, we go over our lines. Every decision is like a new word added to an expanding vocabulary. When we're certain we're all fluent we are ready to construct our structures. Constant rehearsal make the words second nature — let's call it culture.

Don't you get in each others' way?
The three of us are all each others' right hand men. But we aren't taking any chances. If one of us was lost on the job it would throw off the balance. We know that three's a crowd and a basic social unit and we'd hate to be reduced to a couple.

"Three Heads are Better," *FILE* 4:1 (Summer 1978), 14–15

MARSHALL McLUHAN, GENERAL IDEA, AND ME!

I'd like to thank the Art Gallery of Ontario for inviting me to deliver the McCready Lecture on Canadian Art. The invitation tells me one thing: contemporary eventually becomes historical. I am honoured to follow John Raulston Saul, who in this series two years ago spoke importantly of Canada as a *métis* civilization. I am not about to go him one better with a talk tonight about the *queering* of Canada ... or Toronto ... or at least the Toronto art community. No, no, no, tonight I am talking about Marshall McLuhan, General Idea, and me!

What was it about Winnipeg, because is this not the initial connection between Marshall McLuhan, General Idea, and me? Some forty-three years ago when I bought this pocketbook edition of *Understanding Media*, attended architecture school in the wake of Michael Tims (soon to become AA Bronson), and saw an exhibition of Ron Gabe's (soon to become Felix Partz) large-scale hand paintings in some loft in downtown Winnipeg, what was it?—because the McLuhanistic outlook of that time seems so foreign to the insular surrealism that has dominated that city recently, albeit in its rise to attention. However, this is not a talk about Winnipeg but Toronto and the question of the Toronto School: the Toronto School of Communications, that is, which included Harold Innis, Eric Havelock, and Marshall McLuhan—and, why not, General Idea?

Could these original bad boys of Canadian art ever belong to a school—even a night school, the title of one of their 1989 exhibitions? Not that I am trying to get my foot in the door of such an elite institution as the Toronto School by tagging along in this lecture's title. Of course, by "me" I mean everybody. There is some trace in mine, though, of Roland Barthes's initial title to his essay "Longtemps je me suis couché de bonne heure," which was "Proust et moi" ("Proust and I"). But instead of a homosexual coupling of two, my title is a ménage à trois (or ménage à cinq). *Menage a trois*, you know, is also the name of a 1978 General Idea exhibition and publication. There is a reason for maintaining *three* in my title, rather than two: Marshall McLuhan and General Idea ... or, again, General Idea and me. "Two" is the number of rivalry—or mimicry (which are one and the same). The number two ensures that we would talk here of influence: the influence *of* Marshall McLuhan *on* General Idea. The number two would give us our marching orders—one, two, one, two—to traditionally conceive influence, marching straight ahead, as unidirectional, which is often the case only of "mechanical matching," as McLuhan would say (rather than the possibility of the reverse: a posthumous queering of McLuhan, if that is at all possible—probably not!). On the other hand, and by saying this, that is, by saying "on the other hand," we are already caught within the binary logic of handedness (one, two, left, right), the binding logic of either-or, ... (nonetheless) on the other hand, the number three complicates matters: it dispels influence in undermining one of the mainstays of its concept: that of authorship that a collective implicitly denies. Not that this passage from two to three is an *overturning*, which applies the same dualistic language, when we are concerned instead with the flipping or oscillating back and forth of ambiguity as it operates in General Idea's system, an ambiguity that is regulated instead by the contradictory logic of myth. General Idea materially realized this logic in the mirrored venetian blinds of their 1973 prototype *Luxon V.B.*

The numbers two and three underlie everything that I say tonight. They rule it since these numbers as well engender General Idea's system. This is easy to remember, not easy to see. One, two, three, a numeric cosmology rules General Idea's system. Repeat after me, class: One, two, three, a numeric cosmology rules General Idea's system.

Not the least concern in the passage from two to three is the anti-oedipal nature of the transition, which renounces the father figure. I'll leave this question of renunciation and paternity suspended but it does touch upon, in the period between 1975 and 1977, what was abandoned in General Idea's system by arguably turning away, however unconsciously or ironically, from McLuhan. The *threesome*—becoming three—had something to do with this.

General Idea would have been the first to acknowledge the pervasive influence of Marshall McLuhan, as when for instance AA Bronson wrote in a text for the AGO's 1997 exhibition *The Search for the Spirit: General Idea 1968–1975*:

> As children of the Summer of Love (1967) and spectators of the Paris riots (1968), we were well aware of the International Situationists and *Society of the Spectacle* on one hand, and of Marshall McLuhan, drug culture, digger houses, underground papers and free schools on the other.

This is a complex "awareness" for a group that formed in 1969; but McLuhan, or the *name* McLuhan, could be taken *at the time* to sum them all up. And for at least AA, we know that McLuhan was a hero of sorts.

Turning to General Idea's work, one might think that it would make sense to examine McLuhan's influence on the artists through their *media* works, their brilliant television productions, such as *Pilot*, *Test Tube*, or *Shut the Fuck Up*, made between 1977 and 1985. Meant to be broadcast on television, these videos tended to deal with the mechanics not the medium itself—that is, when the artists were not directly talking back to the media, as in *Shut the Fuck Up*. *The 1984 Miss General Idea Pageant* performances were already "television," performed as if in television studios; they rehearsed both the performers *and* audience in their staged cues. They were ceremonies meant to parody the art system's methods of evaluation and elevation as seen through—or commented on by—the format of the beauty pageant. (In the end they were all commentary, commentary being the linguistic basis of much of General Idea's fabrications.) Television was taken over as one other format to parody or plunder. Such nesting of contexts literalizes McLuhan's statement that "the 'content' of any medium is always another medium."

Rather than a specific medium—the television medium, for instance—we need to discover the immersive environment within which General Idea's own system operated, but not necessarily as the *visible* "anti-environments, or countersituations made by artists" as McLuhan called them stressing the importance of artists in revealing the unconscious effects of new technology. When McLuhan wrote that "Environments are invisible. Their ground rules, pervasive structure, and overall patterns evade easy perception," we might apply these comments word for word to General Idea's system itself, which likewise was invisible. Their system was the medium within which their work functioned.

Then again, we might look to *FILE Megazine*, General Idea's picture magazine in the guise of *LIFE* magazine, which began publishing in 1972, and find its source in McLuhan's *Mechanical Bride: Folklore of Industrial Man*, first published in 1951 and reissued in soft cover in 1967 to capitalize on his fame—although by then, admittedly, the book was a bit dated. Yet General Idea always proved that the dated was fertile ground, indeed, camp ground; they took it as a principle of their work. Their retrospective futurity—creating an archaeology of the past's image of the future—based itself on the same type of images McLuhan used (in their case mainly drawn from *Fortune* magazine from the 1940s and 1950s), except these images were contemporary to McLuhan and retro for General Idea. Perhaps McLuhan gave General Idea license to proceed with their own parody of the media in *FILE*, turning the media's devices against them, much the way McLuhan had done later when he stylistically adopted advertising lingo and techniques in his popular editions *The Medium in the Massage* (1967) and *War and Peace in the Global Village* (1968), etc. By the way, *FILE* published from a *Canadian* point of view, which is its own special kind of irony, as we all know. It is important to remember that at a high point in Canadian nationalism, General Idea, too, were nationalists, in spite of their international outlook (another McLuhanistic trait perhaps). Yet General Idea had an advantage over McLuhan in that their criticism was parasitical, not seemingly objective; it was produced from an artistic not academic point of view. It took place as an artwork mimicking the mythmaking processes of advertising or popular culture but at a higher semiotic level. They "criticized" *performatively*, their operations taking place within the mechanisms they put on display. In the essay "Myth Today" extremely influential on General Idea around 1974–75, yet only offering a more sophisticated analytical language for what was already in their work, Roland Barthes wrote:

> It thus appears that it is extremely difficult to vanquish myth from the inside: for the very effort one makes in order to escape its stranglehold becomes in its turn the prey of myth: myth can always, as a last resort, signify the resistance which is brought to bear against it. Truth to tell, the best weapon against myth is perhaps to mythify it in its turn, and to produce an *artificial myth*; and this reconstituted myth will in fact be a mythology. Since myth robs language of something, why not rob myth? All that is needed is to use it as the departure point for a third semiological chain, to take its signification as the first term of a second myth.

The latter proceeded from Barthes's observation of myth as a second order semiological system parasitical on a prior sign. General Idea's Glamour myth was a *third* order semiological system parasitical on a second order myth that it in turn cannibalized. While myth naturalizes, hiding its ideological construction, Glamour does the opposite: it artificializes. It's hard to imagine how an artificial myth can be produced except as an artwork, especially an artwork about artifice. Imagine Miss General Idea's shoes as a model of this artificiality: "They raise the Participant into an unnatural (hence cultured) position in which walking is rendered difficult..."

Not limited in their media analyses to McLuhan, General Idea were incredibly syncretic in amalgamating various influences within their fictional system. And being *mediumistic*, these influences extended, as well, to the Kabbala and Mme. Blavatsky. In the real world, Guy Debord's *Society of the Spectacle* and Roland Barthes's *Mythologies* were equally important as McLuhan, not to mention the wild card of William Burroughs's provocative media speculations, which were more about radical media intervention breaking viral mind control than comfortable academic or ideological analyses of content. After outlining the mix of late sixties influences cited earlier, AA Bronson went on to say: "Now we turned to the queer outsider methods of William Burroughs, for example, whose invented universe of sex-mad, body-snatcher espionage archetypes provided the ironic myth-making model we required." Burroughs offered models, methods, and lingo, even to the advice to simulate a newsmagazine as here in his early 1960s novel *Nova Express*:

> "We need a peg to hang it on," he said. "Something really ugly like virus. Not for nothing do they come from a land without mirrors." So he takes over this newsmagazine.
> "Now," he said, "I'll by God show them how ugly the Ugly American can be."
> And he breaks out all the ugliest pictures in the image bank and puts it out on the subliminal so one crisis piles up after the other right on schedule.

When you look at the ideas in this short dialogue—virus, the subliminal inhabitation of media (i.e., taking over formats such as a newsmagazine), mirrors (although the influence of Robert Smithson should be marked here as well), and image banks—you realize how influential Burroughs was (not to mention his concept of cut-up) not just to General Idea but the whole correspondence network of mail artists.

But to keep our sight on McLuhan, consider this 1973 General Idea reference to McLuhan's *The Medium is the Massage*:

> Concerning the mechanics of vision it is necessary to see that a shift in realities is simply shifting seeing. It is necessary to realize the levels of vision, the split between naturalized and culturalized information and the manner in which culturized (sic) information may become ritualized as natural information to the point where it in turn may be absorbed by the cultural processes as raw material for further processing. The famous "Medium is the Massage" is simply this, media inversion and the raising of vision to additive levels and complexities.

Shifting seeing as shifting focus in order to look at the ways of seeing actually was more about the mapping of word lines on sightlines, a technique whereby the artists directed or, rather, controlled our vision. Both McLuhan's media inversion (the embedding of previous media as content of a new medium) and Barthes's second order semiological system could be seen to be the models here for how cultural information is ritualized, as if it was natural, and then taken to an additive level of parodic complexity by our artists. Yet the very mention of a nature/culture division should cue us to Claude Lévi-Strauss, whose writings on structural anthropology, strongly influential on early

General Idea, also uncover the same mechanisms. Under the influence of Lévi-Strauss, General Idea saw themselves as anthropologists of contemporary myth. In fact, before the influence of Barthes's *Mythologies*, Lévi-Strauss's was General Idea's model of myth.

You're beginning to see that McLuhan was only part of the mythic mix (a subversive mix, one might add). So while I agreed to give a lecture tonight on Marshall McLuhan and General Idea, I don't want to bore you with the traditional tracking down of influences, which makes no sense in a body of work like this, but rather look at the relationship between McLuhan and General Idea in a more diffused way. For instance, listen to McLuhan's pronouncement from his 1968 book *Through the Vanishing Point*:

> Perhaps the mere speed-up of human events and the resulting increase of interfaces among all men and institutions ensure a multitude of innovations that upset all existing arrangements whatever.

Increasing interfaces upsetting all existing arrangements perfectly describes the ethos and methodology of General Idea's early work, which was a radical collage aesthetic, but which owed as much or more to William Burroughs, as I have said, as it did to Marshall McLuhan, and which was shared amongst the short-lived correspondence art movement, and, moreover and significantly, which set up the long-term *systematic* framework within which General Idea's work developed (the *Pageant* and *Pavillion*)—which was a system of myth. In light of McLuhan's quotation above, consider this description from General Idea's May 1973 *FILE* article "Pablum for the Pablum Eaters":

> When a junky when any junky when we art junkies gotta get our fix we gotta make a connection we gotta get a fix we need our correspondences.... The logic of myth is the logic of connections. Image making room for words. Naming of partz, sensing the network working plugged into the subliminal. The key to this logic is the borderline situation, the neither one nor the other, camouflaged indifference, mirror mirror on the wall. Flip flop. Lip flap.... The logic of myth is the moving territory of words, cut word lines, shift linguals. The logic of myth is the sense of image upon image image overdose the network causality affair with ideas raining in the corner.... Image trouble is no trouble at all. Image overdose and suddenly snap you're out there broken through the borderline floating on the dead edge of nowhere with images diving in all directions, a sky full of claws and feathers.... Then there is jumbled jargon, lip flap, loose vowels. Cut word lines shift linguals.

As crazy as this sounds, in its increasing interfaces upsetting all existing arrangements, *all* of General Idea is here, even if we don't recognize their main themes. For, after all, we believe, that as architecture, General Idea's is a stable system. But theirs was a "system in motion" that was only temporarily stable, or was only an illusion of stability based on alternatives:

> In this article seeing art as a system of signs in motion as an archive and indicator and stabilizer of culture as a means of creating fetish objects as residence for the field of imagery defining a culture, seeing all this and more in many ways we have become aware of the necessity of developing methods of generating realizing stabilizing alternate myths alternate lifestyles.

Taking seriously General Idea's early writing would allow us to shake up our understanding of their work—upsetting all existing *interpretative* arrangements. What are the implications of a "system of signs in motion" for interpreting and exhibiting a body of artworks (especially in retrospectives, as here at the AGO)?

The problem with interpreting General Idea's work is that we take the artists at their word and at the same time we *don't* take them at their word. Their work was not just one big joke; it was a coherent system. Moreover, it was a coherent system that can be examined analytically with the period's interpretative tools, which General Idea used, significantly, as well to *construct* their work: Claude Lévi-Strauss's structural anthropology, Roland Barthes's semiology, Marshall McLuhan's media theory, amongst others. General Idea's work appeared as artwork, that is to say visually, but its mode of appearing, or its *event* of appearing, one might say, was performative: it came into being through a language act; the *Pavillion* was erected through language—it did not exist otherwise. The *system* put the *Pavillion* in place (i.e., erected) and kept it standing (i.e., operating). As it was in their work, so it should be in our analyses: a priority given to language, in our case a close examination of their writing.

Seventeen years after the end of General Idea, the systematic nature of their work has still to be addressed. This is a difficult task because the system, in work that was all about presentation, did not show itself. In other words, in work that was all about articulation, the system could not articulate itself—but it was there nonetheless in the telling, as the telling. While not appearing, nonetheless, this *total* system regulates all the operations of General Idea's enterprise, and, as in any system, all these operations are linked.

Because the subject of my book is not the subject of my lecture, you'll have to take my word for now that the system's ruling term Glamour is a *concept* whose *operations* are achieved through the application of *techniques* produced by *strategies* and insinuated by *tactics*. Although there might be a number of sub-categories for each, there is only one concept: *Glamour*; one operation: *reversibility*; one technique: *cut-up*; one strategy: *theft*; one tactic: *camouflage*.

As a substitute for this discussion, here is a structuralist diagram of Glamour's operations, which explains the commutable system of reversibility of General Idea's work. I believe that everything in General Idea is expressed in this diagram (fig. 1).

I can assure you that I did not know the degree of systematicity of General Idea's work when I started to write my book, although its aim was to discover and formalize this system. Moreover, I did not really comprehend for a long time that it also was a "system in motion," which I think is consequential for any interpretation of their work.

So I want here briefly to uncover the early ground that instituted this system, the ground on which the *Pavillion* later stood, which rather was an *abgrund*: an *un*grounding of system at the

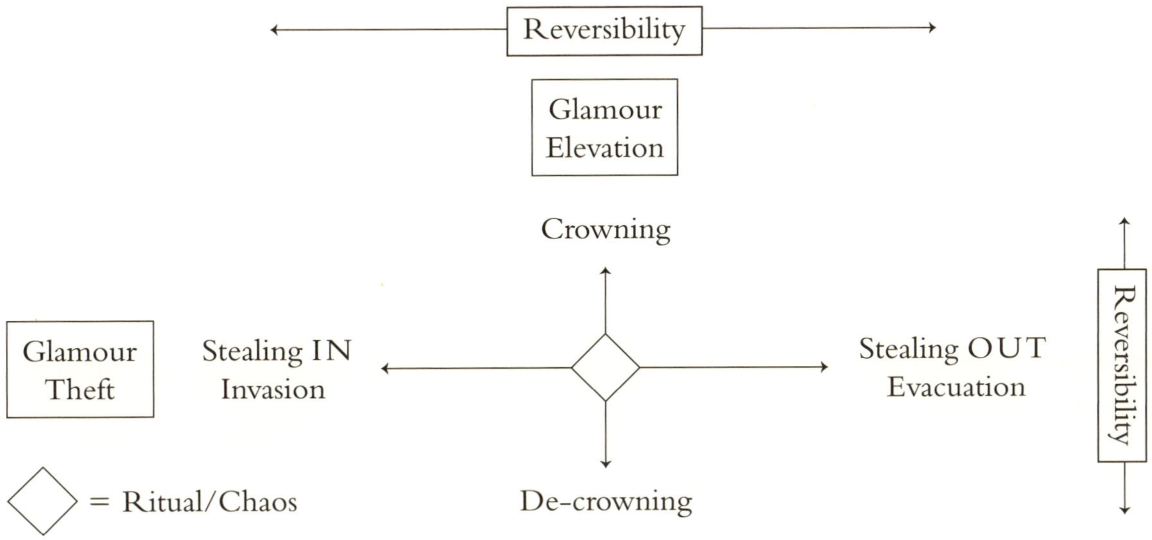

fig. 1. Glamour's operation of reversibility

same time. You see, the *Pavillion* was built on a fault line, a fault line that was both spatial and temporal. A recurring problem of critical interpretation is that we don't go back far enough in figuring out General Idea's work but tend to stop when it was consolidated in the period between 1975–1977: when the *Pavillion*—and its destruction—was most fully articulated. *Articulated.* General Idea were architect-*advocates.* Through their *verbal* advocacy, the *Pavillion* was erected. They were also advocates of their own program; their program was this advocacy, so why shouldn't we believe them? After all, they were persuasive; the *Pavillion* was built by persuasion, as the artists both directed our view of it and thus our understanding of their artistic program: "This is the story of General Idea," they said in 1975. They told this story better than anyone else. And we have believed them. But, we also know that behind every story there is a backstory, even an underground story, or perhaps an ungrounding story.

Even when they were telling stories about others, it was still about themselves: for instance, the article "Pablum for the Pablum Eaters." Ostensibly, this was an article about Vancouver's Image Bank, which, in the process, was intended to describe the methodologies of the correspondence art movement. Without elaborating its complete thesis, which was about describing myth as a total system, what is important for our story here is the idea of alternatives ("alternate myths alternate lifestyles")—but not only hippy alternatives or the alternative myths that artists create through cannibalizing the detritus of commercial capitalistic culture. No, we are talking of the very concept of the alternative itself, the alternative in alternation with itself (what at about the same time in French philosophy began to be called *différance*): that is, a *perpetual* alternation of ideas, words, and images—a cut-up methodology where everything was in constant motion and in perpetual crisis. "Everything is permitted," was a Nietzschean slogan General Idea took from Burroughs.

To return by example to McLuhan, who wrote "We actually live mythically and integrally, as it were, but we continue to think in the old, fragmented space and time patterns of the pre-electric age," General Idea's enterprise was a system of myth produced by the cut-up method. McLuhan's own method was collage-like—and his books were image banks of "what's happening." McLuhan called *The Medium is the Massage* "a collide-oscope of interfaced situations," which is a perfect description of what General Idea were writing about. Even an academic book such as *Gutenberg Galaxy* McLuhan called a collage event: "Thus the galaxy or constellation of events upon which the present study concentrates is itself a mosaic of perpetually interacting forms that have undergone kaleidoscopic transformation." This is what the whole correspondence art movement was all about: image banks were individual myths, archives of like images obsessed upon by artists, which were solicited through the pages of *FILE* and submitted through the mail by fellow subliminal networkers to surface again sometimes in the same pages of *FILE*. Detached from their intended meaning or function within one context, they were perversely put into circulation in another. Belying their symbol of stability (that of a bank), image banks were systems of signs in motion composing varied cosmologies. "Pablum" continued: "Correspondences are the key to the mythical universe, the cosmology of moving bodies, images in collision, classification by jointing." As image banks, not only *FILE*, but also *The 1984 Miss General Idea Pavillion* itself were such precarious constructions.

Perpetually changing, constantly colliding, collage conjunctions were events that brought together, in continual cut-up, different alignments of words and images. Different classifications by alternate jointings led to ever-new configurations. These were momentary events that were hardly visible, or at least visible only as after-images that offered the illusion of stability. Their conjunction was a vacillating borderline that was temporary.

The borderline (really, an interface) was a concept that General Idea shared with McLuhan, not surprisingly given that McLuhan posited it as part of the makeup of the Canadian persona (engendered vis-à-vis our relation to the United States). An ambiguous model signifying between the domains of politics and psychology—as both the boundary between nations and a personality disorder (i.e., borderline personality), the borderline was a major operative concept for General Idea. In their September 1973 *FILE* article "General Idea's Borderline Cases," the artists wrote "Ambiguity is not a symptom of a schizophrenic who travels back and forth across the line but a quality of the border dweller who performs in the stolen moments." Borderlines came into existence *every* time there was a mirror insertion or collage cut. In fact, mirror, cut-up, and borderline were one and the same: silent and invisible, yet engendering the verbosity of myth. ("The vacuum created by your invisibility has got to be filled with words," read a complementary article in the same issue). Unlike the *Pavillion* or *Pageant*, which were containers or formats, the borderline was an operative concept by which and on which the *Pavillion* was erected through means of disguise and theft. The *Pavillion* was built on this unstable borderline where the border dweller (General Idea) performed in stolen moments.

This article was its own case of cut-up correspondence of words and images. The borderline cases were ten exercises in creating seeming symmetries between words and images. Between one and the other, between word and image, though, was the surreptitious insertion of a mirror.

From the start, the mirror image, of course, always added up to two. Between one and the other, between the numbers one and two, were all the resources of mirroring, mimicry, and mockery as language clichés were married to banal images. Here is the text from the second case, titled "Imitation of Life (Mimicry)":

> It's only natural to try to be part of our vision, our culture. Like chameleons at odds trying to be part of it all. Like letting our one hand know what the other is about. When one body is imitating one body lying down its life imitating life. This act of bodies rubbing is merely a shadow of things to come. Was meeting face to face the mother of invention of the looking glass? Was this prop-osal to end our singleness? There's safety in numbers and two can have a mind of its own. Our two hands applauded the engagement and came out dueling. In the crack of dawn a narcissus is blooming. All together now, one two, one two, one two.

Yet, the two, or the mirror image of two, did not mean equality or even actual symmetry. *One* brought forth the other (as if in a mirror), and engendering it gave it life, as simulacral as that life was since it was only mimetic. (Mimicry was viral: indeed, a virus. The point of entry, the mirror act was a viral, replicating invasion.) One preceded two and that one was the word. That is, the word came first and did not merely caption an image after the fact. It took off from its invasion: serially, creating content in the process. Words, too, were mirrors.

Each case was an application: the application of a method through the insertion of a mirror. It was purely artificial. There was no given place to insert a mirror, however. No guideline. The borderline did not preexist. The *act* of mirror insertion created the borderline situation. Only the mirror preceded—as invisible as it was. As invisible as it was, it was an *event*, the instantiation of a case, an instance of now: a collage collision. It was *the* inaugurating act: the origin of *all* General Idea's work.

"The Great Divide was words," they said. Words made images secondary; in fact, they doubled them. Words split images. Or, the proliferation of words split images into mirror images of themselves. Here is case number 3, "Self Conscious":

> Now that we've got our distance we look back over our shoulders. Could this be our skin? Still waters reflect our eyes reflecting still waters running deep. Let's keep this all on the surface. The surface of the silvered glass narcissus. Could this be our connection? Score one for us and chalk it up to experienced. Driving the wedge down deep through the centre and splitting the images in halves. There is two of us to contend with now. Two heads are better than one but it's really just one more mouth to feed on. Casting our image in the mirror revealed a cast of two. Our very own dialogue to talk to ourselves. We're not the one we used to be.

Splitting in half was only a beginning that had no end. Words, like mirrors, were viral.

So in retrospect, when we read the statement from *FILE*'s first editorial ("Every image is a self image. Every image is a mirror."), we must now presume that *between* every image (that is, between every self-same image) is a borderline. This does not just make the image reflect itself (as if in a mirror) but is a fissure of words, indeed, of "cutting remarks." Words were a method of invasion, even of the image.

Identity, too, was viral. Identity—or role—was a mirror effect produced serially: one plus one plus one, which did not add up to three, however. Two was a precarious couple, not really the pillars of social and familial stability we think. As in a tripod, a motif in their late 1970s work, *three* was the stable number as when the 1977 *"Right Hand Man" Showcard* (1-076) reads: "The three of them are all each others right-hand man but they aren't taking any chances. If one was lost on the job it would throw off the balance. They know that three's a crowd and a basic social unit and they'd hate to be reduced to a couple." You know, General Idea were not always a threesome—the three men they became. A loose coalition at the beginning, General Idea did not *conceptually* consolidate themselves into a trio until 1975, when the first of their self-portraits began to appear: first as architects, then as their impersonations of babies, poodles, scholars, baby seals, etc. Is this fact significant? Yes. It is an intentional turn within their work, though not acknowledged: a crisis, you might say. And it pertains to the influence of McLuhan, which in 1975 ends, I would claim. The three-fold corporate stability could be argued as a turning away from both McLuhan *and* the principles of the collage-based correspondence movement, the origins of their early work that subsists throughout, nonetheless, in having set up the ground of their system.

The passage from two to three was a crisis indeed. Until this coup to the rule of three, the numbers one and two dominated in General Idea's system (as I've suggested by selecting the borderline cases cited earlier). Not even that many: the number *one* was above all. (Miss General Idea was the number one above all.) Two was only the effect of a mirror, engendered there as a simulacrum. But what an effect! Their whole system was sustained by it. But in 1975, henceforth the number three began to rule General Idea's work and it would have room for no others. This number, a troika, was all about control: controlling our vision, or, rather, constructing our vision in order to erect the *Pavillion* through these sightlines—and to elevate Miss General Idea at the same time. General Idea's corporate consolidation was consequential. Their fixed point of view, albeit established by a trio and not an individual, was a throwback. Paradoxically, it re-instituted the single-point perspectival system; "fixed relationships in pictorial space" were no longer images in collision. "Fixed relationships in pictorial space," McLuhan claimed, with its accompanying fragmented private point of view, were key to establishing the concept of individual identity during the print epoch, and were at odds with a mythic vision brought about by today's "electric implosion." The latter was the mythic universe of correspondence and collage cut-up—"the cosmology of moving bodies, images in collision" with its collide-oscopic McLuhanistic overtones—that General Idea, having earlier participated in, seemingly gave up. For example, here is one of General Idea's guiding statements produced in that mid-seventies period that evokes their fixed point of view, accumulated, though, to excess:

THE FRAME OF REFERENCE is basically this: a framing device within which we inhabit the role of the general public, the audience, the media. Mirrors mirroring mirrors expanding and contracting to the focal point of view and including the lines of perspective bisecting the successive frames to the vanishing point. The general public, the audience, the media playing the part of the sounding board, the comprehensive framework outlining whatever meets their eye.

That the triadic turn of 1975 re-established identity—that is to say "authorship," even though of a collective nature—when the whole ethos of General Idea's early work was the flouting of copyright is one of the anomalies of this intriguing body of work—but, of course, it was then turned to ironic ends. This is no criticism on my part of the further development of General Idea's work, only a way of designating the end of McLuhan's influence, and the conclusion of my lecture. Not only can we not judge, we cannot argue with a *mythic* system such as General Idea's.

As a corporation General Idea had become what McLuhan had first written about in 1951 in *The Mechanical Bride*: "Ours is the first age in which many thousands of the best-trained individual minds have made it a full-time business to get inside the collective public mind" and in the process creating a "folklore of industrial man, so much of which stems from the laboratory, the studio, and the advertising agencies. But amid the diversity of our inventions and abstract techniques of production and distribution there will be found a great degree of cohesion and unity. This consistency is not conscious in origin or effect and seems to arise from a sort of collective dream." General Idea were all three—a laboratory, a studio, and an advertising agency—and their collective dream was *The 1984 Miss General Idea Pavillion*. •

McCready Lecture on Canadian Art by Philip Monk on Wednesday, November 9, 2012, at Jackman Hall, Art Gallery of Ontario, Toronto

EDITORIAL

YOU — YOU'RE THE ONE

This issue we had to deal, once again, with the impossibility of writing editorials. This issue being General Idea's tenth aniversary, a time for looking back, looking forward, and saying something meaningful about it all, made the writing all the more difficult.

We knew in fact what we wanted to share with you. We wanted to point out the wildly fluctuating interpretations you, our public, impose on us. Under your gaze we become everything from frivolous night-lifers to hard-core post-Marxist theoreticians. We wanted to point out the function of ambiguity in our work, the way in which ambiguity 'flips the meanings in and out of focus', thus preventing the successful deciphering of the text (both visual and written) except on multiple levels. Curiously, many of you choose only to read one side to any story. Since we give a wide range of choices (and we are conscious of the politics of choice) we are never sure which side you, our readers, will take. Which is what makes this editorial so difficult to write. After all, we are not interested in 'capturing' our audience — only in arresting your attention.

The nature of criticism, like the nature of puns, is to pull a 'text' into crisis. The nature of our work then is 'critical', as opposed to descriptive. And the "crisis" is 1984.

WE DO IT ALL FOR YOU

A blow-by-blow description: Hot-head Jorge Zontal takes the cake in this celebration snapshot from General Idea's tenth anniversary party. Felix Partz (left) and AA Bronson (right) combine talents to make a wish for 1984.

FILE *Megazine*, Summer, 1978 7

"Editorial," *FILE* 4:1 (Summer 1978), 7

PERIODIZING GENERAL IDEA

Crises initiated the episodes of General Idea's work. They secretly produced the periodicity of their work. Some crises were acknowledged, others not. This is the story of General Idea as told through their crises.

1. *Mirror Trick*: May 1973

"We began as a mirror of sorts, a transcanada organ of communication within the art scene, a way of looking at the scene and oneself within it," General Idea wrote in 1972, describing the initial function of *FILE Megazine*, which they had commenced publishing earlier that year. But a year later, narcissistically, they stated, "FILE, no longer mirroring a scene, mirrors the mirror." Of course, this "crisis" was a fabrication of their own devising, a necessity, really, to get on with their own project: promoting themselves, not a scene. In abandoning a community, though, and turning the mirror on themselves, they were going against the principles of their own formation—or at least the formation of *FILE*—in the correspondence art system of the Eternal Network. For *FILE* was begun to service this network: it was a vehicle for collecting and disseminating image requests in order that these subliminal assemblages might be captured in individual image banks. Each bank was a myth of contemporary culture.

General Idea were not ready to give up myth, though. Myth was fundamental, indeed foundational, to their system. Myth stabilized alternatives; art was a method of "generating realizing stabilizing alternate myths alternate lifestyles," as they wrote in "Pablum for the Pablum Eaters." Initially, the function of myth was to contain contradictions: "In the myth opposite possibilities become complementary content," stated *FILE*'s first editorial. Yet the stability of myth belied the fact that this art was a "system of signs in motion." The problem is on our end, a problem of perception; for thinking that end products have no process, that artworks are static things and not in motion, is, in effect, a problem of believing in the architectural solidity of the *Pavillion* itself. But the basis of General Idea's work in collage cut-up made theirs a system in *permanent* crisis: myth, rather, was a "cosmology of moving bodies, images in collision." Cut-up was a continual crisis of the stability of the image.

When we realize that a mirror is an image in collision with itself, we understand General Idea's early slogan: "Every image is a self image. Every image is a mirror." Mirrors were divisive. Mirrors were tools of destabilization. They were cutting remarks for dissolving word lines, then erecting the illusion of others: the *Pavillion* itself, which was erected solely through the mirror effect of its language operations. Turning the mirror on itself made this apparatus not only fictional but functional, a machine for keeping a crisis (ambiguity, contradiction) in perpetual motion. Myth, mirror, and collage were one; they were one process of unlimited disruption and reconfiguration.

2. *Dead Letters*: September 1973

The September 1973 issue of *FILE* printed the obituary of the New York Correspondence School, or rather a letter from Ray Johnson (and one from Robert Cumming as well) "resigning" from the correspondence movement. As the first *FILE* editorial expressed that "The New York Correspondence School begun by Sugardada Ray Johnson remains the recognized forerunner of international image exchange now in operation," his abdication was indeed a blow to the movement. Strategically, General Idea published no requests of their own that issue, but it took four more issues of *FILE* before Image Bank Request Lists finally were discontinued, in 1976.

Was it a happy accident that correspondence art imploded, providing a convenient crisis for General Idea? Or the cover of one? We have already witnessed the mirror shift that subtly displaced their image from the crowd of correspondence artists, while not ostensibly elevating General Idea above others, as they stole away to reflect on themselves.[1] Coincidentally, in 1976 the original 1973 *FILE* article "Pablum for the Pablum Eaters," which so brilliantly theorized correspondence art, was reworked and republished. Now the original strategies of correspondence art were extended from individualistic to corporate activities ("in what way different groups continued to generate and stabilize an ongoing body of imagery as myth"), and from individual icons to collective formats ("as such, American mythology is deactivated and included in Ant Farm's [substitute General Idea's] larger mythological structures, their concern with themselves as artists concerned with culture").

Disengagement was subtle: between September 1973 and December 1973, *The 1984 Miss General Idea Pavillion* was no longer a participatory project of collective tender solicited through the mail but solely an articulation of General Idea's platform. The death of correspondence consolidated General Idea's program.

3. *Imitation Then Intimidation of LIFE*: June 1974

In June 1974, the editors of *FILE* received a cease-and-desist letter from TIME/LIFE Incorporated for "unauthorized simulation of the cover of LIFE." After two years of its look being lifted, the empire had struck back. So much for semi-disguised appropriation of popular and corporate culture or for subliminal viral inhabitation—"Like we slipped into your mailbox disguised as LIFE. There you were staring FILE in the face and you couldn't believe it was LIFE." The subliminal was criminal, but here was the real effect of the fictional language of parasitism entering the real world. Typically, General Idea played TIME/LIFE while playing along with them. Yet changes demanded were changes made.

All the same, "the legal battle merely punctuated a change of vision that was already occurring for FILE. The look-alike contest had run its course." So read the spring 1977 editorial that announced the resolution of the conflict. The appearance of *FILE* changed, but its cover girl makeover was still in TIME's face. Cheekily, the 1977 editorial continued: "FILE was entering a no-no-nostalgia age in preparation for 1984 and in keeping abreast of the TIMEs was becoming increasingly concerned with PEOPLE"; that is, appropriating neither the logo nor look but the content of another, recent Time Inc. publication, *People*. General Idea lived to fight another day, but their retreat was still one of Glamour's aggressive strategies of disguise.[2]

So tested legally in the challenging of a brand, they would eventually begin to ask themselves what was an "effective" art of the marketplace. Their response was twofold. Not quite immediate, the first was anti-authoritarian (see section 5). A decade later, the second was "if you can't beat them, join them" (see section 9). The first response was marginal, the second mainstream. The first perhaps was more aggressive than the second, but both meant an end to the "no-no-nostalgia age" of their early work.

4. *Two Becomes You*: September 1975

What was the change of vision that General Idea's legal battle merely punctuated? It was not necessarily what was in evidence in 1977 when the "FILE simulates LIFE" editorial was published, because in 1977 that vision again would change, bringing about a new crisis. The change was in the concept of Glamour—or rather Glamour's displaced looks, a change in its function. It is hard to qualify the concept of Glamour as a crisis, but it is not what Glamour exposes but what it hides or covers over that is the problem. Most people think of Glamour as the epitome of General Idea's system and the 1975 "Glamour" issue of *FILE* as its classic expression. But we are no longer dealing with Glamour as the ritual elevation of Miss General Idea, as in the *Pageant*, but as a *theft* that elevates instead our trio of artists. The discovery of this theft is no crisis, not even the realization that they had plagiarized Roland Barthes to make it. The crisis was ever so slight: only a change or two in number. If the change was slight, the effect, however, was disproportionate to the numbers involved. General Idea had "re-structured"; from a loose conglomerate of about eight members, they were reduced to their core group, and it was time to assert the identity of this brand in the art world. It was only in 1975, starting with the *Showcards*, that the image of a threesome began to be promoted aggressively: hence the collective portraits of them as a trio of architects, etc., that would continue in other impersonations until 1994. Yet we persist in reading back this group identity to their beginnings in 1969, just as, reading forward, we tend to assume that Glamour was an unchanging concept. Altogether different from General Idea's disguises or camouflage, these unacknowledged rifts that continuity smoothes over are crises of interpretation on our part.

Yet, it was not a reduction in number that was a crisis but its augmentation. Until this coup to the rule of three, the numbers one and two dominated in General Idea's system.[3] Not even that many: the number *one* was above all; two was only the effect of a mirror, engendered there as a simulacrum. But what an effect! Their whole system was sustained by it. The *Pavillion* itself was erected on a borderline. The borderline did not pre-exist; it was engendered by an event: by the flash of a mirror or the cut of collage. It was a non-place where suddenly one became two, where the selfsame image transformed into a mirror of itself. (The mirror was a viral replicating invasion: even identity was a mirror effect produced serially.) The borderline was the event itself: a perpetual crisis.

In becoming three, in becoming a threesome, General Idea gave up the borderline risk and hence gave up the crisis. They gave up the event where the one engendered two—all for the triumvirate stability of numbers.[4] This was the beginning of the troika's rule, even though ten years later the poodle disguises of their portrait made the three appear deceptively subservient.

So, after all, number was identity.

This was the beginning of the end, the end of their system as originally conceived. It was the first evidence of the "change of vision that was already occurring for FILE." The number three began to rule General Idea's work, and it would have room for no others.

5. *Punked*: September 1977

The second "people" issue of *FILE* (Fall 1977) was peopled by punks. As people, punks are notoriously disruptive. Punks are destructive. In so publicly embracing punk in this issue of *FILE*, what did General Idea want to destroy? *Themselves*, it seems, and all they previously stood for. There is nothing like self-immolation for a "change of vision"—especially when performed on a public stage, as an editorial pretends to be. Concluding statements are conclusive, especially in editorials. So we must take this admittedly more than three-chord statement from General Idea seriously: "The sentimentalism of late sixties early seventies essentially surrealistic aesthetic has been replaced by a certain pragmatic anarchy which is now the theme of this issue." But at the same time, we have to ask, to whom did this "sentimentalism of late sixties early seventies essentially surrealistic aesthetic" refer?

Was this a little of the anti-authoritarian "up yours" self-reflexively becoming "up ours"? What else could this statement refer to but the youthful merry mythmaking of the subliminal kids and their cut-up hijinks: General Idea and their gang? Here was inspiration in another, younger generation of cut and paste, and slash and burn. But a movement of "no future" was equally a movement of "no-no-nostalgia." The nostalgia age was past. But nostalgia, co-dependent with narcissism, was a bulwark of General Idea's system. Condemning nostalgia condemned the whole system. For instance, "Glamour" was another name for the dual functions of nostalgia and narcissism, just as the term "nostalgia" was interchangeable with "camouflage" and "disguise" in the operations of the system. Moreover, narcissism and nostalgia's implicated relationship implied a "mechanics of vision" that aligned word lines to sightlines and that set up the framework in which General Idea's work could be seen: indeed, the sightlines within which the *Pavillion* itself was erected. Punk was a blunt force that dismantled all this.

Moreover, "nostalgia" was a code word for camp; it was a coping word. Were General Idea dissing their own "pageantry of camp parody," as an earlier leftist art critic had derogated the first issue of *FILE*? Or were they displacing it to the transgressive positions advocated by these "hard-core post-Marxist theoreticians" they proposed to have become? At any rate, this "Punk issue" of *FILE* coincided with the English translation of Deleuze and Guattari's explosive toolbox *Anti-Oedipus* to influence an interesting but little discussed or exhibited period of General Idea's anti-patriarchal work from the late 1970s. Queer was no longer camp but hard-core.

6. *Who Lit the Match?*: October 1977

In October 1977, during one of the rehearsals for *The 1984 Miss General Idea Pageant*, the *Pavillion* burned down. The *Pavillion* had seven more years to go before its scheduled completion in 1984. Had the idea run its course, or were General Idea merely bored as per the contemporaneous "Punk" editorial ("look how bored we all are")? To sum up their work early in a crisis was no big deal; General Idea had been through crises before. Actually, burning the *Pavillion* was an afterthought of 1977. Yet destruction was implicit to their system from the start; it was the mirror inverse of construction. Potentially the biggest crisis of them all, the fire was only a turning point, a conversion process where the artists turned from architects to archaeologists combing the ruins. The ruins seemed terminal, though; and even though General Idea continued to add rooms (*The Boutique*, *Colour Bar Lounge*), they were detached from an overall system and answered to other demands and other principles. The archaeological reinvention of the *Pavillion* in the 1980s had nothing to do with their original system.

7. *No More Myth!*: July 1978

To sum up General Idea in a crisis, as the artists did in their summer 1978 editorial, should by now be no surprise. Their definition of crisis, given here a *textual* inflection, though, was surprising. "The nature of criticism, like the nature of puns, is to pull a 'text' into crisis," they wrote. "The nature of our work then is 'critical,' as opposed to descriptive. And the 'crisis' is 1984." What is *critical* is not necessarily what is a crisis in their work, but this indication of their conversion from mythology to textual criticism was. "Text," of course, was the "different object" of the "science of the signifier," the domain of French theory presided over by Roland Barthes. The reception of French theory in North America in the late 1970s was problematic, to say the least, notably in its staggered and out-of-sync translation of key texts. For instance, in 1975 General Idea "plagiarized" Barthes's essay "Myth Today" from his book *Mythologies*, but this early attempt at semiology had already been surpassed by the author himself even before its 1972 English translation.

Getting with the postmodernist program along with everyone else was no crisis (in Canada, admittedly, General Idea were still ahead of the game). It was what they gave up to get with it that was. Once more, General Idea continued to gang up on themselves, as they had done twice in *FILE*'s 1977 editorials, to reject once again their earlier sentimental nostalgia. Though not named, what was under assault was myth itself. Not just myth but the whole methodology (mythology) of their early work: the image bank, correspondence, cut-up foundation of their system in motion. For *description* was the basis of the mythological system: myth "structures a cosmology through description, not analysis," read the second "Pablum for the Pablum Eaters" article, echoing the first.

Let's not get sentimental about this rejection. Textual theory provided a more exploitable model to justify the system's formalism: for instance, that of reversibility in a project where "ruins are created as quickly as rooms are built."[5]

8. *The Revenge of the Market*: September 1981

For General Idea, editorials were sometimes manifestos, but they were always "recurring statements of position."[6] The fall 1979 editorial on transgression and the March 1981 one on $UCCE$$, with their audacious "flirtation" with neoconservative fascism and capitalism, may have appeared "shocking" in their time—what are manifestos for—but they did not deviate from General Idea's course. The shock of the *old* returned to haunt them in the fall 1981 editorial

"The Re-materialization of the Art Object"—with devastating effect. Devastating because changes in market forces forced them to return to the rubble of the *Pavillion* in order to recover *artifactual* fragments from its ruins. But this was no longer the same ruin; it had been transported in time from a machine-design age to a handcrafted era. The artifacts were handcrafted bijoux for a bygone era when artists were subservient: hence the complementary brilliant parody of themselves as poodles, whose antics paralleled the antiqued poodle acts depicted in fallen plaster fragments.[7]

The antique world of the poodle was no backdoor re-entry to myth, however. "The Re-materialization of the Art Object" was far from the origins of General Idea's work in the "*de*-materialization of the art object." In fact, back then, General Idea even objected to the market-oriented, historically deterministic bias of American conceptual art! On the contrary, as image bank artists, they were mythical rather than conceptual artists. A little myth turns one away from history, one might say, but a lot brings one back to it.

9. *"I Like to Look at America and America Likes to Look at Me"*: 1986

Having moved to New York in 1986, General Idea faced a dilemma. Americans didn't get their irony![8] So much, it seems, had changed with postmodernism, and General Idea were so much ahead of their time. Yet they dumbed it down for America. At a time in New York of appropriation art and neo-geo painting, their work had to be reduced to a one-liner; it had to be in your face. Why not just show the copyright sign, stupid, or a Trinitron television test pattern, or brands stripped of their names? Blatant, their copyright and macaroni paintings blandly fitted in with the tenor of the times. Dumbing it down, however, was not good for the product line; it degraded the overall General Idea image. Frankly, these weren't their strongest works.

10. *AIDS*: 1989

Irony returned with the AIDS works, but the irony was unintended. When it first appeared in paintings and posters, this direct image—a logo in fact revised from Robert Indiana's 1966 *LOVE* painting—was not well received by New York AIDS activists: they thought the logo *was* ironic. But this was a minor crisis of understanding. General Idea reactivated their old Burroughsian viral strategies to suffuse the logo in countless iterations over the next few years throughout the global system. Crises return, the second time round sometimes absorbed and articulated to advantage. Sadly, the crisis could not be managed this time; viral effectivity hit home: both Felix Partz and Jorge Zontal became HIV infected, in 1989 and 1990, respectively. The legacy of this last General Idea project from 1987 to 1994, collectively entitled *Imagevirus*, is its complexity *and* clarity. No crisis can deny this. •

1. "Consider your mirror's feelings. Must it always reflect *you*? A) Coerce all your mirrors to look at each other. B) Now that you've turned them onto the ultimate narcissism, steal away your reflection while they aren't watching. Carefully. It's all done without mirrors. How they'll talk about you! The vacuum created by your invisibility has got to be filled with words. They'll talk and talk. . . ." "Are You Truly Invisible?," *IFEL* 2:3 (September 1973), 35.
2. "Glamour is a passive defense [whose strategies are] simple but evasive:
   1. Concealment, i.e., separation, postured innocence.
   2. Hardening of the Target, i.e., closure of the object, a seeming immobility, a brilliance.
   3. Mobility of the Target, i.e., the superficial image hides an APPARENT emptiness (changing one's mind, shifting stance, 'feminine' logic)."

   "Glamour," *FILE* 3:1 (Autumn 1975), n.p.
3. See General Idea's second and third Borderline Cases: "Imitation of Life (Mimicry): ... There's safety in numbers and two can have a mind of its own. Our two hands applauded the engagement and came out dueling. In the crack of dawn a narcissus is blooming. All together now, one two, one two, one two."
   "Self Conscious: ... Driving the wedge down deep through the centre and splitting the images in halves. There is two of us now to contend with now. Two heads are better than one but it's really just one more mouth to feed on. Casting our image in the mirror revealed a cast of two. Our very own dialogue to talk to ourselves. We're not the one we used to be." "General Idea's Borderline Cases," *IFEL* 2:3 (September 1973), 14, 16.
4. See the 1977 *Showcards* "Three Heads are Better" (1-078), "Three Men" (1-079), "Group Decision" (1-080), and "Right Hand Man" (1-076): "The three of them are all each others right-hand man but they aren't taking any chances. If one was lost on the job it would throw off the balance. They know that three's a crowd and a basic social unit and they'd hate to be reduced to a couple."
5. "Cornucopia: Fragments from the Room of the Unknown Function from the 1984 Miss General Idea Pavillion," *General Idea 1968–1984* (Eindhoven: Stedelijk Van Abbemuseum, 1984), 67. First published in Elke Town, *Fictions* (Toronto: Art Gallery of Ontario, 1982).
6. Hans Ulrich Obrist with AA Bronson, "General Idea," *UOVO* 17 (April/May/June, 2008), 203.
7. "We are the poodle, banal and effete; note our relished role as watchdog, retriever and gay companion; our wit, pampered presence and ornamental physique; our eagerness for affection and affectation; our delicious desire to be groomed and preened for public appearances; in a word, our desire to please: those that live to please must please to live." General Idea, "How Our Mascots Love to Humiliate Us," in *General Idea: 1968–1984*, 23.
8. "The irony disappeared when we moved to New York in 1986. It was the first year we exhibited in the US, at the Albright-Knox Art Gallery in Buffalo, although we had been exhibiting in Europe for ten years. The American audience wasn't prepared to deal with the complexity of our narratives. They didn't want something that couldn't be digested in a split second. We had to completely rethink what we were doing for the work to have any meaning, for it to communicate in any way with the New York audience." Snowden Snowden, "Bzzz Bzzz Bzzz: AA Bronson on General Idea," *Metropolis M*, February/March 2011. Or as AA Bronson said more directly in his interview with Hans Ulrich Obrist, "We had to make that very complex narrative less visible because it was too confusing for America." *UOVO*, 205.

First published in *Fillip 16* (Spring 2012), 106–112, prefaced by a version of Chapter 17, *Crises*.

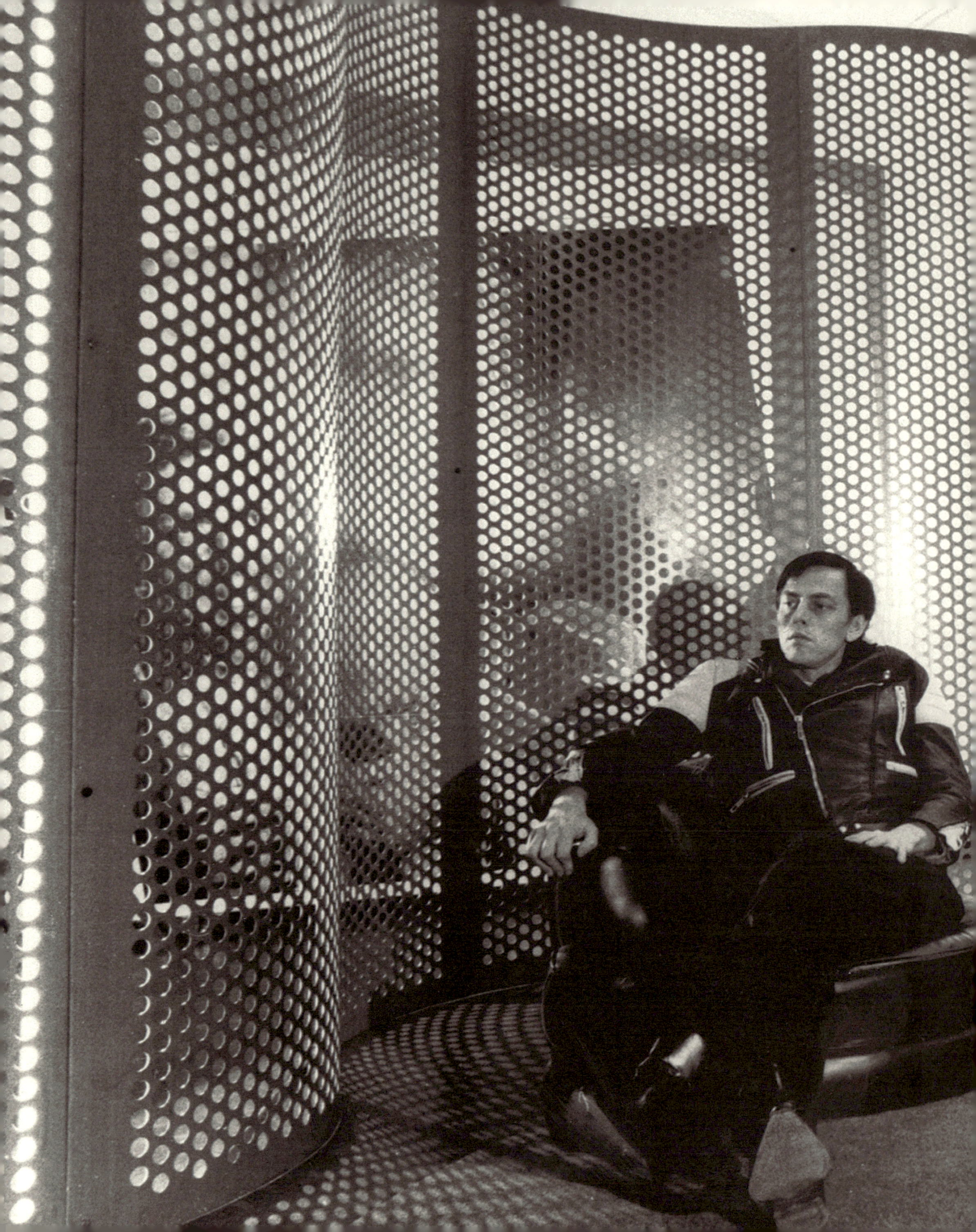

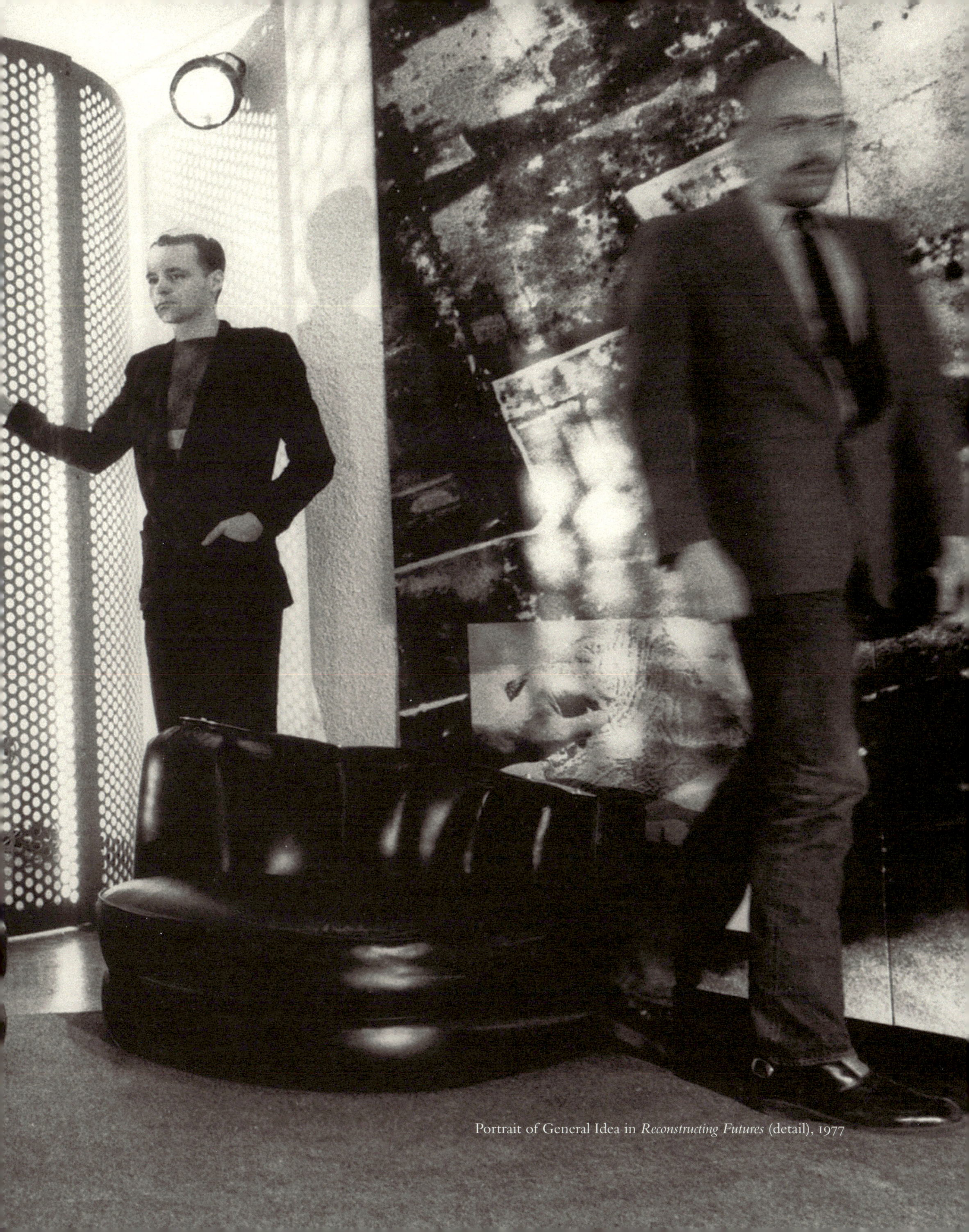

Portrait of General Idea in *Reconstructing Futures* (detail), 1977

EXHIBITIONS

GOING THRU THE NOTIONS

Carmen Lamanna Gallery, Toronto
October 18 – November 6, 1975

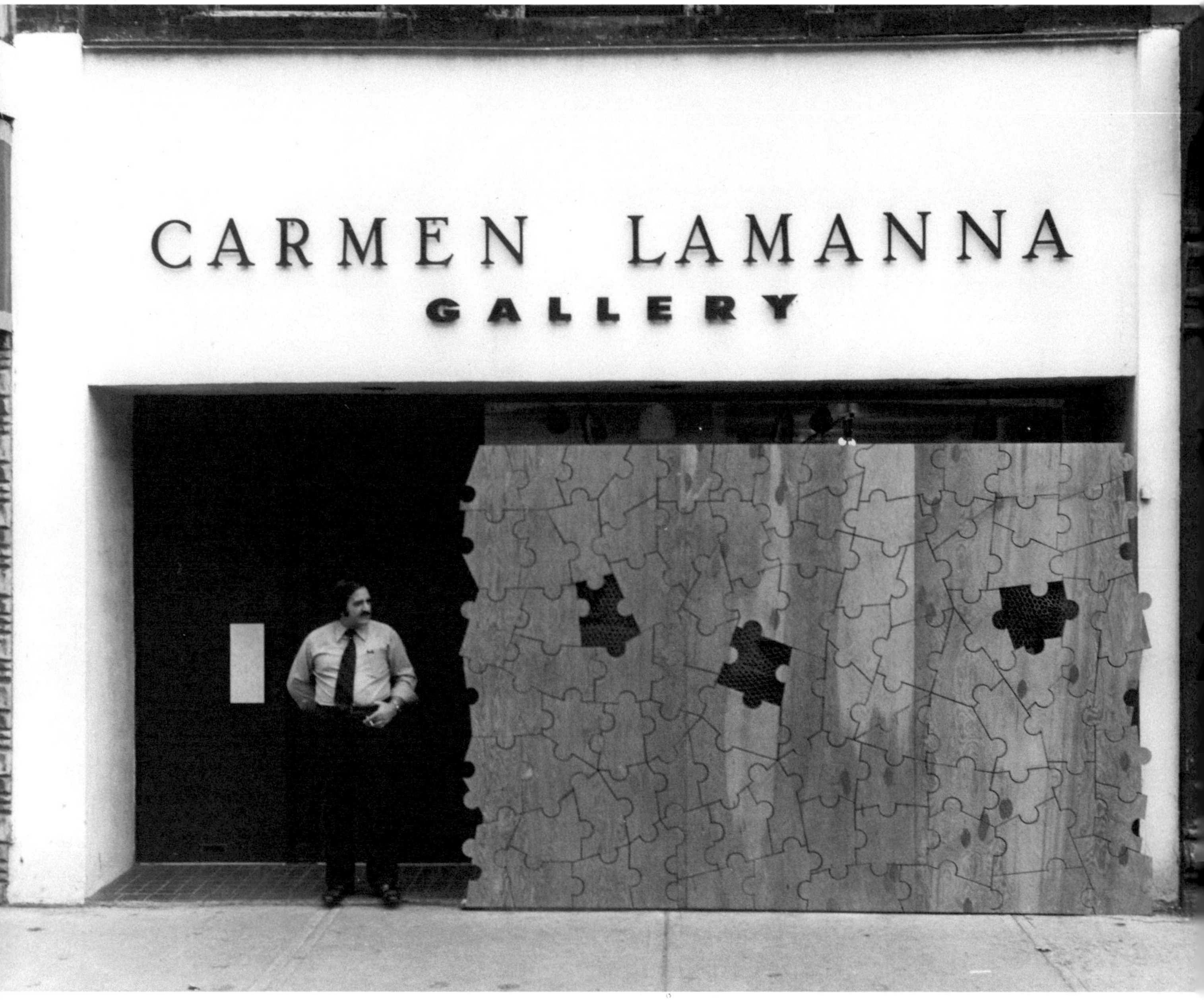
CARMEN LAMANNA
GALLERY

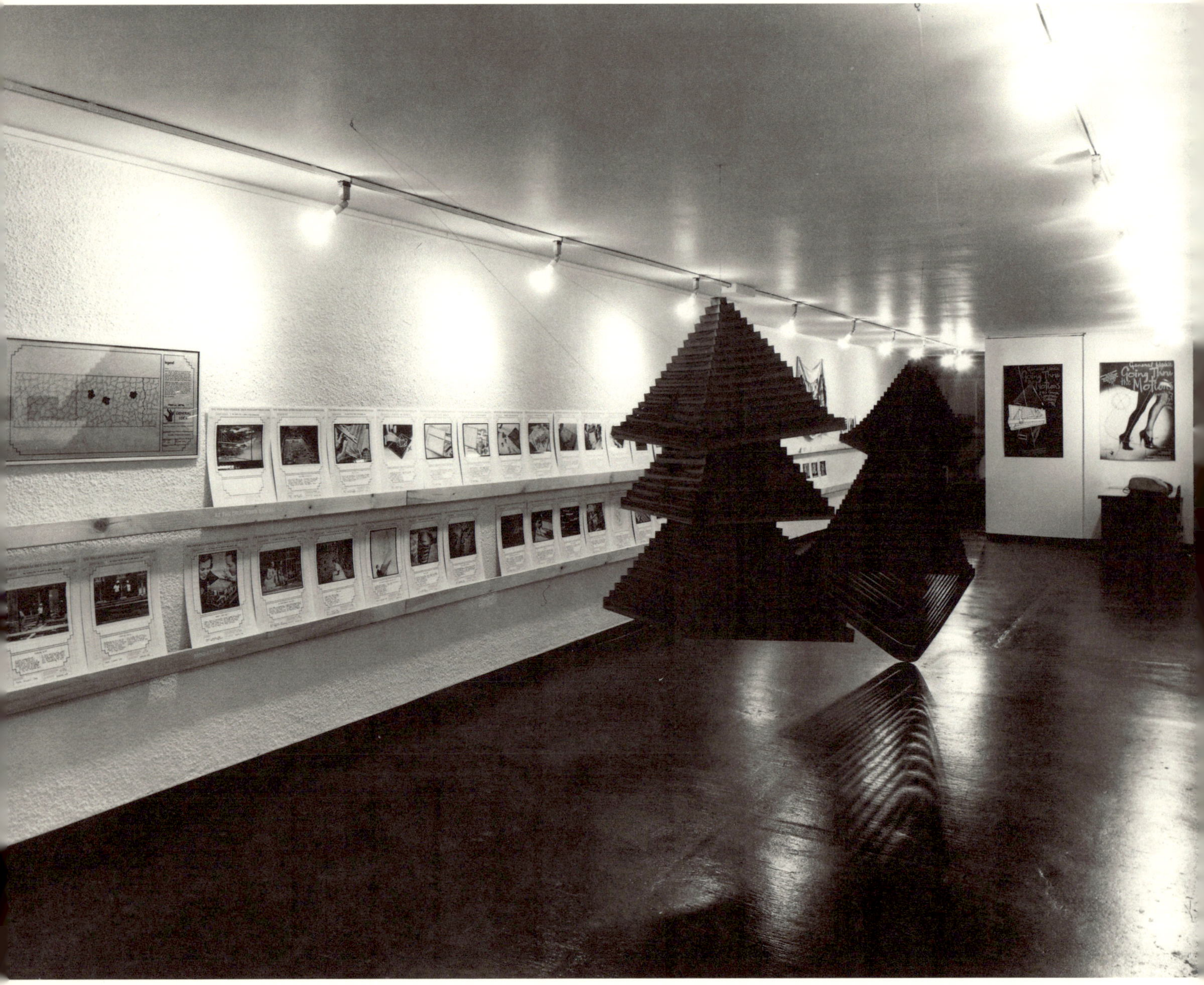
General Idea
Going Thru the Motions

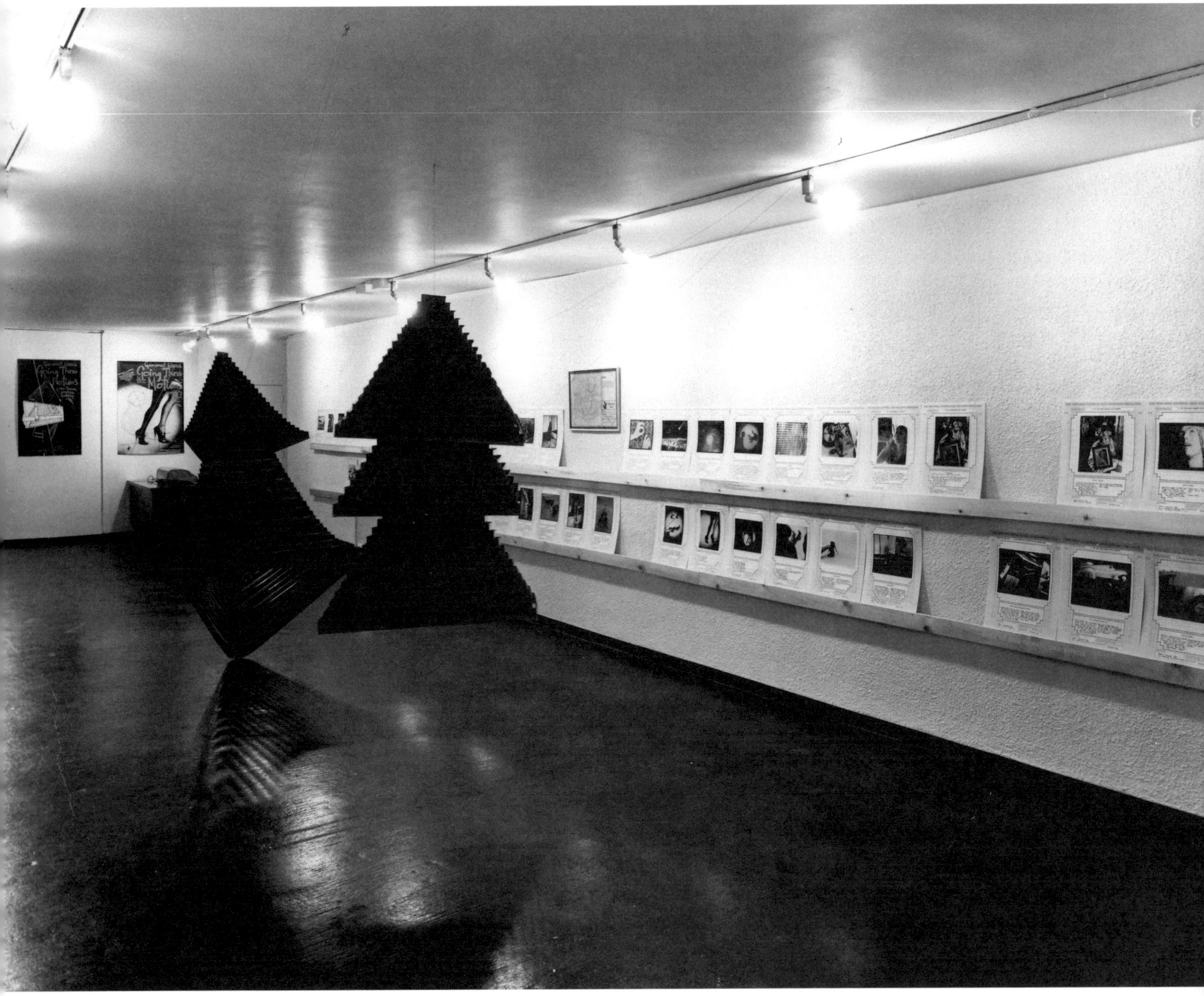
Going Thru the Motions
Going Thru the Motions

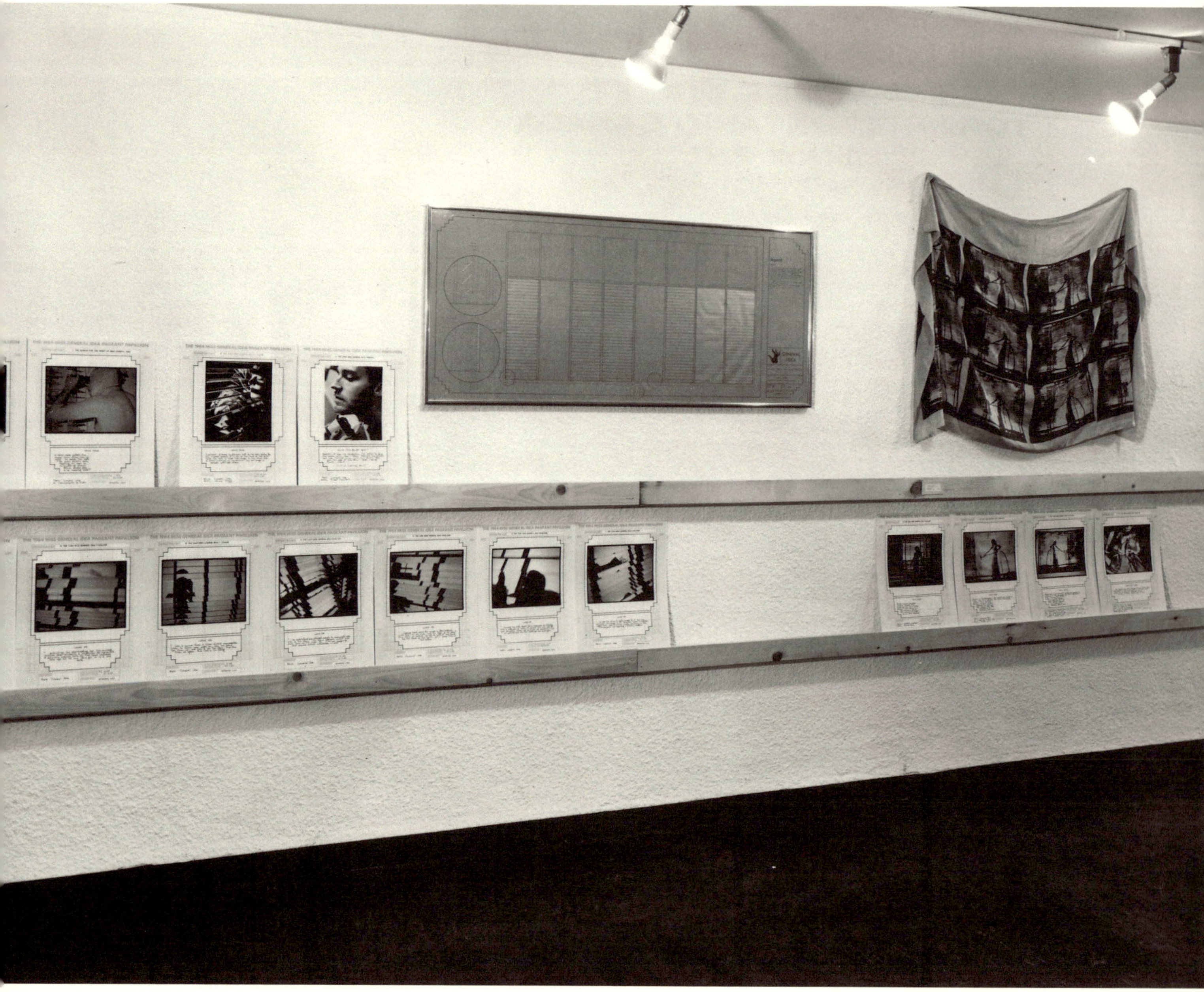

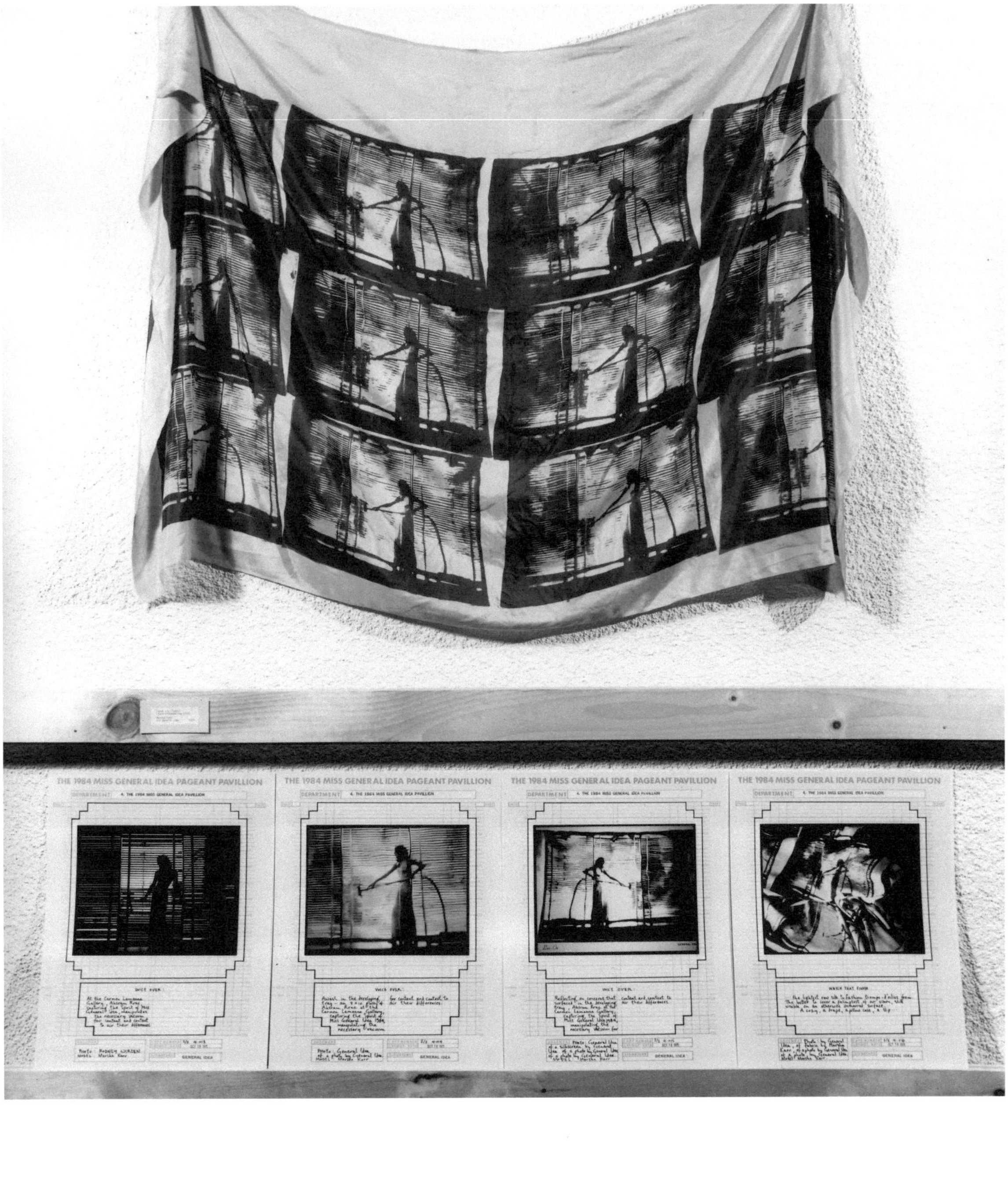
THE 1984 MISS GENERAL IDEA PAGEANT PAVILLION
THE 1984 MISS GENERAL IDEA PAGEANT PAVILLION
THE 1984 MISS GENERAL IDEA PAGEANT PAVILLION
THE 1984 MISS GENERAL IDEA PAGEANT PAVILLION
GENERAL IDEA
GENERAL IDEA
GENERAL IDEA
GENERAL IDEA

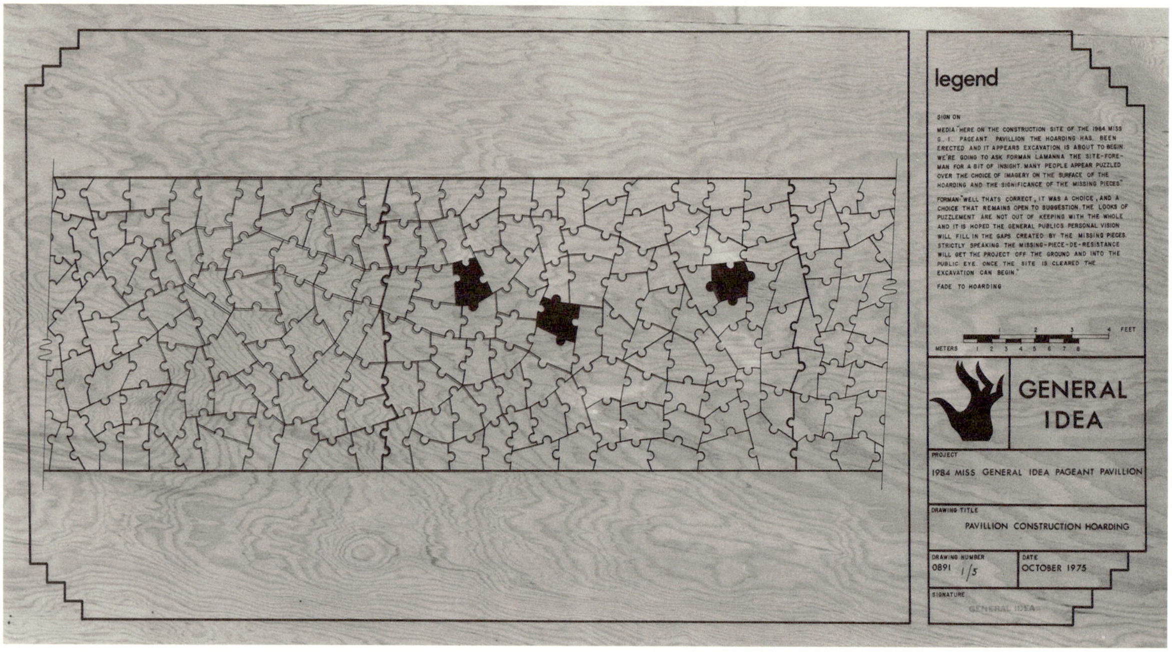

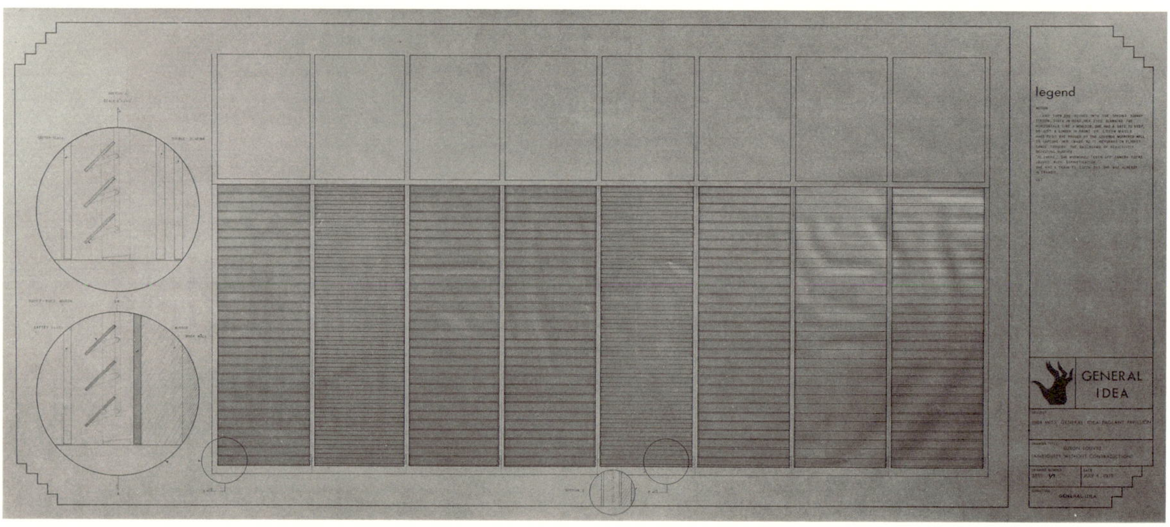

upper left: *Pavillion Construction Hoarding*, 1975
lower left: *Luxon Louvre (Ambiguity without Contradiction)*, 1975
upper right: *Proposed Seating Arrangement (Form Follows Fiction)*, 1975
lower right: *Miss General Idea Glove Pattern (Form Follows Fetish)*, 1975

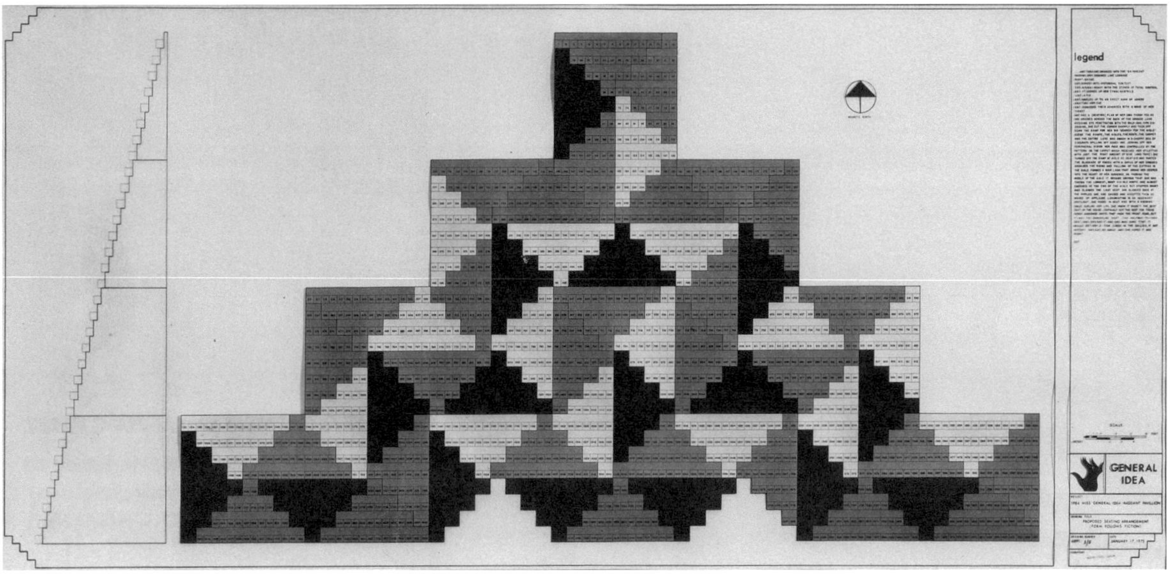
legend
GENERAL IDEA

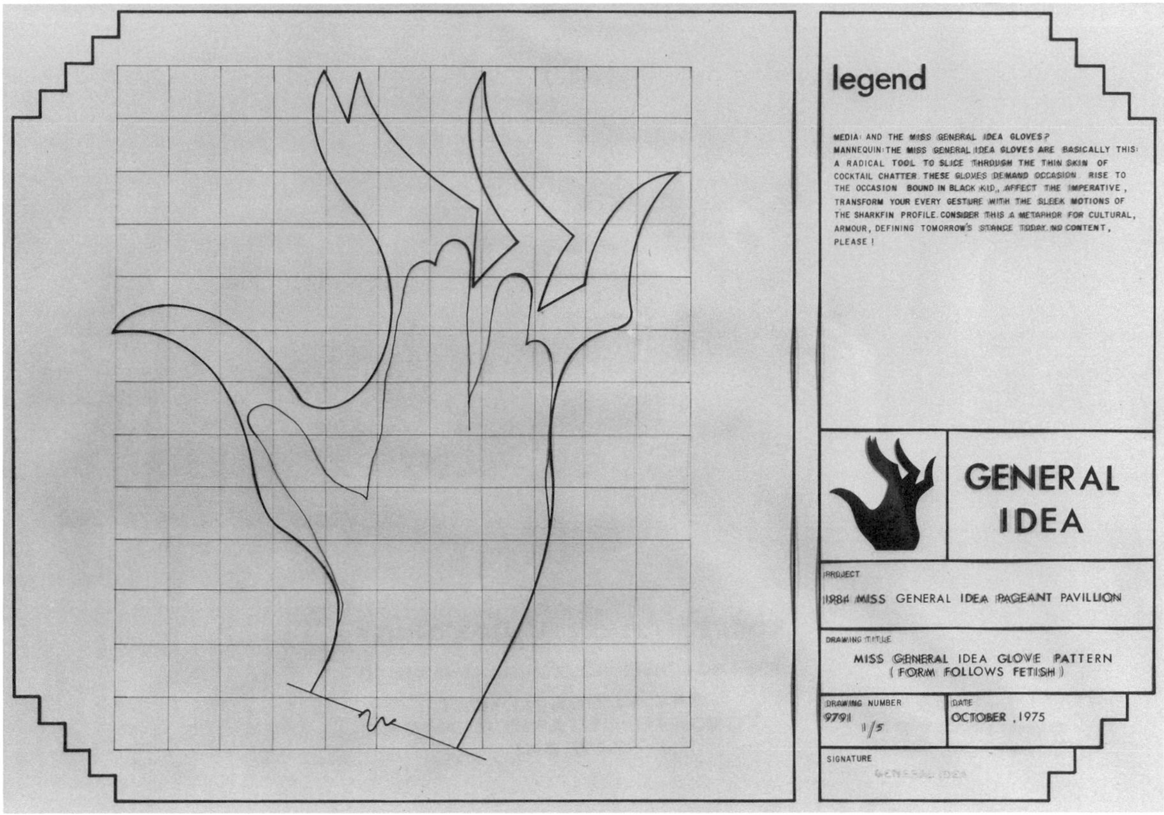
legend
MEDIA: AND THE MISS GENERAL IDEA GLOVES?
MANNEQUIN: THE MISS GENERAL IDEA GLOVES ARE BASICALLY THIS: A RADICAL TOOL TO SLICE THROUGH THE THIN SKIN OF COCKTAIL CHATTER THESE GLOVES DEMAND OCCASION RISE TO THE OCCASION BOUND IN BLACK KID, AFFECT THE IMPERATIVE, TRANSFORM YOUR EVERY GESTURE WITH THE SLEEK MOTIONS OF THE SHARKFIN PROFILE. CONSIDER THIS A METAPHOR FOR CULTURAL, ARMOUR, DEFINING TOMORROW'S STANCE TODAY. NO CONTENT, PLEASE!
GENERAL IDEA
PROJECT
1984 MISS GENERAL IDEA PAGEANT PAVILLION
DRAWING TITLE
MISS GENERAL IDEA GLOVE PATTERN
(FORM FOLLOWS FETISH)
DRAWING NUMBER
9791
1/5
DATE
OCTOBER, 1975
SIGNATURE
GENERAL IDEA

RECONSTRUCTING FUTURES

Carmen Lamanna Gallery, Toronto
December 10, 1977 – January 5, 1978

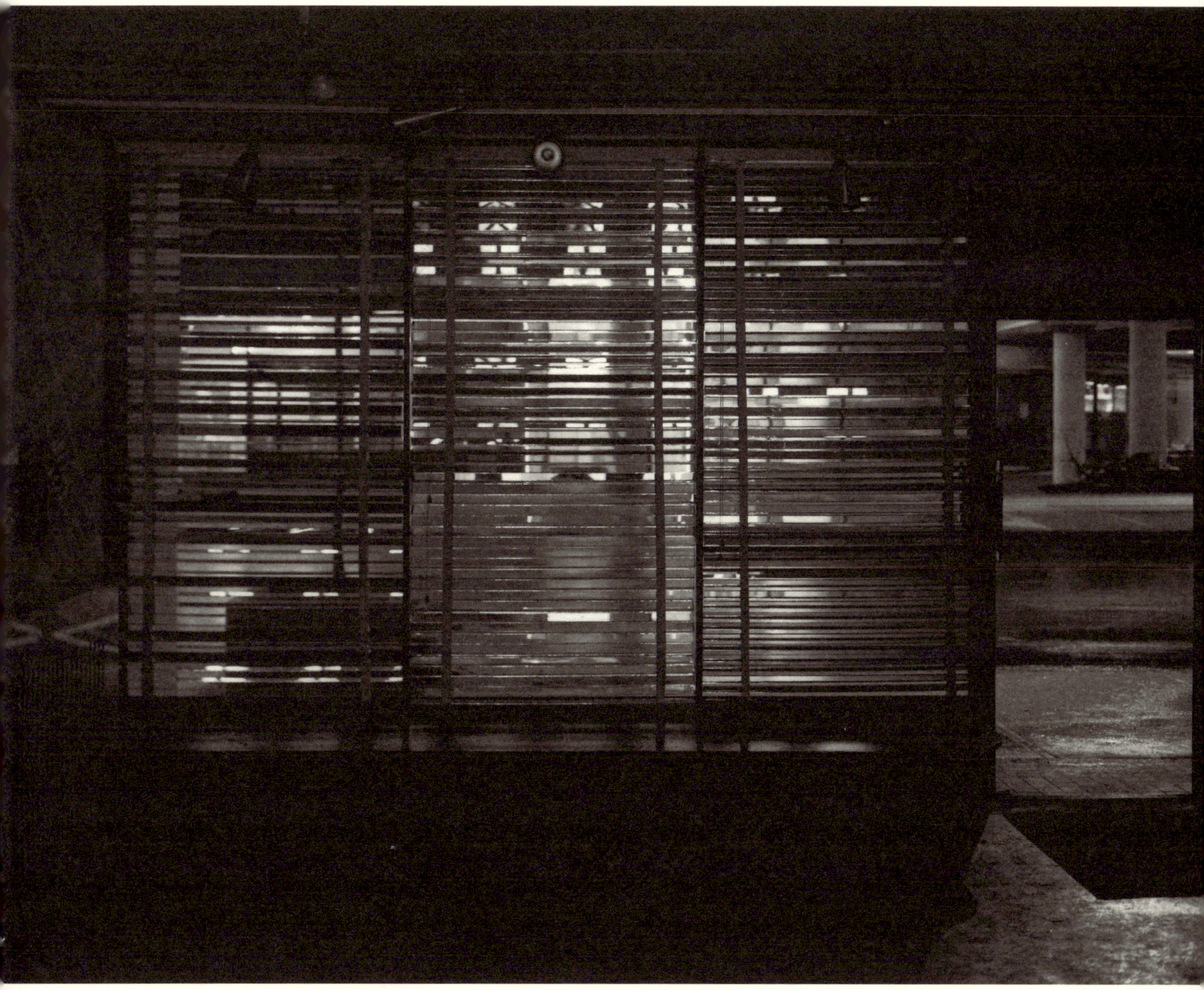

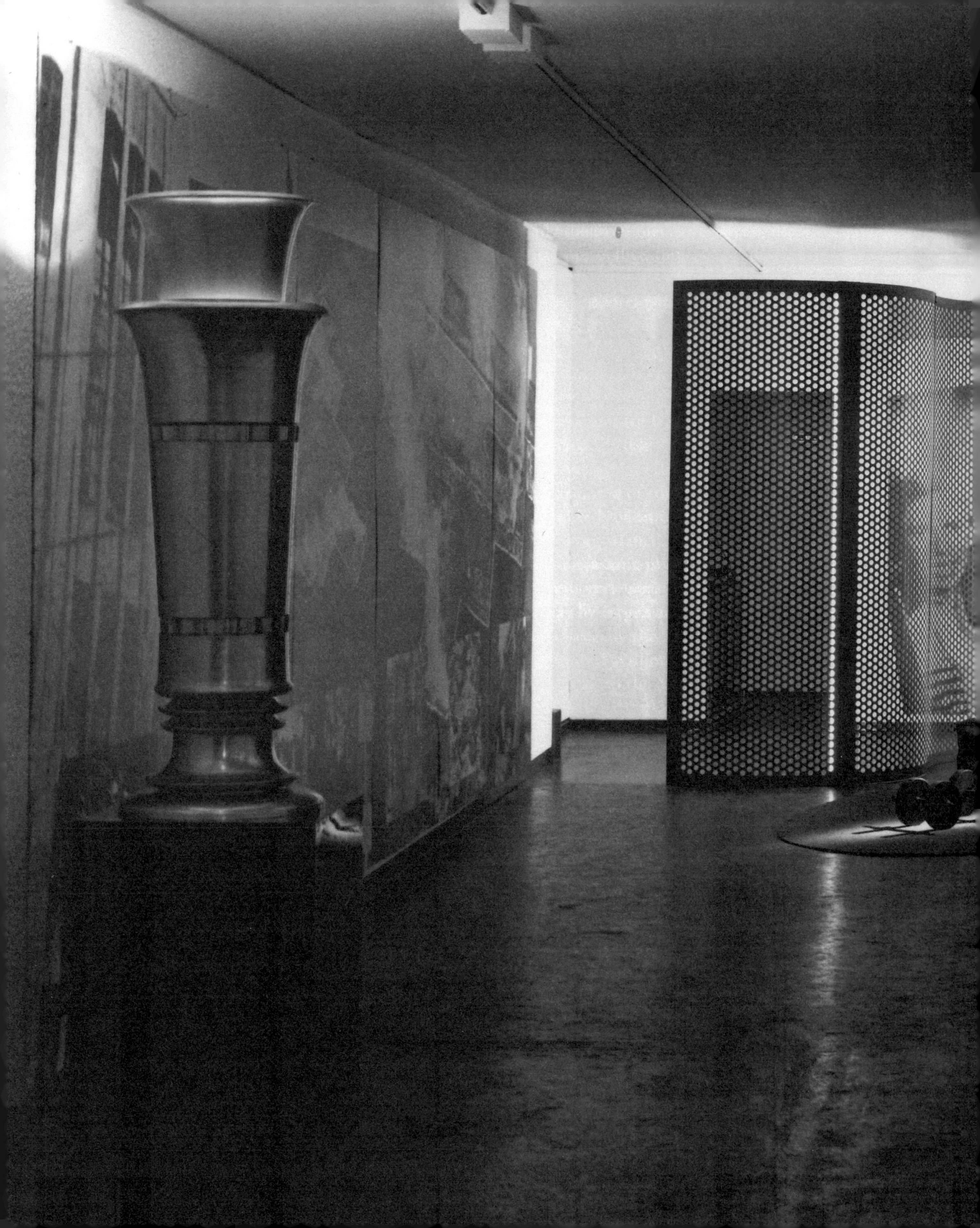

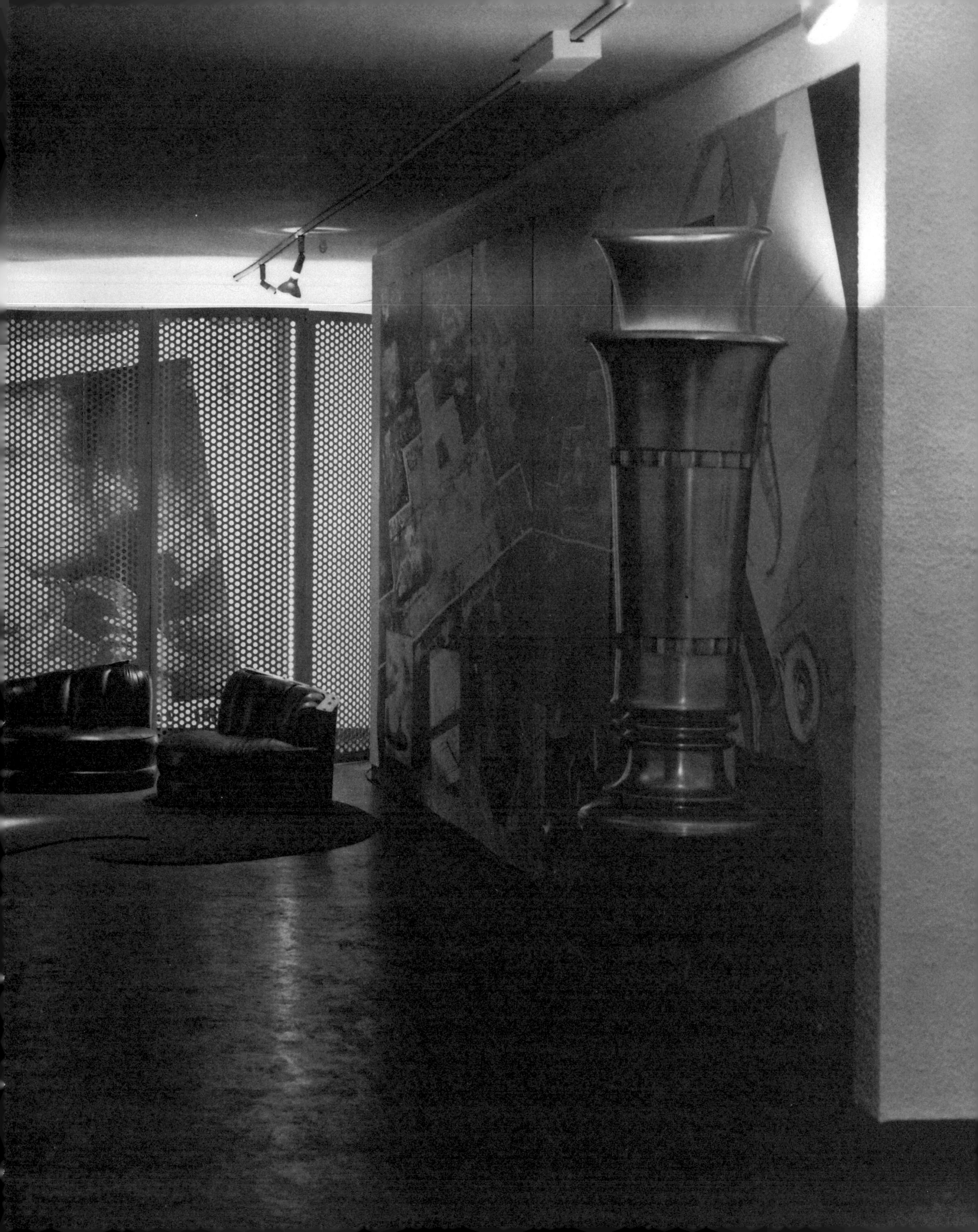

THE 1984 MISS GENERAL IDEA PAVILLION

Art Gallery of York University, Toronto
September 15 – December 6, 2009

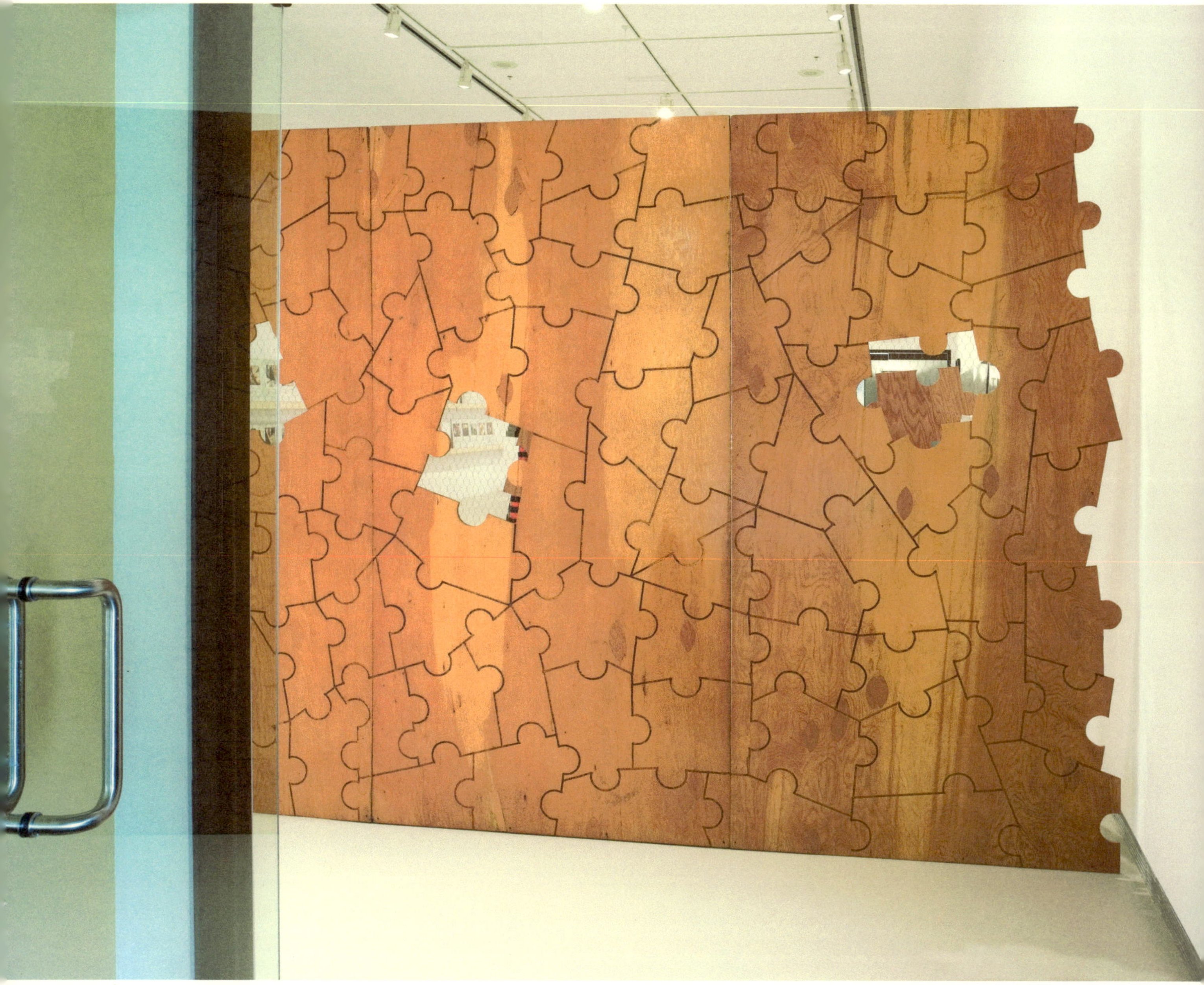

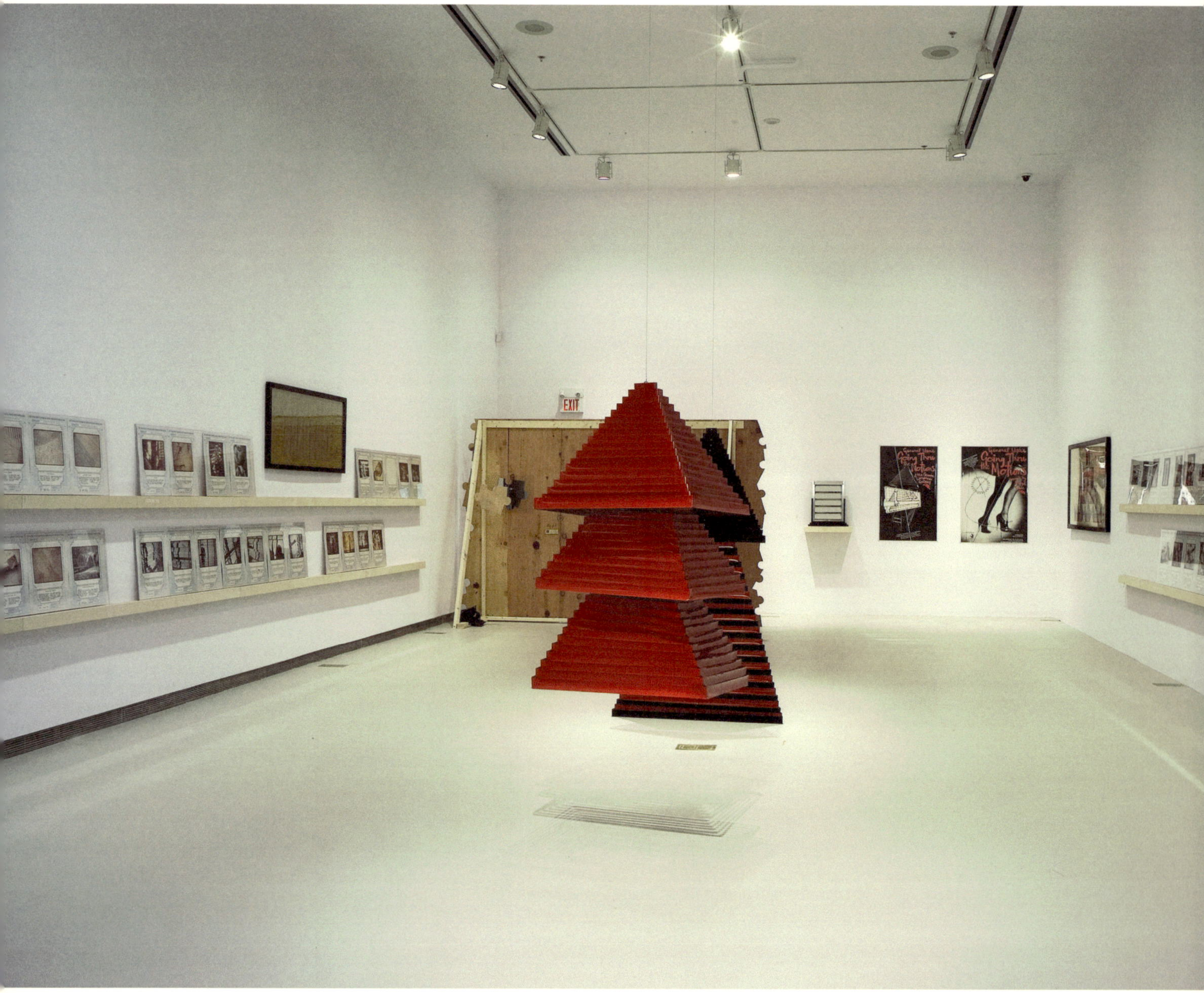
EXIT

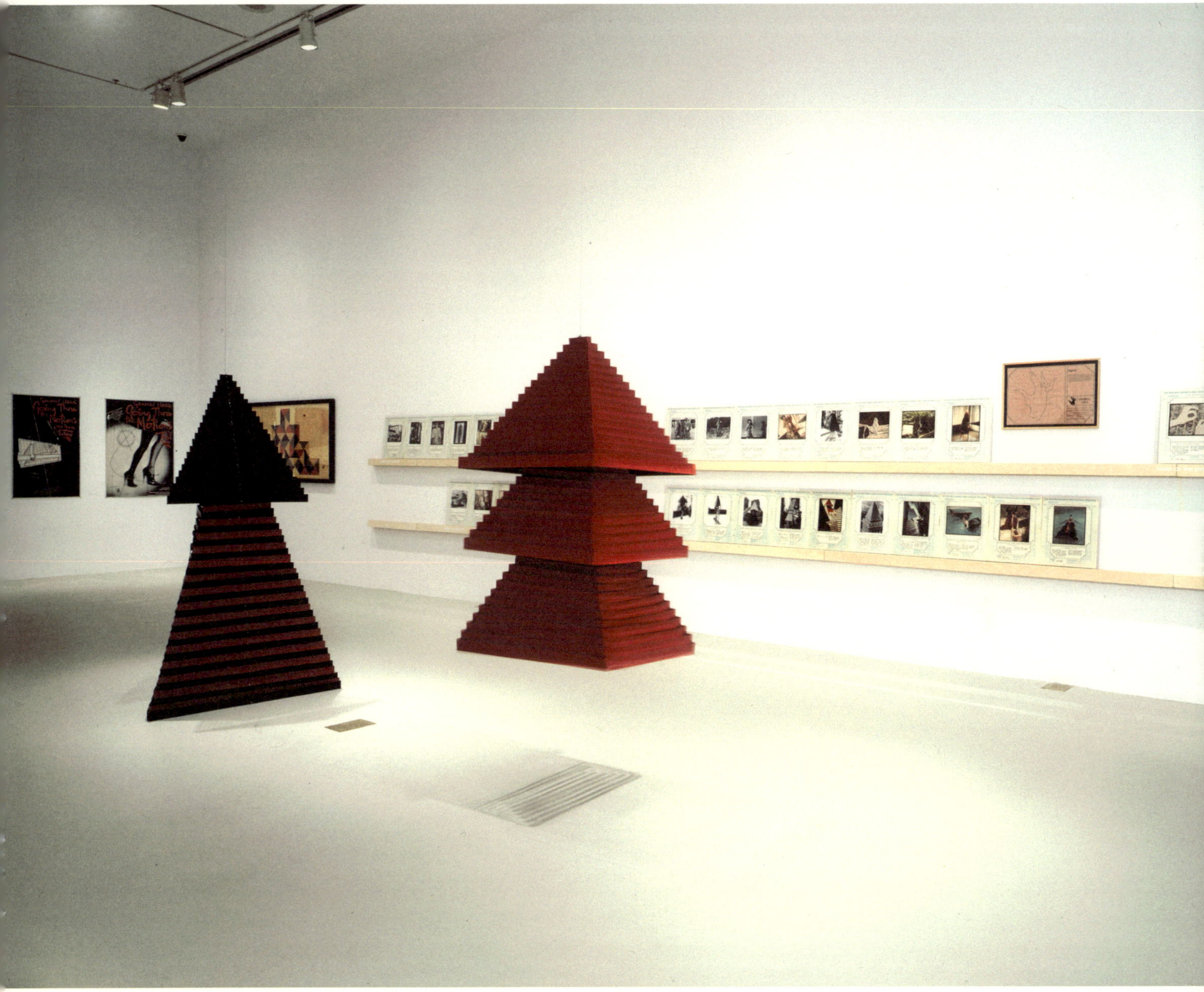

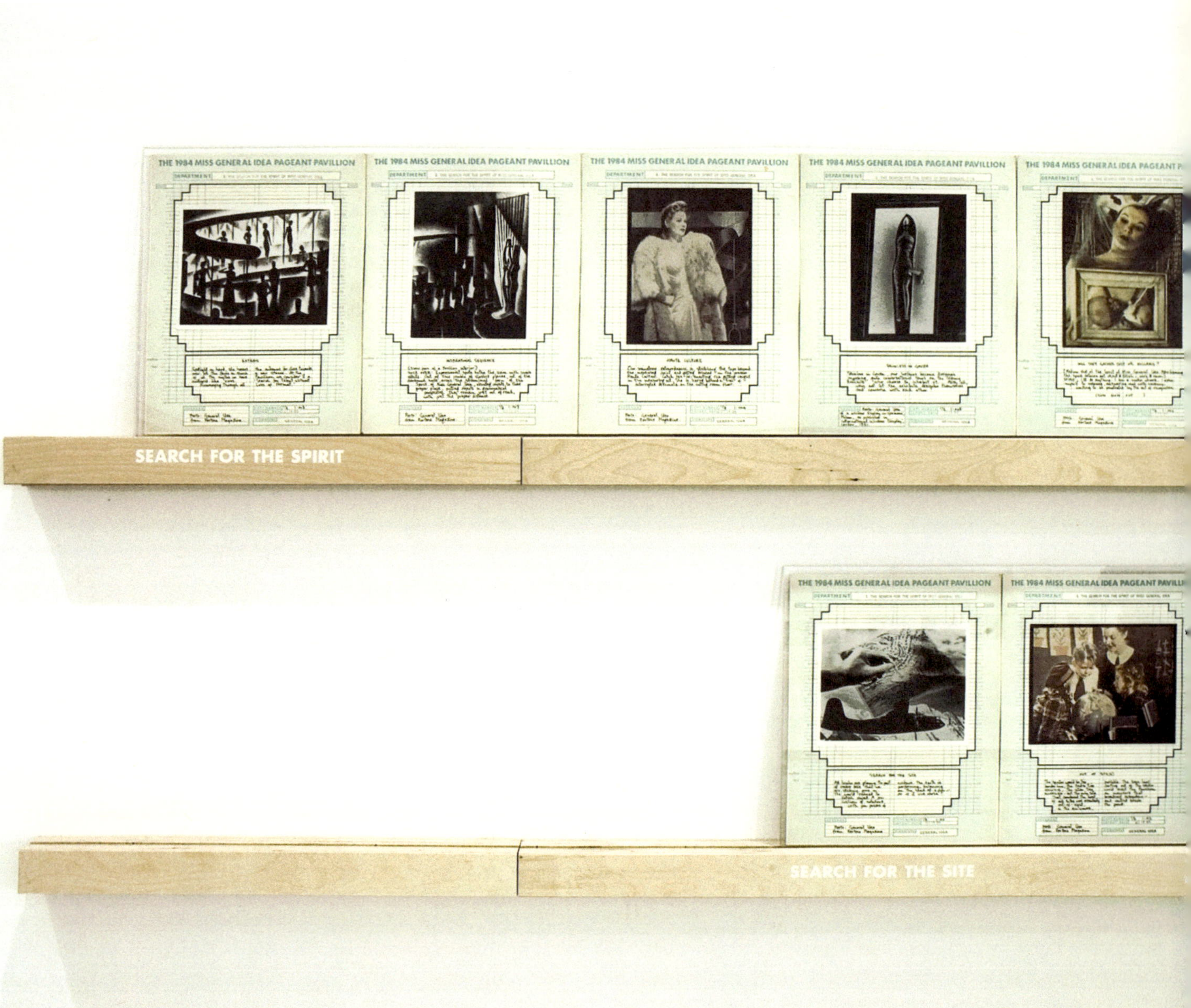
THE 1984 MISS GENERAL IDEA PAGEANT PAVILLION
THE 1984 MISS GENERAL IDEA PAGEANT PAVILLION
THE 1984 MISS GENERAL IDEA PAGEANT PAVILLION
THE 1984 MISS GENERAL IDEA PAGEANT PAVILLION
SEARCH FOR THE SPIRIT
THE 1984 MISS GENERAL IDEA PAGEANT PAVILLION
SEARCH FOR THE SITE

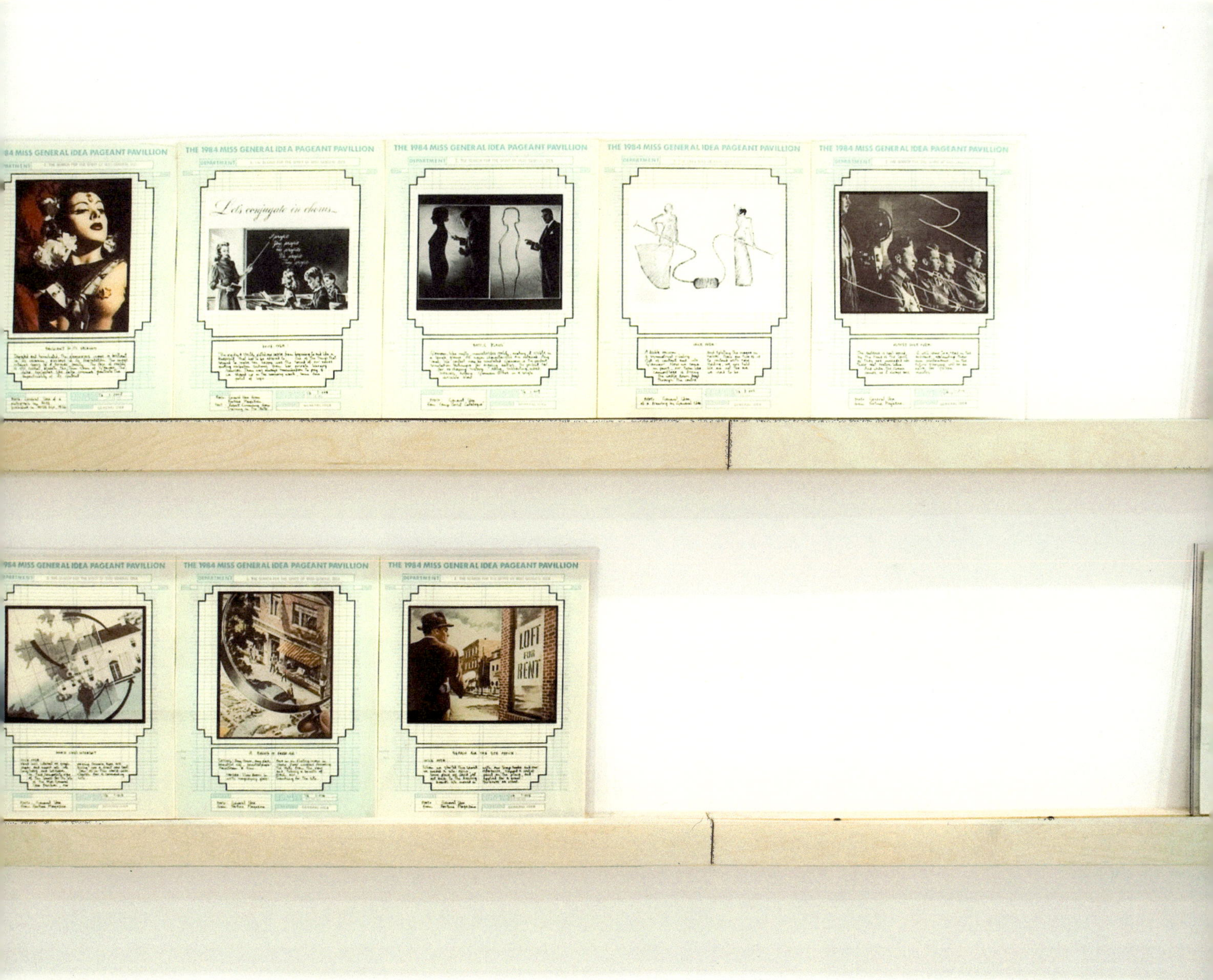
THE 1984 MISS GENERAL IDEA PAGEANT PAVILLION
Let's conjugate in chorus
LOFT FOR RENT

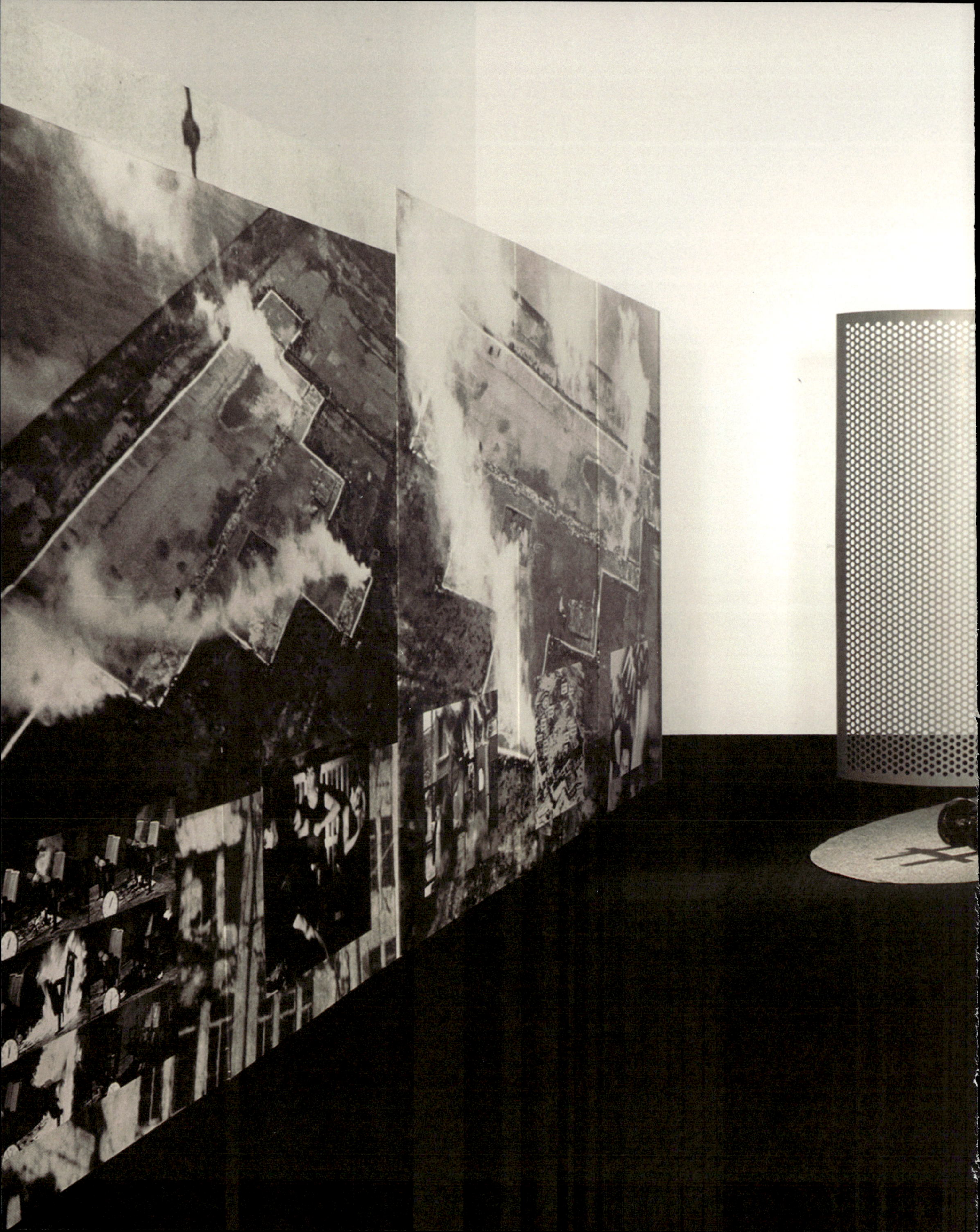

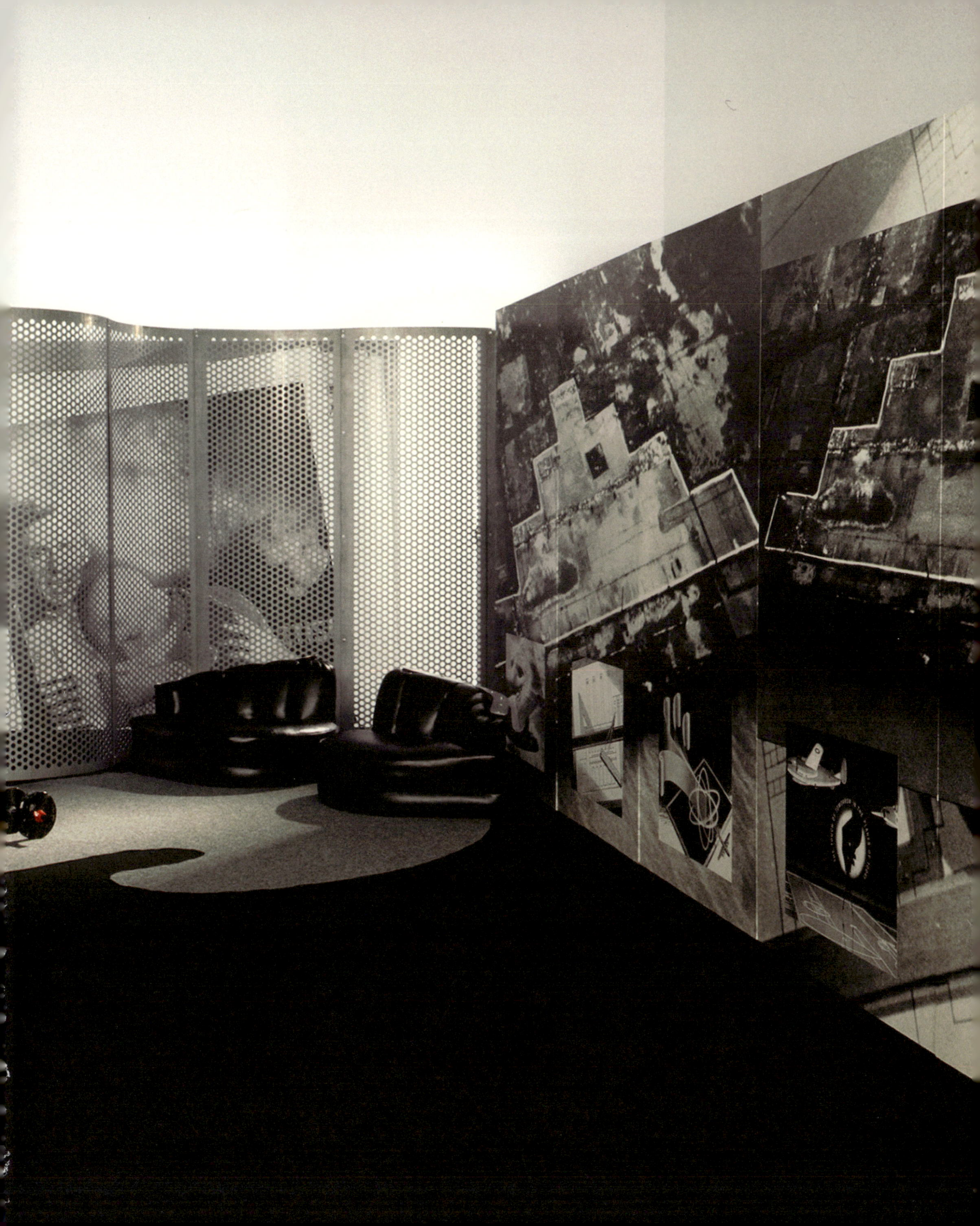

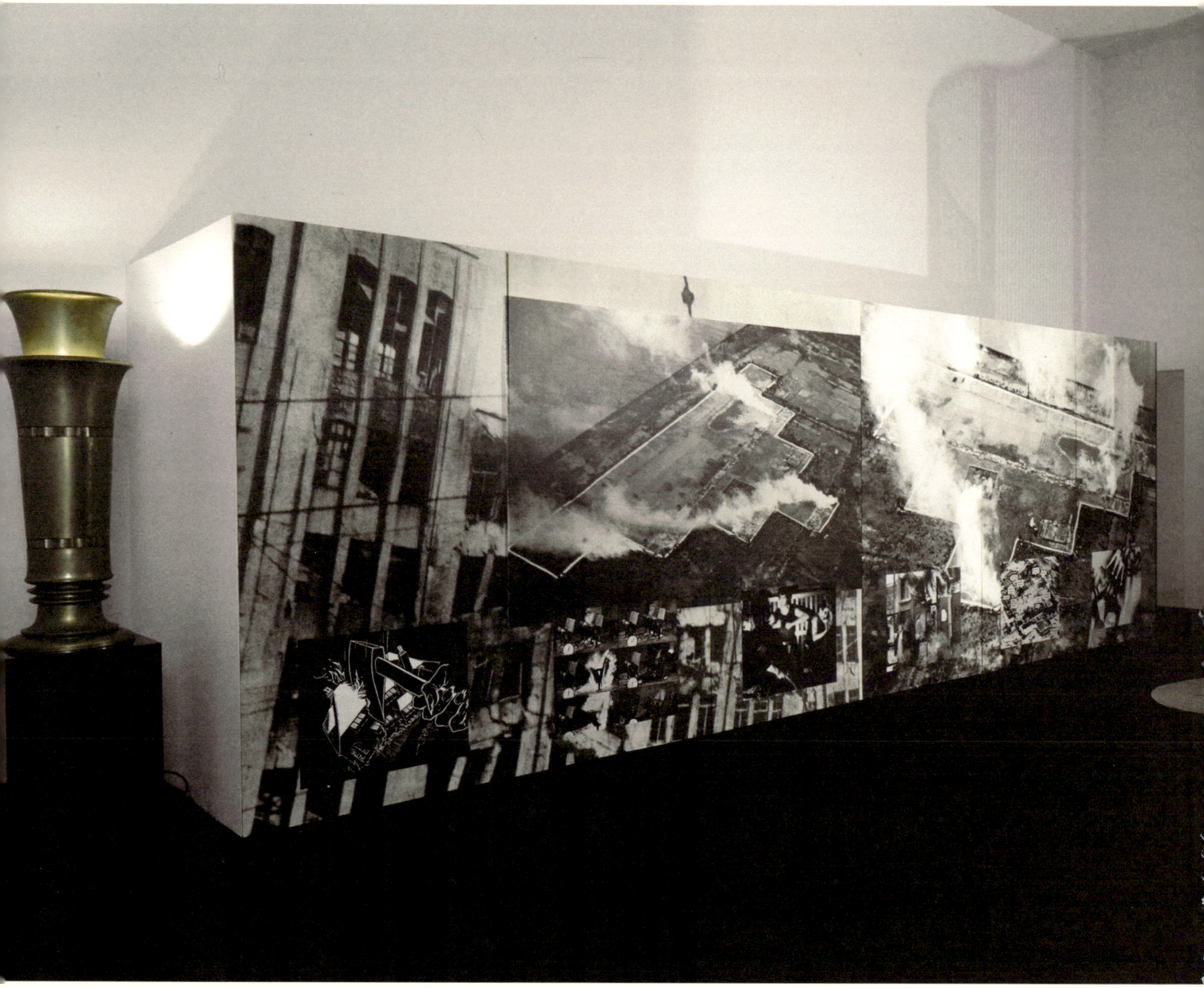

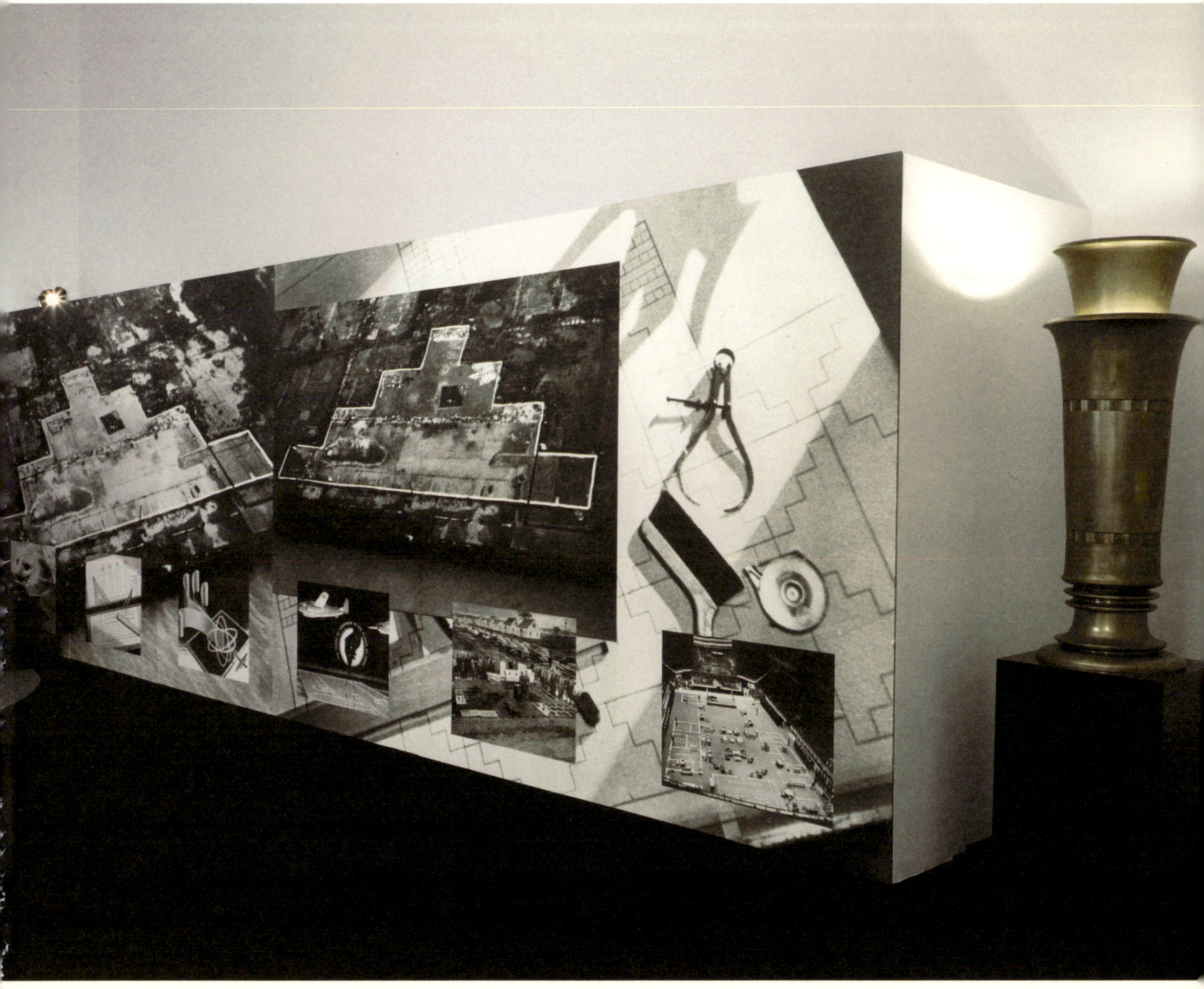

LIST OF WORKS AGYU EXHIBITON

Going thru the Notions

Showcards, 1975
122 serigraphed cards with photographs
45.7 x 35.6 cm (each)
Collection of Art Gallery of Ontario, Toronto.
Gift of Vivian and David Campbell, 1994

Showcards 1-041, 2-018, 2-019, 2-046, 4-009
Carmen Lamanna Collection

The Dr. Brute Colonnade (Dominant Imagery), 1975
diazotype and enamel on acetate over craft paper
62.0 x 116.0 cm
Collection Art Gallery of Ontario, Toronto
Purchase, 1987

Luxon Louvre (Ambiguity without Contradiction), 1975
diazotype and enamel on acetate over craft paper
66.3 x 148.4 cm
Collection Art Gallery of Ontario, Toronto
Purchase, 1987

Miss General Idea Glove Pattern (Form Follows Fetish), 1975
diazotype on acetate over paper
44.0 x 61.0 cm
Carmen Lamanna Collection

Pavillion Construction Hoarding, 1975
diazotype on acetate over plywood
43.2 x 81.9 cm
Collection Art Gallery of Ontario, Toronto
Purchase with assistance from Wintario, 1976

Proposed Seating Arrangement (Form Follows Fiction), 1975
diazotype on acetate, hand coloured with enamel, card
97.0 x 201.0 cm
Collection Art Gallery of Ontario, Toronto
Purchase, 1987

The Hoarding of the 1984 Miss General Idea Pavillion, 1975
3 parts, grooved and shellacked plywood with pine nails, chicken wire, wooden support
Courtesy AA Bronson, Toronto/New York

Hoarding cutouts [three pieces], 1975
shellacked plywood
35.0 x 44.0 x 1.27 cm; 44.5 x 34.5 x 1.27 cm; 42.5 x 30.5 x 1.27 cm
Carmen Lamanna Collection

Luxon Louvre Mock-up, 1975
mirrored glass, aluminum, and wood
58.5 x 51.0 x 16.5 cm
Collection of Lonti Ebers, New York

Massing Studies for the Pavillion #1, 1975
red and black baked aluminum venetian blind slats with chains
193 x 113.5 x 115.5 cm
Carmen Lamanna Collection

Massing Studies for the Pavillion #2, 1975
red baked aluminum venetian blind slats with chains
137 x 73.5 x 86.0 cm
Carmen Lamanna Collection

General Idea's Going thru the Motions, 1975
screenprint on paper
124.5 x 83 cm
Courtesy AA Bronson, Toronto/New York

General Idea's Going thru the Notions, 1975
screenprint on paper
123.0 x 74.5 cm
Courtesy AA Bronson, Toronto/New York

Reconstructing Futures

Reconstructing Futures, 1977
14 photo-montage panels, 2 vinyl-upholstered seats, 2 marble and steel barbells, synthetic carpet, 2 copper- and metal-plated lamps, 6 perforated steel panels, recorded soundtrack, tape recorder, 4 fluorescent lights
2.74 x 4.32 x 10.17 m
Collection National Gallery of Canada, Ottawa
Purchased 1983

ACKNOWLEDGEMENTS

A project of this scope, which includes an exhibition as well as this book, owes debts to many people. In its mimicking fiction, the book is written first of all as homage to General Idea's strategies. But the book is also a serious acknowledgement of what General Idea achieved in twenty-five years of working and of what they contributed to the artist-run system in Canada in particular and accomplished for Canadian culture in general.

My first thanks are to the living inspiration of AA Bronson. The book is written in memory of his two partners Jorge Zontal and Felix Partz. Researching and writing, one cannot delve so deeply into this material without frequently hearing their singular voices amongst this collective enterprise.

Nobody can write in depth on General Idea without acknowledging the diligent role Fern Bayer has played in cataloguing the artists' archive deposited at the National Gallery of Canada and writing detailed Series Descriptions. Fern has assisted with this book in many ways. My appreciation is also owed to Cyndie Campbell, Head, Library and Archives at the National Gallery of Canada. Michael Maranda took on the arduous task of editing this big book and Barr Gilmore beautifully designed it. From 1991–1995, Barr was Studio Assistant to General Idea; thus familiar with their work and practice, he is well suited to lend a sympathetic design.

The book is the end product of an exhibition process where General Idea's two exhibitions at the Carmen Lamanna Gallery in Toronto—the 1975 *Going thru the Notions* and the 1977 *Reconstructing Futures*—were precisely recreated at the AGYU. I would like to thank Carmen Coangelo and the Carmen Lamanna Estate for their help, with assistance from Lonti Ebers. The exhibition would not have been possible but for two of Canada's museums that made major loans: The Art Gallery of Ontario and The National Gallery of Canada. I am grateful to their two Directors, respectively Matthew Teitelbaum and Marc Mayer, for supporting these loans.

To Emelie Chhangur, Michael Maranda, Suzanne Carte, Karen Pellegrino, and Allyson Adley, staff at the AGYU, I would like to express my ongoing appreciation. Thanks as well to *ELF!* designer Ken Ogawa.

This book is testimony to a shared history, even though I might not have realized how closely we would be entwined when General Idea first published my writing in *FILE* in early 1982. On my part these engagements have taken different shapes in writing and curating over the last thirty years: from severe critique to forming the collection of their work at the Art Gallery of Ontario. The exercise of return that this project marks—the assessment of General Idea and the discovery of their system—is also a return to that beginning in recognition of a time when altering temporalities in performative fictions came together in a commitment to Canadian art—whether that of established artists as General Idea were or a young writer as I was.

Art Gallery of York University
4700 Keele Street, Toronto, ON Canada M3J 1P3
www.yorku.ca/agyu

The Art Gallery of York University is supported by York University, the Canada Council for the Arts, the Ontario Arts Council, and the City of Toronto through the Toronto Arts Council.

Edited by Michael Maranda
Designed by Barr Gilmore
Printed and bound in Canada by Flash Reproductions and Anstey Bookbinding, Toronto
Distributed by D.A.P. / Distributed Art Publishers, Inc.
http://www.artbook.com

All artwork and photography by General Idea unless otherwise noted.
Pages 4, 8, 20, 23, 27, 43, 44, 102, and 114 photographed by Peter MacCallum
Page 12–13 photographed by Rodney Werden
Page 17 photographed by Mary Canary
Page 174 courtesy the Art Gallery of Ontario
Pages 233–39 and 241–43 photographed by Henk Visser
Pages 245–53 photographed by Cheryl O'Brien

cover image: *Untitled*, 1973-74 (Sandy Stagg models *The Miss General Idea Shoe* and the *Hand of the Spirit* against the backdrop of *Luxon V.B.*)
back cover image: *Untitled*, 1973-74 (Sandy Stagg models the *Hand of the Spirit Make-up*)

Library and Archives Canada Cataloguing in Publication

Monk, Philip, 1950-
Glamour is theft : a user's guide to General Idea, 1969-1978 / Philip Monk.

Includes bibliographical references.
ISBN 978-0-921972-66-2

1. General Idea (Firm). 2. General Idea (Firm--History. 3. Art, Canadian--20th century. I. General Idea (Firm) II. York University (Toronto, Ont.). Art Gallery III. Title.

NX513.Z9G46 2012 700.92 C2012-907425-X